Universal Principles of Color

Universal Principles of Color

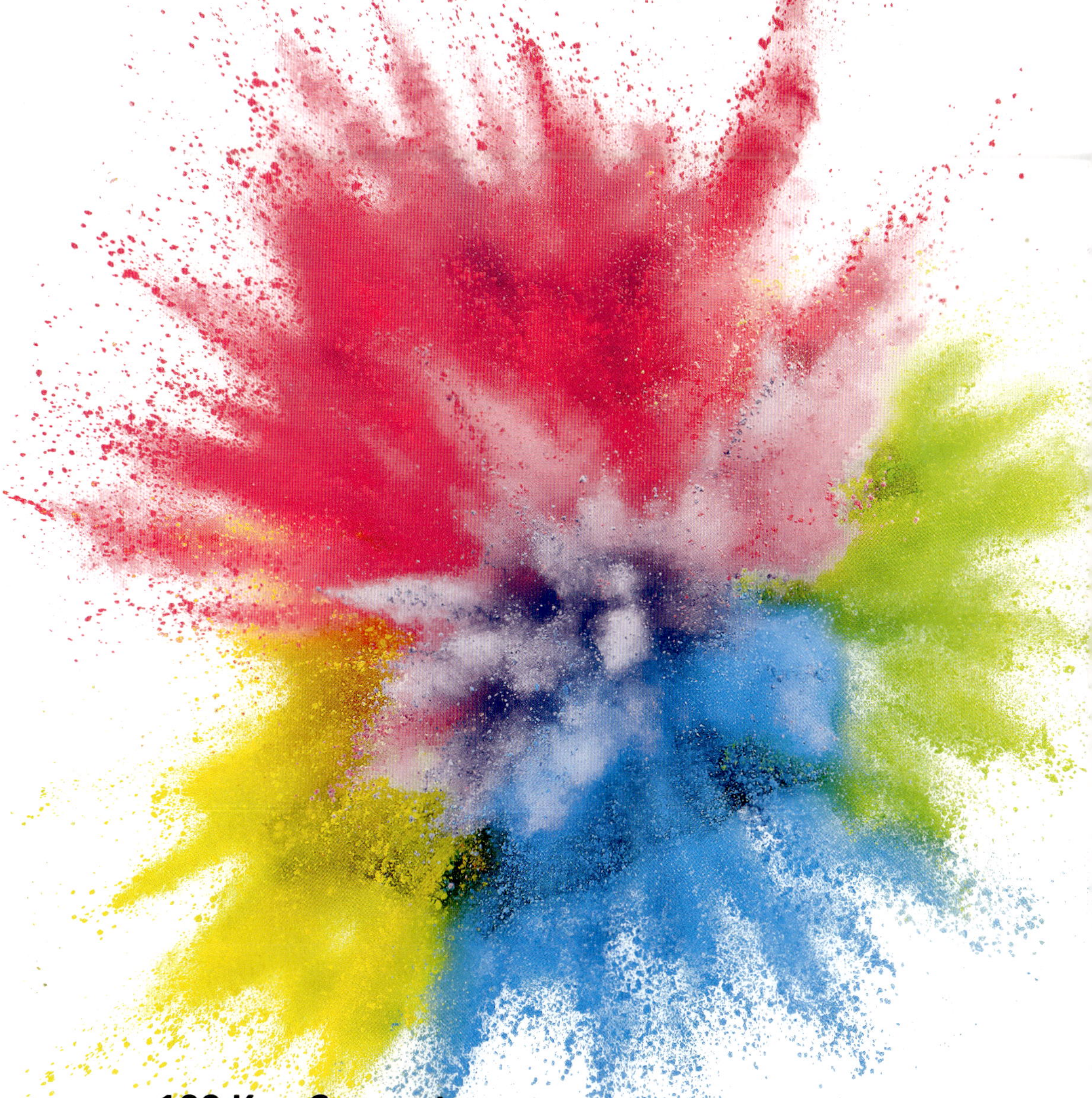

100 Key Concepts

for Understanding, Analyzing, and Working with Color

ROCKPORT

Stephen Westland
and Maggie Maggio

Quarto.com

First published in 2023 by Rockport Publishers, an imprint of The Quarto Group,
100 Cummings Center, Suite 265-D, Beverly, MA 01915, USA.
T (978) 282-9590 F (978) 283-2742 Quarto.com

Rockport Publishers titles are also available at discount for retail, wholesale, promotional, and bulk purchase. For details, contact the Special Sales Manager by email at specialsales@quarto.com or by mail at The Quarto Group, Attn: Special Sales Manager, 100 Cummings Center, Suite 265-D, Beverly, MA 01915, USA.

10 9 8 7 6 5 4 3 2 1

ISBN: 978-1-63159-925-5

Digital edition published in 2023
eISBN: 978-1-63159-926-2

Library of Congress Cataloging-in-Publication Data available

Page Layout: Sporto

Printed in China

Dedication

This book is dedicated to the late Marjorie Ingalls, a longtime member of the international color community, who shared her vast color library and collection of resources with me when I started my research on the history of color education.

—Maggie Maggio

CONTENTS / ALPHABETICAL

CONTENTS / PATHWAYS

Light

Order

Communication

Object

Mixture

Application

Observer

Composition

History

INTRODUCTION

"In a flower, in a beetle, every line, every form, every color has arisen from a deep necessity," wrote the Swiss artist Sophie Taeuber-Arp. How different our lives would be without the gorgeous reds and yellows of a sunset, the blinding blues and yellows of a beach holiday, and the effervescent greens of a rain forest. Color is vital to our emotional well-being. Yet, in art and design it also imparts meaning, conveys information, contributes to aesthetics, and induces affective responses in the viewers of artwork.

Arguably the most important thing to understand about color is that it is a perception. Although from our everyday experiences it seems as though color is the property of objects in the world, we see color with our brains rather than our eyes. Color is neither a property of light nor a property of objects, but rather it is our brain's response to light reflected by those objects. Isaac Newton understood this more than 300 years ago when he famously wrote that "the rays are not coloured." Despite the incredible advances made in the science of color over the past two centuries, it is impossible to understand how colors work together without an appreciation of the advances made by artists as well. The realization of the natural connection between color and light is summed up by Paul Cézanne: "Color is the place where our brain and the universe meet." Too often, the words of both Newton and Cézanne are overlooked. It is unfortunate that the mainstream teaching of color throughout the twentieth century became increasingly disassociated with exploration and reverted to ideological principles with an overdependence on color theories that confuse rather than illuminate. But the groundbreaking advances in science and technology over the past fifty years are shaking the foundation of color education. It is time to reconnect color and light.

Universal Principles of Color presents one hundred essential topics that are critical to understanding the effective use of color, pairing applications of each principle with visual examples from practice. Color is a meta-discipline, and a thorough understanding of color requires appreciation of ideas from a wide range of academic disciplines including, but not limited to, art, philosophy, design, biology, physics, chemistry, and cognitive science. The authors have both straddled the art/science divide throughout their long careers and deliberately present concepts from a wide range of disciplines to challenge the reader to reexamine historical ideas that they may have never questioned before. In presenting concepts through the contemporary lens of how color is understood in the twenty-first century, some topics are not given the prominence that might be expected.

Presented in both alphabetical and categorical order, *Universal Principles of Color* provides an essential foundation for anyone wishing to begin their journey toward understanding how to use the science and art of color to enhance their work and for everyone who wishes to expand their use of color beyond the rainbow.

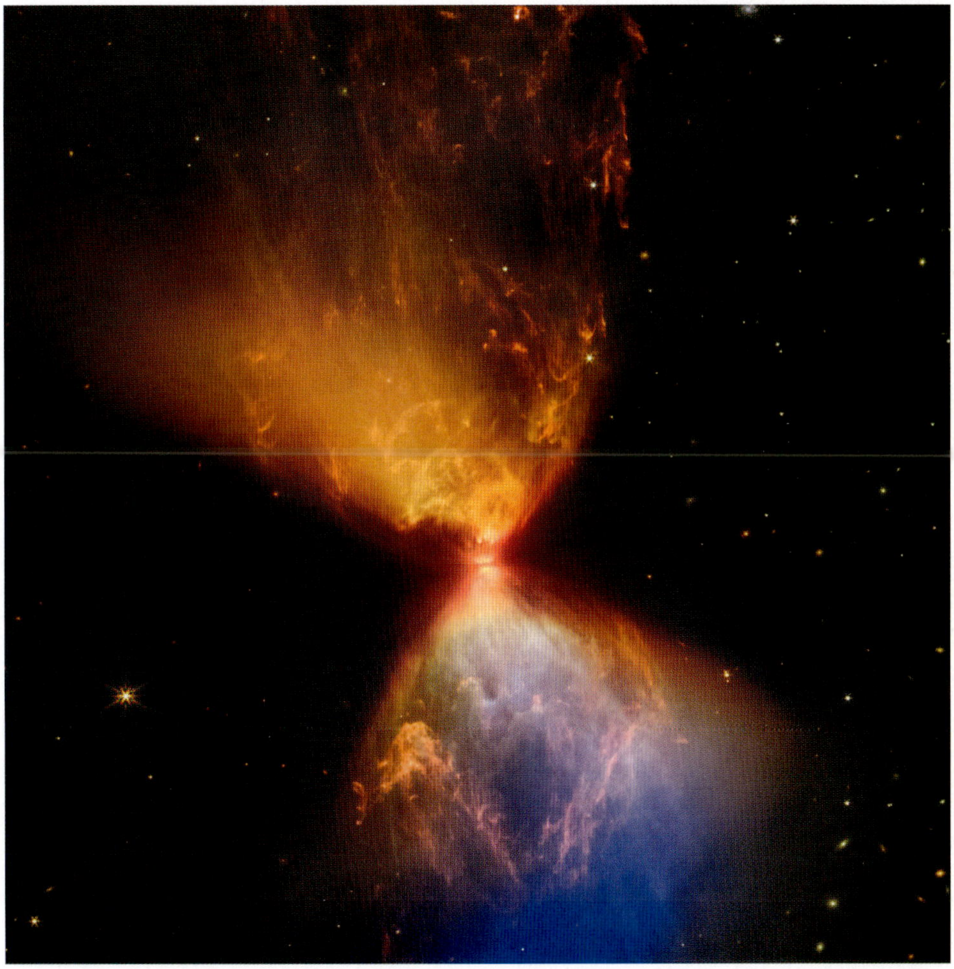

L1527 and Protostar (2022).
A photo from the Webb telescope.

PATHWAYS

We have designed this book to be used in two ways. First, you can simply dip in and read any entry in random order. Each entry is self-contained, though we provide references to other related entries. Second, we have curated the entries into distinct pathways based on nine topics of color study ranging from science, art and design, and industry. Each pathway provides a sequence of entries color-coded by topic area. We suggest reading entries in each topic area in the order given in our Content/Pathways page. We think of this as a color itinerary, with road maps that you can follow on your color journey.

1. Light
2. Object
3. Observer
4. Order
5. Mixture
6. Composition
7. Communication
8. Application
9. History

01 #THE DRESS

An internet meme in 2015 in which people saw a digital photo of a two-color dress as either blue and black or white and gold

The photo of the dress became an internet sensation because it appeared to have different colors to different people at different times. The original digital image was taken by Cecilia Bleasdale of Scotland and showed a dress she intended to wear at her daughter's wedding. Very quickly it emerged that people disagreed about whether the dress was blue and black or white and gold. The image found its way onto the Tumblr page of *New York* magazine's BuzzFeed and attracted more than 10 million tweets within a week.

SEE ALSO:
Color Constancy
Human Visual System
Perception Triangle

The image of the dress garnered huge interest from the public because it countered their inherent assumption that objects have a fixed color. The fact that the dress appeared to be different colors to different people, and even to the same person at different times, revealed the remarkable truth that color is a perception rather than a fixed property of an object. Nevertheless, color perception is complex, and there is currently no consensus on exactly what feature or mechanism of human color vision caused this phenomenon. The fact that the image was closely cropped and overexposed was a likely factor; it is unlikely that such controversy would have resulted from people looking at the actual dress in person.

The furor over the dress prompted vision scientists and neurologists to ask new questions concerning our perception of color and the role of color constancy. Research is ongoing.

#TheDress is a reminder that objects don't have a single fixed color and that the context in which a color appears in a design can have a profound effect on its appearance.

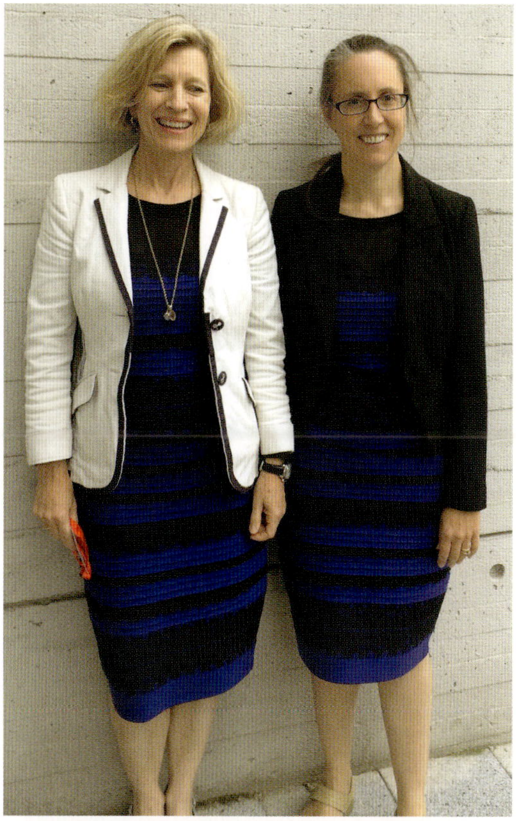

Professor of Visual Neuroscience Anya Hurlbert and Professor of Vision Science Jenny Read, Newcastle University, (left to right), at The European Conference on Visual Perception (ECVP) 2015, Liverpool, UK. It was the digital image of the dress (which was overexposed) rather than the dress itself that caused people to see different colors.

Curious about how to settle the online debate, BuzzFeed posted the photo with a poll: white and gold versus blue and black. The poll triggered millions of responses that ended up with the vote split 2:1 for white and gold. The actual dress was blue and black.

So let's settle this: what colors are this dress?

67% 2.5M votes

White and Gold

33% 1.2M votes

Blue and Black

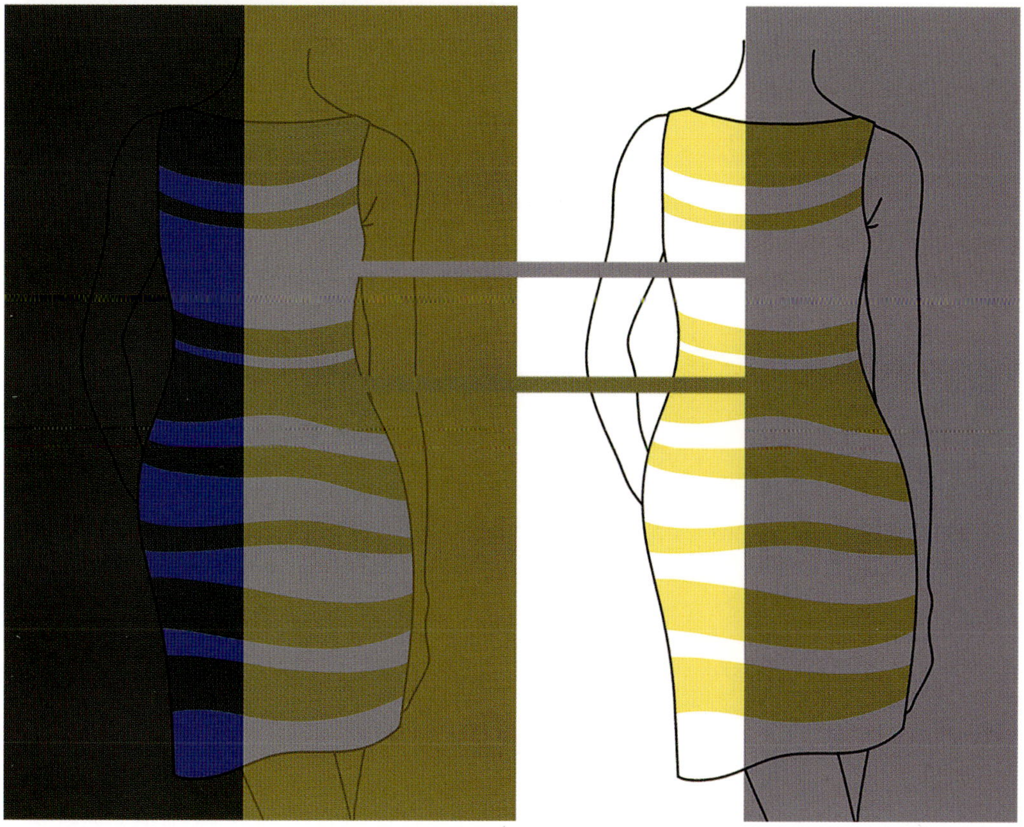

Each individual's interpretation of the colors of the dress depended on their assumptions about the lighting conditions.

02 ACCESSIBILITY

Design color combinations with enough contrast so that the content is clearly legible for people with limited vision

There are many forms of limited vision including low vision, which cannot be corrected by glasses, contacts, or surgery. Eyesight often gets worse with age, and vision impairment caused by glaucoma, cataracts, or diabetes is a leading cause of disability. In addition to low vision, approximately 1 in 12 males and 1 in 200 females have limited color vision, colloquially known as color blindness. People with this condition can see color, but in the most common types of this condition, red and green colors cannot be discriminated from each other.

In terms of web design, accessibility is assessed by the Web Content Accessibility Guidelines (WCAG). WCAG 2.0 was introduced in 2008, and the latest version of the framework awards three accessibility-level standards (AAA, AA, and A).

It is important to consider accessibility in the design stage and to avoid the situation where text and background are similar in lightness.

SEE ALSO:
Contrast
Lightness
Limited Color Vision
Trichromacy

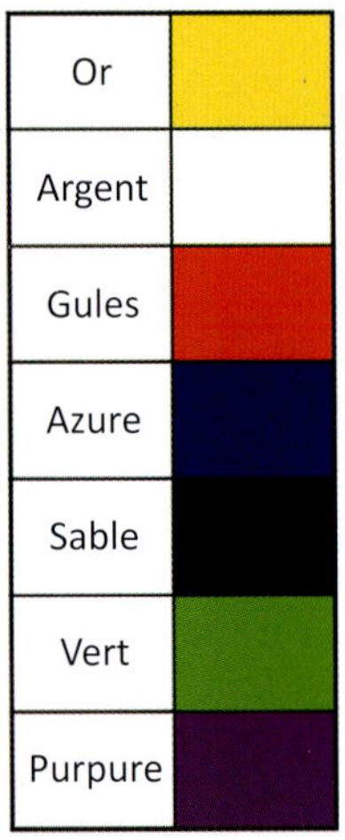

RULE OF TINCTURE

"Metals shall not be put on metals, nor colors on colors."

The medieval rule of tincture is based on the fact that most of the vivid hues have a mid to low lightness and do not contrast with black, while vivid yellows have a high lightness and do not contrast with white.

This practical rule was originally used in heraldry to ensure the legibility of the design on a coat of arms. It can still be used today as a simple and useful guide in graphic design.

Metals: The first metal is Or (yellow); the second metal is Argent (white).
Colors: The third color is Gules (red); the fourth, Azure (blue); the fifth, Sable (black); the sixth, Vert (green); and the seventh, Purpure (purple).

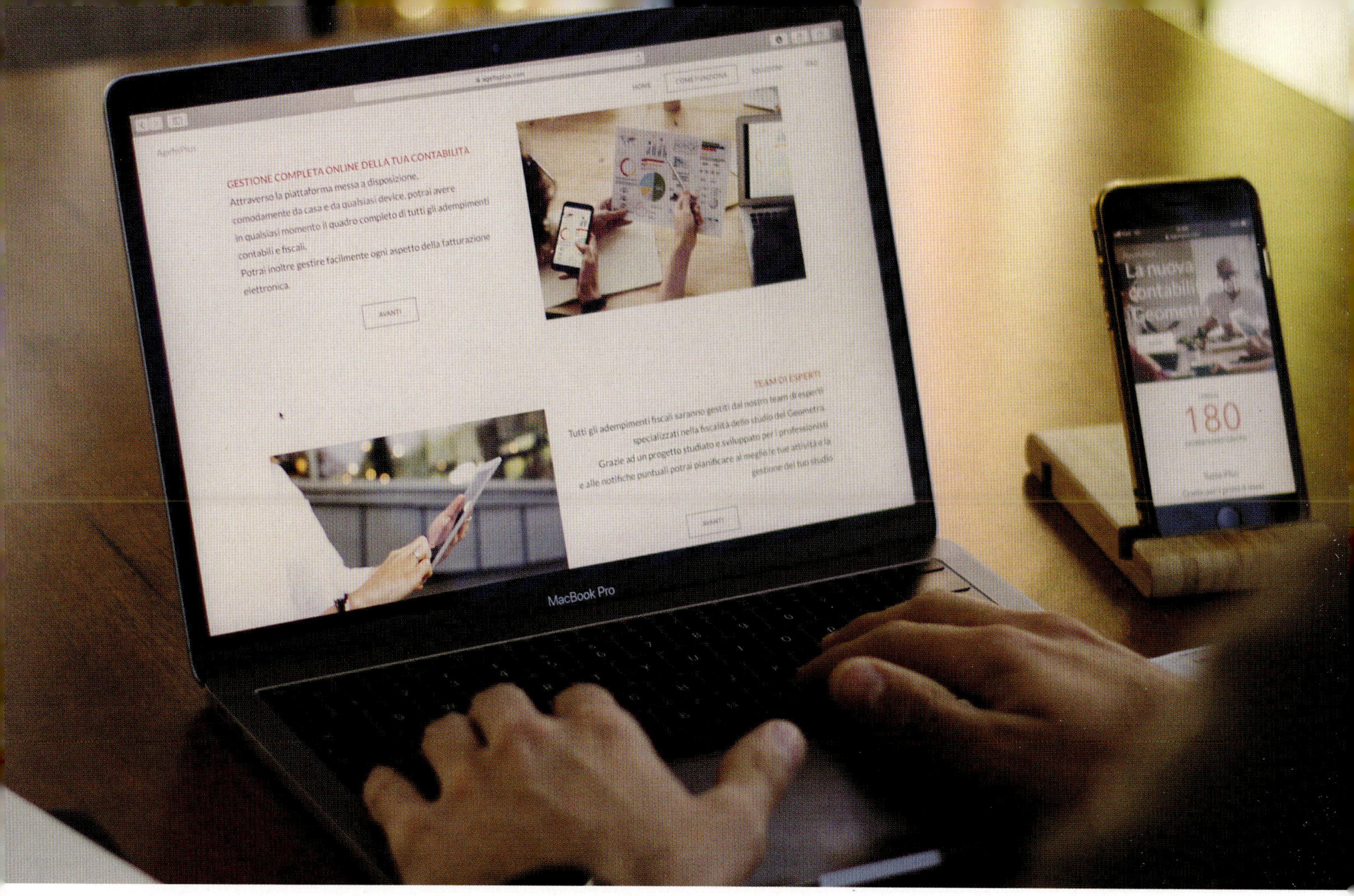

Checking online content using the Web Content Accessibility Guidelines (WCAG) can help ensure legibility for all users. WCAG considers both the contrast between foreground and background and the text size.

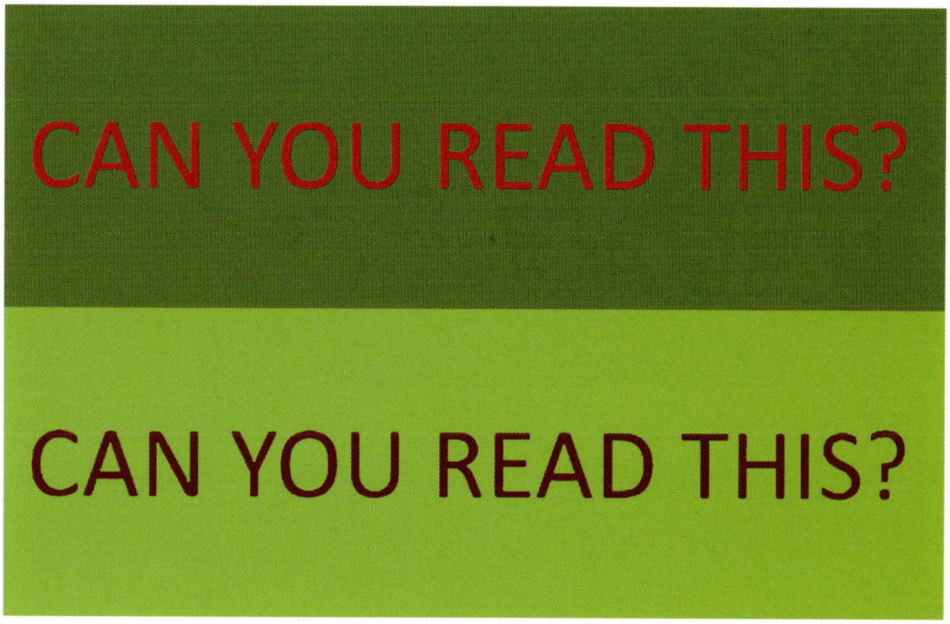

Red on green? Although there is hue contrast in this image, the top text example "Can You Read This?" does not follow the rule of tincture. One solution is to lighten the background and darken the text. This makes the text more accessible.

03 ADDITIVE MIXTURE

The process and effect of combining colored lights

Additive mixture describes the process by which different lights appear to be combined and the colors that result from this process. The term mixing is a bit of a misnomer; what is more accurate is that the lights are spatially coincident or so close together that they cannot be resolved by the eye.

The fact that when lights are combined new colors are created is not a property of light; it is a property of the human visual system. The visual system is not able to resolve the spectral property of light emitted by a source or reflected by an object but instead records the response of three classes of light-sensitive cells in the retina called cones.

The optimal set of three primaries that results in the largest color gamut in light are red, green, and blue. Although this set can generate all hues it cannot generate all the variations of the hues that we can see.

Different manufacturers of displays often use slightly different red, green, and blue primaries in their systems. This makes color fidelity challenging with images that are moved from one imaging device to another. Nevertheless, the three-primary principle of additive color mixture has allowed the development of color imaging technologies such as TV, cameras, projection systems, and emissive displays.

The default color space for working with digital designs is RGB because they are the optimal additive primaries of light.

SEE ALSO:
CMYK
RGB
Subtractive Mixture

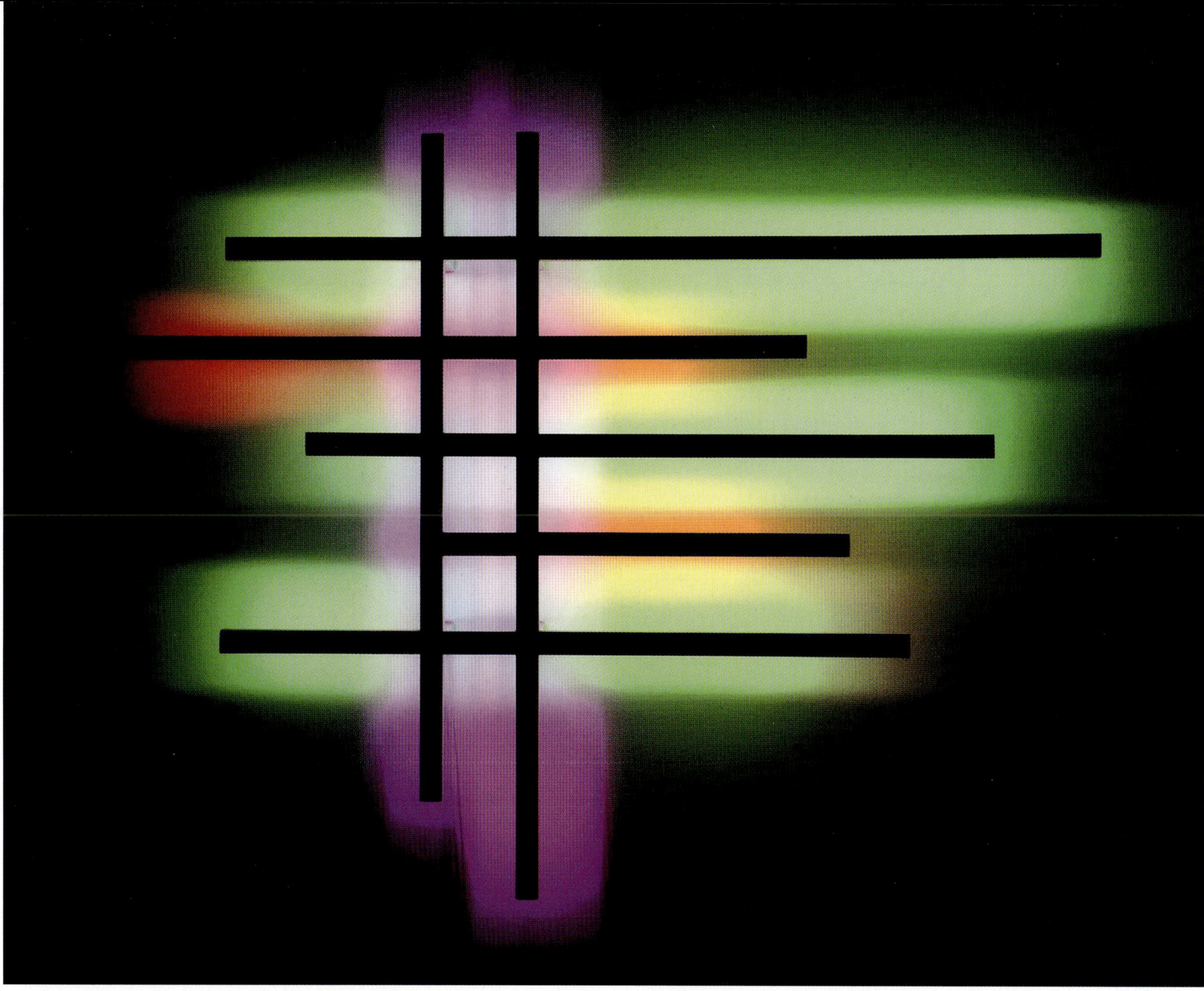

Know Where Your Exits Are (2019), sculpture by Dave Meeker. Aluminum, LEDs, theatrical gels. The white sections in the vertical center are the result of the additive mixture of white LED light shining through green and magenta gels.

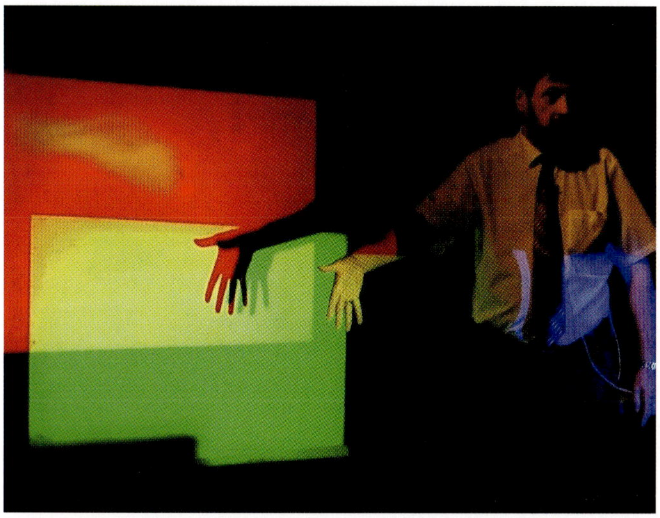

Projected light: additive mixture of projected lights (red + green = yellow). The overlapping of projected lights is an example of additive mixture. In this case, the additive mixture of red and green produces yellow.

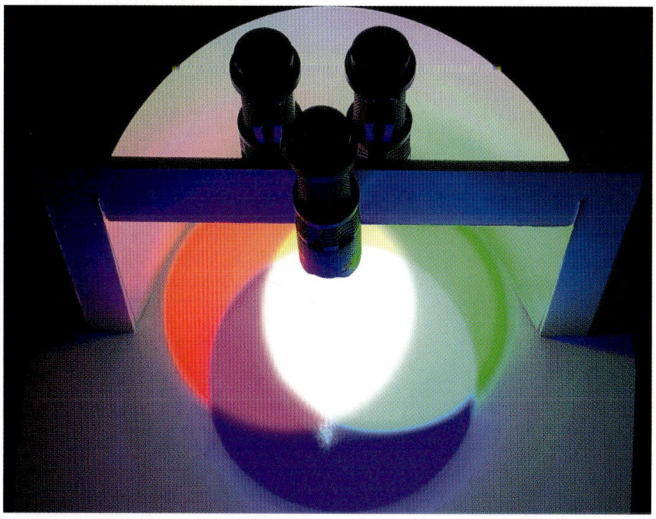

The overlapping of RGB LED flashlights produces the additive mixture of white.

04 ADVANCING AND RECEDING

Colors can appear to be in front of or behind one another, creating the illusion of depth in two dimensions

It is often stated that warm colors advance and cool colors recede. While it may be true that a vivid red swatch will appear to be closer than the same-sized vivid blue swatch, this is not a factor of hue but of chroma.

Vivid blues are lower in chroma than vivid reds. The reverse effect of blue advancing and red receding is possible if the chromatic relationship is shifted, as seen in the design opposite by master weaver Michael Rohde.

There is much more than hue involved in intentionally manipulating color to create a sense of depth. Attention must be paid to the relative lightness and chroma as well as the relationship of figure and ground.

SEE ALSO:
Atmospheric Perspective
Chroma
Warm and Cool

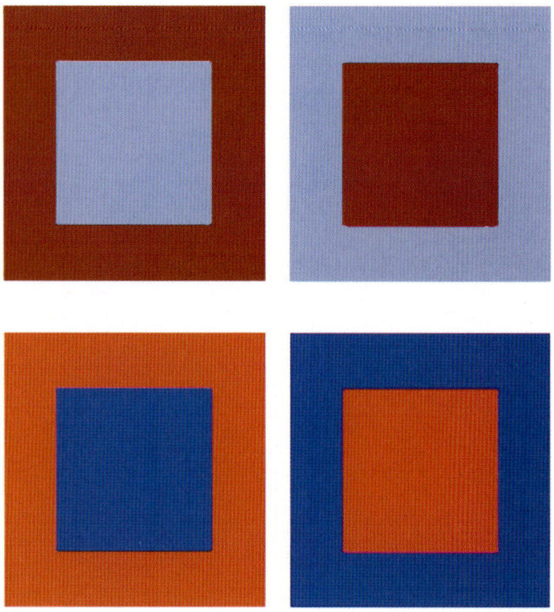

Compare the figure-ground relationships of each of the four variations on the left. Do the smaller squares appear to be on top of the larger squares or behind the frame created by the larger squares?

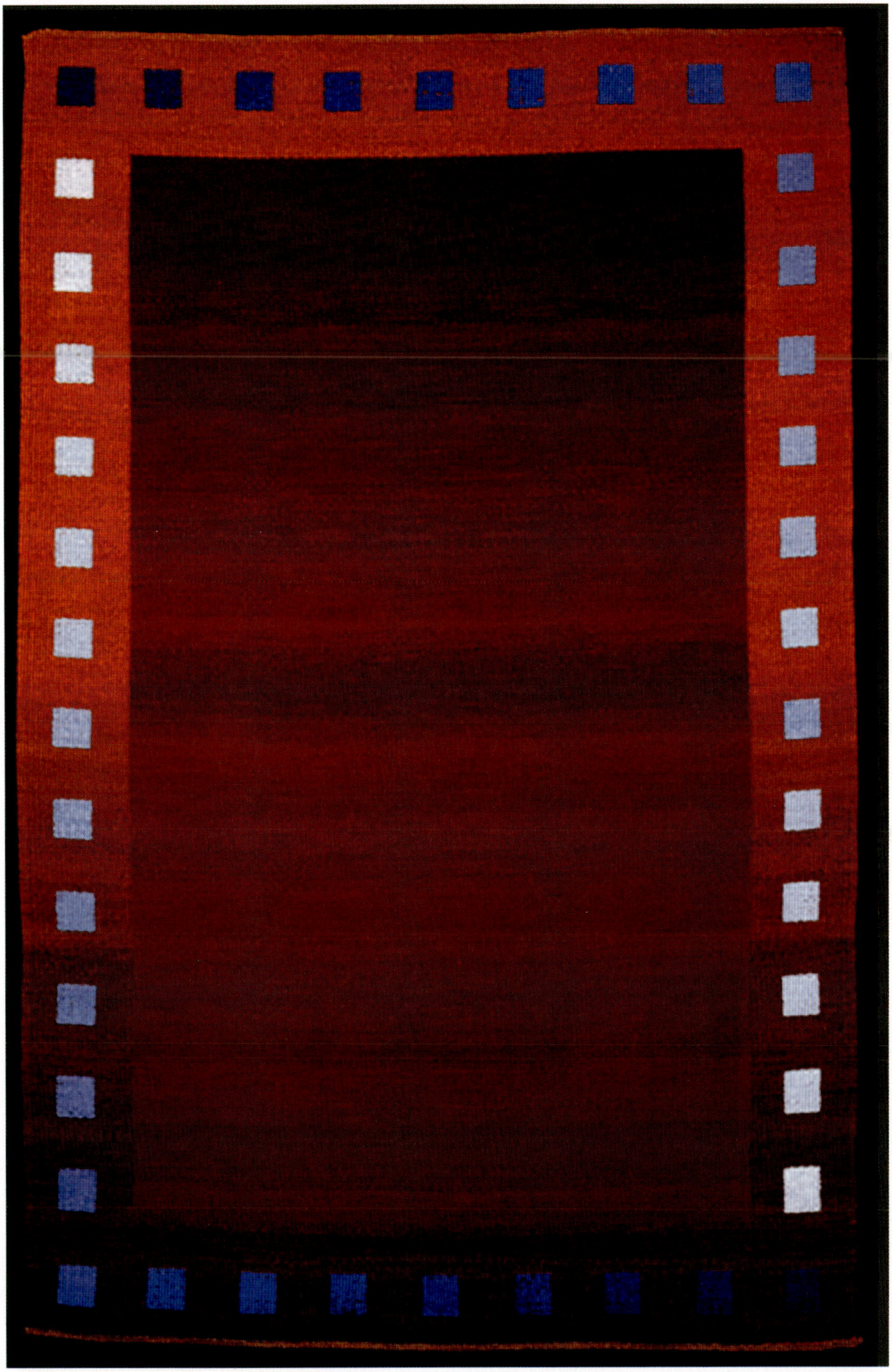

Danse (2002), a hand-dyed wool rug on linen warp by Michael Rohde: Are the blue squares windows or swatches—or both? (photo credit: Andy Neuhart).

05 ALBERS'S *INTERACTION OF COLOR*

The seminal text on color in context by Josef Albers published in 1961

Trained as an art teacher, Josef Albers was a student and then a teacher at the Bauhaus in the 1920s and early 1930s. At the Bauhaus his teaching methods included "... construction experiments with straw, matchboxes, paper and wire." Following the closure of the Bauhaus in 1933, Josef and his wife, Anni, left Germany to teach at the newly formed Black Mountain College in North Carolina.

His course at the college focused on color phenomena rather than on mixing and used paper instead of paint as the medium of choice. Josef and Anni Albers moved to New Haven, Connecticut, in 1950 when he accepted the position of director for the Department of Design at Yale University. He taught the drawing and color courses at Yale, and his teaching approach, experiential and based on perception, influenced generations of artists and designers who went on to teach in programs throughout the United States.

In *Interaction of Color* Albers wrote, "In visual perception a color is almost never seen as it really is—as it physically is. This fact makes color the most relative medium in art. To use color effectively it is necessary to recognize that color deceives continually."

Although the notion that color is physical is contentious today, the key idea that color perception is relative has stood the test of time.

SEE ALSO:
Simultaneous Contrast
Warm and Cool

FURTHER READING:
Interaction of Color (1963), by Josef Albers

"... color is the most relative medium in art."
—*Josef Albers*

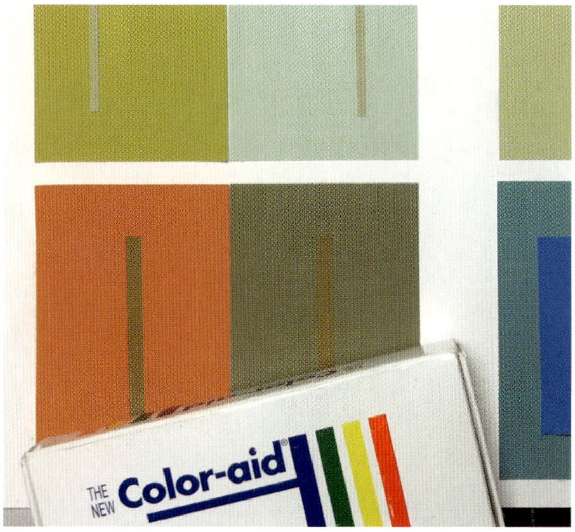

Albers's early color exercises were completed using a collection of all sorts of papers. In the late 1940s he started ordering Color-aid paper to supplement the collection. Color-aid soon became a requirement for an Albers color course.

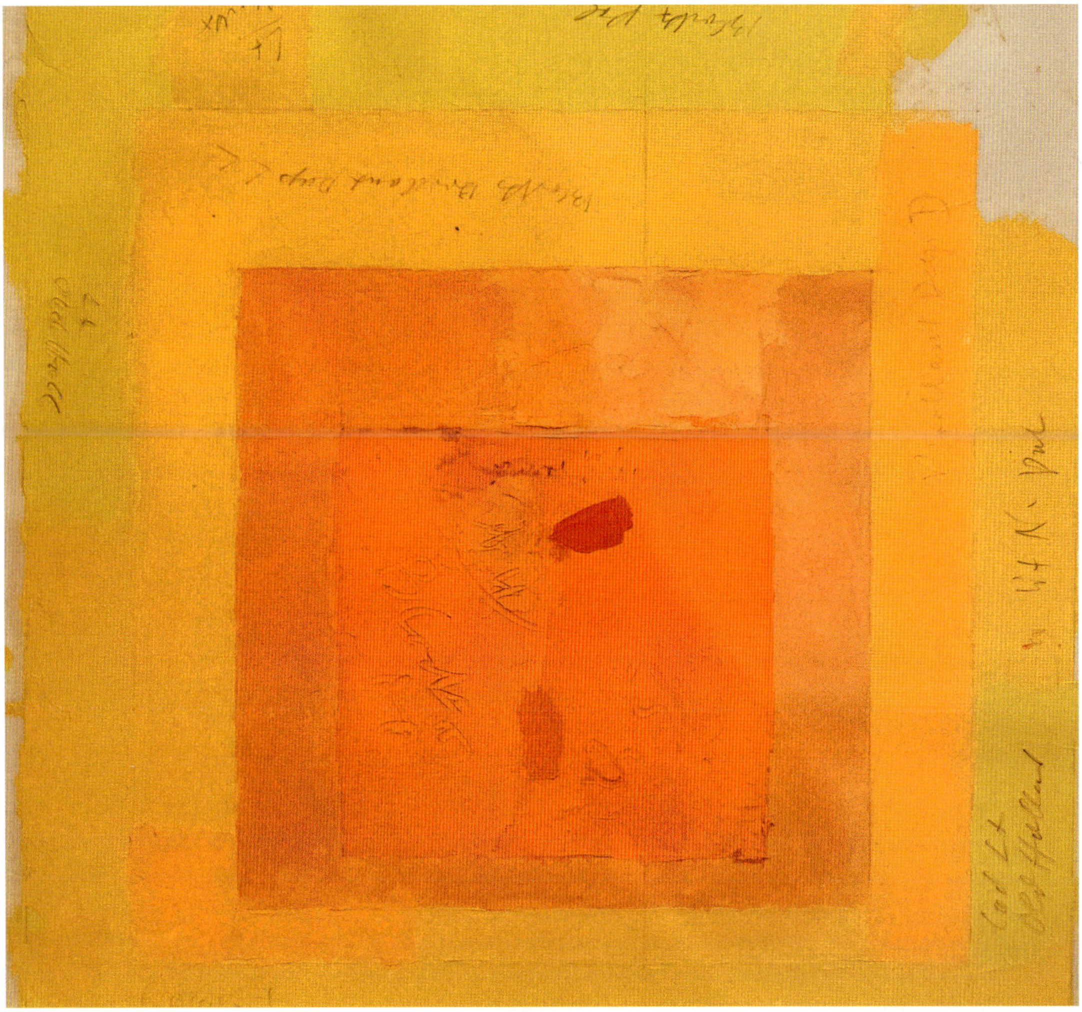

Color Study for Homage to the Square by Josef Albers.
In the world-famous series of paintings, Homage to the Square, Albers explored the relationship of colors in more than a thousand paintings between 1950 and his death in 1976.

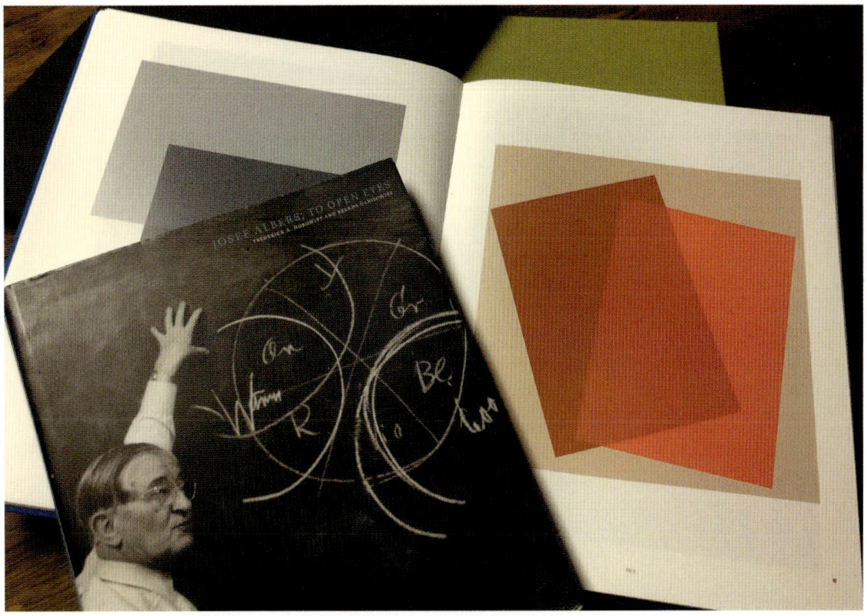

Albers's exercises were published in 1961 in a two-volume set with illustrations in color. The book is open to illustrations of the transparency effect. On top is the book *Josef Albers: To Open Eyes*, a comprehensive history of Albers's life and care by Brenda Danilowitz, chief curator of the Josef & Anni Albers Foundation, and Frederick A. Horowitz.

06 ATMOSPHERIC PERSPECTIVE

The technique of representing more-distant objects as less distinct, bluer, and more muted

Also known as aerial perspective, this technique simulates changes in the appearance of colors in the distance in the scene because of the Earth's atmosphere.

Artists and designers use this technique to create the illusion of depth in their work. The illusion is enhanced by softening edges, limiting detail, and reducing the lightness contrast between objects in the distance.

Based on his observations of nature, Leonardo da Vinci wrote about this principle in *A Treatise on Painting*: "Colors become weaker in proportion to the distance from the person looking at them."

In the "Blue" chapter of *The World According to Color*, James Fox wrote, "Horizons are often blue because of a phenomenon related to Raleigh scattering called aerial perspective: as objects recede from us, they are veiled by ever more scattered light, appearing progressively bluer, before terminating in a hazy cerulean horizon."

In summary, objects in the distance appear to become progressively:

- Smaller in size
- Less detailed
- Weaker in chroma
- Faded and lighter
- Bluer, depending on time of day

SEE ALSO:
Chroma
Rayleigh Scattering

"In an atmosphere of uniform density the most distant things seen through it, such as the mountains, in consequence of the great quantity of atmosphere which is between your eye and them, will appear blue. Therefore you should make the ... wall which is more distant less defined and bluer... five times as far away, make five times as blue."

– Leonardo da Vinci

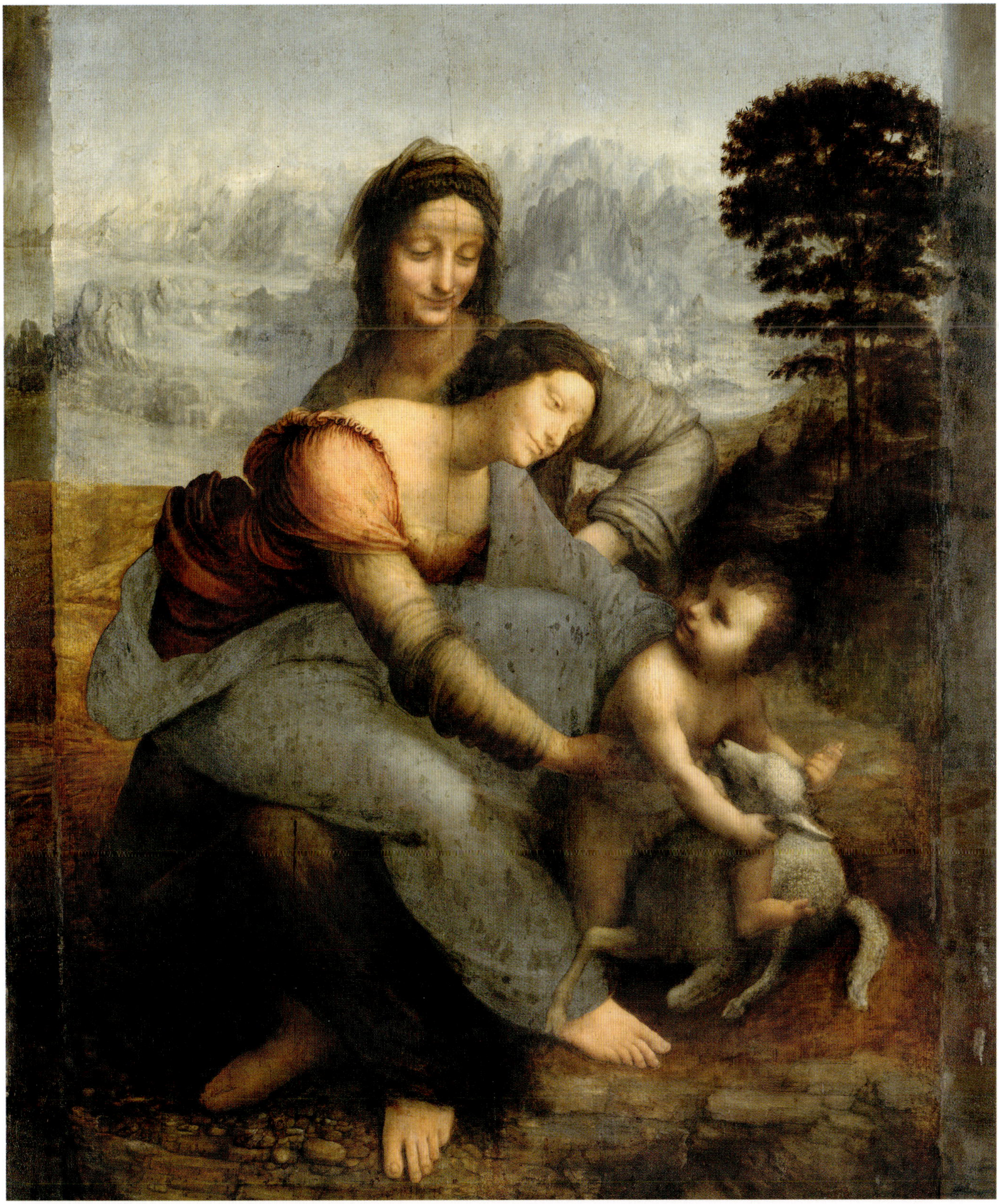

The Virgin and Child with Saint Anne (1510), by Leonardo da Vinci.
The mountains fading into the distance are an example of atmospheric perspective.

07 BALANCE

The subjective perception of unity combining proportion and the visual weight of colors

Balance is one of the key elements of design. While there are many historic references that suggest ways to create balance, there are no fixed rules that will guarantee that a design feels balanced. Some references suggest developing a color scheme based on set proportions of complementary colors; others suggest selecting dominant, supporting, and accent colors. While these concepts may provide a starting point, in the long run putting colors together is a process of trial and error. What feels balanced to one person may feel unsettling to another.

SEE ALSO:
Color Schemes
Complementary Colors

One issue with illustrations of the traditional guidelines or rules is that they usually show only the vivid hues. But if you visualize balancing colors using an imaginary scale, then hue is only part of the equation. Variations in the lightness and chroma, such as pale, muted, and dark versions of the hue, each have different visual weights that affect the overall balance.

It is more effective to balance color by considering not only the hue contrasts but also the relative proportions of lightness and chroma.

PROPORTION

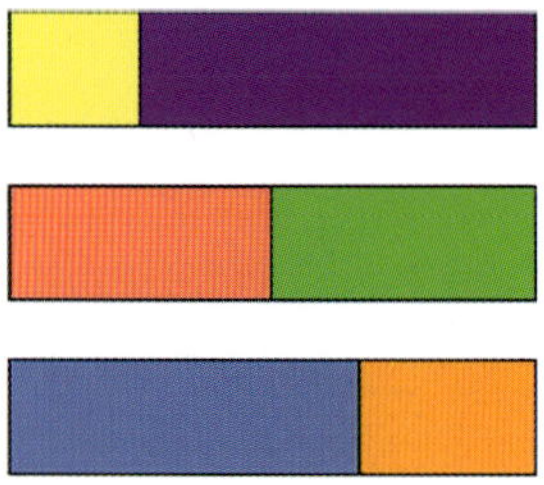

Traditional Complements

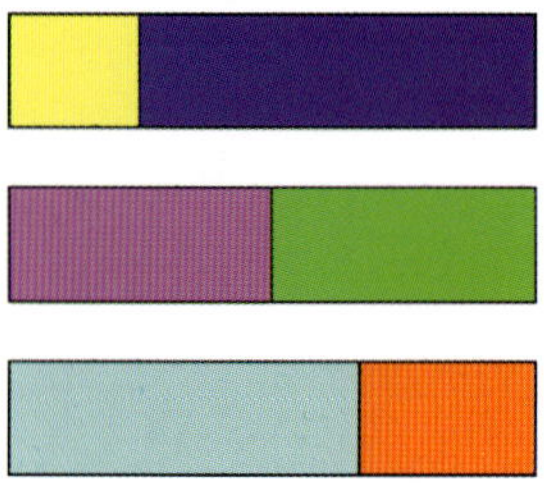

Digital Complements

Traditional color theory recommends set proportions of the six opposing, or complementary, hues. These proportions have less to do with hue and more to do with natural differences in chroma of the vivid hues.

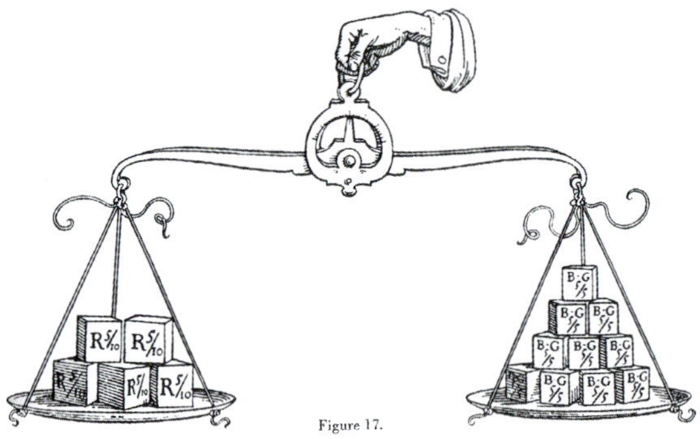

Balancing the visual weight (chroma) of opposing Munsell hues. From *A Grammar of Color* (1921) by T. M. Cleland.

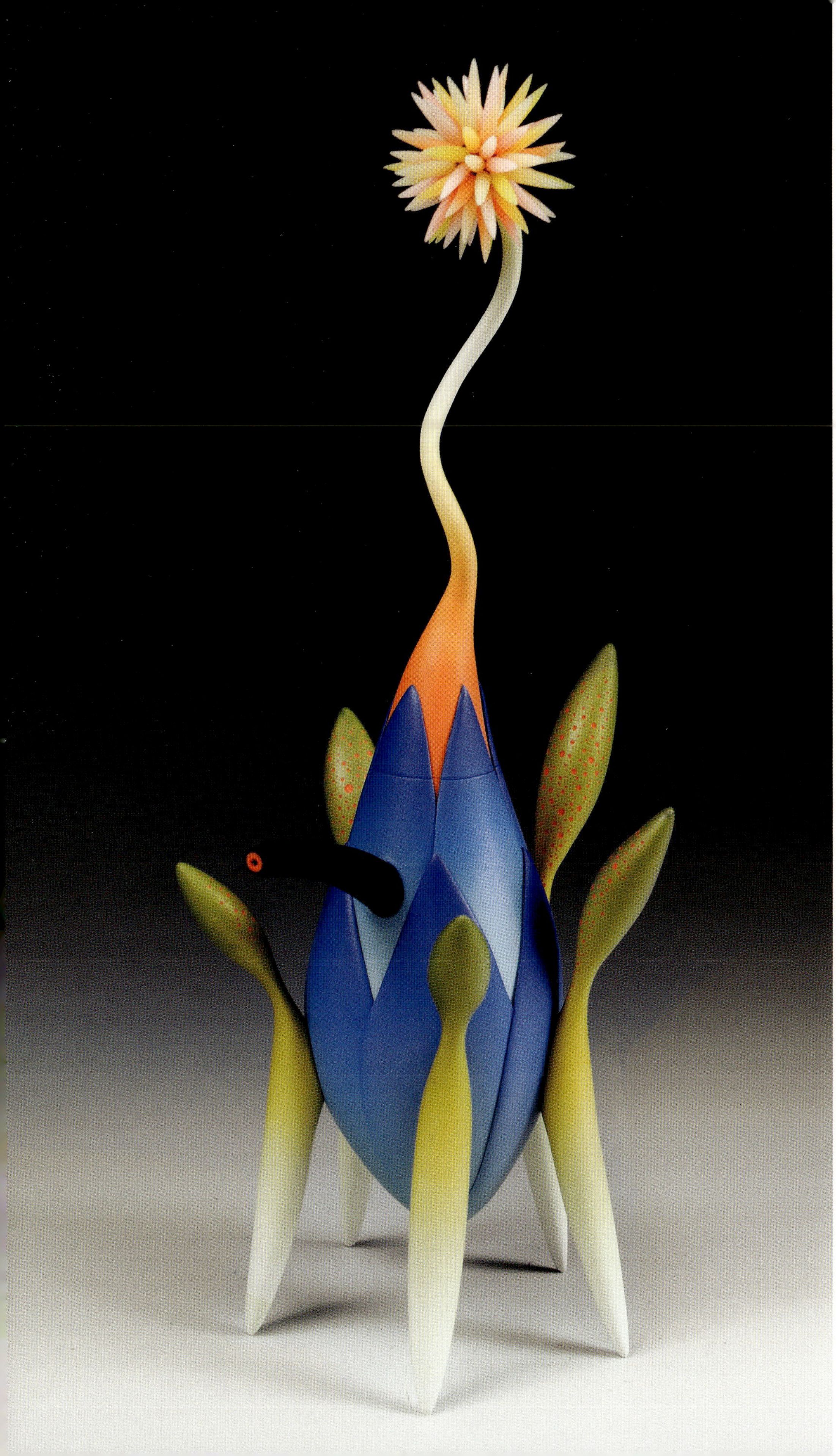

La Joie du Printemps (2014), a polymer teapot by Jeffrey Lloyd Dever.

08 BASIC COLOR TERMS

The eleven basic color terms—white, black, red, yellow, green, blue, brown, pink, purple, orange, and gray—are widely understood irrespective of culture and language

Many studies have explored the relationship between language and color. One study by Brent Berlin and Paul Kay in 1969 explored the notion of basic color terms. They noted that some languages are more developed than others in terms of the available words to describe colors. They also noticed that there was a consistency in the language development between the different cultures; for example, a culture that has a word for *blue* always has an existing word for *red*. The study led to the theory that there are eleven basic color terms that are widely understood: white, black, red, yellow, green, blue, brown, pink, purple, orange, and gray. These terms are more salient than color names such as, for example, fuchsia.

SEE ALSO:
Character Zones
Munsell System
Three Dimensions of Color

The Berlin and Kay study contributed to the debate on linguistic relativity in the context of color and supports universalism. Universalists believe that color perception is the same for all of us irrespective of our language and culture; relativists, on the other hand, subscribe to the Sapir-Whorf hypothesis, which assumes that the language we speak affects how we think. In the context of color perception, relativists would argue that our color perception is influenced by our culture and language. Since 1969 further studies have been done and the original Berlin and Kay study has been critiqued. There are likely universal constraints on color naming, but at the same time, differences in language may affect color perception to some extent.

An online color-naming experiment conducted in 2015 by Dimitris Mylonas and Lindsay MacDonald makes the case for adding two additional colors to the list of basic terms: turquoise and lilac.

Once we move beyond the basic color terms, language becomes much less precise. It is necessary to learn additional terms to describe lightness and chroma to describe color accurately.

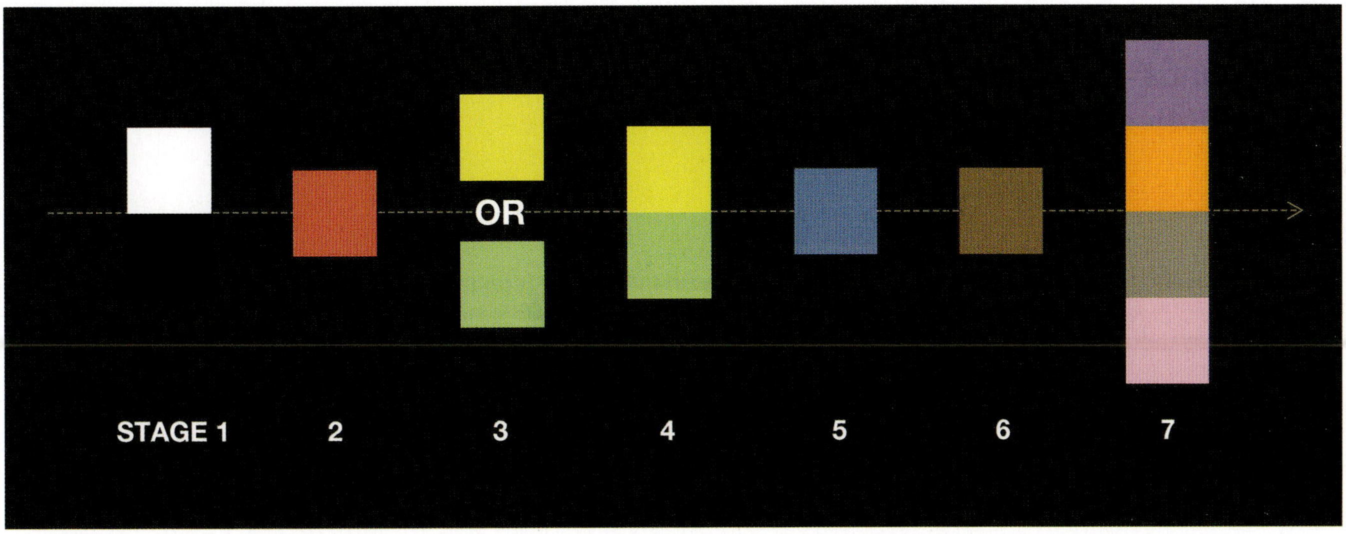

The seven stages of language development for color terms according to the Berlin and Kay study: black and white (stage 1); red (stage 2); yellow or green (stage 3); yellow and green (stage 4); blue (stage 5); brown (stage 6); and purple, orange, gray, and pink (stage 7). There is on-going controversy about how many basic color terms there are and whether these apply to all cultures and languages.

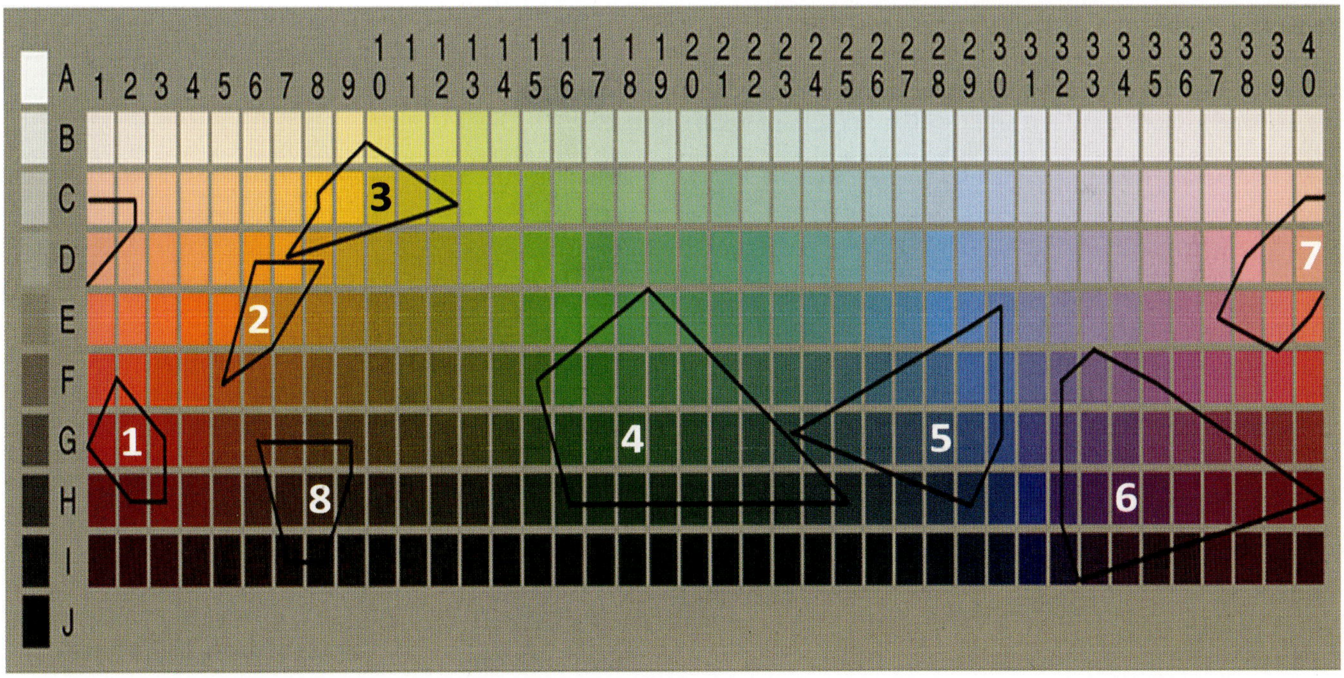

The Munsell color chart and the resulting areas defining 11 basic color terms in the 1969 Berlin and Kay study. Black, white and grey plus: 1. Reds. 2. Oranges. 3. Yellows. 4. Greens. 5. Blues. 6. Purples. 7. Pinks. 8. Browns.

09 BAUHAUS

An influential German art and design school that made seminal contributions to twentieth-century architecture, design, and color education

The Bauhaus—also known as *Staatliches Bauhaus*—was founded in Weimar Germany in 1919 by the architect Walter Gropius. Famous for its interdisciplinary approach to art, craft, and design, the comprehensive program influenced modern thinking and practice in many areas of design, including color.

Four prominent artists related to the Bauhaus—Johannes Itten, Wassily Kandinsky, Paul Klee, and Josef Albers—made notable contributions to color theory. Itten was known for his emphasis on warm and cool colors and for the development and use of a color wheel. Itten's wheel was based on red, yellow, and blue primaries and is now quite dated because it is understood that the combination of red, yellow, and blue is a poor choice for subtractive primaries.

Josef Albers also made important and lasting contributions, and his book *Interaction of Color* remains hugely relevant today. Albers was particularly known for his emphasis on the relativity of color. He produced many beautiful studies of how colors change depending on the colors that surround them.

When the Bauhaus closed in 1933, many faculty emigrated to the United States, including Albers and architects Ludwig Mies van der Rohe and Gropius.

SEE ALSO:
Albers's *Interaction of Color*
Itten's *The Art of Color*

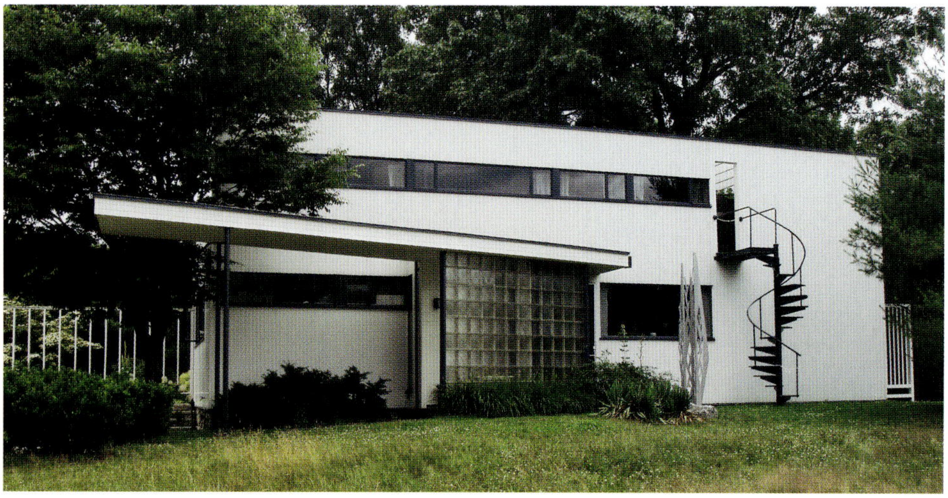

An icon of the Bauhaus influence on the modernist movement in architecture, the Gropius House in Lincoln, Massachusetts, was built in 1938 while Gropius was head of the architecture faculty at Harvard University.

The Bauhaus operated in three German cities. This building in Dessau, designed by Bauhaus founder Walter Gropius, was the most iconic location.

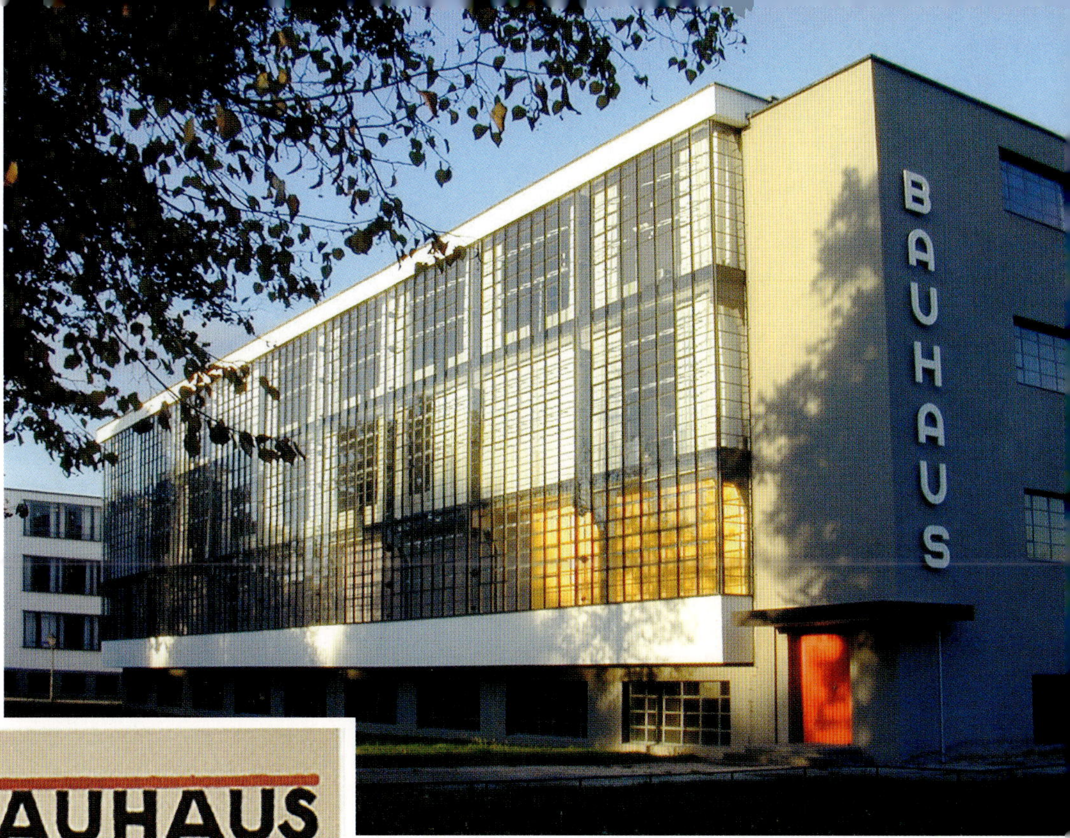

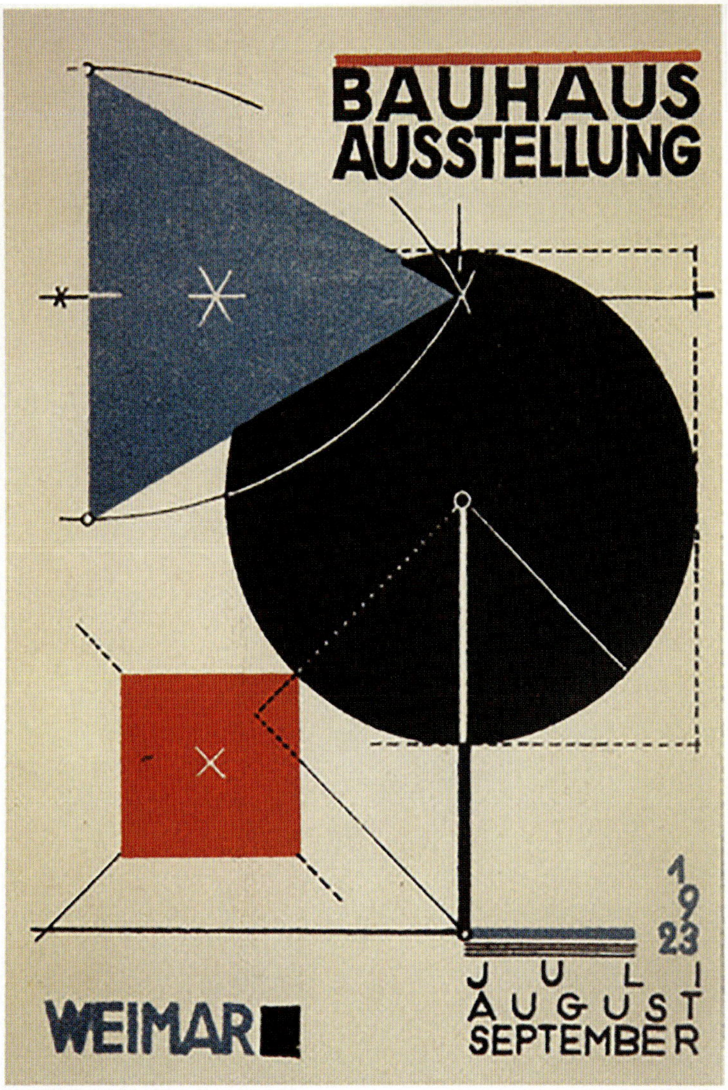

Poster for the 1923 Weimar Bauhaus Exhibition by graphic designer Herbert Bayer.

10 BEZOLD EFFECTS

The substitution of a single color causes every other color in the design to shift in relationship

The Bezold Effect is named after the German professor Wilhelm von Bezold (1837–1907), who observed in the nineteenth century that a color may appear different depending on its relation to adjacent colors. The Bezold Effect refers to the phenomenon where changing a single color in a design causes the perceptual color of every other color in the design to shift. The apparent changes to the other colors in the design are not always consistent; for example, some of the colors in the pattern may become darker and others lighter.

One version of the Bezold Effect is shown opposite. It is an example of how just changing the outline color of a pattern can dramatically alter the appearance.

Effects such as Bezold and simultaneous contrast are all similar in that they demonstrate that color perception is relative. This relative property of color has been known for centuries but is not widely understood. Nevertheless, it is a critical component of many 2D design processes.

Understanding that form affects color and color affects form is of particular significance in 2D design (e.g., textiles and wallpaper).

SEE ALSO:
Partitive Mixture
Simultaneous Contrast

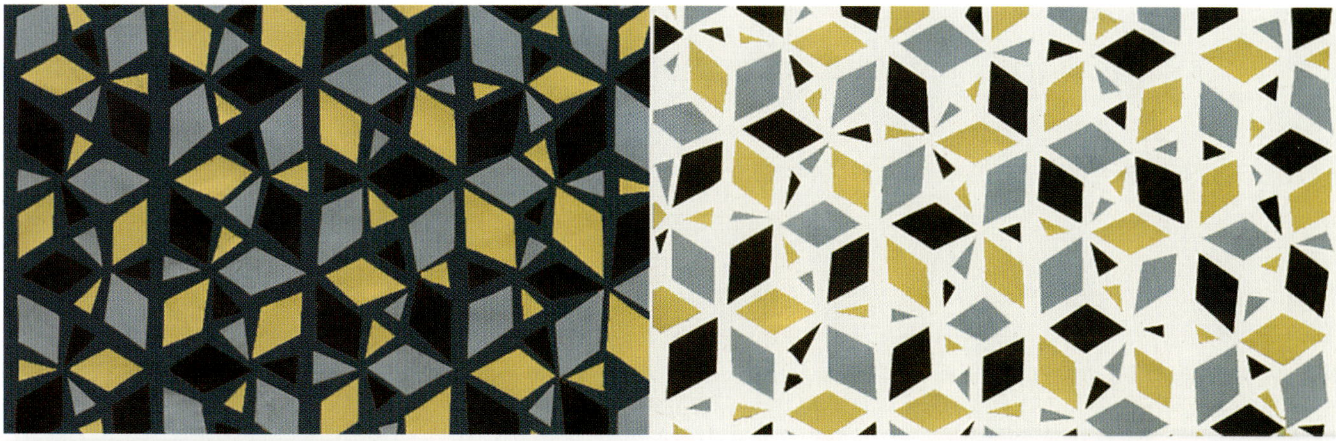

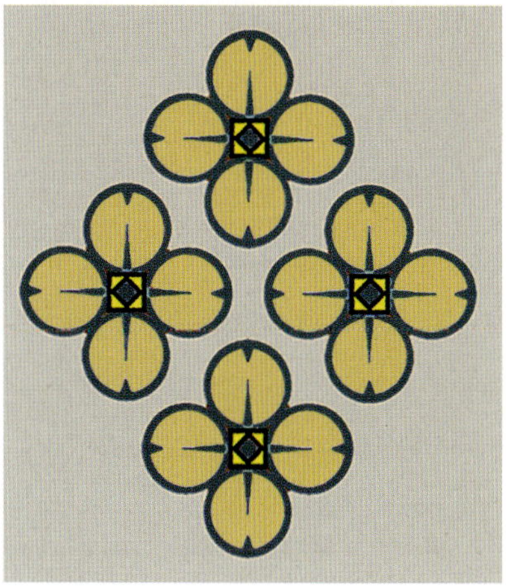

Outline effect: Changing the color of the outline in the pattern above affects the overall perception of the color scheme.

Spreading effect: The yellow is the same in both flower designs but appears different due to perceptual blending.

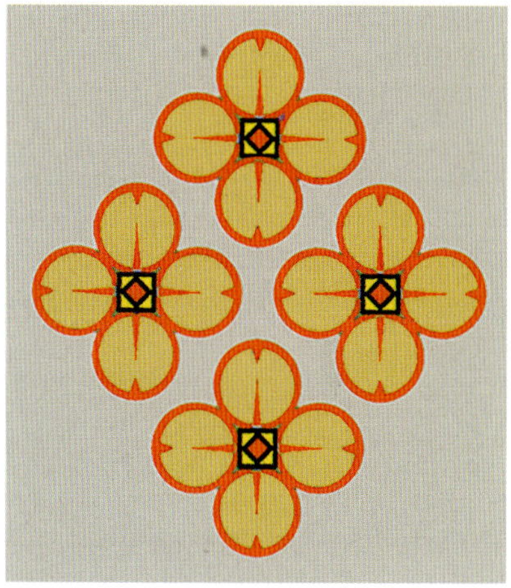

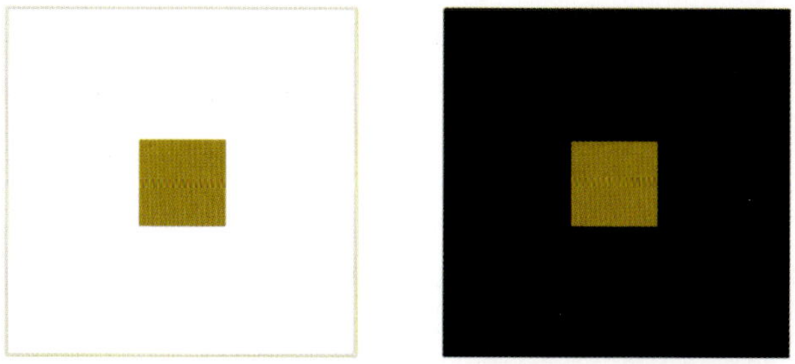

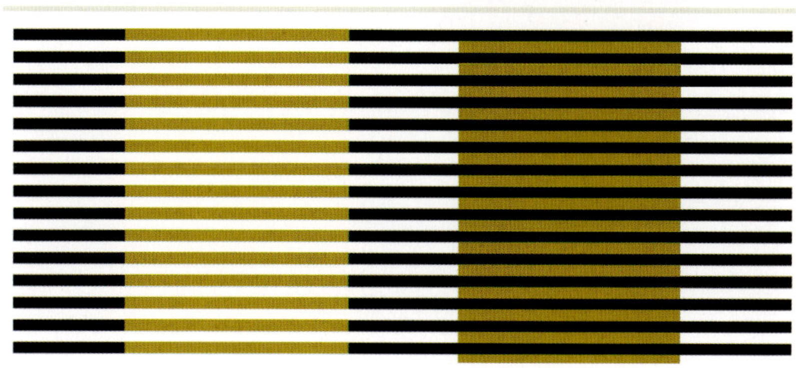

Simultaneous contrast (top) compared with Assimilation (bottom).

Simultaneous contrast: Showing that the gold appears darker on white and lighter on black.

Munker-White illusion showing that the gold appears lighter alternating with white and darker alternating with black.

11 BLACK AND WHITE

The darkest and lightest of the colors

The simplicity of black and white is classic. The controversy over the relative merits of drawing over painting in Renaissance Italy (*disegno* vs. *colore*) positioned the use of color as a less noble art than working in black and white. To this day, value studies in black and white are often the first step in creating a work of art or design because they are the quickest way to evaluate the lightness contrasts and "make it right in black and white."

Are black and white colors? Yes, they are colors with neither chroma nor hue. In other words, they are achromatic colors. The gray colors between black and white are rarely achromatic in practice, since they often have an undertone of hue that can be identified when they are compared with neutral grays. These very low-chroma colors are called chromatic grays.

Most black paints reflect about 4 percent of the light that falls on them across the visible spectrum. Recently, a super-black coating called Vantablack was developed. Vantablack, invented by Ben Jensen, has a reflectance of less than 1 percent. It is not a pigment but rather is constructed from a nanomaterial. The search for the perfect black pigment has ramped up in recent years with the latest version, Musou, developed at MIT, announced in 2019.

In 2022 researchers at Purdue University announced the results of tests carried out on their ultra-white paint made using barium sulfate. Tests showed that it reflected more than 98 percent of sunlight compared with the 90 percent reflectance of the next whitest white paint. Further testing for permanence and cost-efficiency are underway, but the scientists are hopeful that the new "whitest white" could help save energy and fight climate change.

SEE ALSO:
Colorants
Grisaille

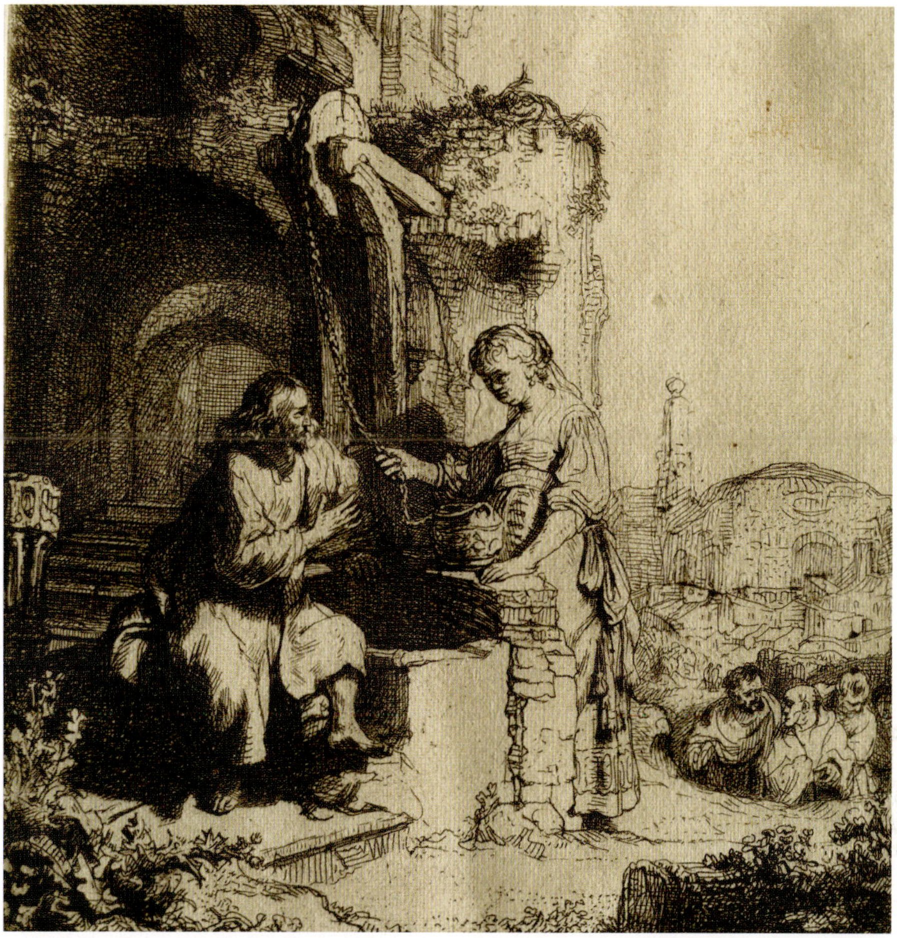

Christ and the Woman of Samaria among Ruins (1634). Etching by Rembrandt van Rijn.

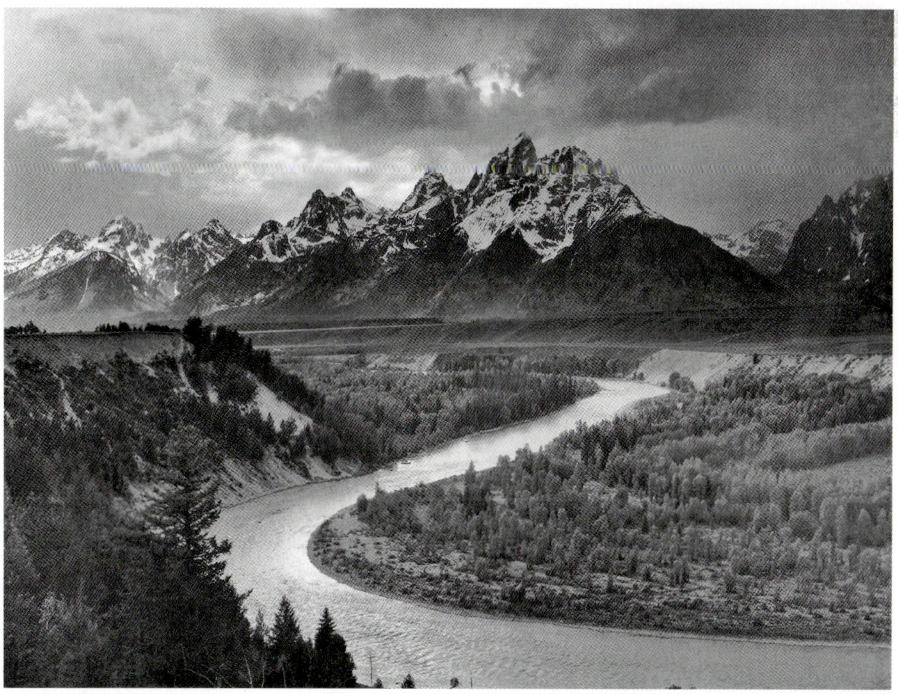

The Tetons and the Snake River (1942), a photograph by Ansel Adams. Adams' Zone System achieved the desired final print through understanding how the tonal range of an image depends on exposure, development, and printing in photography.

12 BLUE LIGHT

The intensity and color of light can interfere with natural sleeping patterns and overall well-being

In 2013 an academic paper reported that the installation of blue lights on the subway platforms of stations in Tokyo led to a reduction of suicides by 84 percent. Although the implications of this claim are not clear, the story did generate a plethora of similar stories about the health benefits of color and light and the potential harmful effects.

Until around 2000 it was believed that the human visual system contained four photopigments: three that mediated color vision, and one that was involved in low-level night vision. In the last couple of decades, we have seen the discovery of a fifth photopigment (melanopsin); retinal ganglion cells that contain this light-sensitive pigment send signals to the hypothalamus in the brain, which regulates the human circadian system.

Exposure to very intense light sources (particularly blue light) may cause damage to the visual system. However, light emitted from computer displays is unlikely to be sufficiently bright to be a problem. Nevertheless, it is now established that patterns of light and dark over a 24-hour period help to entrain the human circadian system, which is critical for healthy sleep. Exposure to too much light in the hours before sleeping and/or insufficient exposure to light in the hours just after waking are likely to negatively impact sleep and well-being in general.

Our increasing understanding of the effect of light on health and well-being is impacting how lighting is being used in the design of our homes and workplaces.

SEE ALSO:
Human Visual System
Lighting

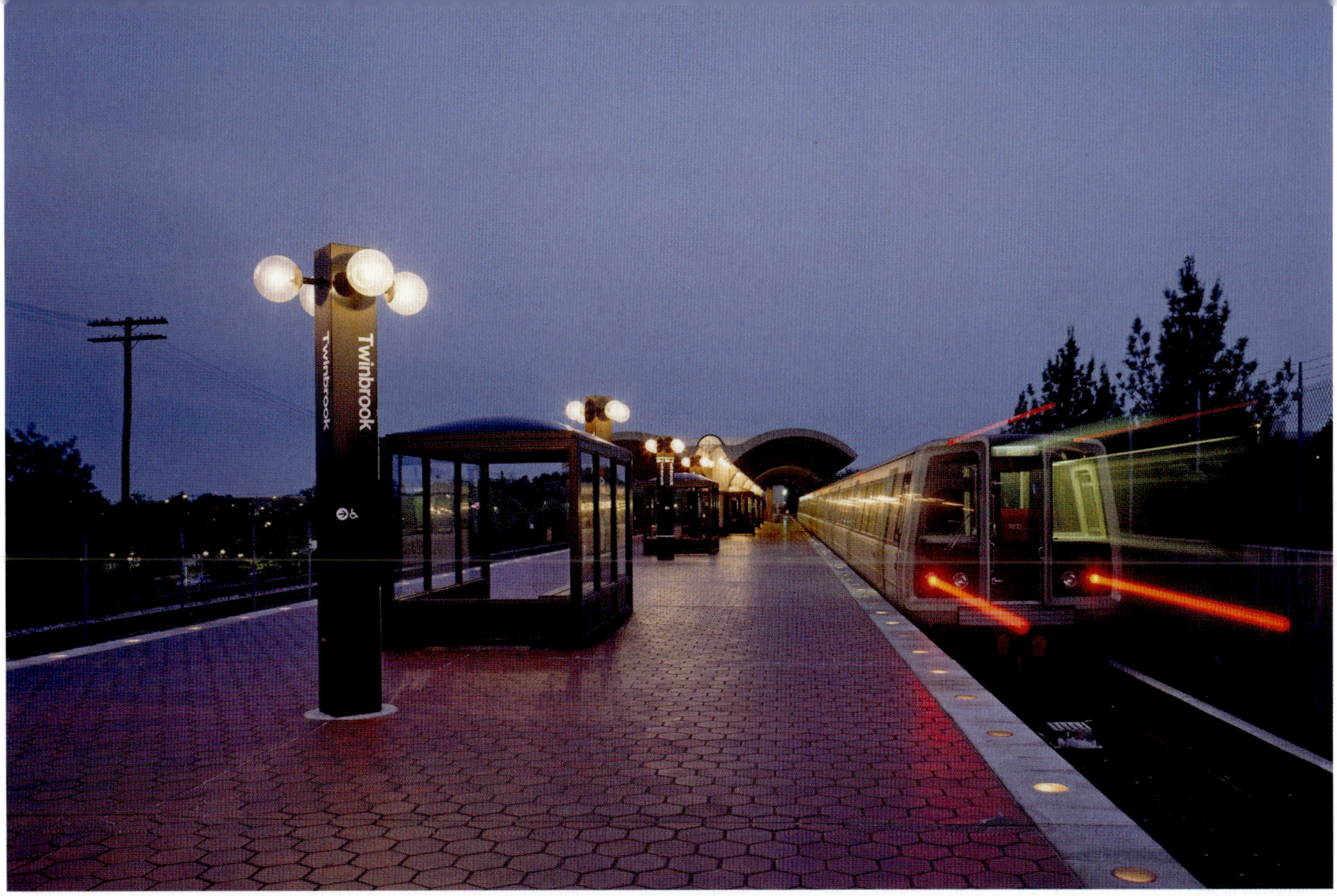

Installation of blue light at subway stations in Tokyo has led to various installations of light systems in several locations globally with claims about effects on human health and performance. Whether these effects are genuine is still being researched.

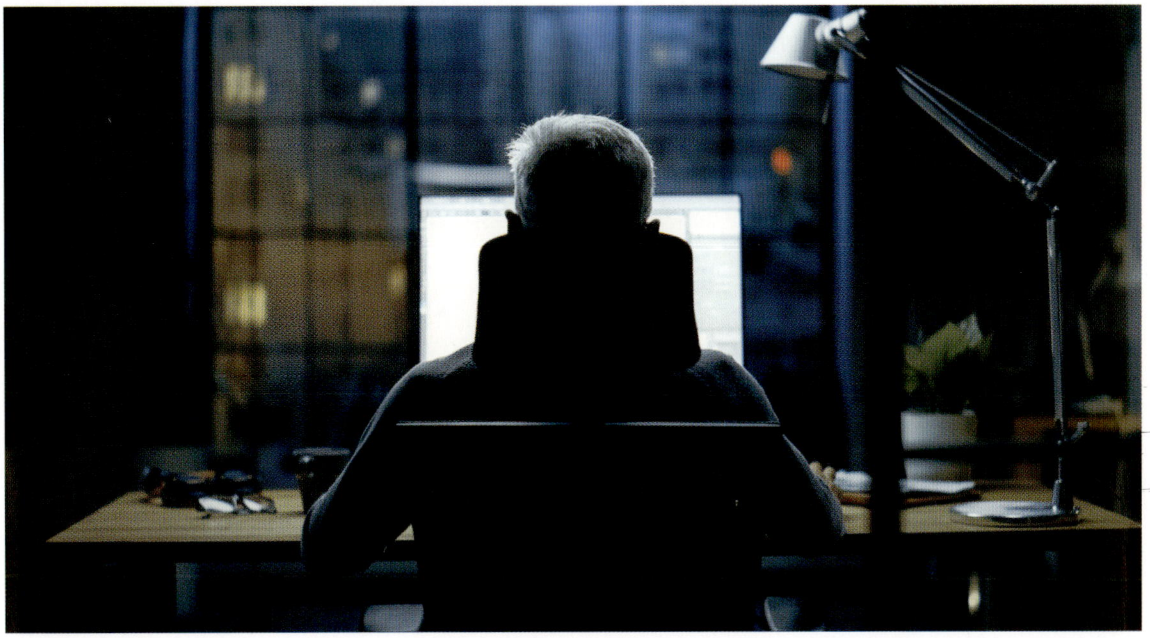

Blue emitted from computer screens is unlikely to damage the eyes directly because it is insufficiently bright. However, concerns remain about the use of emissive displays in the hours before sleep and the potential negative effect on sleep, health, and well-being.

13 BRAND COLORS

A small set of specific colors that are strongly linked with a company or institution

Vision is often the most important of the senses in terms of the effect on consumers. Although there are products for which other senses are equally important, or even more important, for many products the choice of color for the product or the packaging is vital for the product's success.

Studies suggest that the use of color can aid brand recognition and recall. Colors can also successfully represent a brand, and this is achieved most frequently in terms of the brand's visual identity. In many countries it is possible to protect the use of specific colors through a trademark. The most successful visual identities or logos use colors that communicate ideas and emotions that are consistent with the brand's values.

The red Coca-Cola uses is one of the most famous uses of color for branding, and the company has used that color from the very early years, when barrels of Coca-Cola were painted red so that they could be easily distinguished from barrels of alcohol. The use of red by Coca-Cola has been so successful that the use of red (and white) is firmly established as a generic color code for sweet soft drinks. The unique hues (red, yellow, green, and blue) are used to represent brands more than other colors because they help to generate strong and clear identities.

Tiffany Blue was first used on the cover of Tiffany & Co.'s "Blue Book" in 1837. In 2001 the company worked with Pantone to standardize a custom color for use around the world.

Color is a vital component of the visual identity of brands and can aid brand recognition and recall.

SEE ALSO:
Color Forecasting
Color Meaning
Symbolic Color

"No one can own color. Color exists. It's just a phenomenon of nature. How can you own an experience that your eyes have when they see something?"
—*Stuart Semple*

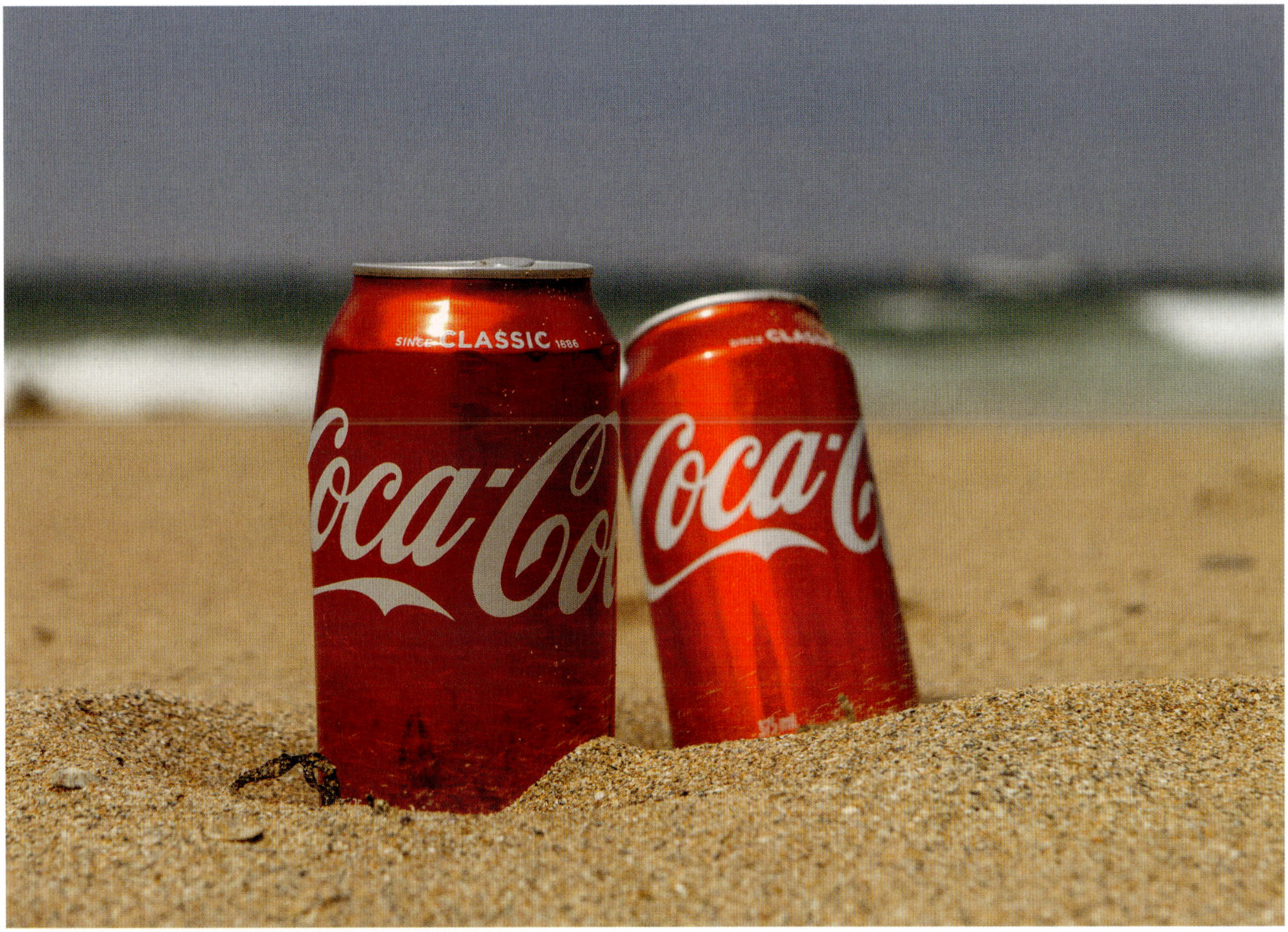

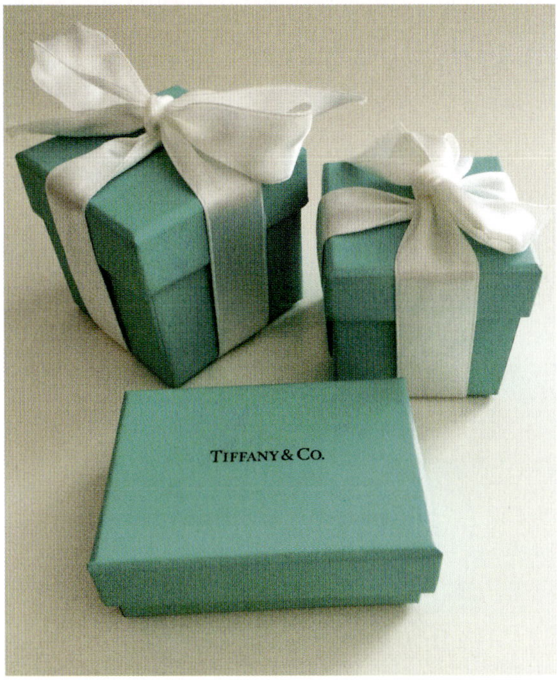

The use of red and white in the Coca-Cola can is firmly established by the market leader and is a generic color code in this product category.

The iconic Tiffany brand of blue was standardized as a Pantone color in 2001 as 1837 Blue.

14 CAMOUFLAGE

Pattern designs inspired by animals in nature who often avoid detection by blending with their surround

Camouflage, one of the oldest examples of biomimicry, is a principle widely found in nature whereby animals use colors that match their environment to make it difficult for them to be seen. In some cases (e.g., chameleons and cephalopods), animals can modify their body color to suit a changing environment.

The idea of using camouflage for military applications became widespread during World War I. France is believed to be the first country to create a dedicated camouflage unit in 1915. (The word *camouflage* comes from the French verb "to make up for the stage"). Originally used to hide guns and vehicles, today camouflage is ubiquitous in military clothing.

The potential for use of camouflage in fashion was picked up by *Vogue* in 1943 and became mainstream when Andy Warhol produced a series of camouflage prints in the 1980s. Popular through the 1990s and the early aughts, the camo trend in fashion is once again on an upswing.

Camouflage is just one example of how artists and designers can be inspired by what we observe in nature.

SEE ALSO:
Chemistry of Chromophores

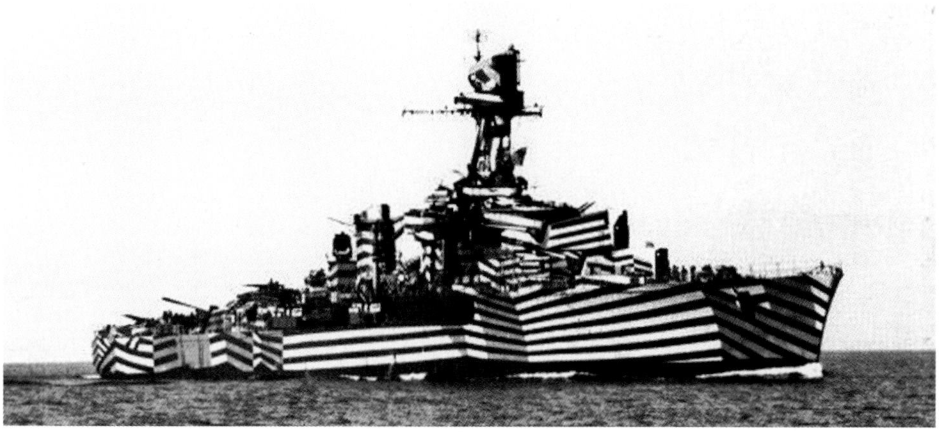

Dazzle is a form of disruptive camouflage inspired by the patterns of prey animals. Because the patterns make it difficult for predators to determine speed or direction, dazzle designs were painted on battleships during World War I.

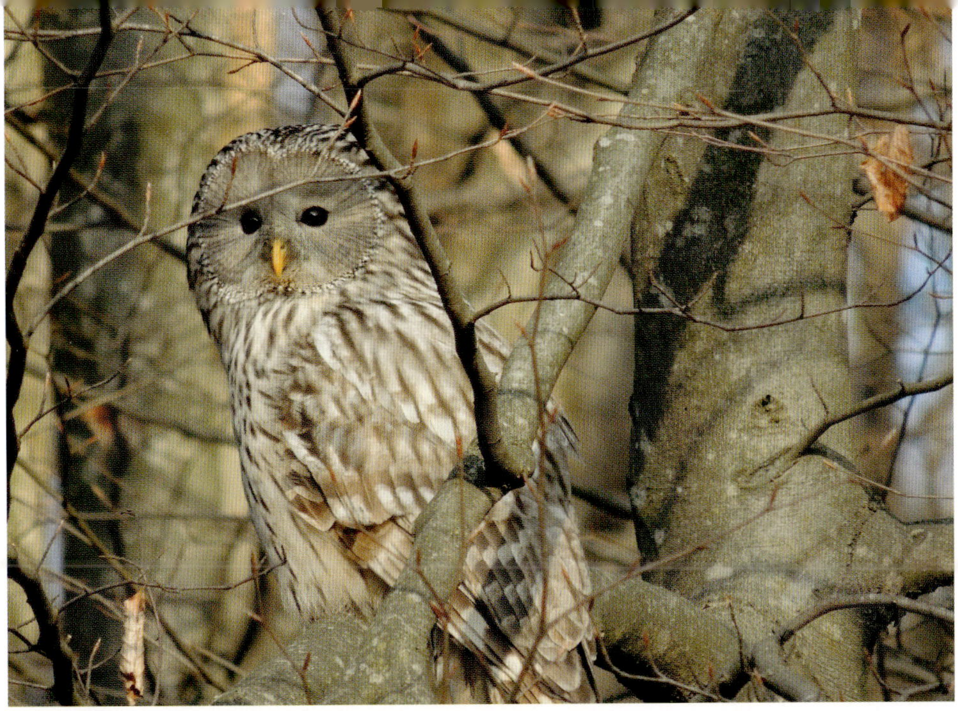

An owl blends into the background by clever use of camouflage.

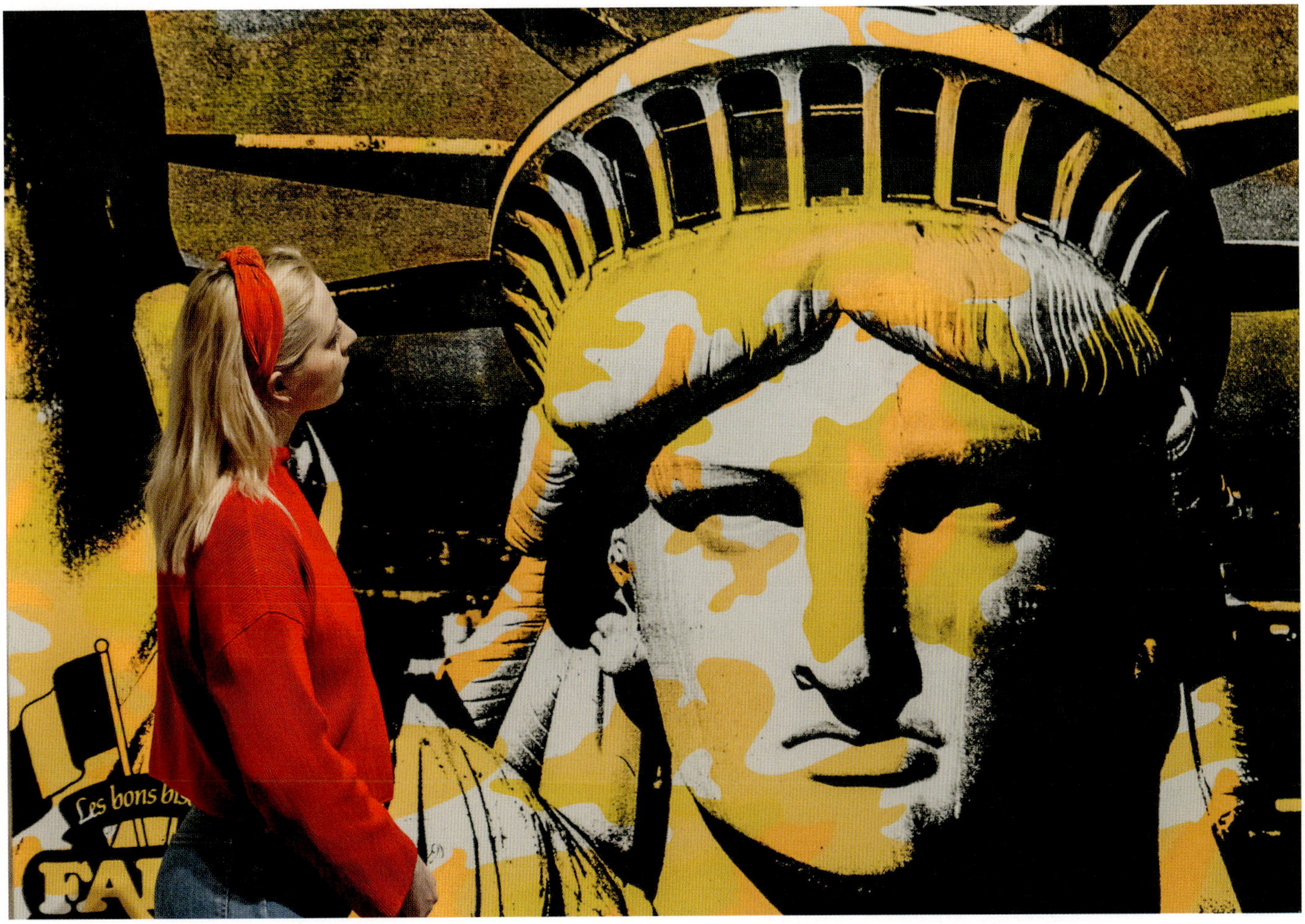

Statue of Liberty (1962–63), a camouflage print by Andy Warhol for whom New York was his home throughout his life.

15 CHARACTER ZONES

The areas of a color space that share perceptual similarities independent of hue

The basic character zones are vivid, pale, muted, and dark. Colors in the pale zone appear to be noticeably lighter than the most vivid version of the same hue. Colors in the muted zone appear to be grayer, and colors in the dark zone appear to be darker than the most vivid version of the hue. Achromatic colors are in a fifth zone: the neutral zone.

Many color order systems use two terms, in addition to hue, to locate colors in a 3D space. A color's position in Munsell is determined by value and chroma, and in RAL by lightness and chroma. In these asymmetric systems the nomenclature doesn't identify the character zone of the color. For example, a muted yellow and a pale blue have the same value and chroma in the Munsell system but fall into different character zones.

Some systems have a single term for the combination of two dimensions: In the Natural Color System (NCS) the term *nuance* refers to the combination of blackness and chromaticness that, together with its hue, locates a color in a specific zone within that system. Colors with the same nuance code fall into the same character zone.

In Japan the Practical Color Coordinate System, developed by the Japan Color Research Institute in 1991, and the Hue and Tone System, developed by Shigenobu Kobayashi in 1981—both based on Munsell—use the English word *tone* for the combination of value and chroma. In these systems, colors of the same tone also fall into the same character zone.

In 1969 Faber Birren used the term *tone* together with *tint*, *shade*, and *full color* to characterize specific variations of colors. "Color and white combine to create tint. Color and black combine to create shade. Color, white, and black combine to create tone." Birren's terms describe how to make variations of any color, but they also relate to the character zones. All pale colors are tints of vivid hues, all muted colors are tones, and all dark colors are shades of the most vivid version of the hue.

In designing a color scheme, it is often the dominant character zone, rather than the hue, that communicates the most meaning.

SEE ALSO:
Color Meaning
Munsell System
Natural Color System
Tint, Tone, and Shade

Although we can see millions of colors, they can be divided into achromatic—or neutral colors—and chromatic colors. The chromatic colors can be further divided into four basic character zones: vivid, pale, muted, and dark.

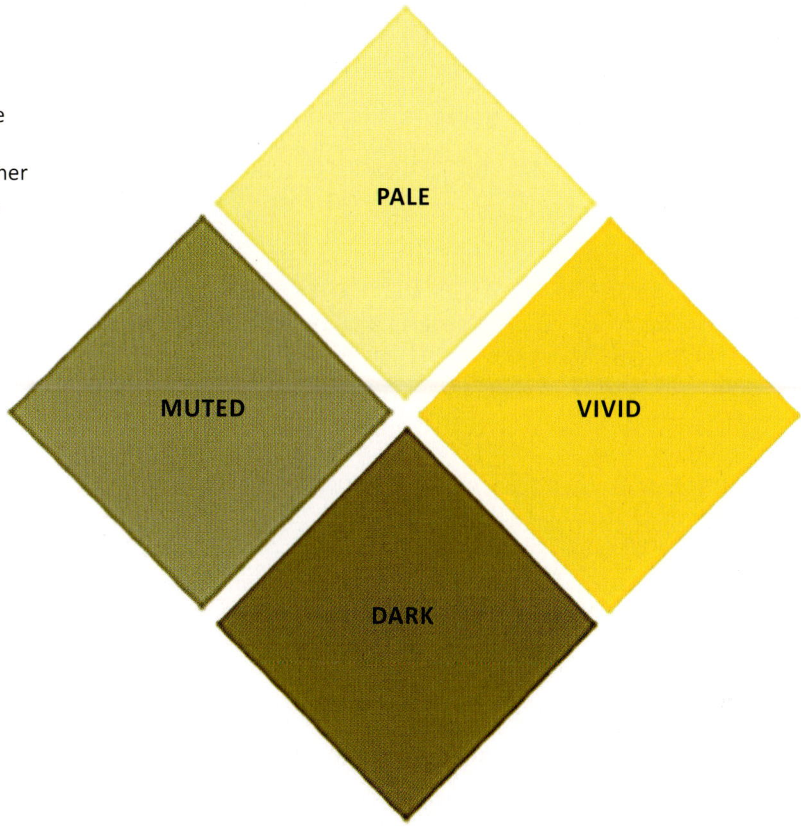

NUANCE

A combination of blackness and chromaticness in the Natural Color System (NCS) of Sweden

Nuance is specified by four numbers: The first two are the percentage of blackness; the second two are the percentage of chromaticness. Colors with the same set of four numbers share a similar appearance.

The triangular NCS hue plane can be divided into four nuance zones and in this way could be considered similar to the four character zones (vivid, pale, muted, and dark).

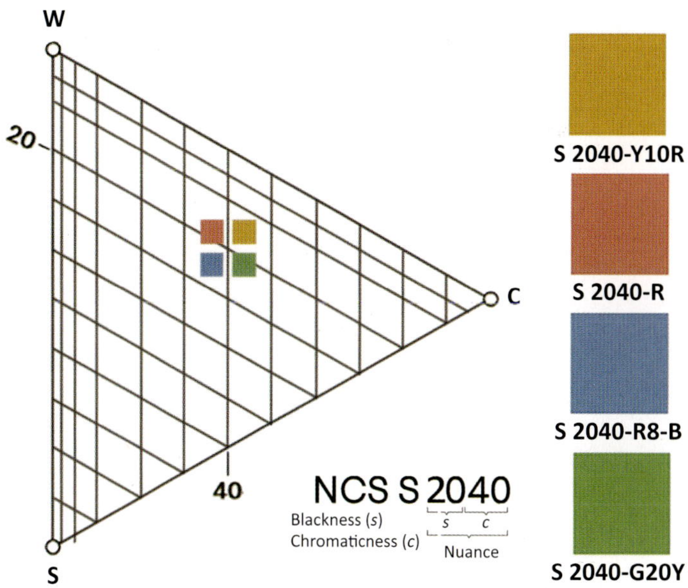

16 CHEMISTRY OF CHROMOPHORES

The part of a molecule that is responsible for its color

The absorption of light by dyes and pigments is primarily due to electronic transitions. The part of the molecule that enables an electronic transition is referred to as the molecule's chromophore.

Many molecules have electronic transitions that enable them to absorb electromagnetic radiation that is outside of the visible spectrum. Such molecules might absorb ultraviolet or infrared light but only molecules that absorb in the visible spectrum will likely be colored.

Color chemists are able to design molecules that primarily absorb in different parts of the visible spectrum; often they are inspired by chromophores that occur naturally. Note that chromophores tend not to absorb at only one wavelength (which corresponds to the difference in energy for the electronic transition). The molecule can rotate and vibrate, so this can lower or raise the amount of energy required for the transition and is why dyes and pigments tend to have absorption spectra spanning a range of wavelengths.

An auxochrome is a chemical group that can be added to the chromophore to change the wavelength where light is primarily absorbed. For example, the chemical benzene absorbs in the ultraviolet region and appears colorless. However, if a nitro group is added to it, this shifts the wavelength of maximum absorb to the blue region, and as a result the compound appears yellow.

In nature, the chromophore is often used to detect light; for example, in humans the light-sensitive cells in the eye contain pigments whose chromophores are naturally tuned to allow them to absorb certain wavelengths of light. In coloration, chromophores (and auxochromes) result in the range of vivid colors that we see in the natural and manufactured world. The mechanism of light absorption explains why the gamut that can be obtained from dyes and pigments is limited.

Chromophores (and auxochromes) result in the range of vivid colors that we see in the natural and manufactured world.

SEE ALSO:
Colorants
Sustainability

Chromophores almost always result from conjugated pi systems or metal complexes. In this case—a dye known as acid sodium red—the conjugated pi systems are denoted by the dotted lines.

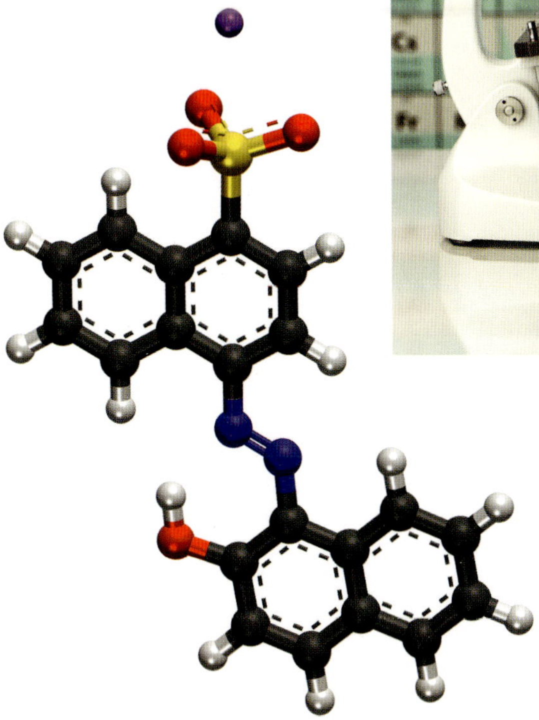

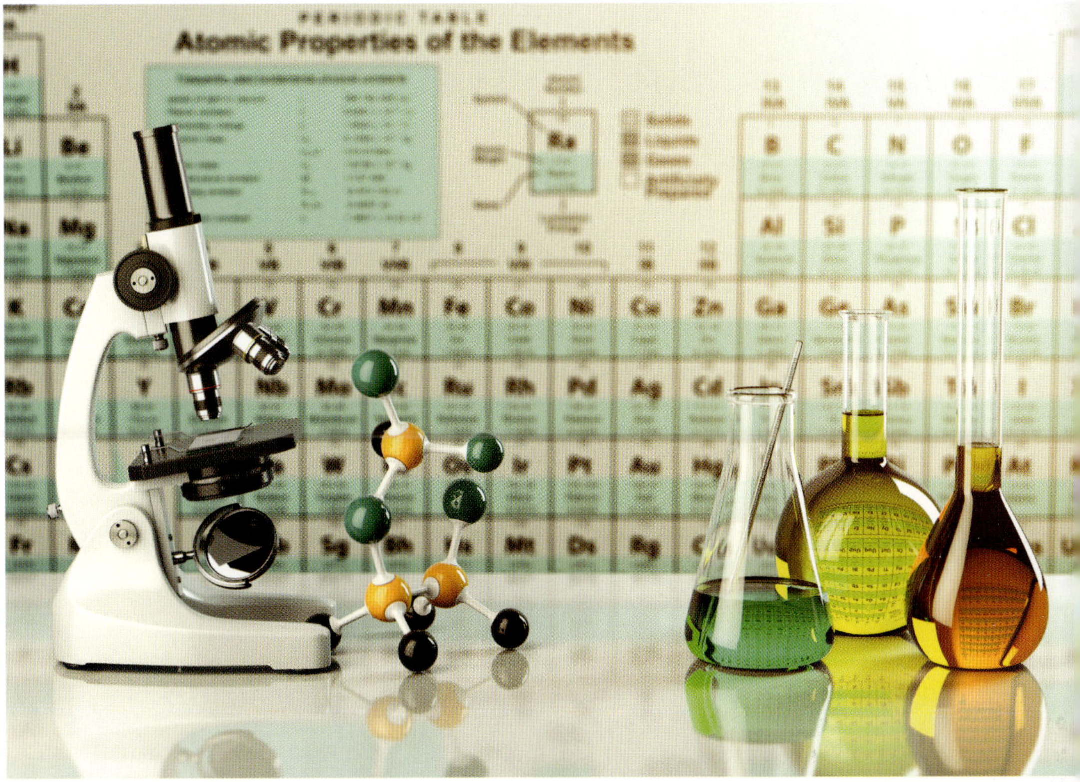

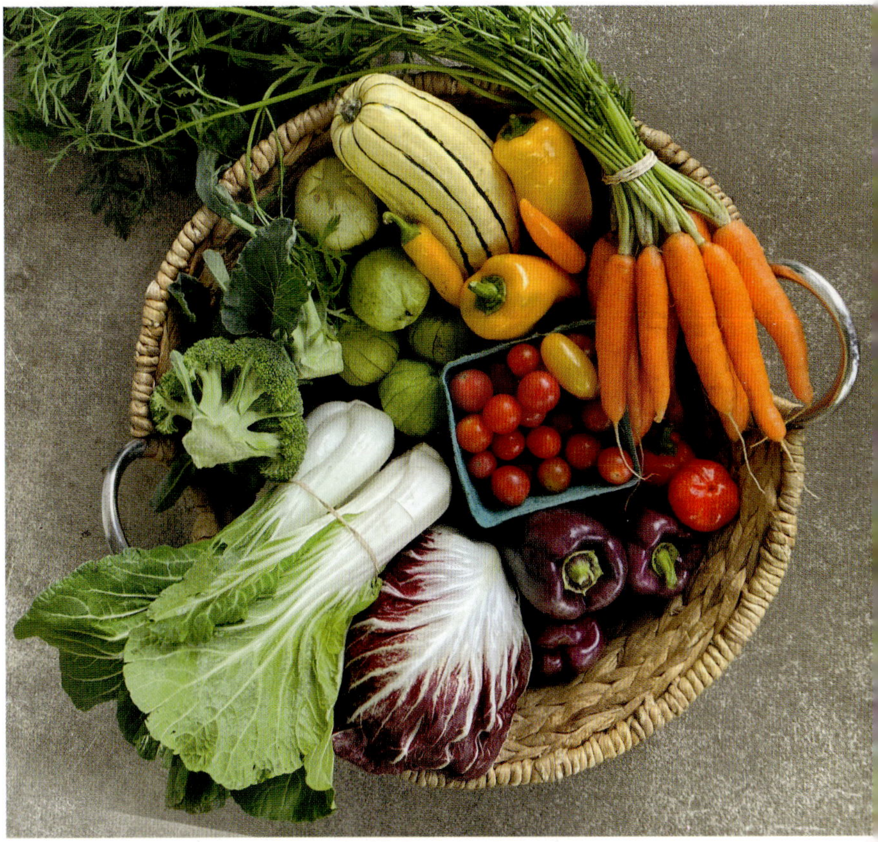

The bright colors found in many foods are caused by chromophores in natural pigments such as carotenoids (yellow, orange, and red) and anthocyanidins (red, blue, and purple).

17 CHIAROSCURO

The intentional emphasis on contrasting light and shadow

The term *chiaroscuro* comes from the Italian word for light: *chiaro* meaning bright, and *scuro* meaning dark. Though versions of the technique date back to Ancient Greece, the use of chiaroscuro became prominent during the Renaissance. Renaissance artists who were particularly known for this technique include Leonardo da Vinci, Rembrandt, and Caravaggio. Chiaroscuro remained popular through the mannerist and baroque periods as artists such as Rembrandt and Vermeer used the technique to add drama and intensity to their painting.

The Chiaroscuro movement was influential in encouraging artists to increase the contrast between light and dark in paintings. This could be achieved by so-called up-modeling using mixtures with white and down-modeling using mixtures with black. Mixing chromatic pigments together was avoided for a long time because of the loss of chroma that would result.

Traditionally there was always resistance to mixing pigments in art. Rather, artists preferred to use pigments in their purest form, known sometimes as a masstone. In Western art, many egg tempera paintings from the fourteenth century and earlier, for example, used pigments at full strength or (occasionally) mixed with white. Over time, artists became more familiar at mixing either white or black with masstone pigment to create depth in paintings.

SEE ALSO:
Contrast
Lighting
Shadows

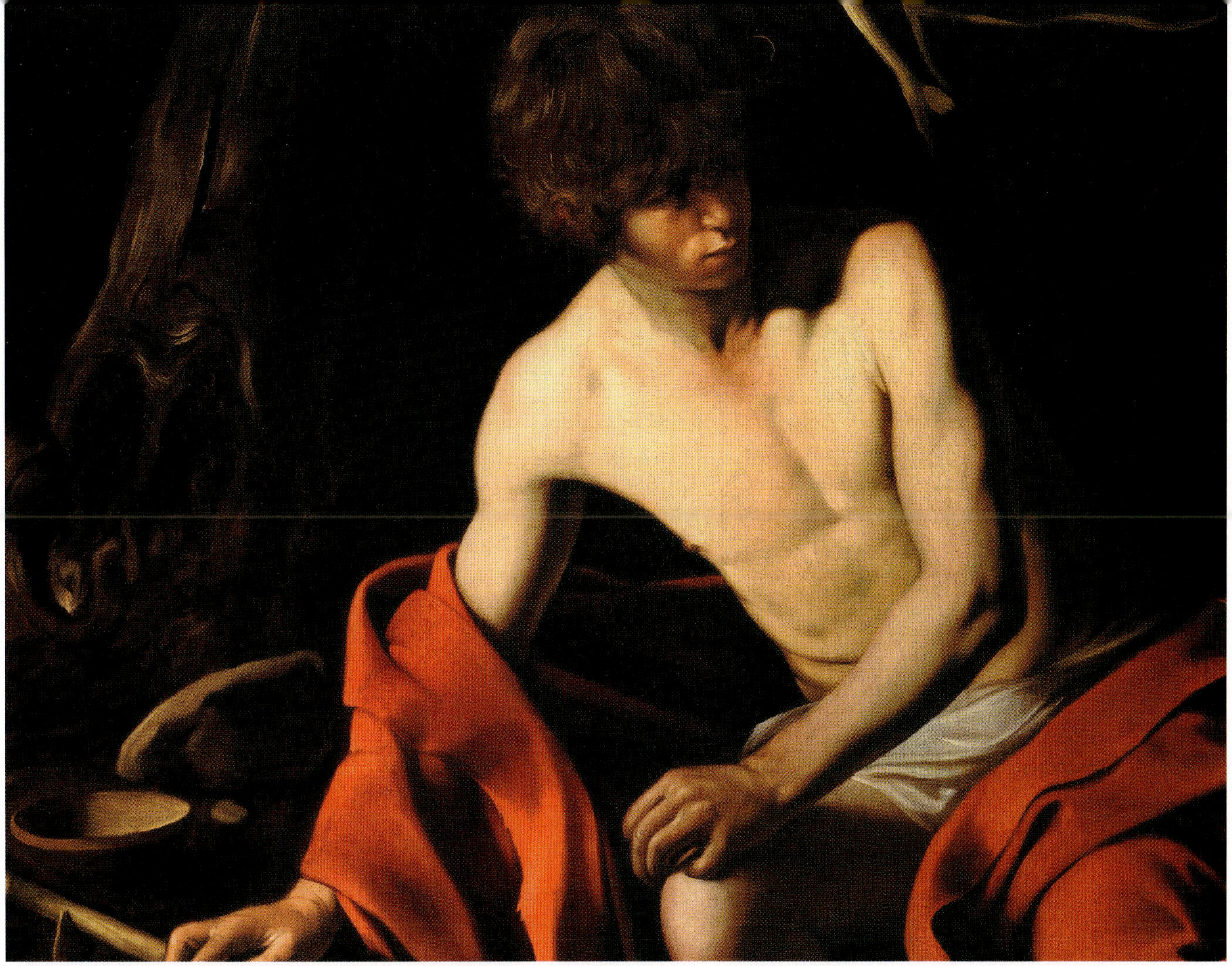

Caravaggio's *Saint John the Baptist in the Wilderness* (1605) is a prime example of the use of the chiaroscuro painting technique.

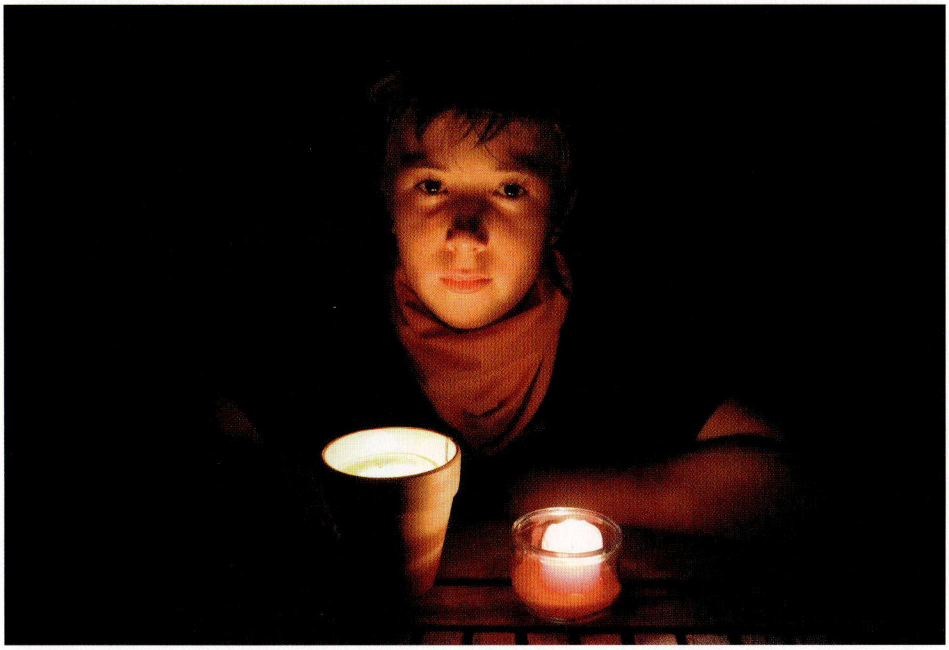

A photograph by Emmanuel Douzery showing the high contrast between light and shadow that is characteristic of the chiaroscuro technique

18 CHROMA

A measure of visual color strength and one of the three dimensions of color

Chroma is a measure of the visual strength of a color and is related to the perceived difference between a gray sample and a chromatic sample of the same lightness. It is one of the three attributes of color perception, although in certain circumstances it is more appropriate to refer to colorfulness or saturation, which are related but subtly different terms. Strictly, chroma refers to a color property of objects; saturation is used to describe light sources.

Albert Munsell was one of the first people to introduce this important concept of color, and his Munsell system was based on value (which we might now refer to as lightness), chroma, and hue. Ever since the introduction of the Munsell system, it has been evident that the lightness of a color at its maximum chroma varies with the hue. For example, highly chromatic yellows have high lightness, but highly chromatic blues have low lightness. The idea that perceived colors can be arranged in a sphere is approximately true but simplifies the actual shape of color perception space, which is more irregular.

Chroma is one of three dimensions of color that can be used to describe color experience. The other two are hue and lightness (also known as value). Consistency in the use of these terms provides a more systematic language to describe color in art and design than would otherwise be possible.

SEE ALSO:
Hue Angle
Lightness
Munsell System
Three Dimensions of Color

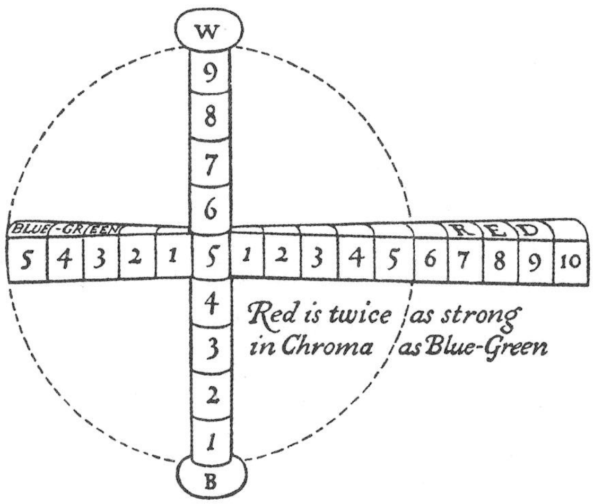

Munsell chroma from *A Grammar of Color* (1921), by Albert H. Munsell and Thomas M. Cleland. It shows that red is twice as strong in chroma as blue-green.

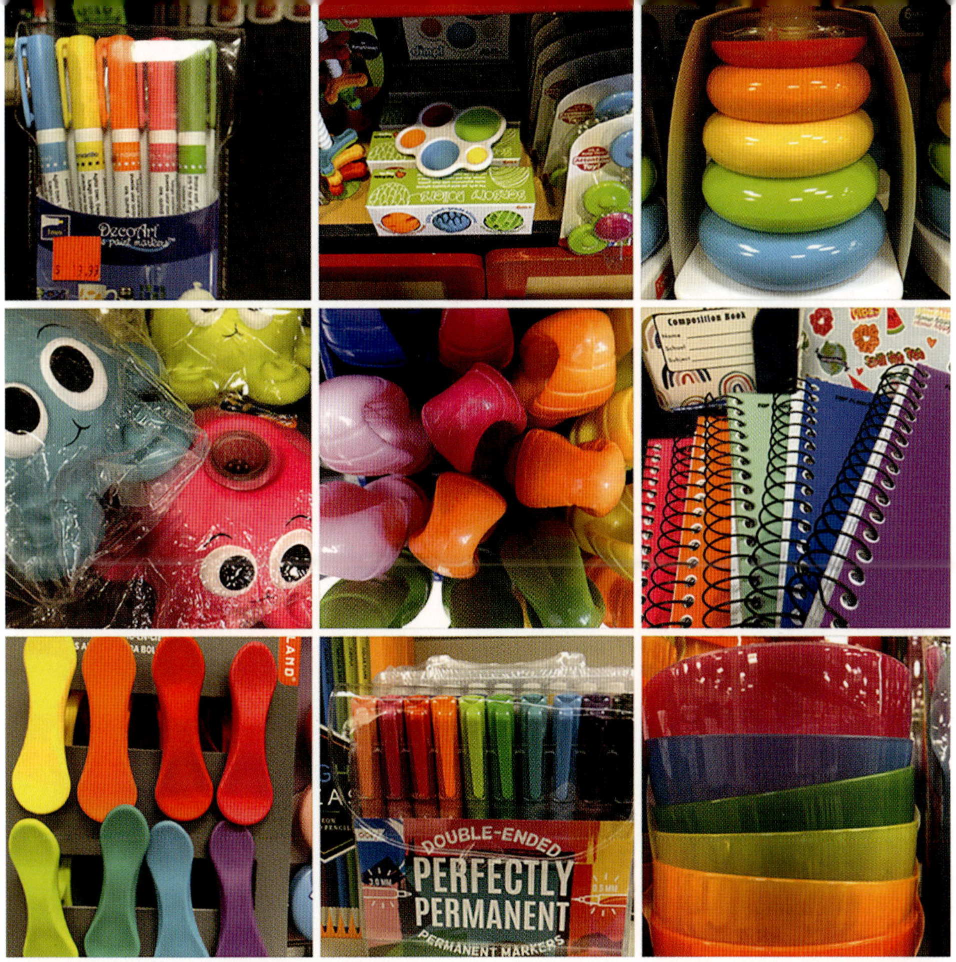

High chroma: In addition to the traditional six ROYGBV vivid hues, manufactured products in the twenty-first century now include high-chroma hues such as turquoise, lime, and magenta.

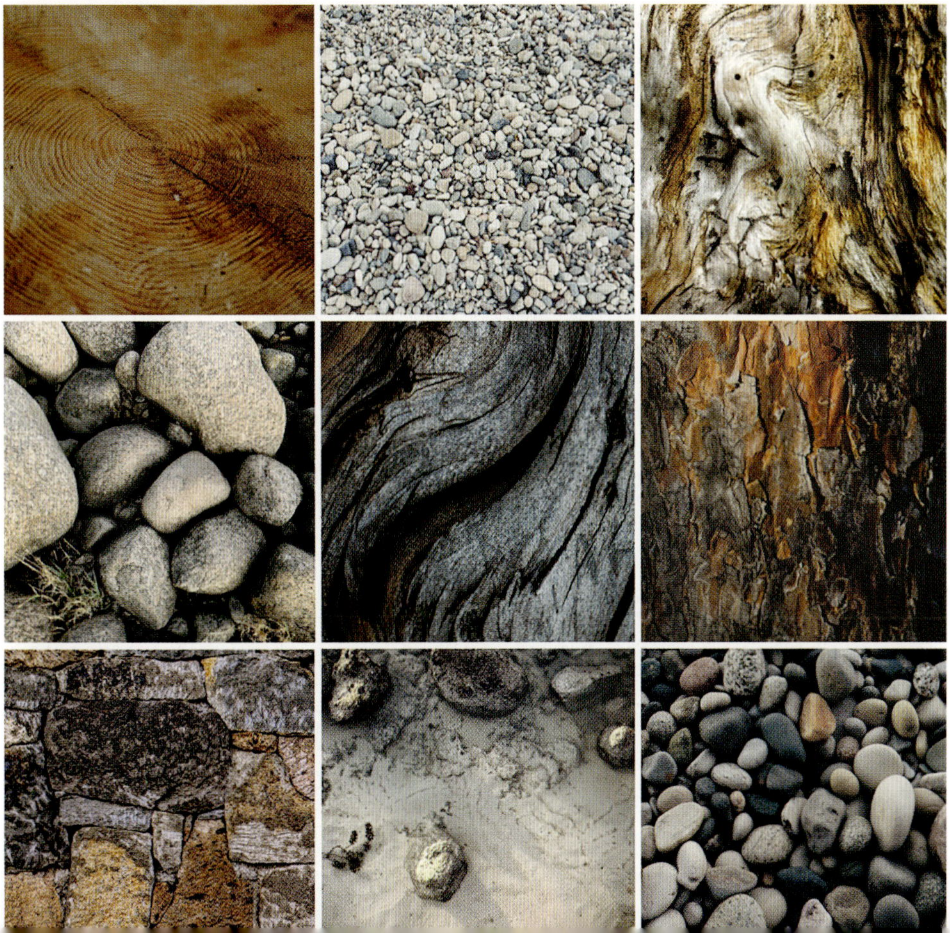

Low chroma: the natural colors of wood and stone.

19 CHROMOPHOBIA

A persistent, irrational fear of, or aversion to, color

In artist David Batchelor's influential book, *Chromophobia*, he argues that over many centuries Western civilization has treated color as something to fear or something that is juvenile and unsophisticated. The misconception that classical Greek and Roman architecture and sculpture were unpainted led to a reverence for white that is evident to this day.

Bright and vivid colors are frequently seen in products marketed for children, whereas the use of black and white is seen as being more sophisticated and suitable for products aimed at older people. Indeed, one could even say that the pre-Newtonian belief that color emerges when a white light is passed through a prism because it picks up impurities from the glass is early evidence of the association of color with something distasteful.

We may argue that the penchant for fashion designers to wear black and the persistent Hollywood images of white statues in Ancient Greece and Rome are examples of chromophobia.

Although a clinical phobia to color is rare, there are cases of psychological fear of or aversion to color. For example, a fear of red is called erythrophobia.

Chromophobia often results in an aversion to using high-chroma colors that can be seen in both designers and the public.

SEE ALSO:
Color Meaning
Symbolic Color

FURTHER READING
Chromophobia (2000), by David Batchelor

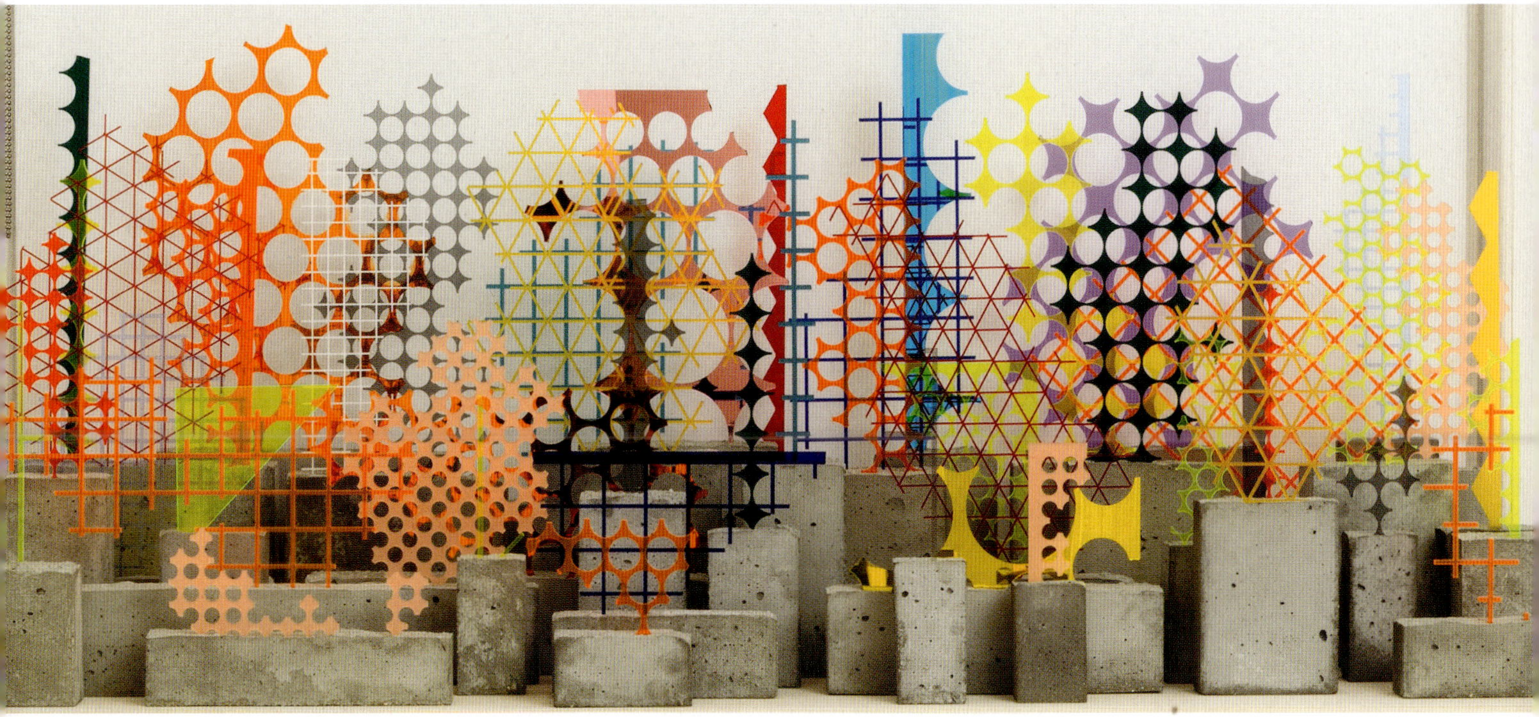

Reef (2016), assemblage of repurposed plastics and concrete by David Batchelor.

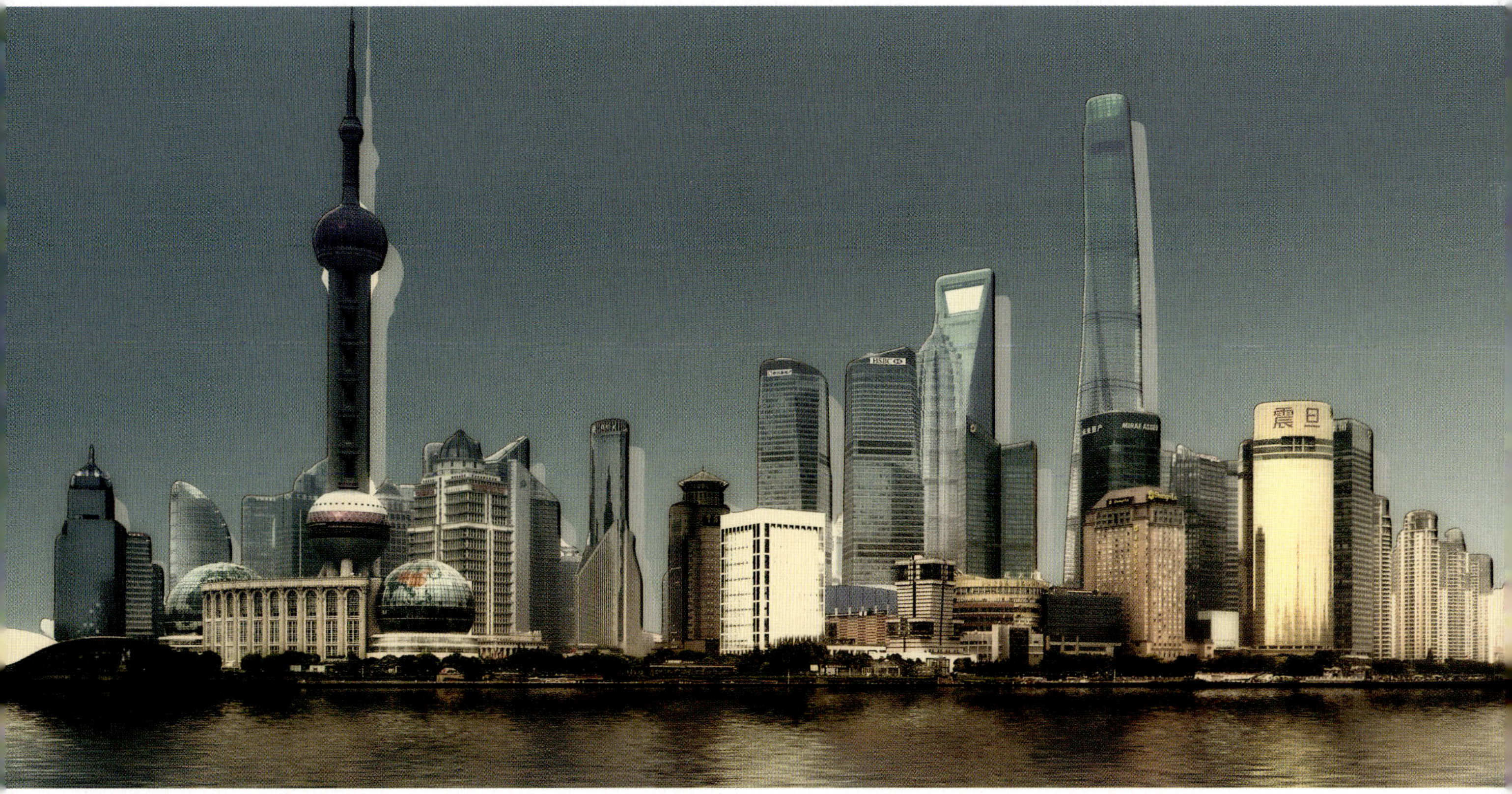

Modern cities are predominantly constructed of low-chroma building materials even though the range of colors available is greatly expanded. Why?

20 CIE SYSTEM

A system of color specification introduced by the *Commission Internationale de l'Éclairage* in 1931

In 1931 the *Commission Internationale de l'Éclairage* (the International Lighting Commission) introduced a system of colorimetry for color specification. Strictly speaking, the system was designed to determine whether two colored stimuli (two lights, for example, or two illuminated objects) match for a so-called standard observer. The CIE standard observer is an average human response that was measured in the early twentieth century.

The main point of the system was to be able to measure the spectral reflectance or emission for a color stimulus and calculate three numbers that are called tristimulus values (usually referred to as XYZ values). If two stimuli have the same CIE XYZ values, they are considered to be a visual match for the CIE standard observer.

In 1976 the CIE introduced a transformation of the XYZ values that generated three new values that are referred to as L*, a*, and b*. The L* represents the lightness of a sample, and the a* and b* values represent the redness/greenness and yellowness/blueness, respectively. CIELAB was introduced because the CIELAB values were more intuitive than the XYZ values and more useful for many industrial applications. Today, CIELAB is still widely used as a color specification system in industry.

SEE ALSO:
Hue Angles
Munsell System

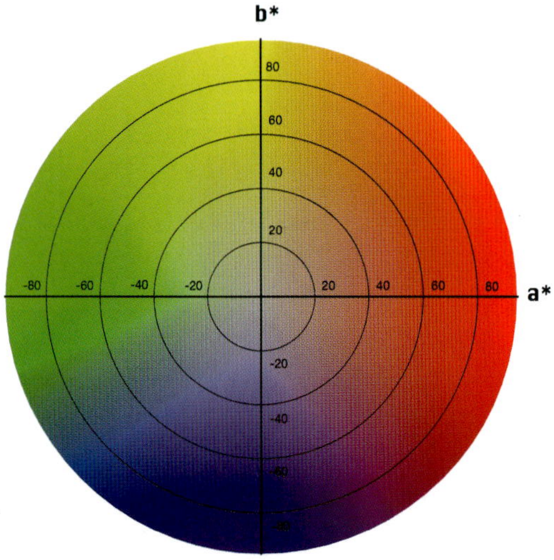

CIELAB hue circle.

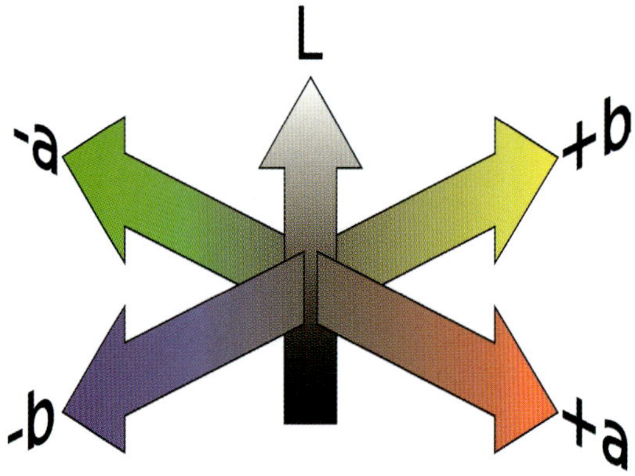

CIELAB color space coordinates.

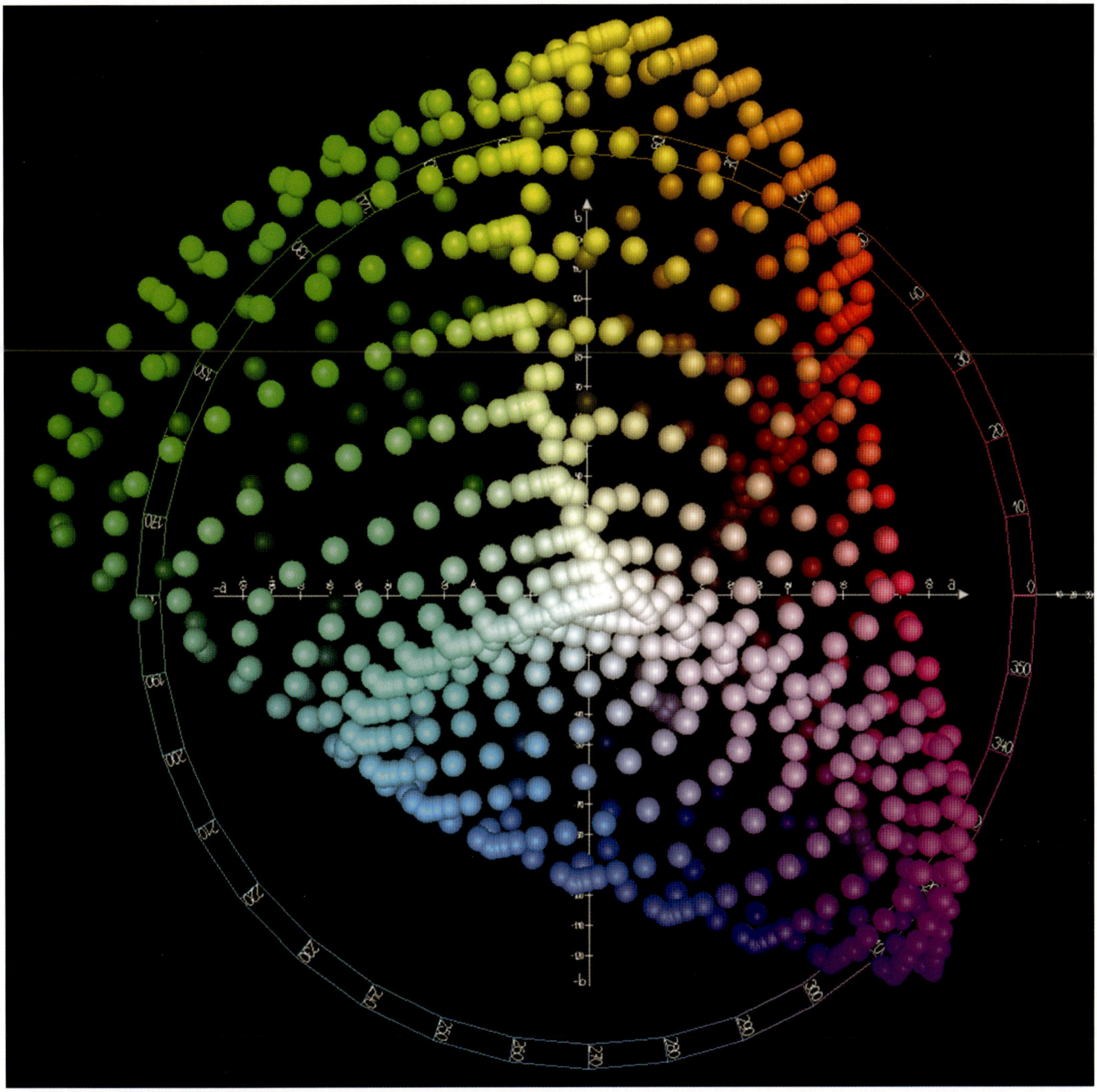

CIELAB color space from above showing a distribution of colors in the space that can be achieved by a particular color-reproduction device.

21 CINEMATIC COLOR

Color used in cinematography to ensure that the intended atmosphere, style, or emotion is conveyed to the viewer

A color script developed for a film ensures that the colors of objects, clothes, and scenery are carefully selected to convey the appropriate feel of each scene.

In the 1999 movie *The Matrix* there is a dark green color wash throughout that denotes a futuristic and scientific feel. This example contrasts with the soft pink feel of the 2014 movie *The Grand Budapest Hotel*. Color grading is very important but cannot compensate for poor set composition or filming. Considerable energy is expanded before a single scene is recorded to ensure the color harmony of the scene. This might involve consistent lighting or use of a single color, or two- or three-color palettes that convey the appropriate messages. Use of color in cinematography is therefore strongly related to color meanings.

There are two important post-production concepts in cinematography: color correction and color grading. Color correction is a process related to color management to ensure that the colors that occur in the cinema are the ones intended by the director. Color correction is normally carried out by colorists who may, for example, adjust for lighting in various scenes to ensure consistency throughout the movie. Color grading, on the other hand, is an artistic process that is primarily concerned with the emotional feel of the movie.

Color plays a vital role in setting the atmosphere for any particular scene in movies and is controlled through various processes including set composition, color correction, and color grading.

SEE ALSO:
Color Management
Color Meaning
Palettes

In *The Matrix* (1999) the color green was dominant throughout the movie to convey a futuristic feeling and to reinforce the idea of computer code that was traditionally written with green screens.

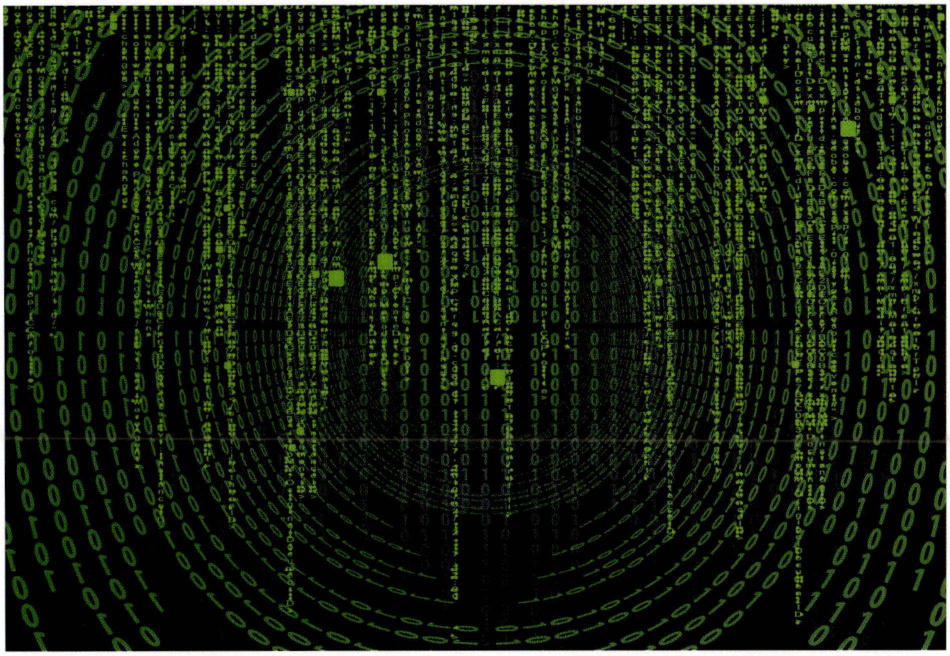

WES ANDERSON | **HAYAO MIYAZAKI** | **CHRISTOPHER NOLAN**

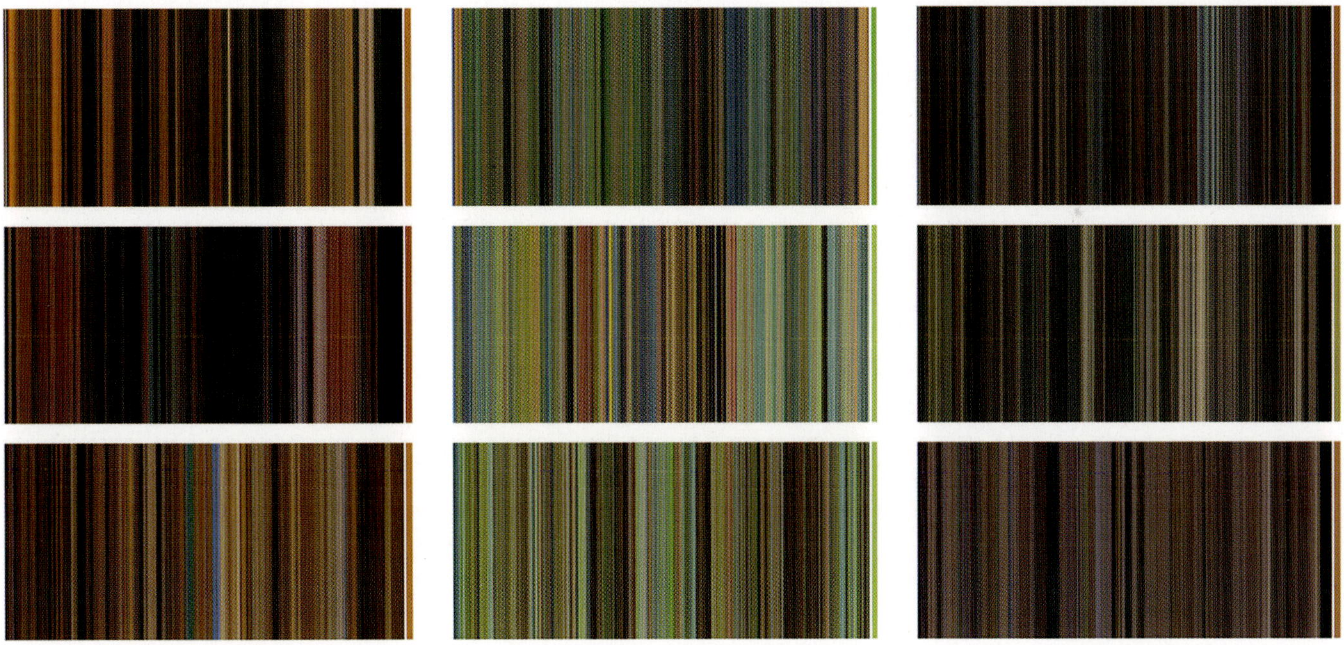

WES ANDERSON	HAYAO MIYAZAKI	CHRISTOPHER NOLAN
Fantastic Mr. Fox	My Neighbor Totoro	Inception
The Grand Budapest Hotel	Ponyo on the Cliff by the Sea	Interstellar
The Life Aquatic with Steve Zissou	The Wind Rises	Memento

Color fingerprints of three contemporary directors compiled by Tommaso Mario Buonocore.

22 CMYK

The standard cyan, magenta, yellow, and black inks used in four-color process printing

Printing inks are based on the optimal subtractive primaries of cyan (C), magenta (M), and yellow (Y), with black (K) added to create a four-ink system. The black ink is referred to as K because it is the key color used to add detail to an image.

There are several practical reasons why CMYK is preferred to CMY. First, it is difficult to get a pure black by mixing cyan, magenta, and yellow inks. Second, if dark colors are produced by mixing CMY, the amount of ink laid down is substantial and can cause the paper to ripple. Third, black ink is less expensive than the other three.

The idea of trichromatic or tetrachromatic printing systems was introduced by Jacob Le Blon (1667–1741), who famously used an RYB (red/yellow/blue) model to make reproductions of fine art paintings. Le Blon's revolutionary process was ultimately a commercial failure. However, RYB continued to be used by other processes until the early twentieth century, when it began to be replaced by CMYK, which enabled a much larger color gamut to be produced.

Although CMYK can create a reasonable color gamut, it is nevertheless limited. High-end printing will use additional colored inks known as spot colors or multiprimary ink systems that use six or more inks. For example, the Hexachrome system was used by Pantone to allow a larger gamut and added orange and green inks to the process colors.

Because CMYK, like RGB (red/green/yellow), is a device-dependent color space, there is no simple conversion formula between RGB and CMYK. However, color fidelity can be achieved by defining International Color Consortium (ICC) profiles. Standardization of printers and inks can, however, allow some profiles to be predefined and used to achieve reasonable success with little effort. An example of this is the SWOP (Specifications for Web Offset Publications) profile.

SEE ALSO:
Partitive Mixture
RGB
Subtractive Mixture

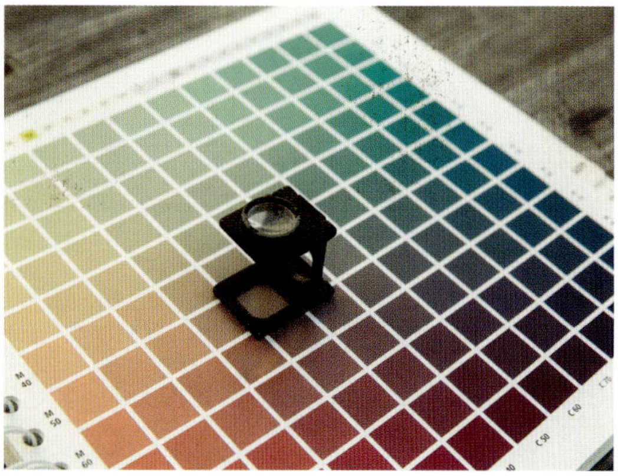

CMYK is widely used in low-cost printing systems to generate a wide range of colors.

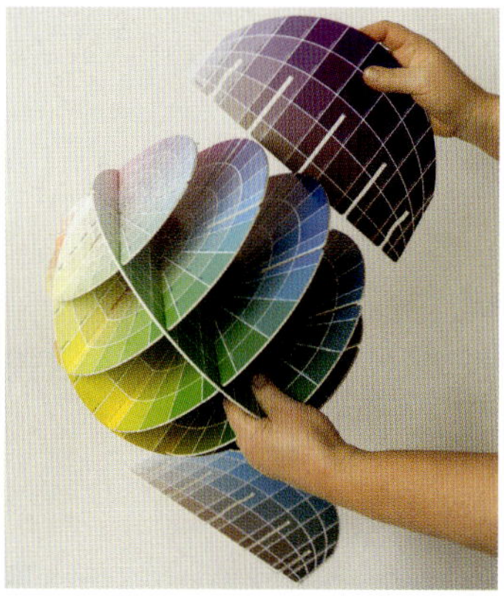

The Kolormondo model is similar to the historic Runge color sphere. It is printed using only CMY with no black.

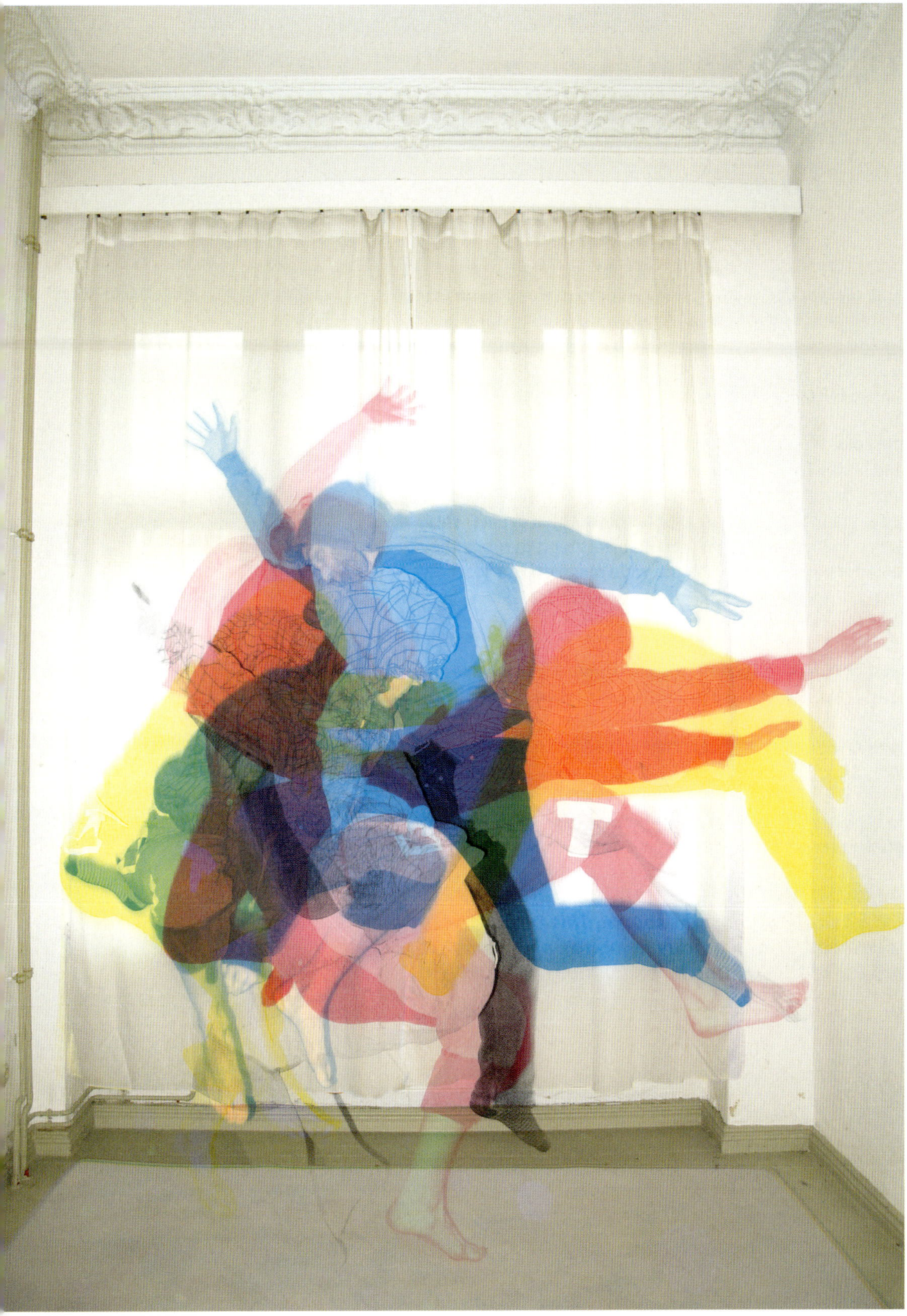

Passing Four (2007), by Elin Hansdottir & Darri Lorenzen. Four digital photographs, each corresponding to one of the colors in CMYK printing, recombined in Photoshop.

23 COLOR CONSTANCY

The tendency to perceive a familiar object as having the same color under different conditions of illumination

We see the color of objects in the world as a result of visual processes in response to light that is reflected from or emitted by the objects. An object viewed under a bluish light source reflects more of the blue light to the eye than the same object viewed under a reddish light of the same intensity. Would we therefore expect the color appearance of objects to change as we change the color of the light that we view them in?

Studies have shown that the color of most objects does change in appearance as the light source is changed. Sand on the beach may look a little redder when viewed under sunset than at noon. However, the perception of the changes in color appearance that occur when the light source is changed is much smaller than we would expect. This is due to a visual process called color constancy by which objects tend to retain their approximate daylight appearance when viewed under a wide range of light sources.

There are two effects of color constancy on our perception of color:

1. Our perception of the color of familiar objects does not change due to changes in illumination.

2. Our perception of the color of unfamiliar objects is influenced by assumptions of illumination based on experience.

One of the first attempts to explain color constancy was proposed by Johannes von Kries in 1905. The von Kries coefficient law is still used today in vision science.

The visual system is adaptive and can partially discount the effect of changes in the color and intensity of the light source. This is thought to have evolved so that we can easily and quickly recognize objects by their color appearance regardless of the lighting in which they are viewed.

SEE ALSO:
#TheDress
Context
Memory Color

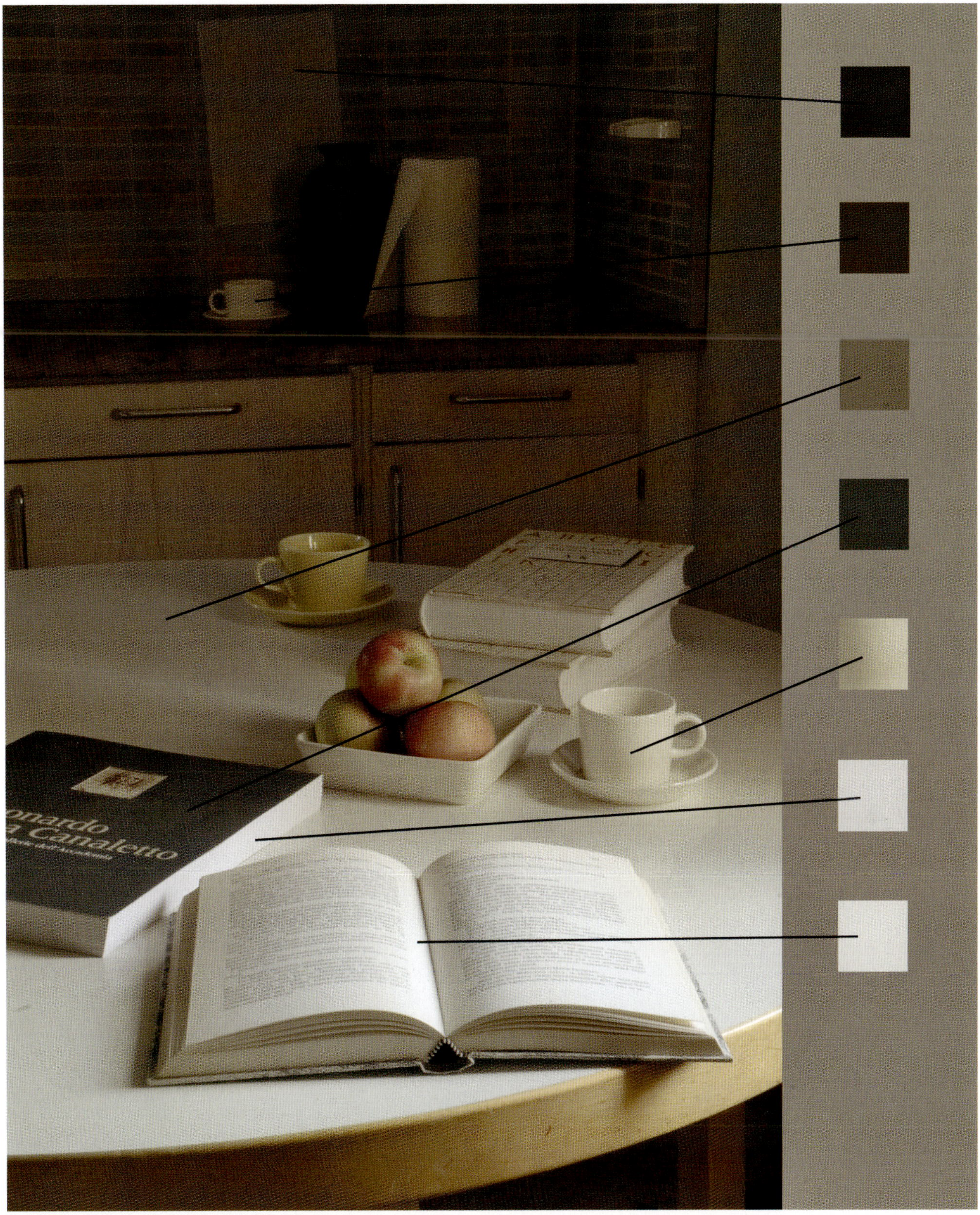

Many variations of white and one of gray. Note the difference in the appearance of the two coffee cups. How do you know they are the same color?

24 COLOR FIELD PAINTING

A style of abstract painting that emerged in New York City during the 1950s characterized by large fields of color

The term *color field painter* was coined by the art critic Clement Greenberg and originally applied to three prominent artists: Mark Rothko, Barnett Newman, and Clyfford Still. This painting style was a type of abstract expressionism that aimed to strip away suggestions of recognizable forms and express raw emotion through color. Other painters who worked in this style include Lee Krasner, Morris Louis, Joan Mitchell, and Kenneth Noland. Much of the work is associated with an attempt to strip away, for example, religious or mythical connotations in art.

In many of these paintings, foreground and background are one and consist mainly of a single uniform hue typically applied to a huge canvas. Still was arguably the first to arrive at this new style, and he applied rich earthy hues in thick layers to the canvas using a palette knife. Rothko did not consider himself to be a color field painter but also painted in this style with the stated aim of using color to evoke emotion.

In the 1960s other artists adopted the color field style in an even more abstract way as part of a second wave of color field painters including Helen Frankenthaler, Sam Gilliam, and John Hoyland. The movement inspired the French artist Yves Klein, who became famous for his paintings using a single color: blue.

SEE ALSO:
Albers's *Interaction of Color*
International Klein Blue
Op Art

"We are creating images whose reality is self-evident and which are devoid of the props and crutches that evoke associations with outmoded images, both sublime and beautiful."

—*Barnett Newman*

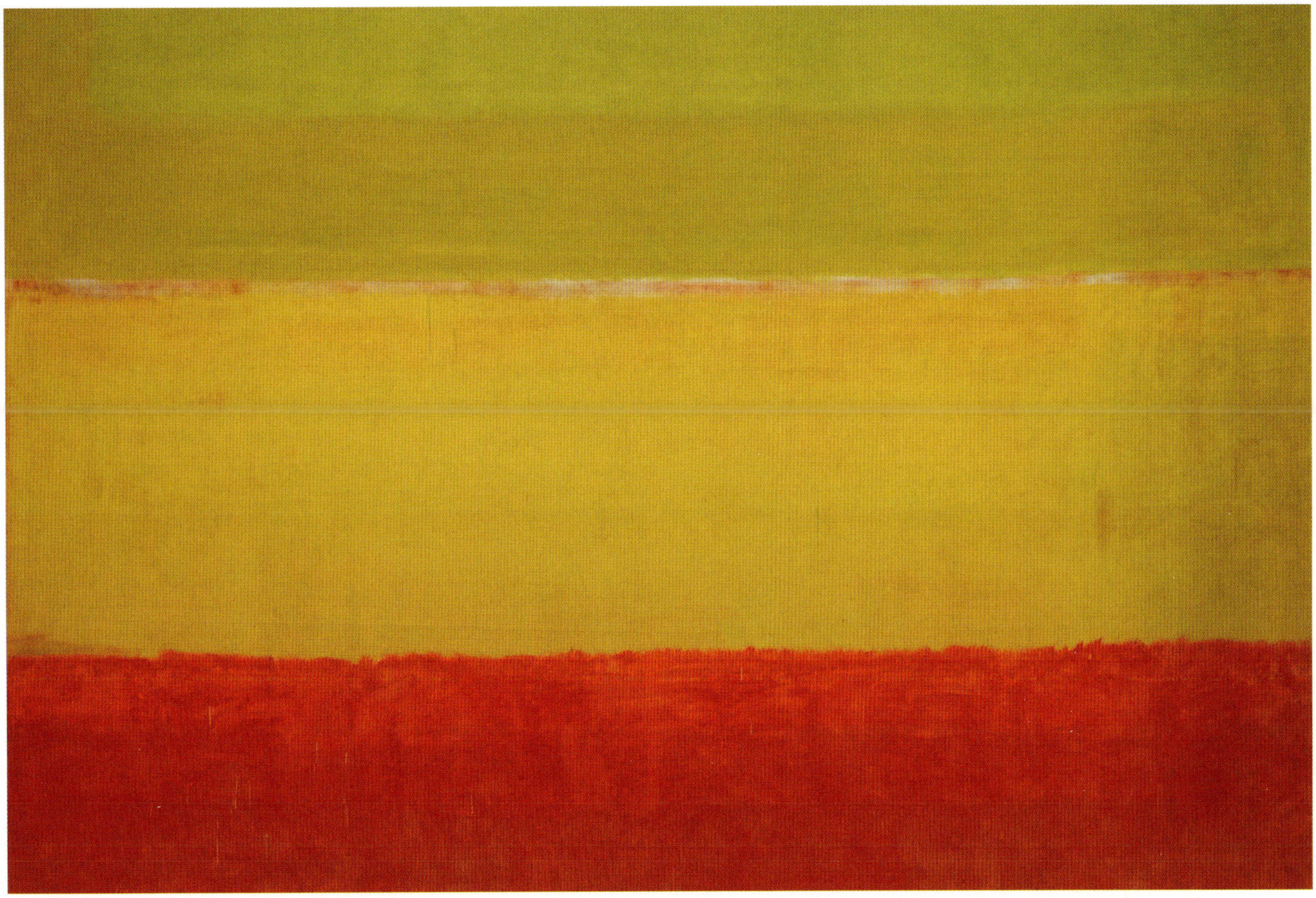

Untitled (1952-53), a painting by Mark Rothko juxtaposing large areas of color. Another painting, *White Center* (1950), was sold at auction by Sotheby's for $73 million in 2007.

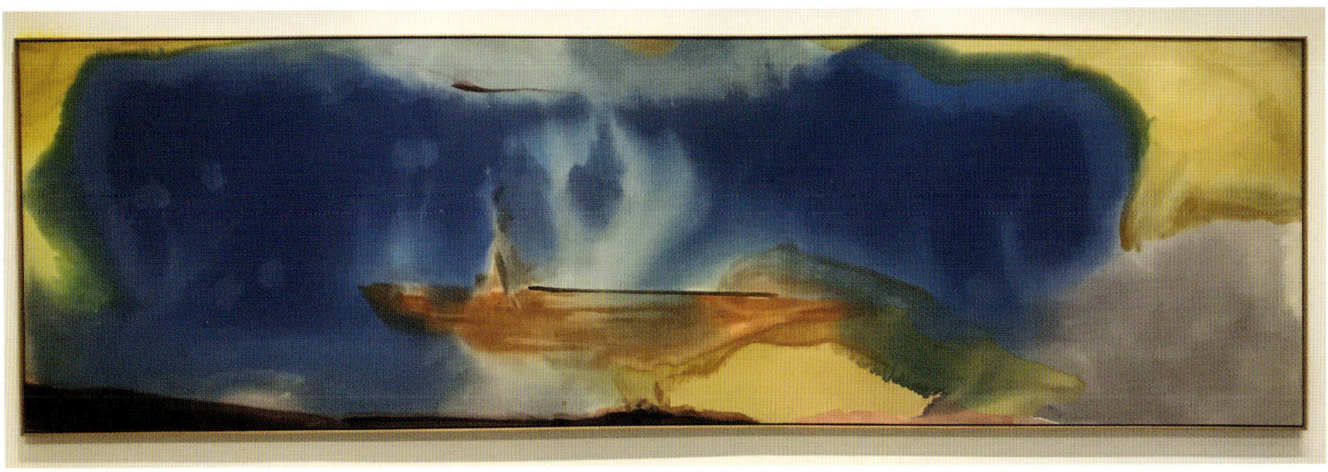

Moveable Blue (1973), by Helen Frankenthaler. Her work was characterized by hues of similar lightness and chroma and the use of large-format canvases.

25 COLOR FORECASTING

The marketing process of selecting colors that are likely to sell well in upcoming seasons

Forecasts are made by groups of color consultants from specific industries who work together to collect data, anticipate cultural trends, and "predict" product colors that will be popular with consumers in the future. To meet manufacturing schedules, forecasts are finalized anywhere from one to two years in advance for fashion and up to five years in advance for the automotive industry. The rise of online shopping and the closer relationship between manufacturers and retailers (e.g., ultra-fast fashion) has started to shorten the forecasting schedule.

The most influential color forecaster of the 1920s and 1930s was Margaret Rorke (1883–1969). According to Rorke, "New quirks in color may be found anywhere; in news events, history, art or music." In other words, the underlying assumption is that new color trends reflect changes in the zeitgeist that naturally occur, and the function of the color forecaster is to notice and assimilate these trends and represent them by color.

Color forecasting (and the broader activity of trend forecasting) as we know it today developed in the 1960s and began to target specific product categories such as women's wear or children's wear. A new concept in the last couple of decades is to put particular focus on one new color. Pantone announced their first Color of the Year in 2000, and other industries and agencies followed.

The narrative produced by a color forecaster is almost as important as the colors themselves. But there is a growing concern about the accuracy of the color-forecasting process, with an increasing spotlight on products that are manufactured and cannot be sold (so-called dead stock). Indeed, some voices claim that our obsession with seasonal changes in color trends is detrimental to the planet and contributing to overconsumption and waste.

SEE ALSO:
Brand Colors
Color Meaning
Colorways
Pantone

FURTHER READING
The Color Revolution (2012), by Regina Blaszczyk

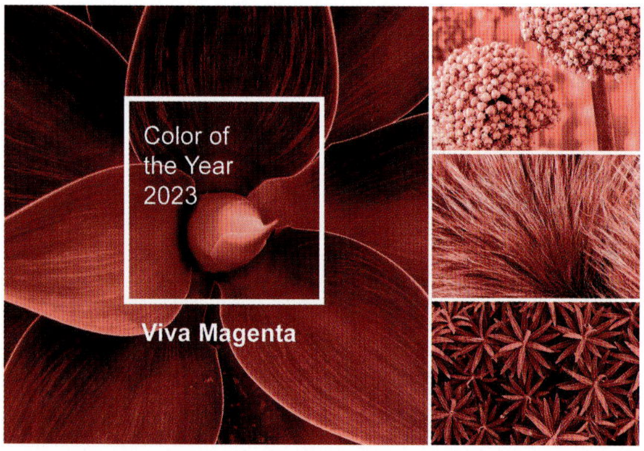

Viva Magenta—the 2023 Pantone Color of the Year. Past variations of magenta that were featured as Color of the Year are Honeysuckle in 2011, and Fuchsia Rose in 2001.

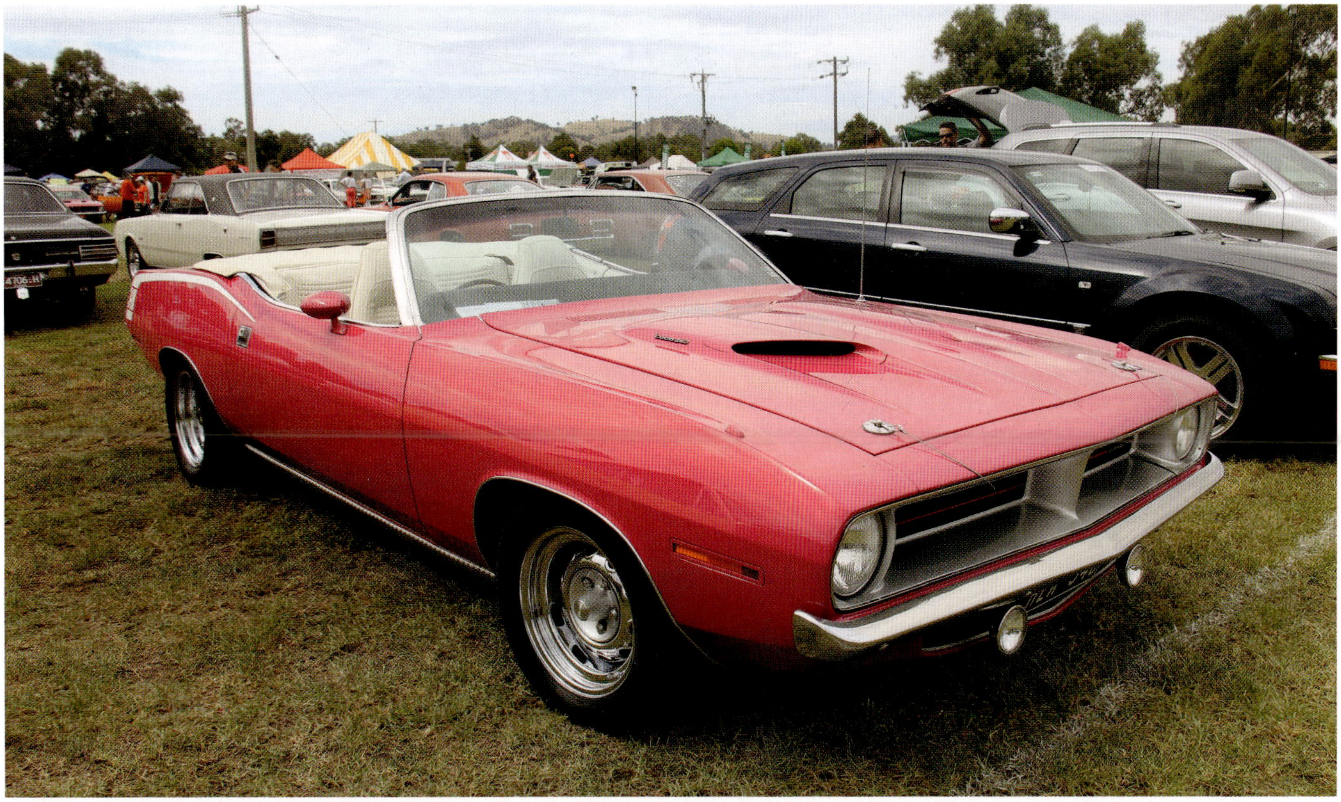

Advances in color chemistry are partly driven by the auto industry. Panther Pink and Moulin Rouge were the "hot" colors in 1970 for American muscle cars.

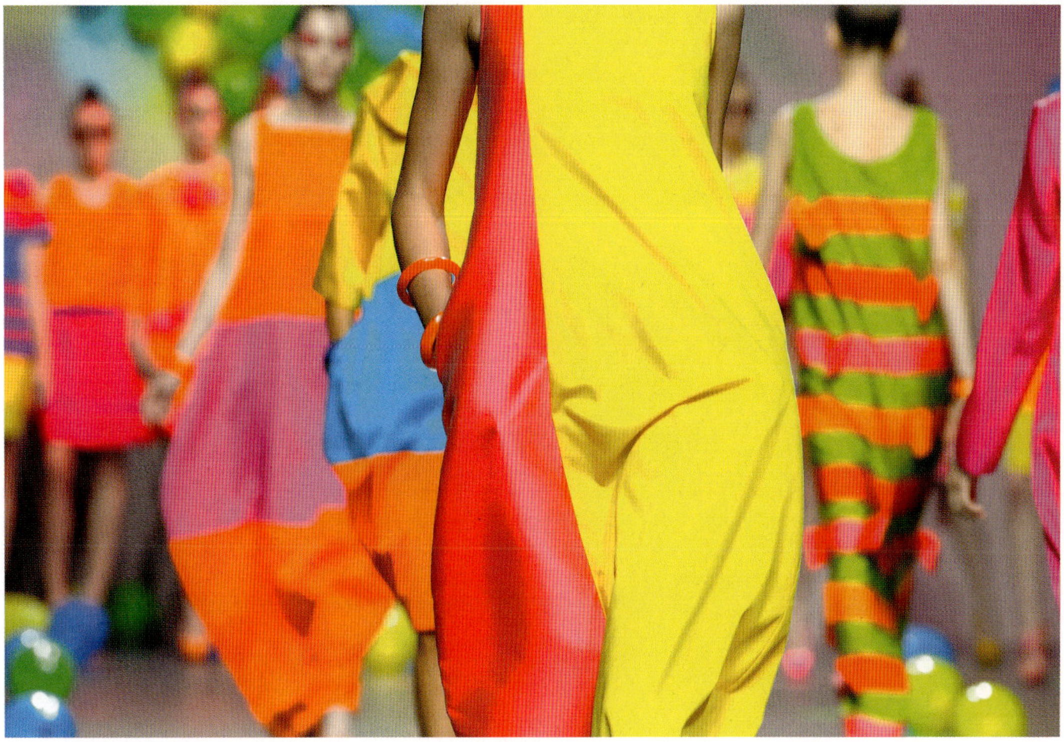

The Agatha Ruiz de la Prada catwalk during the Cibeles Madrid Fashion Week runway show in 2011 in Madrid, Spain.

26 COLOR LITERACY

The ability to use color effectively by achieving a level of knowledge, competence, and practical application of color

One of the benefits of improved color literacy would be to close the gap between the scientific understanding of color and the traditional approach to color that has been practiced in art education.

The first step in expanding color literacy is an appreciation for the complex role color plays in our daily lives. Color literacy is not simply a science or an art and design subject. The basics of color bridge many disciplines. Color literacy includes an expansion of our understanding of color and a growing awareness that the impact of color is cultural and environmental as well as aesthetic.

There is currently much interest in STEAM education, which builds upon STEM academic subjects (science, technology, engineering, and mathematics) but adds the arts to the STEM disciplines. Color is an ideal STEAM subject. It is an inherently multidisciplinary subject that is well suited to introducing children to education based on exploration, observation, and critical thinking.

An initiative supported by the International Colour Association and the Inter-Society Color Council, the Colour Literacy Project is exploring innovative ways to improve the quality of color education by beta-testing and developing a curriculum that combines science literacy and visual literacy.

SEE ALSO:
Human Visual System
Perception Triangle

FURTHER READING
The Colours We Share (2021), by Angélica Dass

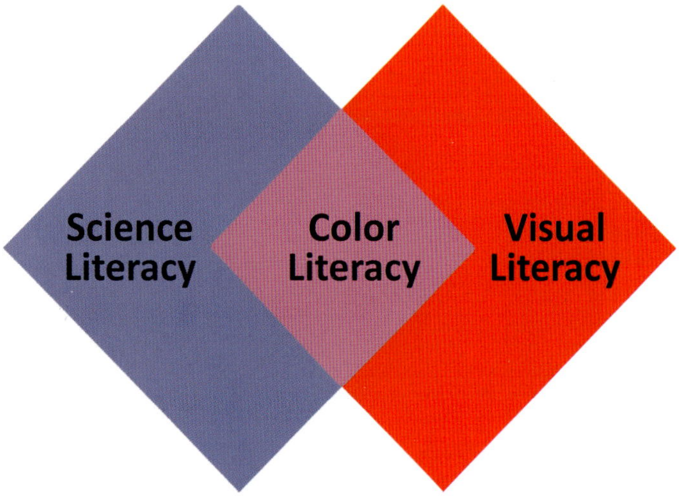

Color literacy can be viewed in a similar way to the concepts of science literacy and visual literacy but draws upon both of these related ideas.

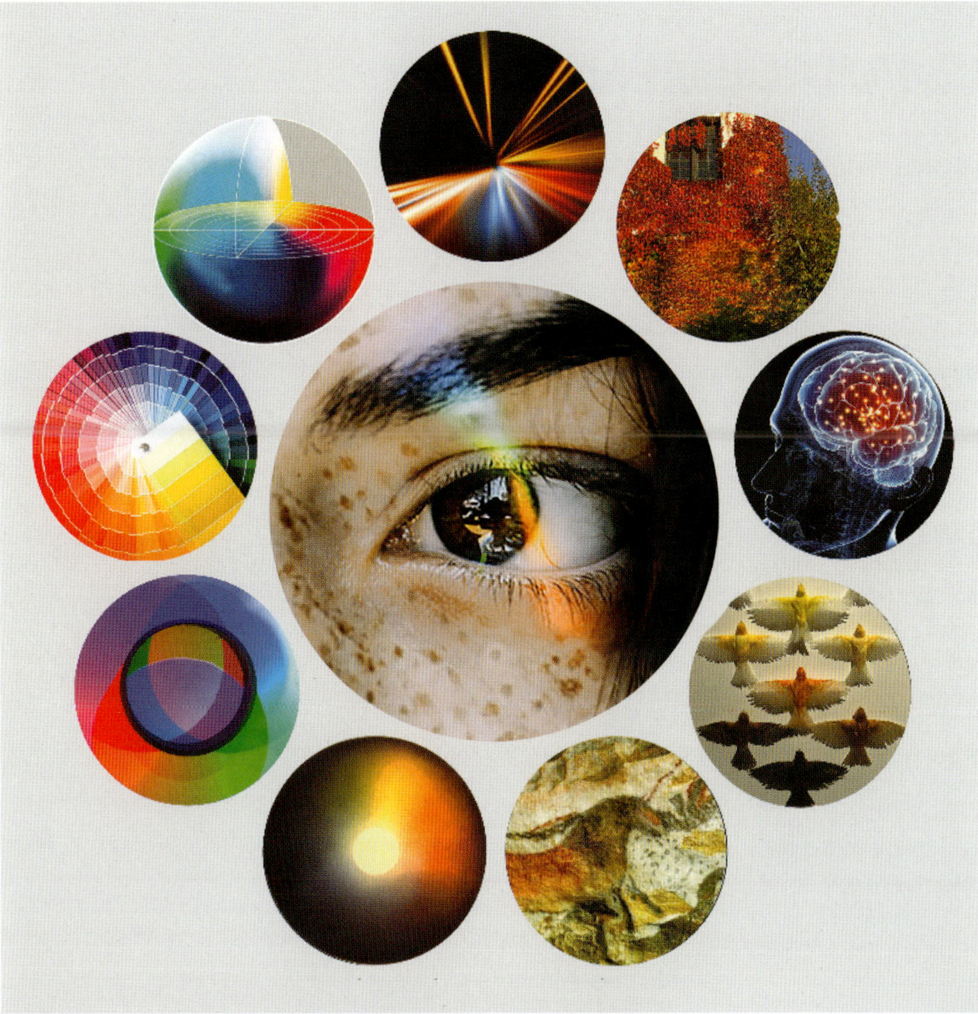

Color literacy begins with paying attention to the impact of color in many areas of our daily lives.

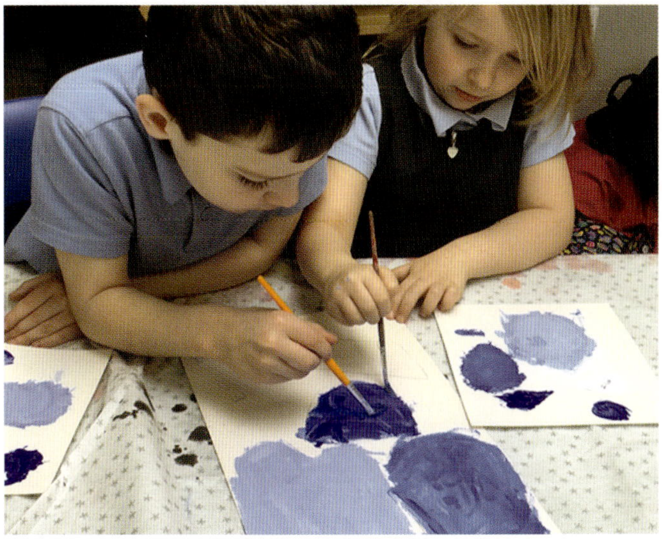

The ability to explore, explain, and predict color phenomena is a key competency of science literacy.

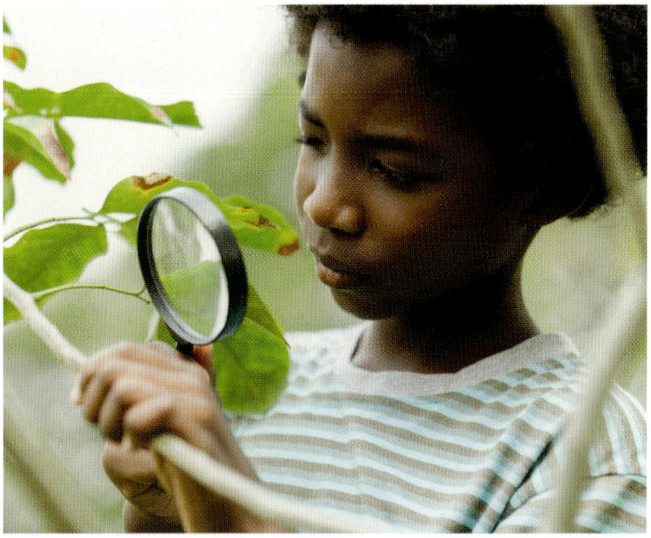

The ability to observe and describe the variety of colors that surround us is a key concept of visual literacy.

27 COLOR MANAGEMENT

The process of aligning color specifications across devices to ensure color fidelity

Emissive displays generate a wide range of colors by combining light from three so-called primary sources. The usual primaries are red, green, and blue because they generate a large range (gamut) of colors. This means that digital color is represented by three numbers (RGB) at each pixel position in the image. However, differences between the actual primaries in different displays and differences in settings (such as contrast, brightness, and color temperature) mean that, without adjustment, the same RGB values will generate different colors on different displays. Color management is the process of making adjustments to achieve color fidelity and ensure consistent color even when images are moved from one device to another.

Color printing involves additional complexity because printers use colorants that absorb light. For printing, the optimal three printing primaries are cyan (red-absorbing), magenta (green-absorbing), and yellow (blue-absorbing) inks. Most printers use a fourth primary (black) for various practical reasons (CMYK). High-end printers use six, twelve, or more primaries to make a wider range of colors. However, when we restrict ourselves to three (or even four) primaries, we can mix all hues, but not all the variations of hues irrespective of whether we use additive color mixing (e.g., displays) or subtractive color mixing (e.g., printers).

Today, color management is ubiquitous but invisible to most consumers. Modern displays and printers can share color information thanks to the work of the International Color Consortium (ICC). ICC profiles are used by the operating system and by applications to enable color fidelity. However, perfect color fidelity is still a "holy grail." There are several reasons why perfect color fidelity is hard to achieve, but one of the most important is that all imaging devices have a limited color gamut, and the gamuts of different devices do not perfectly overlap; consequently, a display can show some colors that cannot be produced by a printer because they are outside of the printer's color gamut, and vice versa.

Color management is an imperfect but vital process that helps to ensure color fidelity in many areas of color reproduction.

SEE ALSO:
CMYK
Color Measurement
Gamuts
RGB

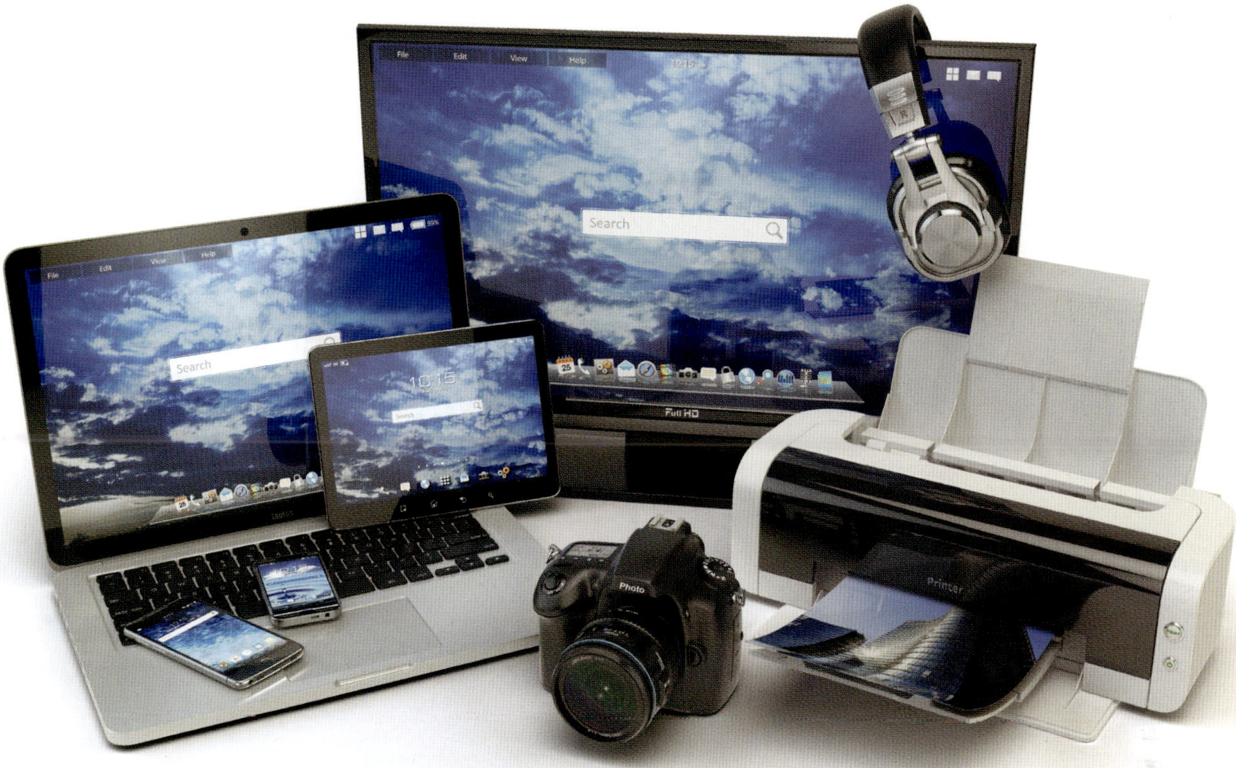

Color management is required to enable color fidelity as color information is transferred between various devices (e.g., cameras, displays, and printers).

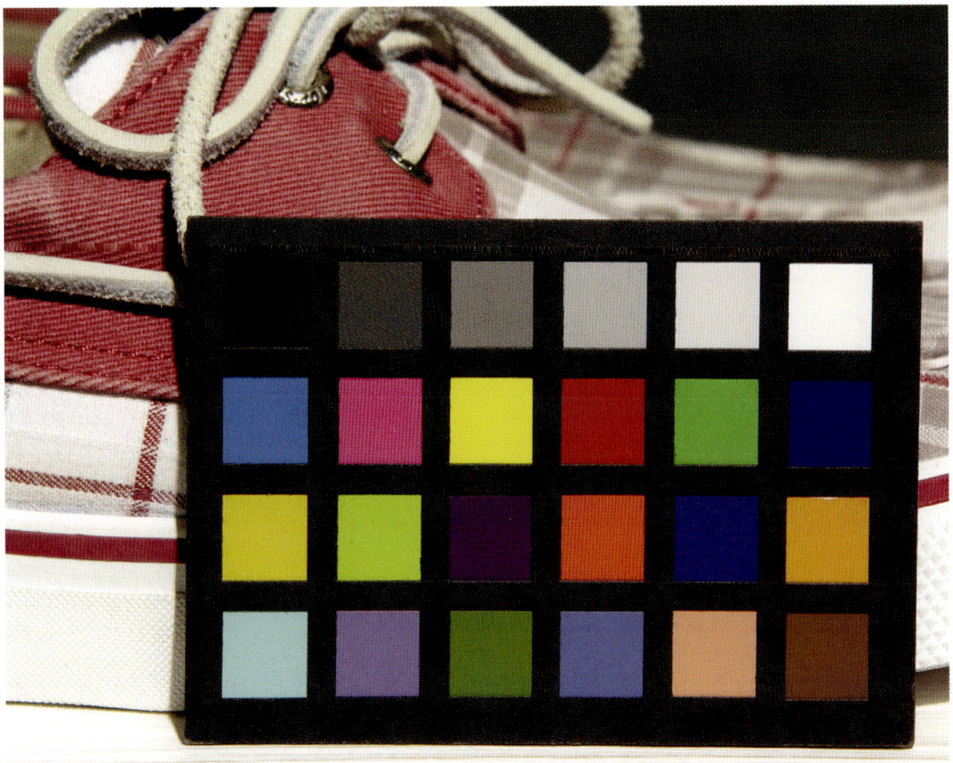

Standardized calibration charts, such as the classic Macbeth ColorChecker, can be used to build an International Color Consortium (ICC) profile for a device.

28 COLOR MEANING

Color is used to communicate ideas and concepts through cultural associations and psychological effects

Color meaning is an intentionally broad term that encompasses all efforts that help us understand both obvious and subtle ways that color permeates our lives.

People associate meaning with color in multisensory and complex ways. Although we often try to isolate aspects of human experience to study them (e.g., cognitive, emotional, behavioral, affective, physiological, spiritual, linguistic, etc.), our response to color is not always orderly and may involve several of these at once. Complicating matters is the fact that a person's response to the same color may also vary according to context, as in the case where we may like wearing a particular color but would not like to see it on a wall in our living space.

An alternate approach is to simply accept that our response to color is complex and to redirect our search to patterns of meaning instead. Color meaning happens when we have an experience with color that is processed in the mind, which enables us to describe it using language. We form literal associations with everyday objects (e.g., blue with sky); use color symbolically on the basis of cultural and historical associations (e.g., purple for royalty, white for mourning in China); or make basic judgments about a color's character (e.g., pleasing, strong, cheerful). Researchers are discovering that meaning can also be found in general categories of colors (e.g., dark colors are strong, pale colors are delicate, vivid colors are intense), not just in single colors.

Color meanings are arguably as important as color aesthetics for the successful use of color in art, design, and packaging. Effective color design is often achieved when the meanings communicated by the colors are consistent with the meanings expressed by the typography, imagery, and content.

SEE ALSO:
Symbolic Color
Three Dimensions of Color
Warm and Cool

"Mere color, unspoiled by meaning, and unallied with definite form, can speak to the soul in a thousand different ways."

—*Oscar Wilde*

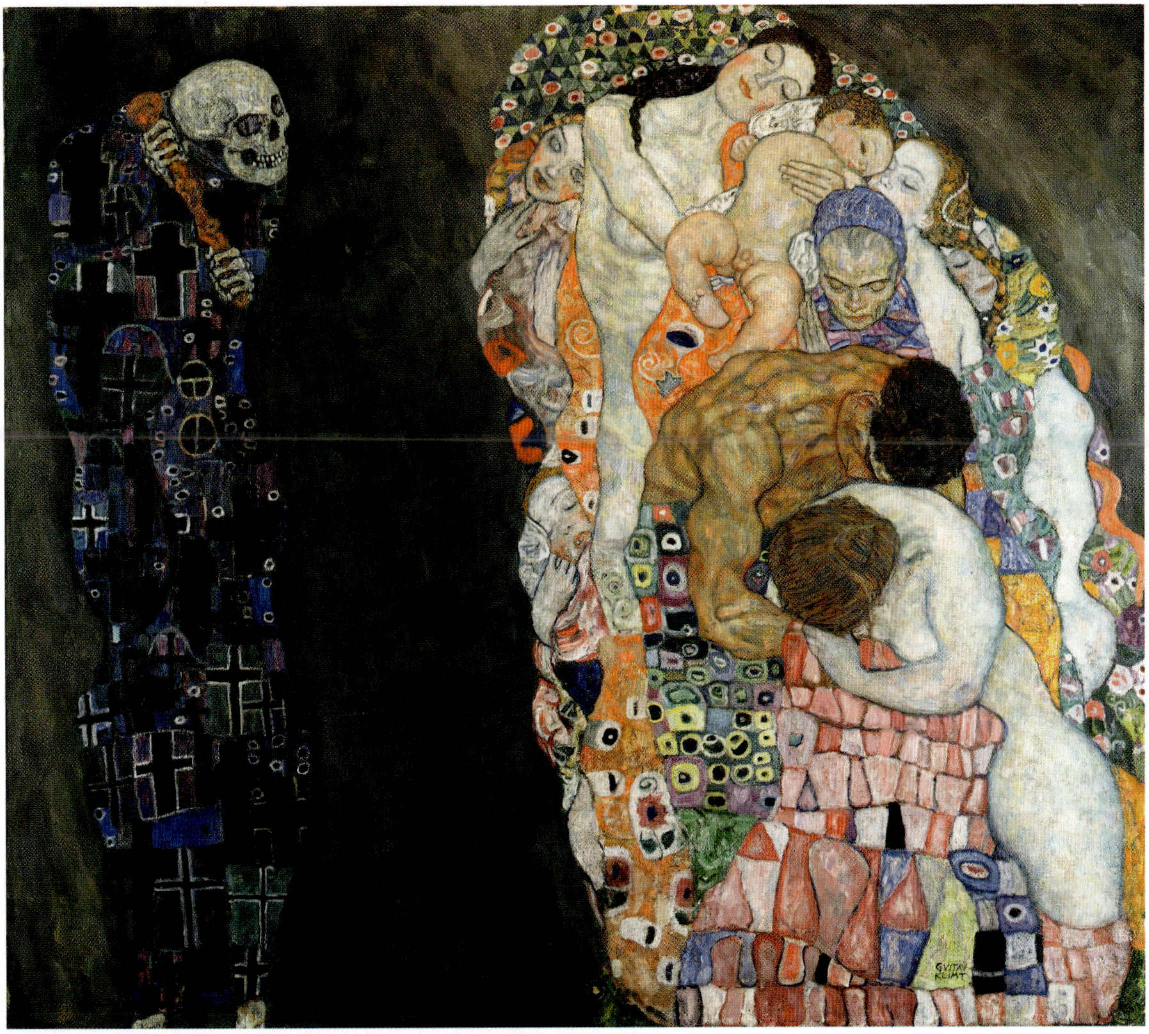

Death and Life (1908-1915), painting by Gustav Klimt.

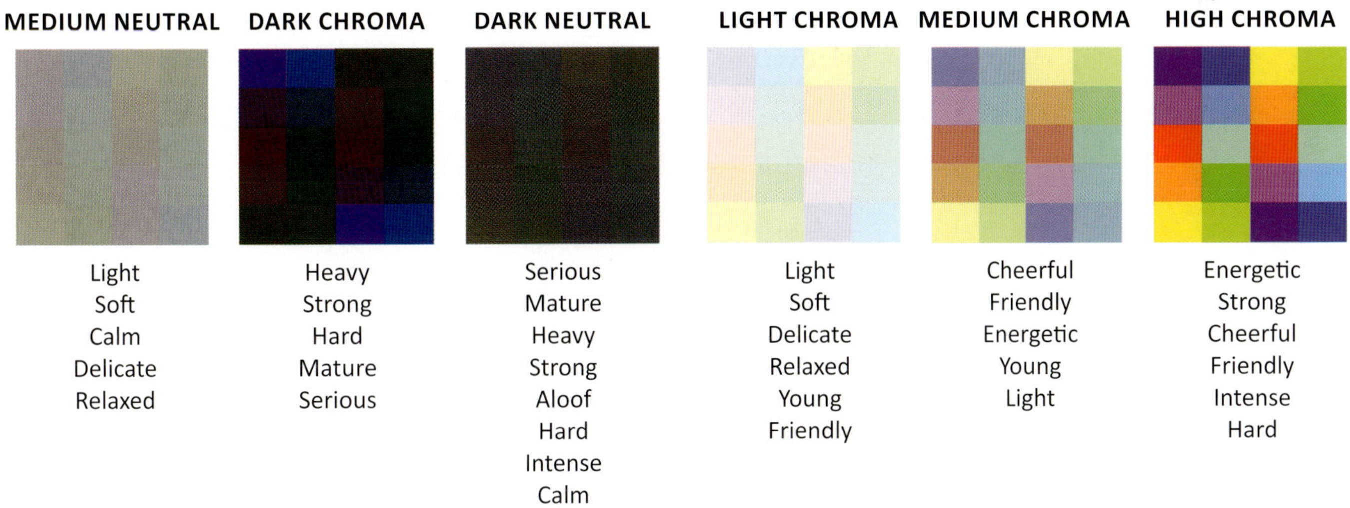

Colorsets (2021), by Ellen Divers. The combination of lightness and chroma can have more consistent meanings than those connected to hue.

29 COLOR MEASUREMENT

The practice of instrumental measurement and specification of color

Color measurement is the science of colorimetry and allows three numbers to be measured to specify a color. It was made possible because of work by color pioneers such as David Wright and John Guild in the early twentieth century. The CIE system of colorimetry was internationally adopted in 1931.

The fundamental concept of the CIE system is that through measurements of reflected, emitted, or transmitted light, it is possible to calculate three numbers that specify color. These three numbers are called tristimulus values and are represented by the letters XYZ. Two color stimuli can match even if their spectral properties are different. However, the critical value of the CIE system is that if two color stimuli have the same XYZ values, they will be a color match when viewed by an average observer. The ability to do this was very important in manufacturing because it provided an objective method to determine whether a production sample would match the color standard provided by a client.

The second half of the twentieth century saw the rapid deployment of color measurement in the manufacturing industry and retail supply chain. The system was concerned with determining whether two objects, for example, were a visual color match. Currently, more sophisticated systems are being developed that attempt to predict color appearance; that is, what something actually looks like rather than whether two things match in color. In 1976 the CIE introduced CIELAB, which, unlike the original 1931 system, was a color appearance model. However, color appearance is complex and depends on many factors. Much research is ongoing to develop color appearance models that can predict color appearance in a wide range of conditions.

Affordable instruments costing only a few hundred dollars are now available and being used for color communication by designers in interior design and architectural applications.

SEE ALSO:
CIE System
Color Management
Electromagnetic Spectrum

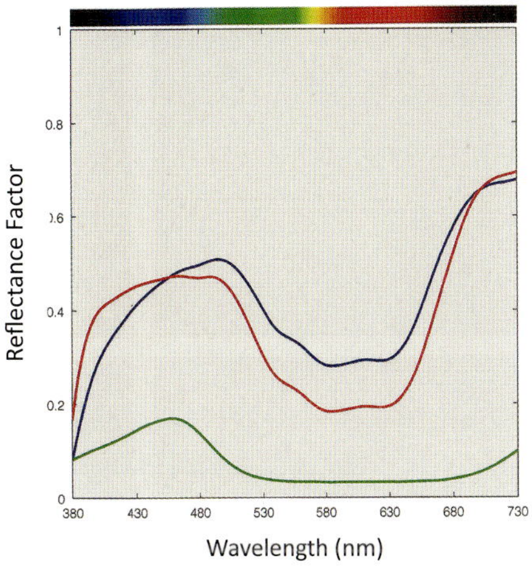

The spectral curves from measurements taken of the left side door for three different bedroom paintings by Van Gogh. The data collected provided information about the pigments used for each painting.

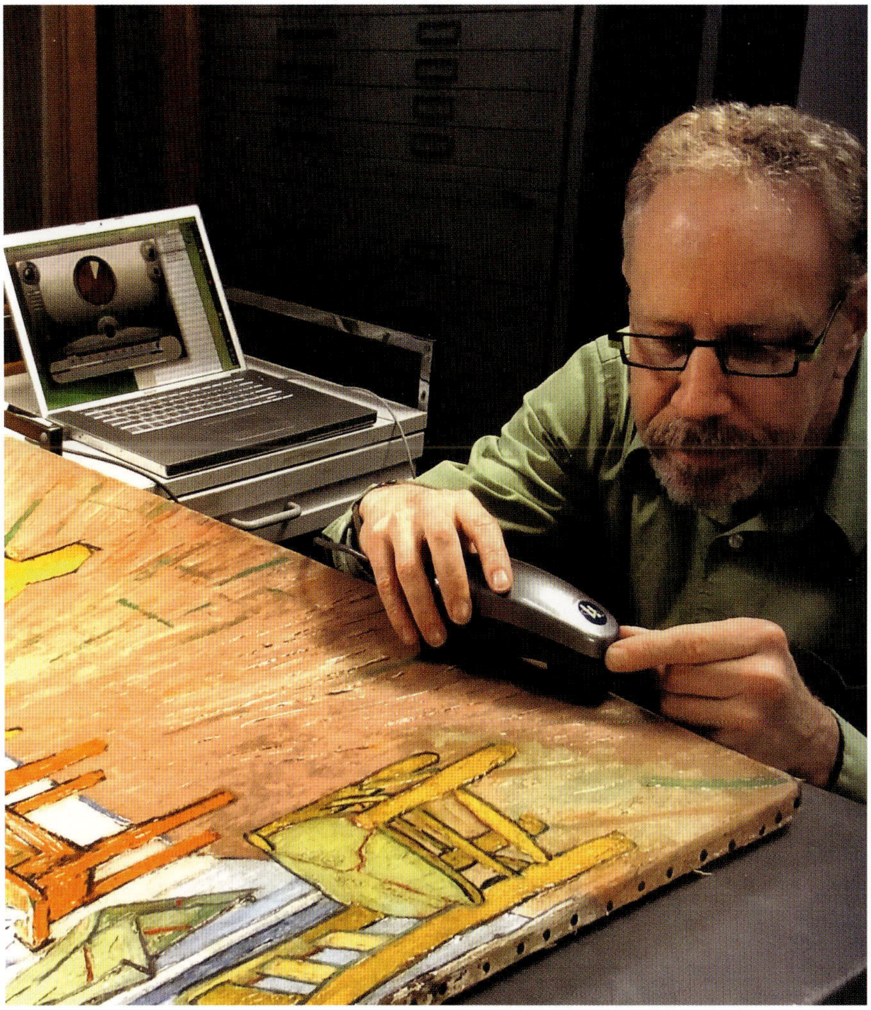

Color scientist Roy Berns measured three of the bedroom paintings by Van Gogh as part of a conservation program.

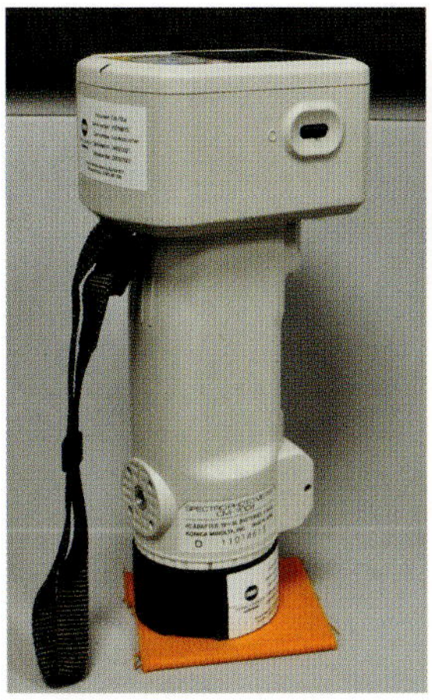

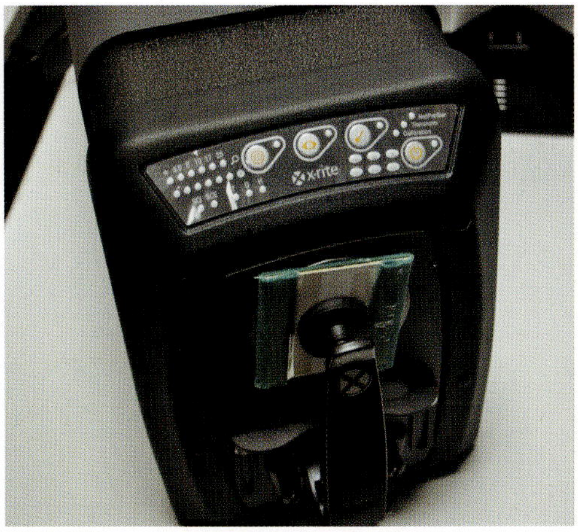

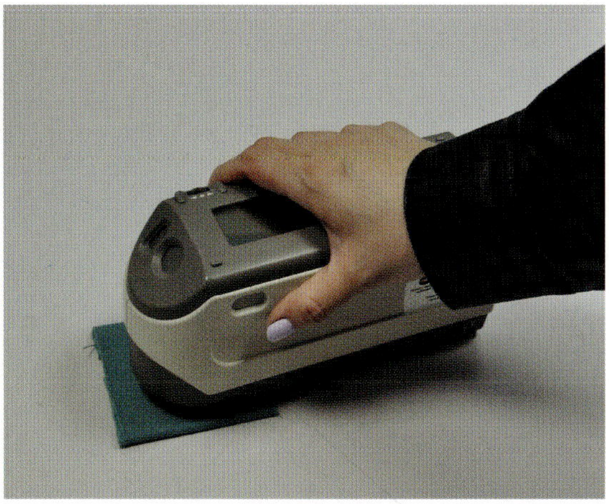

Reflectance spectrophotometers allow spectral reflectance factors to be measured. Onboard software allows CIE values and color differences to be calculated.

30 COLOR ORDER SYSTEM

A systematic method of arranging colors for specification

Over the centuries, many people in many cultures have attempted to conceptually organize colors. Tetradic thinking in Ancient Greece led to the idea of four important colors from which it was assumed all other colors could be made. However, the idea of there being seven important colors also emerged and was linked to the fact that seven bodies in the solar system could be seen with the naked eye. Aristotle arranged these seven colors from lightest to darkest. Meanwhile, Chinese tradition focused on five colors (blue, red, yellow, white, and black), which related to their five elements and were arranged according to the directions east, south, center, west, and north. Newton was the first to understand that hues should be arranged in a circle. Following Newton there were many 3D arrangements of color, beginning with a spherical arrangement published in 1810 by Philip Otto Runge.

Today we distinguish between color order systems that are conceptual and those that can also be physically realized. The Munsell system is perhaps the most well-known physical color-order system. By contrast, the CIE color space known as CIELAB is a mathematical construct. Both systems are helpful for specifying and communicating color because they allow colors to be referred to by the position they occupy in the space.

The Pantone color-specification system is a hugely successful method for color communication in a wide range of industries. However, unlike similar systems such as the Natural Color System (NCS), it does not have a conceptual color space associated with it and is therefore strictly not a color order system.

Color order systems are widely used as color communication tools in fashion, interior design, and graphic design applications.

SEE ALSO:
Munsell System
Natural Color System
RAL System

FURTHER READING
Color Ordered (2008), by Rolf G. Kuehni and Andreas Schwarz

Three Proprietary Systems

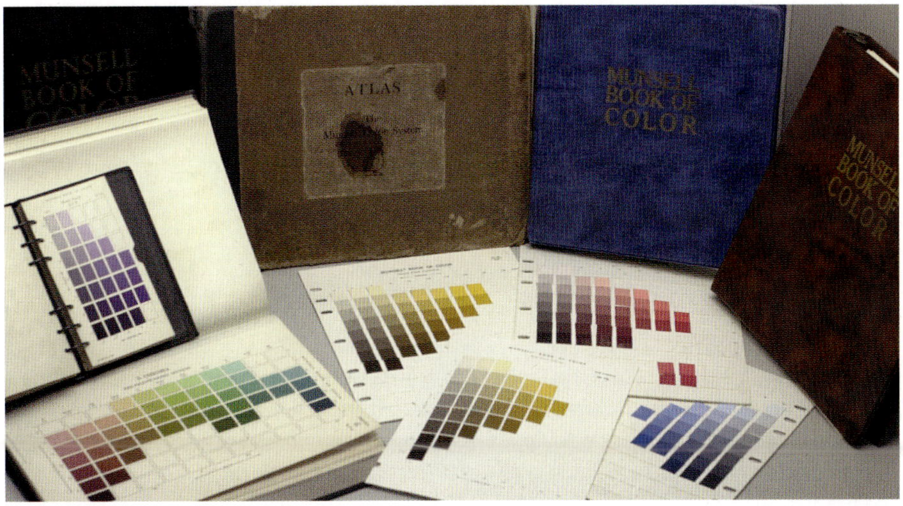

Munsell system, a 3D system devised by Albert H. Munsell, was designed to have samples that were arranged so that the steps between the samples were perceptually equal. Notation: Hue, Value, Chroma (Vivid Yellow = 5Y 8.5/14).

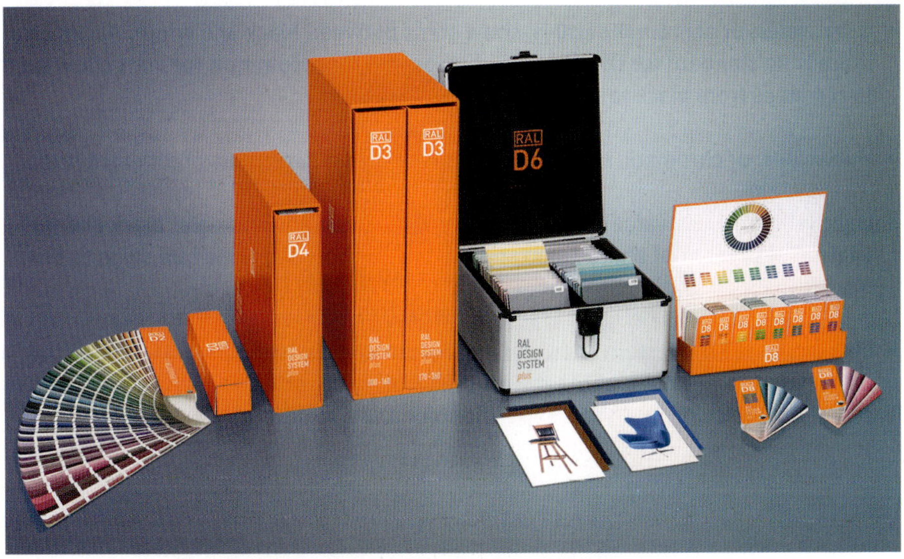

The RAL system, created in Germany, defines colors for paints, coatings, and plastics. Notation: Lightness, Chroma, Hue Angle (Vivid Yellow = 085 80 85).

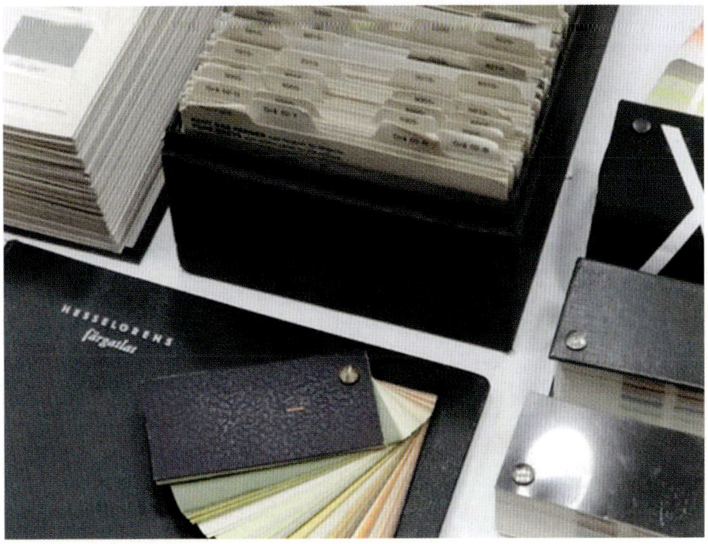

The Natural Color System is a Swedish system based on the color opponency hypothesis of color vision first proposed by Ewald Hering. Notation: Blackness, Chromaticness, Hue (Vivid Yellow = S 0080-Y).

31 COLOR SCALES

A measured sequence of colors illustrating the steps between two colors

Often assigned to learn about the properties of paint mixing, color scales can be made in any media to illustrate the range of colors possible between two specific colors. Methods for making color scales vary depending on the medium, and both physical and digital media offer strategies to add graduations between the steps. Types of color scales include:

- **Gray scales**, or achromatic scales, show steps between black and white. Although there is no standard for the number of steps, the most common versions show eight to ten steps from black to white.
- **Hue scales**, or chromatic scales, show steps between two colors of different hues.
- **Lightness scales**, or value scales, show steps between any color and black and/or white. These types of scales can combine to show how a specific hue steps to both black and to white.
- **Chroma scales** show steps between any color and gray. Technically they show the steps between any color and a gray of the same value, or lightness level, but they can also show the colors between a specific color and a middle gray.

SEE ALSO:
Gradients
Tint, Shade, and Tone

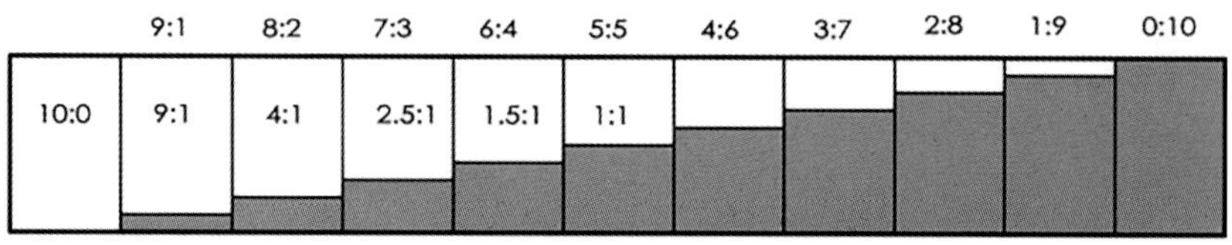

ARITHMETIC SCALE

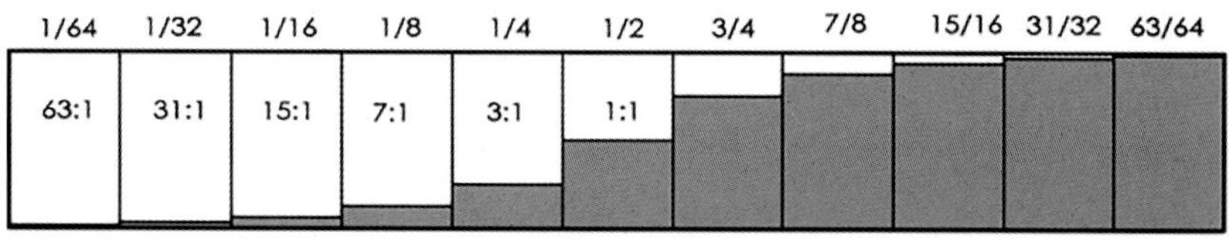

GEOMETRIC SCALE

Gray scales are commercially available for use by artists and designers. Note that, in most media, the gray that is visually halfway between black and white is not a half-and-half mixture.

WEBER-FECHNER LAW

The relationship between the actual change in physical stimulus and the perceived change.
A geometric scale will be closer to the perceptual steps between two colors.

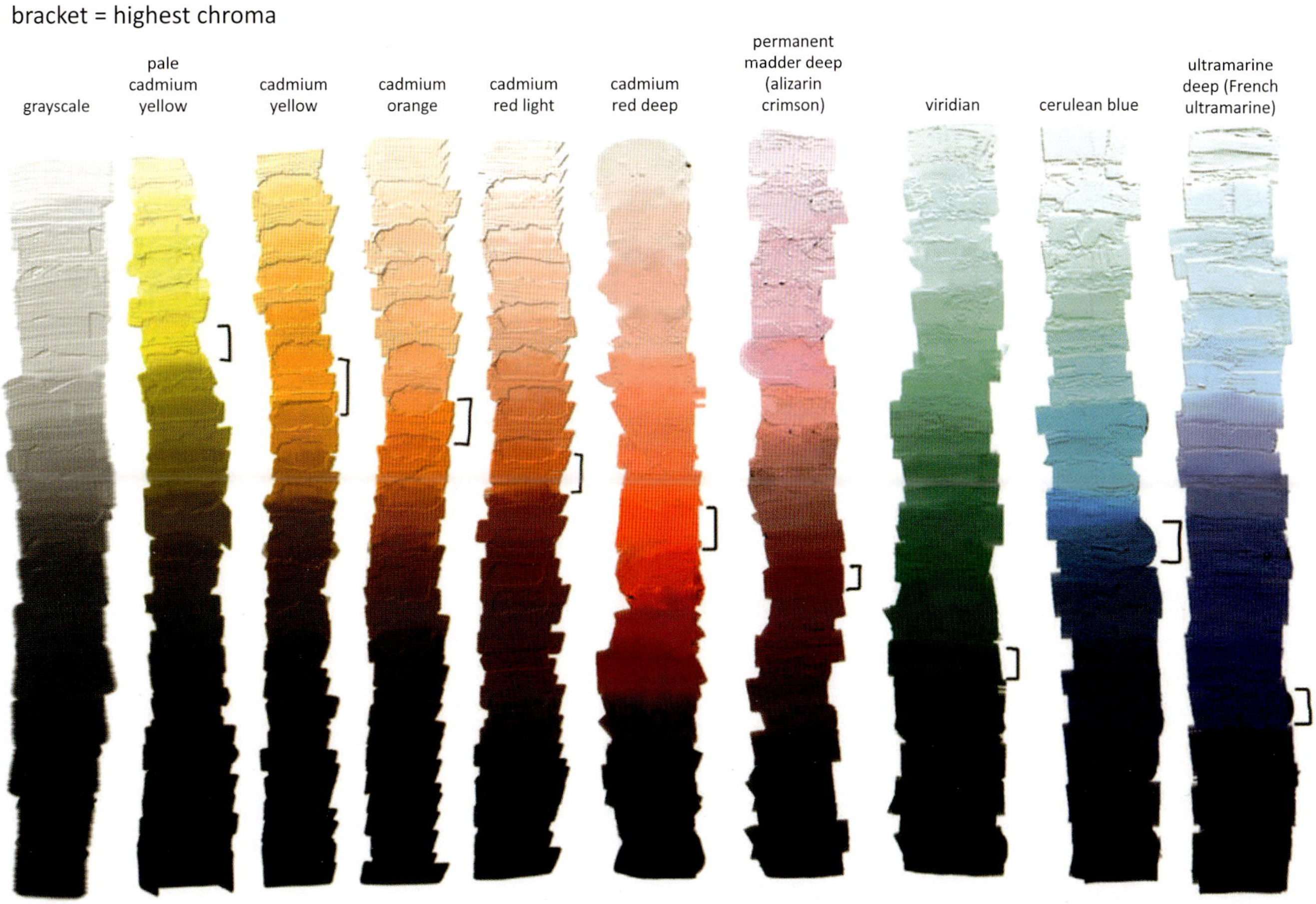

A collection of quick value scales by the Third Cartel showing the steps from the highest chroma of each hue mixed in steps to white and black.

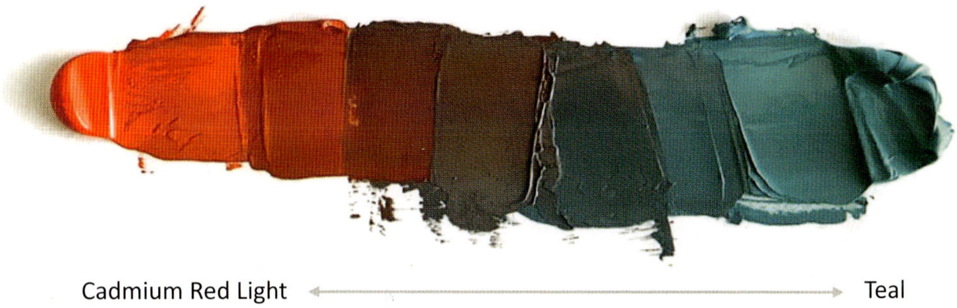

Chromatic acrylic paint scale from red to teal (Golden paint company).

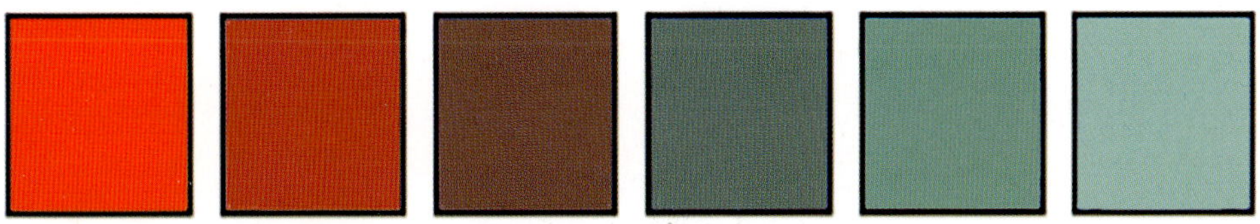

Digital scale from red to teal.

32 COLOR SCHEMES

A limited selection of colors chosen intentionally to create a work of art or design

In traditional color theory a color scheme is often identified using formulaic types of color harmony. For example, monochromatic (where all the colors have the same hue), complementary (where the colors have opposite hues), and split-complementary (one color plus two others that are on either side of its complementary color) are typical types of color schemes. Such color schemes purport to provide artists and designers with a harmonious set of colors, but they are not fail-safe. Many other factors contribute to the success of a color scheme including, but not limited to, the lightness key, chroma levels, placement, and proportion.

SEE ALSO:
Color Meaning
Gamuts
Palettes

It is also possible to choose a color scheme from an image or a piece of art. This is based on the notion that such a color scheme would likely be aesthetically pleasing in any media. For example, Sonia Delaunay's *Electric Prisms* has a polychromatic color scheme that includes many low-chroma colors to balance the vivid hues.

Sometimes the terms *color palette* and *color scheme* are used interchangeably; however, a color palette is the larger set from which to pick colors to create color schemes.

The combination of lightness and chroma are as important as hue selection in setting the tone of a color scheme.

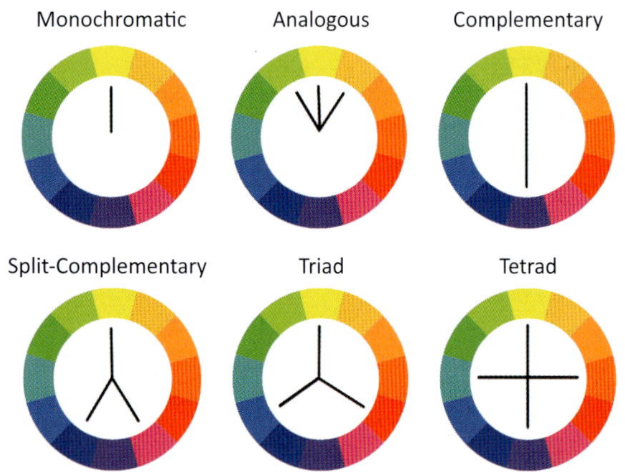

Traditional hue harmonies are typically illustrated with only vivid hues.

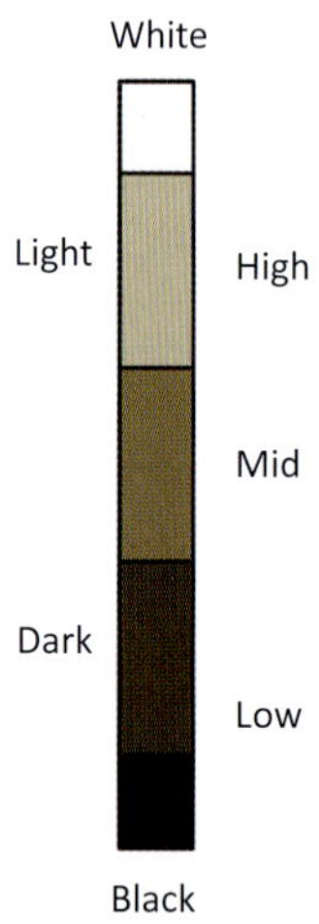

Lightness Keys

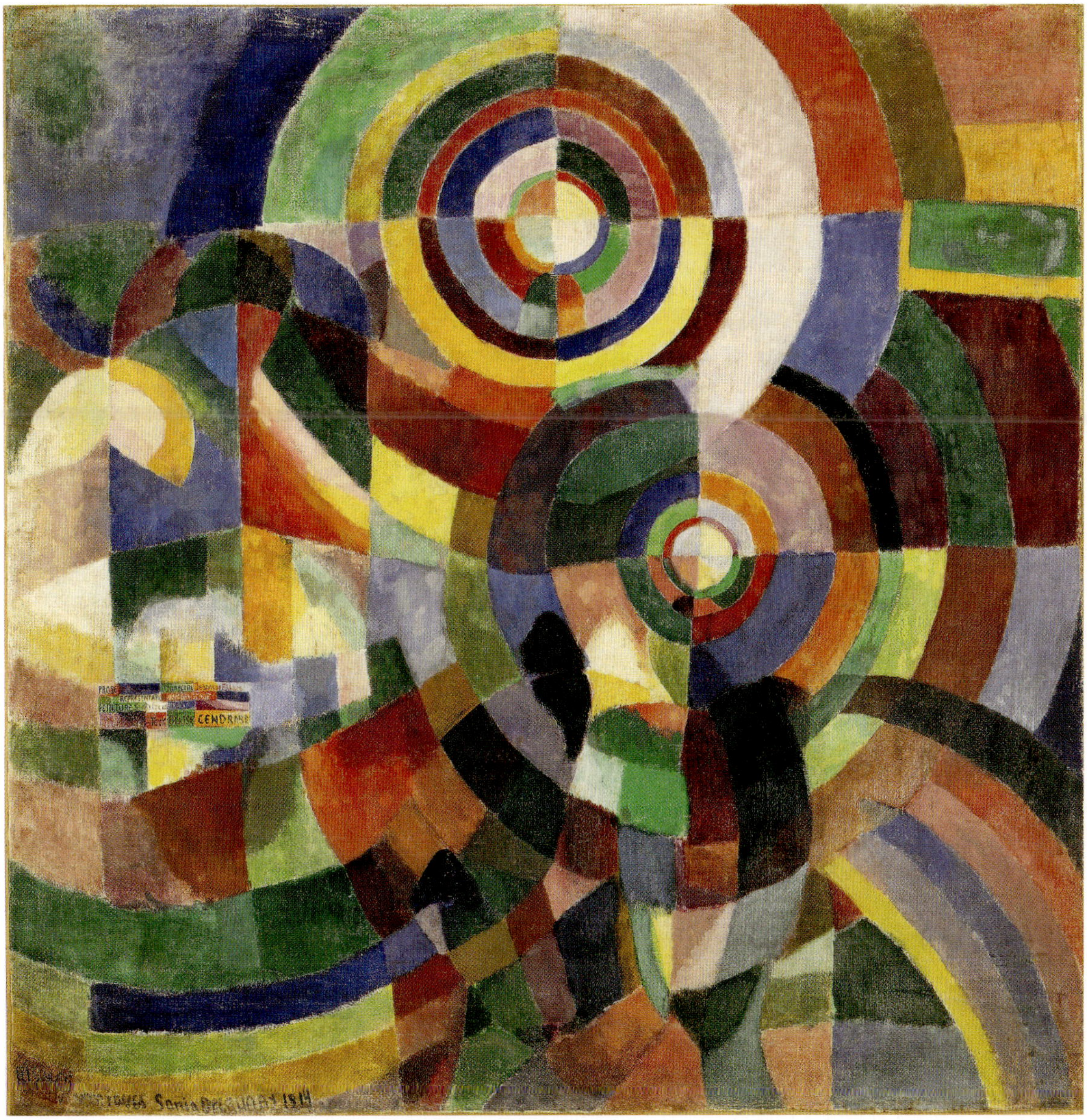

Prismes électriques (1914), oil painting by Sonia Delaunay.

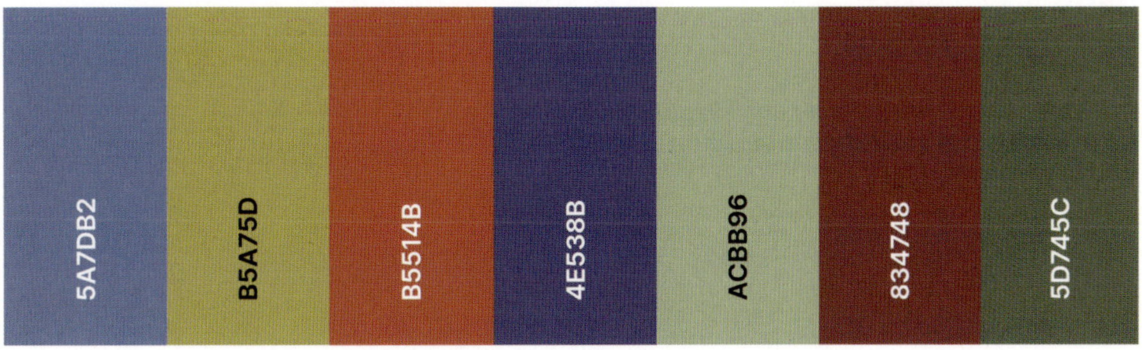

How would you define this digitally extracted color scheme of Sonia Delaunay's painting?

33 COLOR TEMPERATURE

A measurement used to describe the color appearance of a light source

Color temperature is an important concept that is used to describe the color of a light source in terms of whether the appearance of the light is warm or cool. It is based on a theoretical construct developed by the physicist Max Planck in the early 1900s called a black body. A black body is an object that emits radiation as it is heated. As the temperature of the black body increases, the spectral distribution of the emitted radiation changes. At low temperatures the radiation contains more long wavelengths and looks warm; at high temperatures the radiation contains more short wavelengths and looks cool.

SEE ALSO:
LED Color
Lighting

We use the term *correlated color temperature* (CCT) to characterize a light source. The CCT is the temperature of a black body that the spectral distribution of a light source is most similar to in terms of color appearance. The Kelvin temperature scale (K) is used to designate the CCT.

Candlelight typically has a CCT of about 2,000K, incandescent light has a CCT of about 3,000K, and daylight often has a CCT of about 6,500K. Daylight with a higher CCT than 6,500K (e.g., 7,500K) will appear cooler, and daylight with a lower CCT than 6,500K (e.g., 5,500K) will appear warmer than 6,500K daylight.

The introduction of LED lighting over the last twenty years or so has led to greater variation in spectral properties for light sources with the same CCT. Consequently, some researchers claim that CCT is now inadequate to describe the color-rendering properties of light sources and that we need new ways to characterize these light sources, which are increasingly being used today.

Methods exist to quantify the effect of a light source on the color constancy of objects. One such method is called the color rendering index (CRI), which is often cited on commercial light sources. The proliferation of new LED sources, however, is bringing into question the suitability of such indices to correctly quantify the quality of modern commercial light sources.

The ability to adjust color temperature is an ongoing area of research in the lighting industry as well as a critical consideration in designing interior spaces at home and in the workplace.

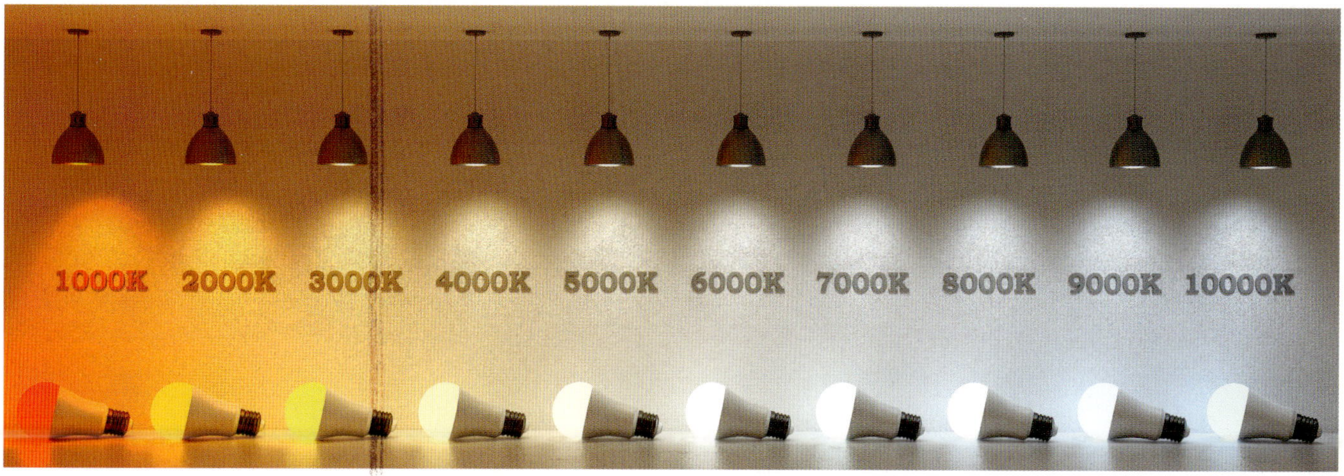

Here we can see the color appearance of light at lower color temperature (left) and higher color temperature (right).

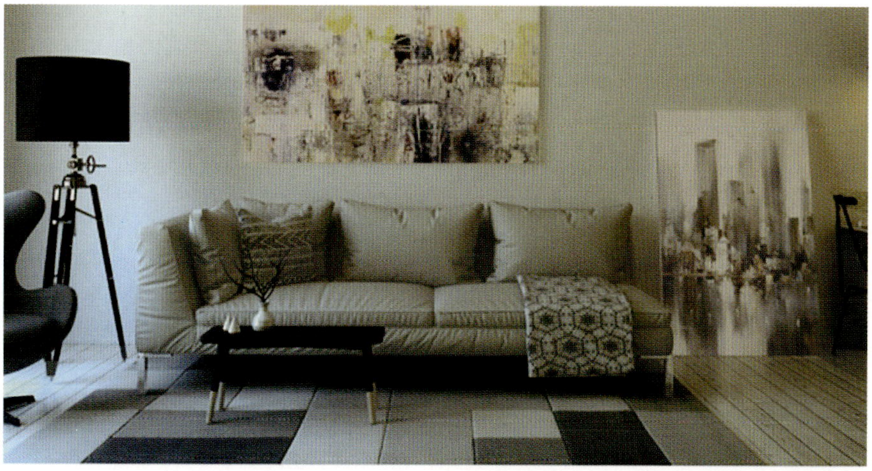

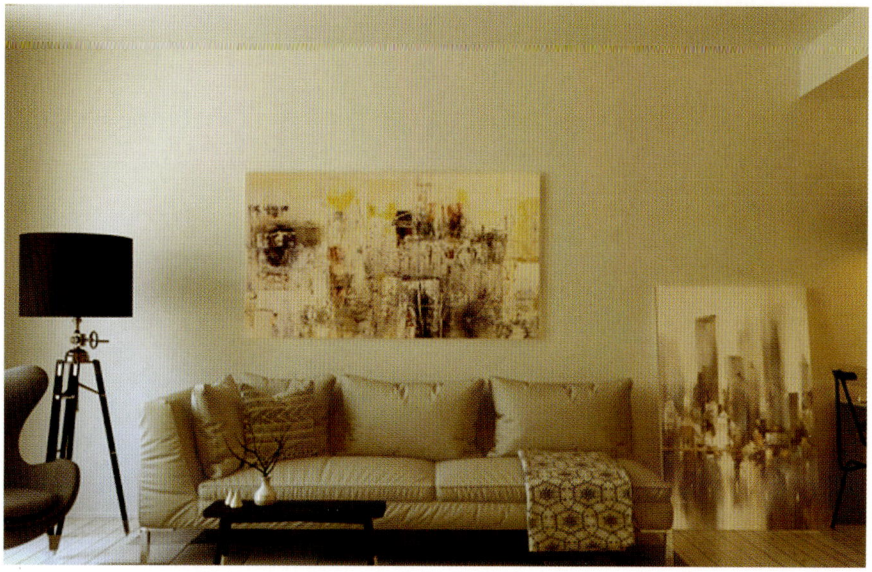

The same scene illuminated by lights of high CCT (upper) and low CCT (lower). Notice the very different feel of the room in each case.

34 COLORANTS

A material that can impart color. Dyes and pigments are examples of colorants

Organic colorants are based on molecules that contain the element carbon, whereas inorganic colorants are generally based on minerals. Early humans used both organic and inorganic colorants that were naturally available. An example of an early organic colorant would be blood, which was probably first used for body decoration. However, inorganic pigments (such as red and yellow ochre and chalk) could easily be found in the ground. Inorganic colorants generally have better light fastness compared with organic ones.

A separate way to categorize colorants is to use the terms *dye* and *pigment*. A dye is a colorant that is applied in a solution (usually, but not always, water), and a material such as a textile is dipped into the dye solution. A chemical reaction often occurs by which the dye binds to the fiber so that the textile is imparted with a stable color. By contrast, pigments are insoluble compounds and often applied as a suspension in a medium (such as a polymer) that hardens as it dries to leave a durable, colored layer of polymer. Textiles are typically colored using dyes, whereas paints and plastics are usually colored using pigments. Printing inks normally use dyes, but pigments can sometimes be used; when pigments are used, the large pigment particles scatter light that strikes them and this can make the ink less translucent or, in some cases, opaque.

Both dyes and pigments primarily impart color by selectively absorbing some wavelengths of light more than others. A yellow dye, for example, absorbs the shorter wavelengths much more than the longer wavelengths. The longer wavelengths are primarily reflected to the eye and perceived as color.

Although natural colorants are still used today, in most cases fossil fuel–based synthetic colorants have replaced them because they are often less expensive and of better quality.

SEE ALSO:
Black and White
Chemistry of Chromophores
International Klein Blue

FURTHER READING

Bright Earth: Art and the Invention of Color (2001), by Philip Ball

The Brilliant History of Color in Art (2014), by Victoria Finlay

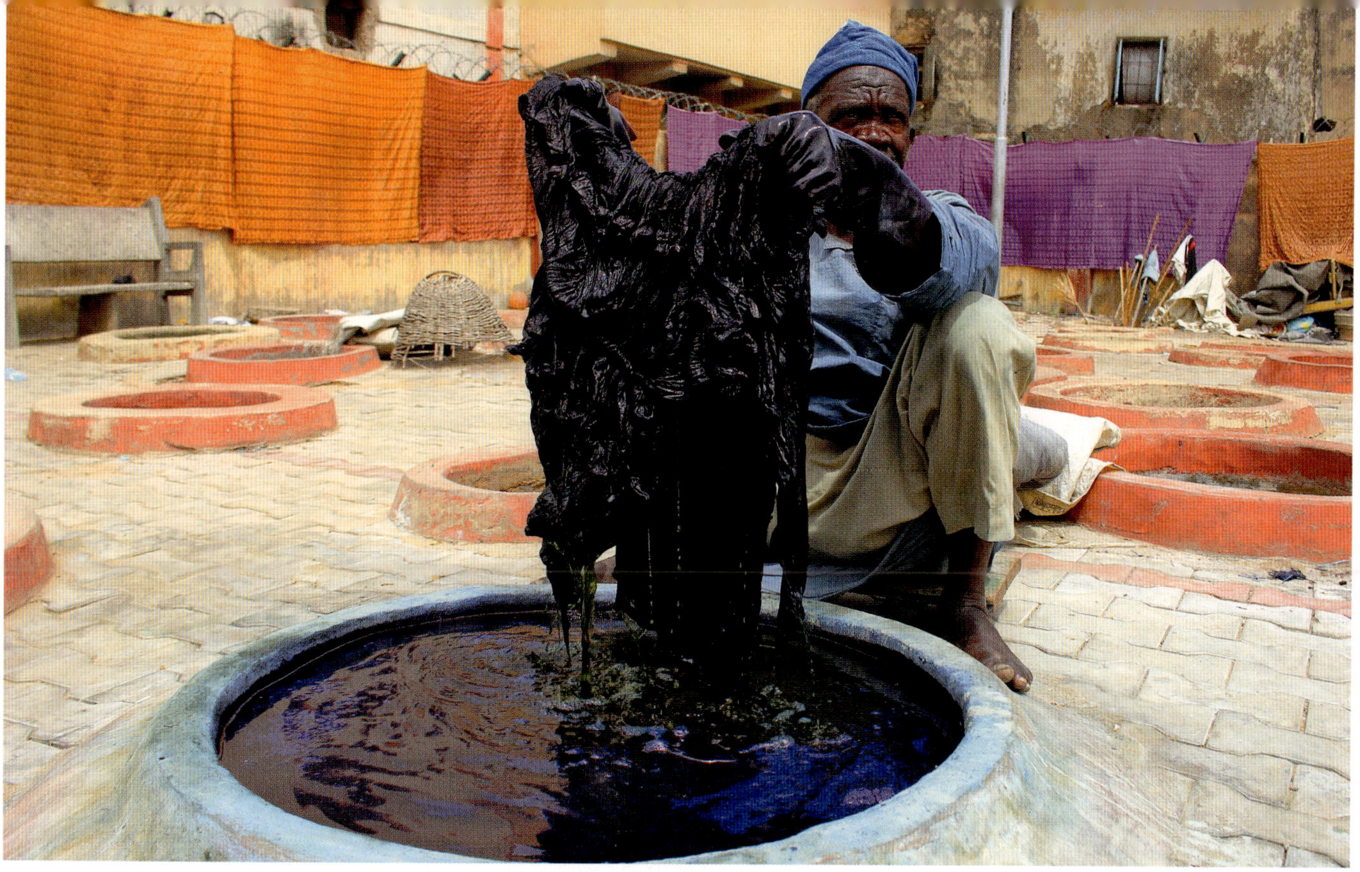

One of the most common uses of dyes is to impart color to textiles. Dyes are usually applied from solution in water and become attached to the fiber during the dyeing process. The dye pits at Kano, Nigeria, are more than five hundred years old, but there is evidence that humans have dyed textiles for at least fifty thousand years.

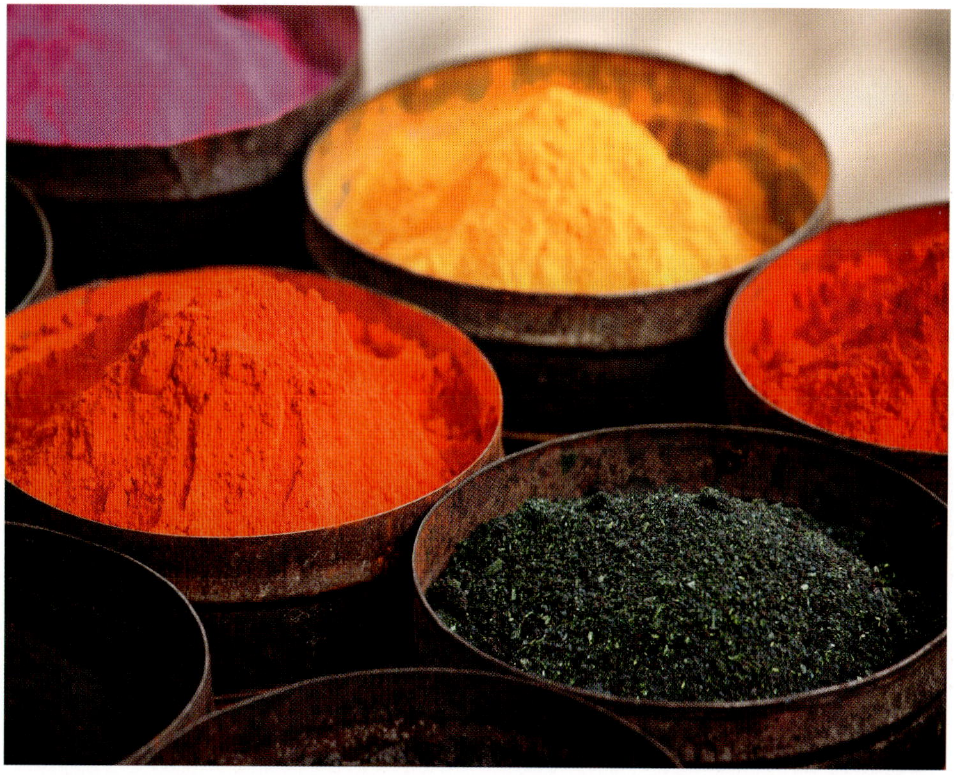

Whereas dyes are soluble and applied from a solution, pigments are typically suspended in a polymer layer when they are applied (e.g., in a paint). Pigments are identified by numbers. See the online Color of Art Pigment Database.

35 COLORWAYS

Different combinations of colors in which a design can be produced

The use of different colorways enables the same pattern or design to be reproduced in many ways. The choice of colorway can dramatically change the feel of the design, and some research has shown that different colorways can change how people perceive the forms or shapes within the design.

Typically, a designer will produce a printed design on paper or textile in three or four different colorways. Although different colorways are easily implemented in digital printing processes, different colorways can be produced in woven fabric using a blanket warp. Thus, often the design solution is not a single design but a collection of related designs where the colorway and even aspects of the pattern may vary.

The development of digital computer-aided design (CAD) software has allowed designers to explore different colorways quickly and effortlessly. Often (but not always) this experimentation takes place toward the end of the design process. The use of such software is now ubiquitous in textile design education and commercial design operations.

SEE ALSO:
Bezold Effect
Color Schemes
Palettes

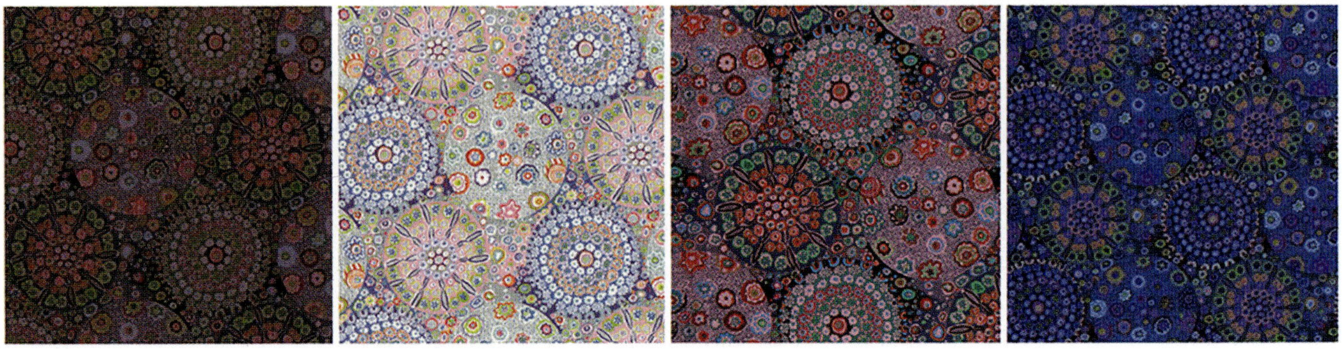

Millefiore fabric by Kaffe Fassett. The same design is illustrated using four different colorways.

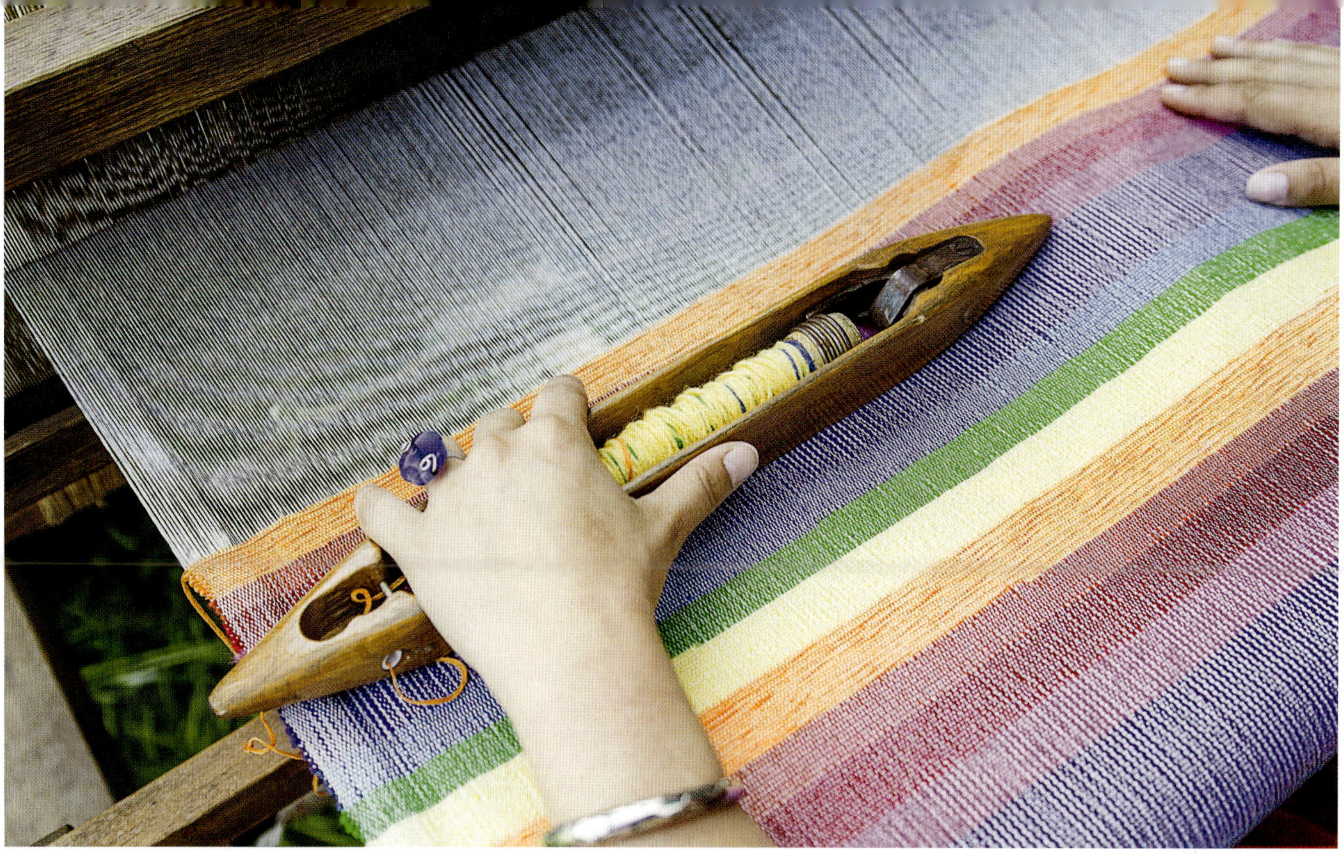

Colorways can be worked out using CAD software and tested by digital printing on paper before going into production by hand or machine.

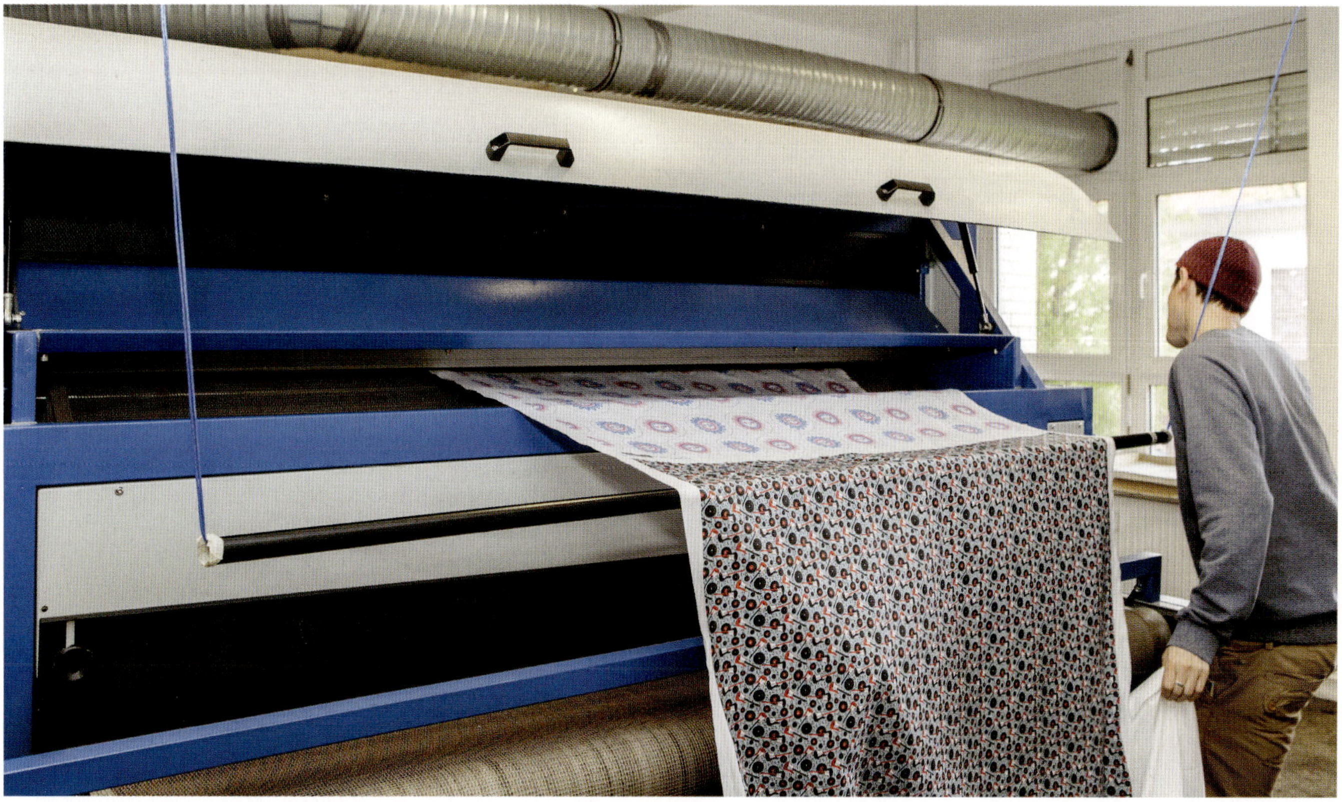

Digital printing of fabrics and wallpapers has made short runs of multiple colorways affordable.

36 COMPLEMENTARY COLORS

Hues that are opposite to each other in some sense

Complementary colors—sometimes referred to as opposite colors or opposing hues—are one of the most contentious concepts in traditional color theory. Sometimes complementary colors are said to be colors (hues) that are opposite to each other on the color wheel, but unfortunately, there are many different versions of color wheels and they do not all show the same hues as complementary.

Complementary hues are sometimes defined as afterimage colors. If we stare at a vivid swatch for a period of time and then remove that swatch and stare at a neutral color, we will often perceive a color that is the opposite of the original color. This effect is referred to as an afterimage or successive contrast.

A related concept describes complementary colors as pairs of colors with maximum contrast when placed side by side. This concept was used by the impressionists in an attempt to create the most vivid visual sensations of color possible.

In mixing ideology, complementary colors are defined as colors that neutralize each other; in other words they reduce the chroma of each other to practically zero. In practice it is extremely difficult to make a neutral by mixing two lights (additively) or colorants (subtractively). Whether two colorants can be mixed to create an approximate neutral color will depend on the spectral properties of the two colorants and not just on their color appearance.

Which hue opposes which other is more complicated than is often presented in traditional color theory.

SEE ALSO:
Subtractive Mixture
Successive Contrast

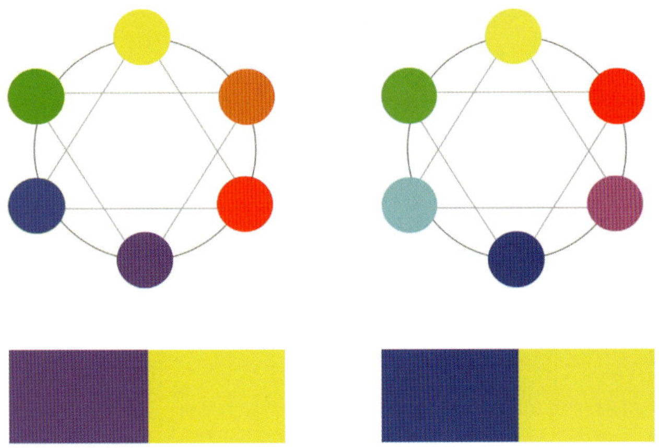

Six-hue color wheels based on a subtractive RYB system (left) and an additive RGB system (right). Notice blue is opposite to orange in one system and opposite to yellow in the other system. Do we get maximum contrast when blue is placed next to orange or next to yellow?

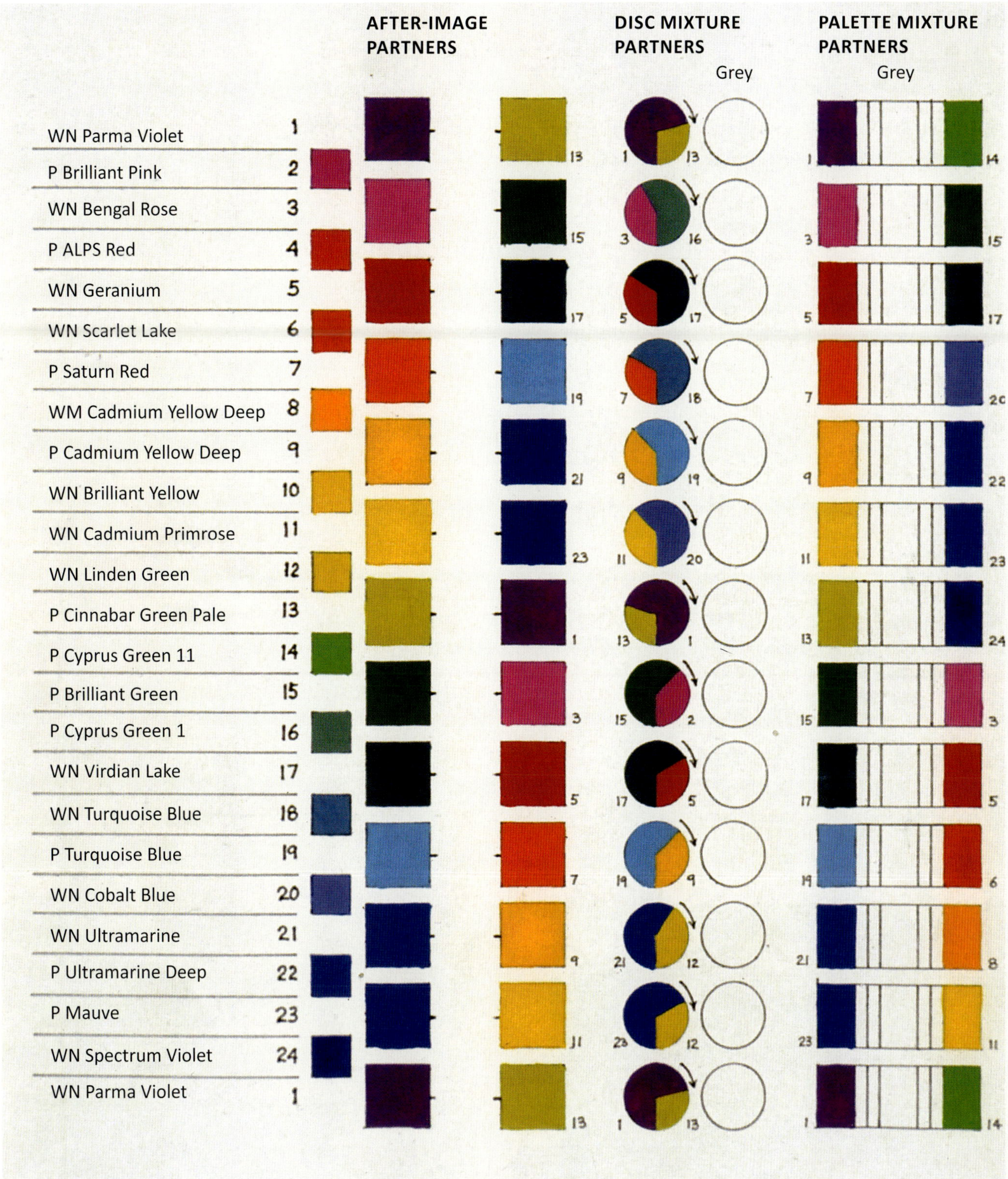

Comparison of complementarity based on three different definitions—afterimages, disk mixture, palette mixture partners—by Paul Green-Armytage

37 CONTEXT

Colors are almost always seen in context, surrounded by colors that affect their appearance

Color perception is relative. Objects, for example, don't have fixed colors. Rather, the color that we see when we look at an object (or part of an object) depends on the context in which we view this color. Perhaps the most common effect of context is the relationship between the surrounding colors on the appearance of a color patch. These effects are described by phenomena such as simultaneous contrast and assimilation.

Similar effects can also occur in a temporal context (e.g., afterimages). Even the colors we see for the spectral colors (when we look at individual wavelengths of light) depend on the surround against which they are viewed. Surround colors—in either a spatial or temporal sense—are not the only factors that affect the context of color perception. Other phenomena such as memory color can also be observed.

In almost all practical applications, color is relative. The term *related color* is sometimes used to generally describe the effects that have been mentioned. However, unrelated color perception can also occur. For example, if we look down a tube and see an emissive patch of spatially uniform color at the end of the tube, this is an unrelated color.

SEE ALSO:
Atmospheric Perspective
Bezold Effect
Simultaneous Contrast
Successive Contrast

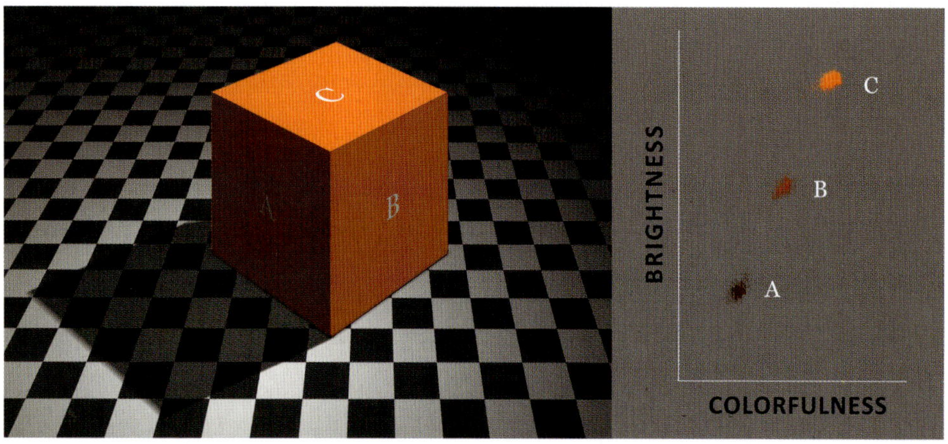

Due to the lighting context, the faces of the orange cube vary in appearance.

Left: The cube is perceived to have a uniform orange color, as if it was painted all over with the same paint but appears progressively brighter and more colorful on its left, right and top planes (A, B, and C).

Right: Brightness and Colorfulness of planes A, B, and C, as quantified by the lightness (L*) and chroma (C*), respectively, in CIE L*a*b* color space.

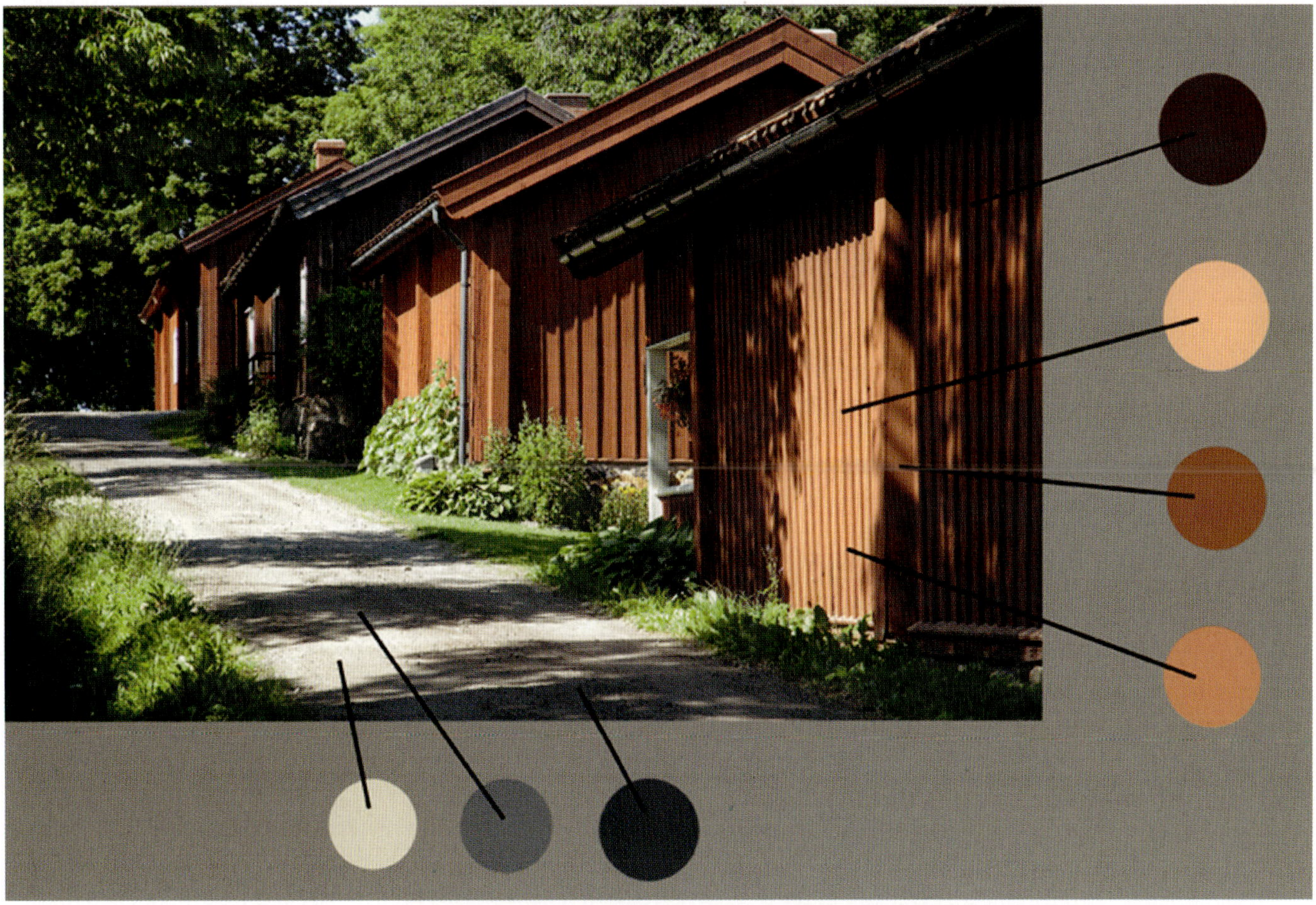

Unrelated colors seen through a tube are like a palette for re-creating the image. We perceive and experience many levels of color simultaneously: We apprehend the uniform red-earth coloring of the houses and the grayness of the gravel road. At the same time, we perceive the colors' modulation in light, shadow, and space.

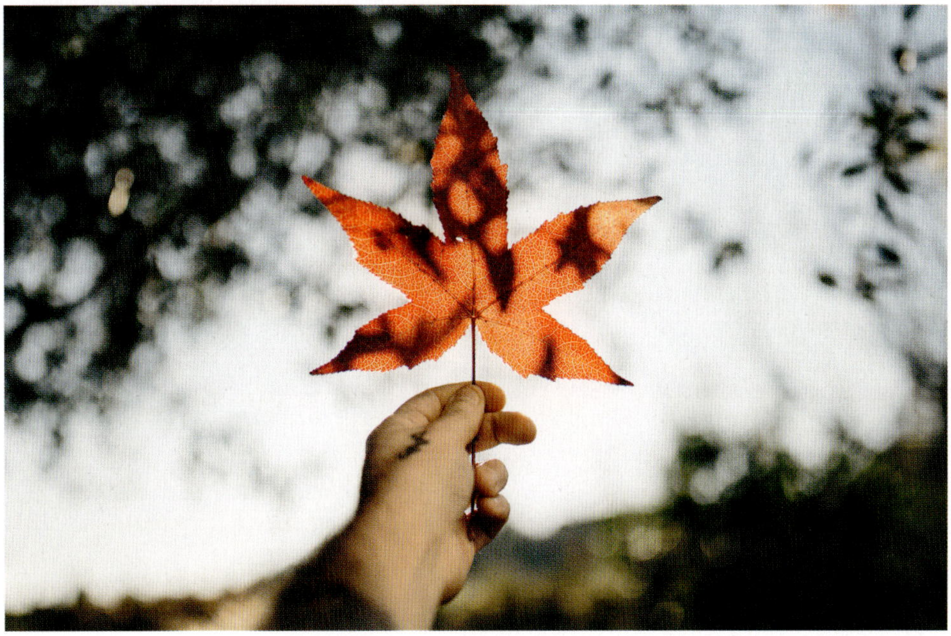

The type of materials affects the appearance of objects. Light shining through a translucent leaf heightens the chroma.

38 CONTRAST

The amount of difference in the color appearance of colored lights and surfaces compared with the surround

One of the earliest references to contrast was by the physicist Ibn al-Haytham (965–1040), who noticed that spots of paint on a white background looked blacker than their "true" color. Later, Goethe (1749–1832) noted that a gray on a white background looks darker than the same gray on a black background.

Since the days of Hermann von Helmholtz and Ewald Hering, there have been arguments about whether contrast can be explained by mechanisms in the eye (favored by Helmholtz) or by more cognitive processes in the brain (proposed by Hering). Today it is believed that both retinal and cortical activity may contribute toward contrast.

It is also possible for temporal contrast to occur when color appearance contrasts with what has previously been seen. Commonly known as successive contrast, temporal contrast is responsible for the phenomenon of afterimages.

In *The Art of Color*, Johannes Itten listed seven types of contrast. Although choosing one type of contrast is often recommended as a starting point in designing a color scheme, a variety of contrasts are often used to greater effect.

Consideration of contrast enables artists and designers to enhance the effect of color combinations. Lightness contrast is the most important consideration for legibility, while hue and chroma contrasts provide additional opportunities for visual emphasis.

SEE ALSO:
Complementary Colors
Simultaneous Contrast
Successive Contrast

ITTEN'S SEVEN CONTRASTS

1. Contrast of hue
2. Light-dark contrast
3. Cold-warm contrast
4. Complementary contrast
5. Simultaneous contrast
6. Contrast of saturation
7. Contrast of extension

Although Itten's seven contrasts are often explored in introductory color courses, the underlying concept of contrast is much more complex in practice.

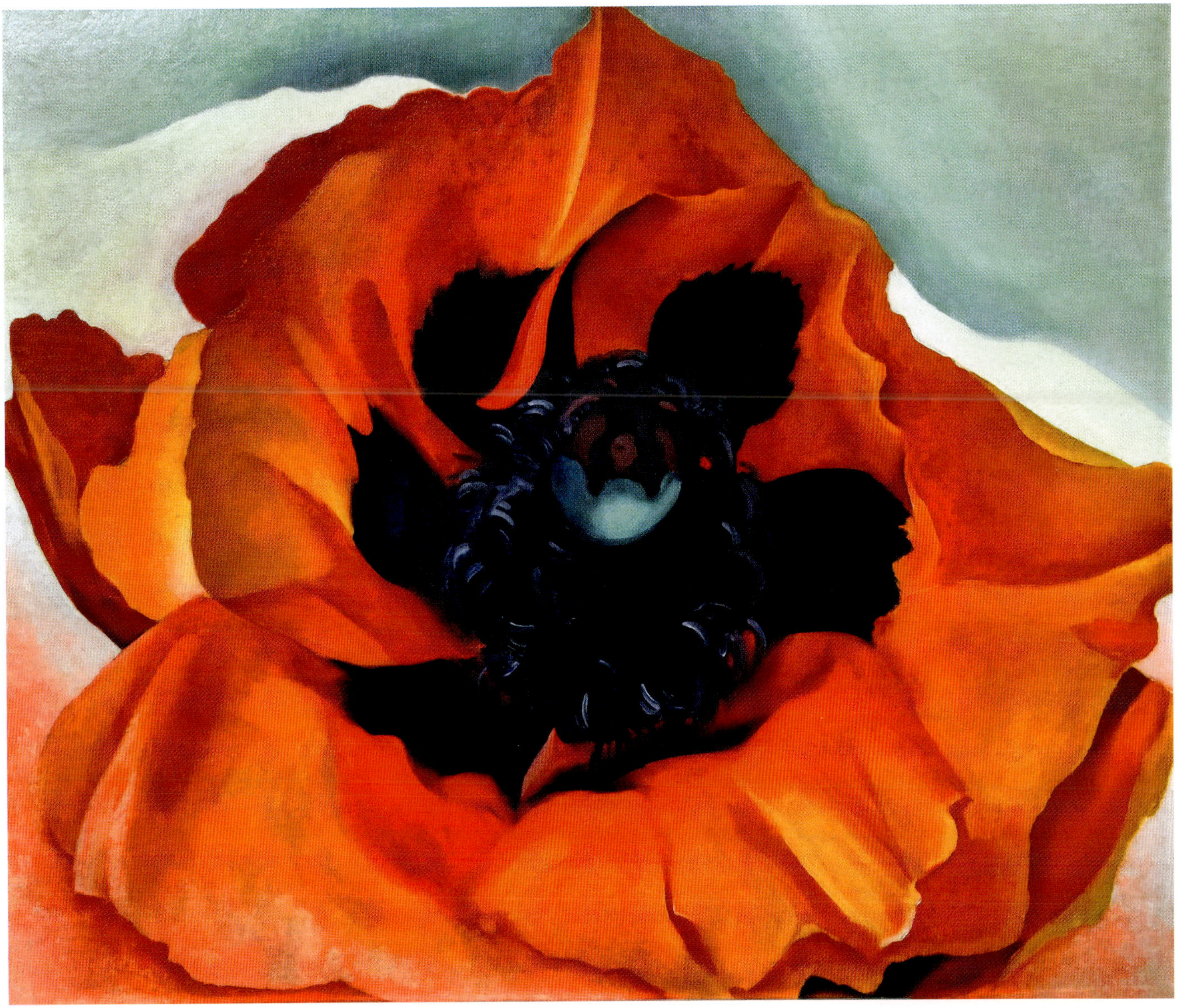

Poppy (1927), oil painting by Georgia O'Keeffe.

In an example by Andreas Schwarz, all of Itten's color contrasts apply to the combination of these two colors—a slightly yellowish green of high lightness and medium chroma, and a slightly bluish red of low lightness and higher chroma.

39 ELECTROMAGNETIC SPECTRUM

The range of wavelengths or frequencies over which electromagnetic radiation extends

Electromagnetic radiation is a form of energy that can be characterized by wavelength. Some of the radiation has very long wavelengths. For example, an FM radio station broadcasting at 90 MHz has a wavelength of 3.3 meters. However, at the opposite end of the spectrum, some of the radiation has a very short wavelength. Gamma rays, for example, have a wavelength of about 100 picometres (a picometre is one-trillionth of a meter).

Our visual systems are sensitive to a very narrow band of electromagnetic radiation in the approximate range of 360 nm to 780 nm (a nanometer is one-billionth of a meter). The CIE system defines this range of radiation as light. Some physicists, however, use light in a broader sense to include all electromagnetic radiation. According to this definition, the range from 360 nm to 780 nm is visible light. Note that in certain conditions some humans have been known to be sensitive to electromagnetic radiation at wavelengths as short as 300 nm and as long as 1,000 nm.

All electromagnetic radiation—including light—has aspects of being both a wave and a particle. The idea that light is a particle—which we call a photon—was known in the nineteenth century. But Louis de Broglie (1892–1987) first introduced the idea that light could also behave as a wave and subsequently received the Nobel Prize for this work. Wave-particle duality is an essential component of the field of quantum mechanics.

The particle nature of electromagnetic radiation is important because as the photon size increases in energy, the radiation becomes intrinsically more hazardous for us. Radiation with wavelengths less than about 400 nm are dangerous, and gamma rays are life-threatening. This explains why UV radiation is dangerous and can cause skin damage and even skin cancer.

Our definition of light (or visible light) is human-centric, based on the range of wavelengths to which human photoreceptors in the eye are sensitive. Some insects such as bees have sensitivity to UV (ultraviolet) light and can see patterns on flowers that are invisible to humans. On the other hand, bats and mosquitoes have visual sensitivity extending into the IR (infrared) range.

SEE ALSO:
CIE System
Color Measurement
Spectral Hues

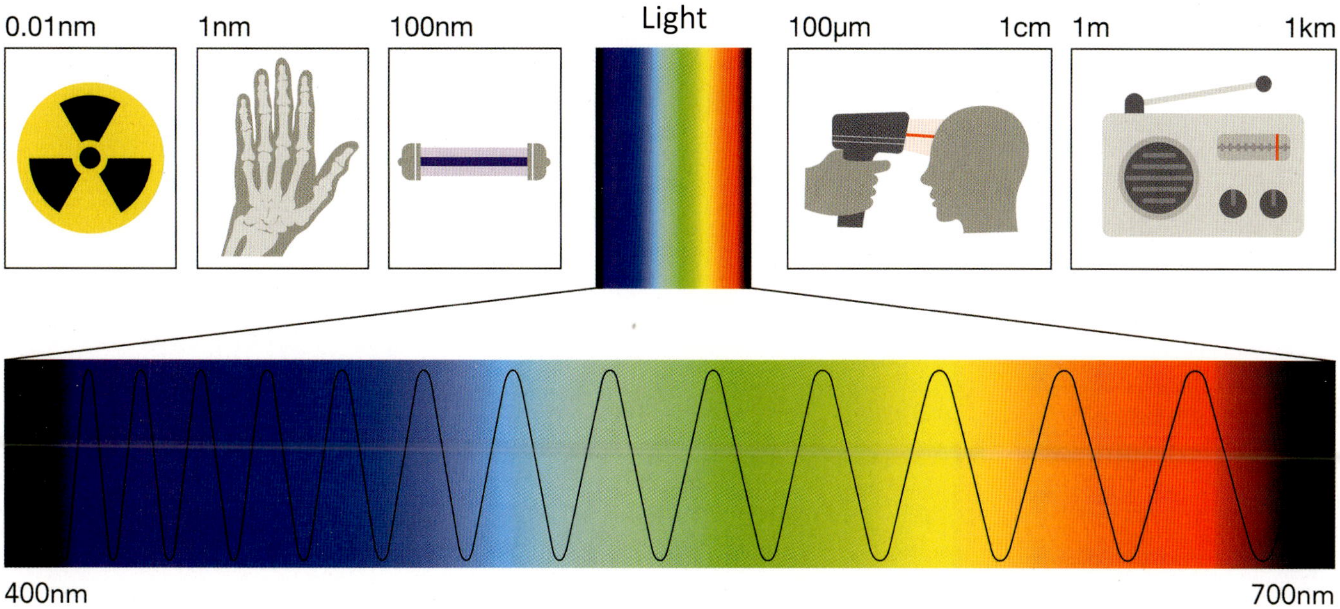

Visible spectrum: Human range is between 400 nm and 700 nm. A bee's range is between 300 nm and 600 nm.

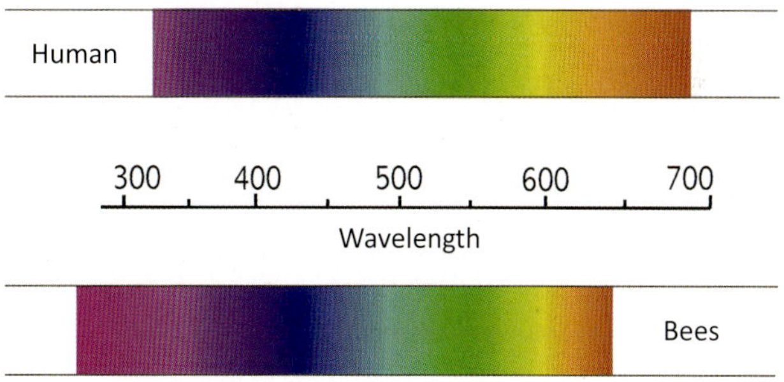

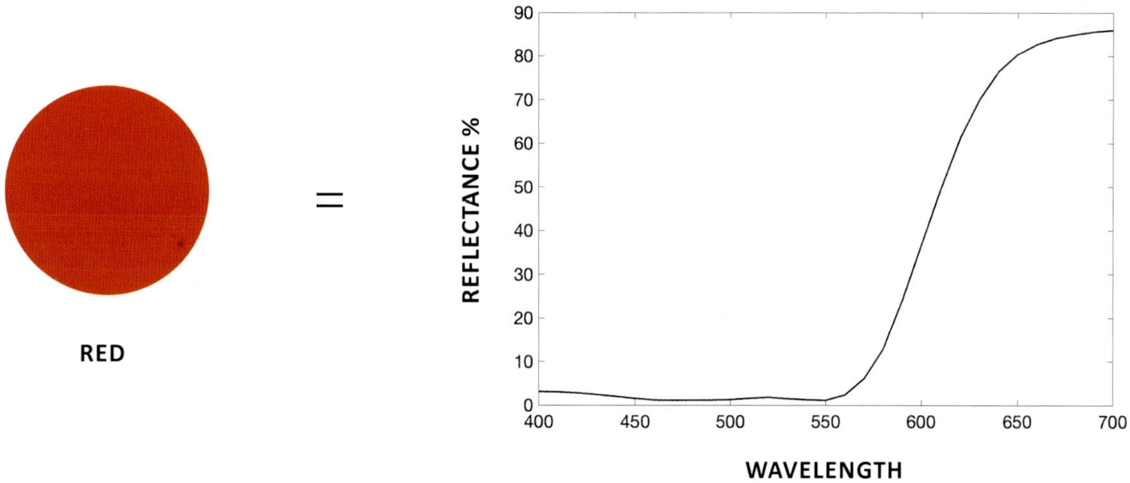

Spectral reflectance curve: a graphical representation of the amount of light that an object reflects at each wavelength in the visible spectrum.

40 EMOTION AND COLOR

Color is historically thought to have an affective response that is linked to human emotion

In the past century popular psychology reinforced the notion of a one-to-one correspondence between vivid hues and people's emotions, an idea that paralleled theories about the existence of basic emotions (e.g., joy, anger, fear, sadness, disgust, surprise), each with its own neural pathway in the brain. However, this view of emotion has come into question, not only because of new findings in neuroscience but because this paradigm does not account for the myriad of less intense internal responses ("feelings") that people have to everyday events, places, people, and objects.

Research methodology on color and emotion has ranged from measuring physiological responses (heart rate and blood pressure), to observing behavior, to recording subjects' verbal or written responses. However, many studies have been plagued by methodological concerns that make it difficult to arrive at solid conclusions about the relationship between color and emotion.

Adding to the problem is the fact that researchers have typically studied the chromatic hues and neglected the many variations in lightness and chroma that exist within a hue. One would be hard-pressed to generalize about how red feels to you when confronted with a pale pink or a deep mahogany, each of which conveys a different character. Also, colors are typically studied in isolation, one at a time, which does not explain their effect when experienced in combination with other colors.

Fortunately, researchers are beginning to address these issues, so clearer answers about color and emotion may be forthcoming in the future. In the meantime, some researchers have shifted their focus to the broader topic of color meaning.

SEE ALSO:
Character Zones
Color Meanings
Symbolism

"Color directly influences the soul."
—*Wassily Kandinsky*,
Concerning the Spiritual in Art

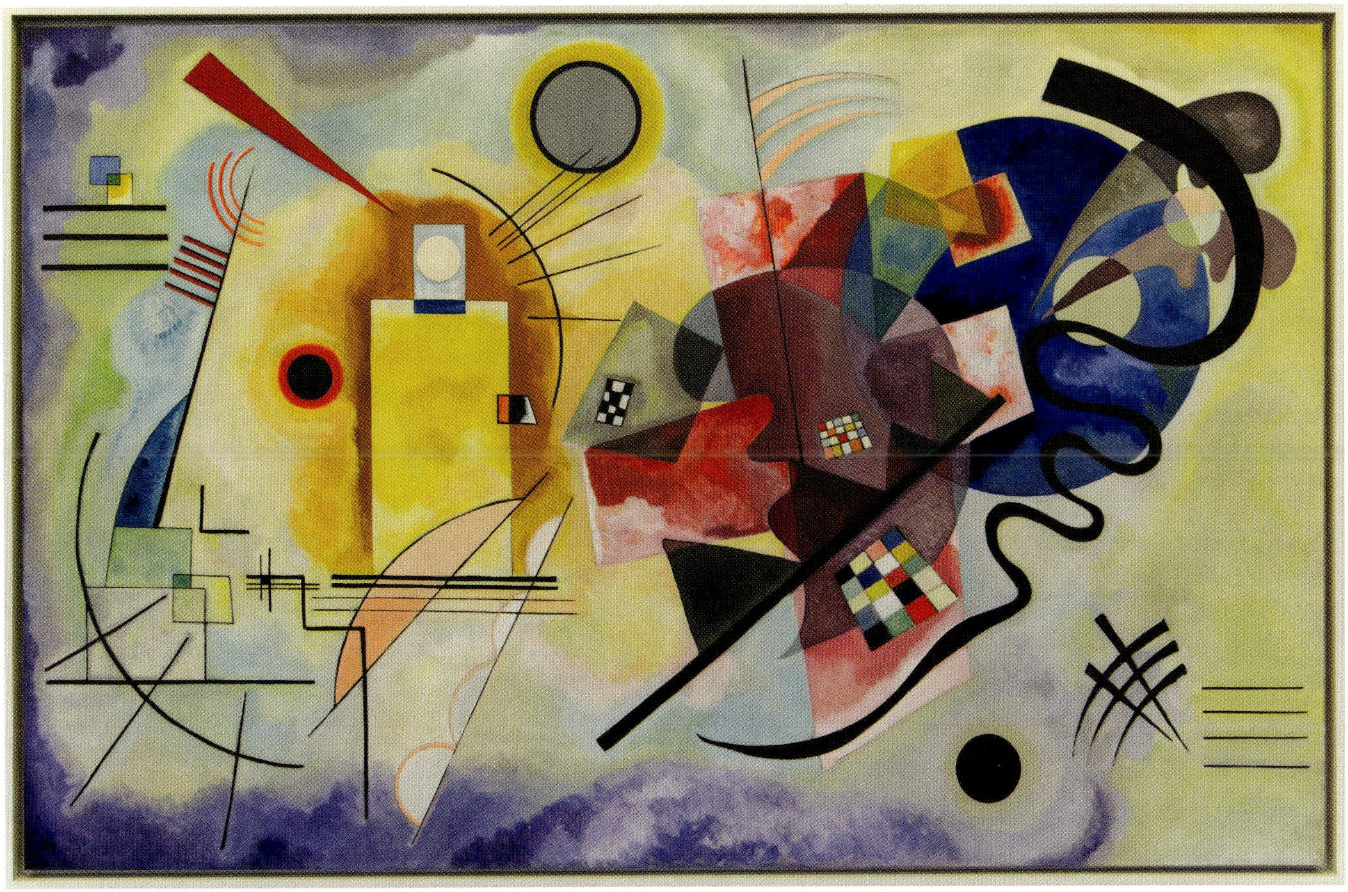

Yellow-Red-Blue (1925), by Wassily Kandinsky

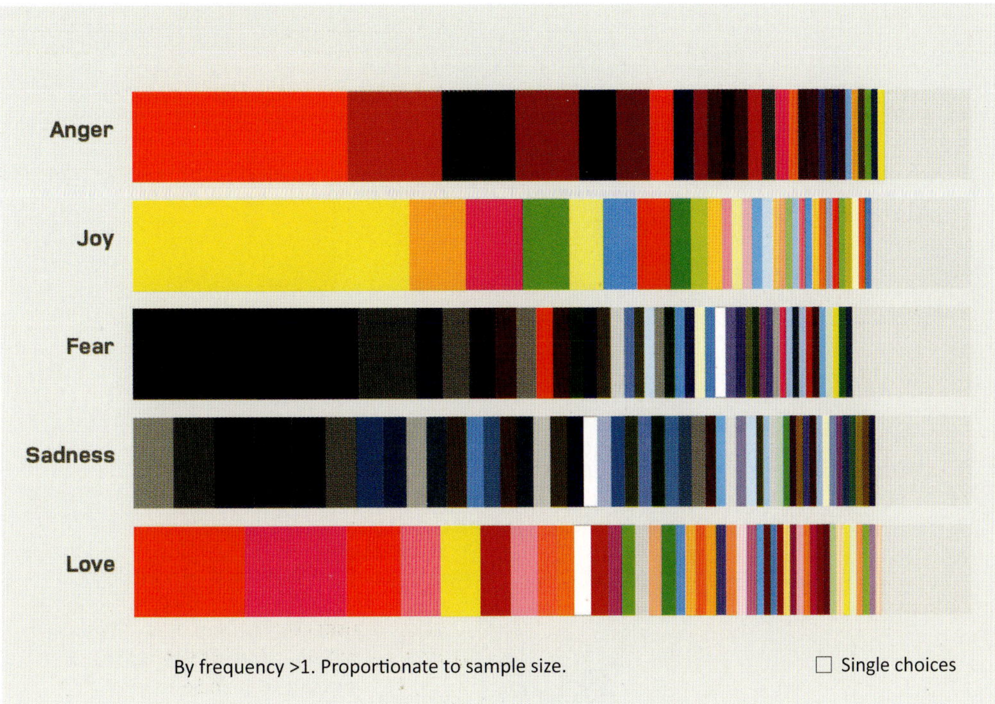

Color associations of 250 participants, part of Emotionally}Vague, a visual research project by Orlagh O'Brien conducted worldwide between 2006 and 2012. The labels are in English as those were the words participants responded to, even when they spoke different languages.

41 ENVIRONMENTAL COLOR DESIGN

Design focused on the intentional use of color and light in the built environment

Environmental design includes architecture, landscape design, urban planning, interior design, industrial design, graphic design, textile design, and fashion design. Environmental color design involves the intentional use of color to support and enhance the design objectives.

Colored environments and lighting can influence physical responses in both positive and negative ways. Research on the range and degree of environmental effects of color and light on human emotions, cognition, and behavior is ongoing.

SEE ALSO:
Geography of Color
Sustainability

"My goal is to formulate a new color theory based on the full spectrum of visible light."
—*Olafur Eliasson*

FURTHER READING
Color for Architects (2019), by Juan Serra Lluch

I Don't Have a Favorite Color (2016), by Hella Jongerius

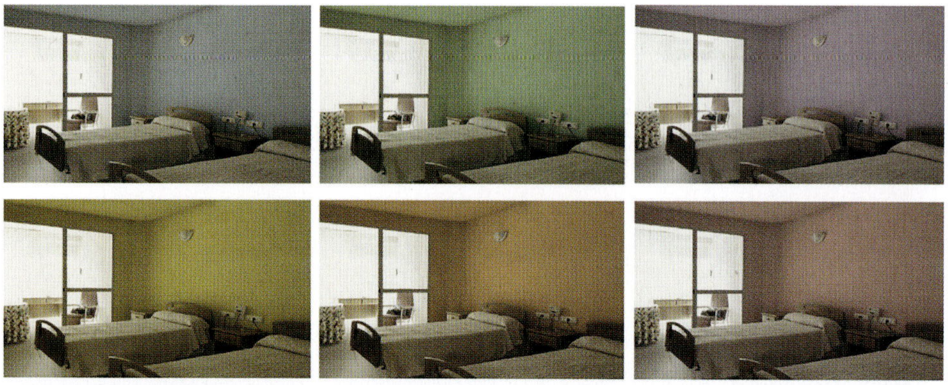

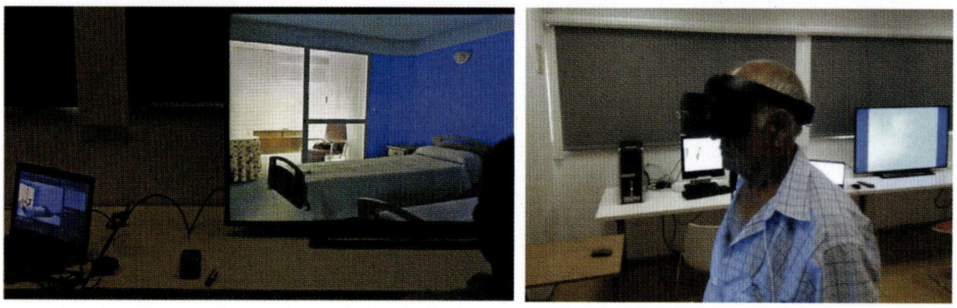

Recent research in care facilities utilized virtual reality to access the user color preferences in bedrooms, hallways and activity spaces. Ana Torres and Juan Serra Lluch.

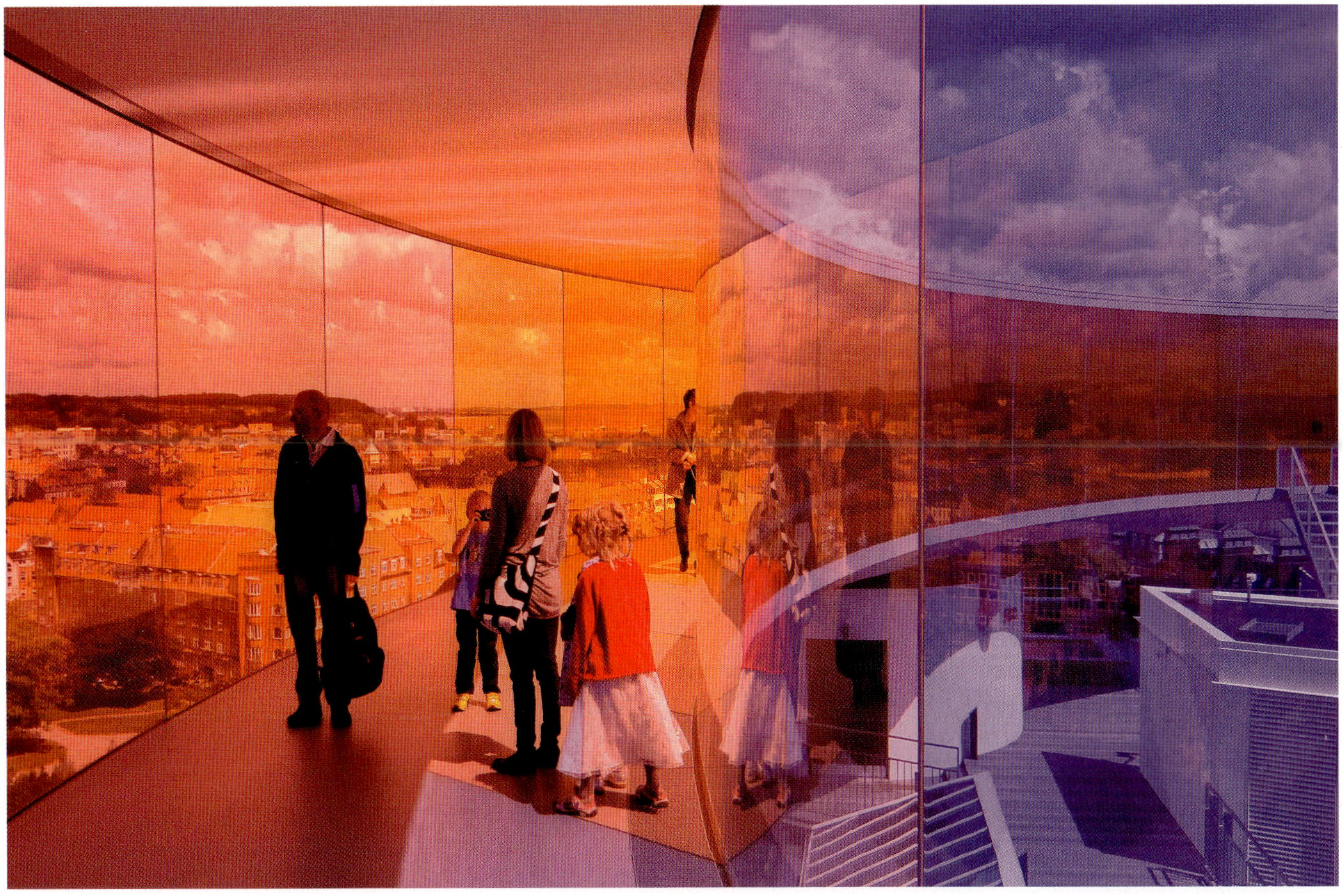

Your Rainbow Panorama (2011), a rooftop walkway by Olafur Eliasson in Aarhus, Denmark.

CMF DESIGN

Color, Materials, and Finish (CMF) design is an area of industrial design that focuses on the chromatic, tactile, and surface appearance of products and environments.

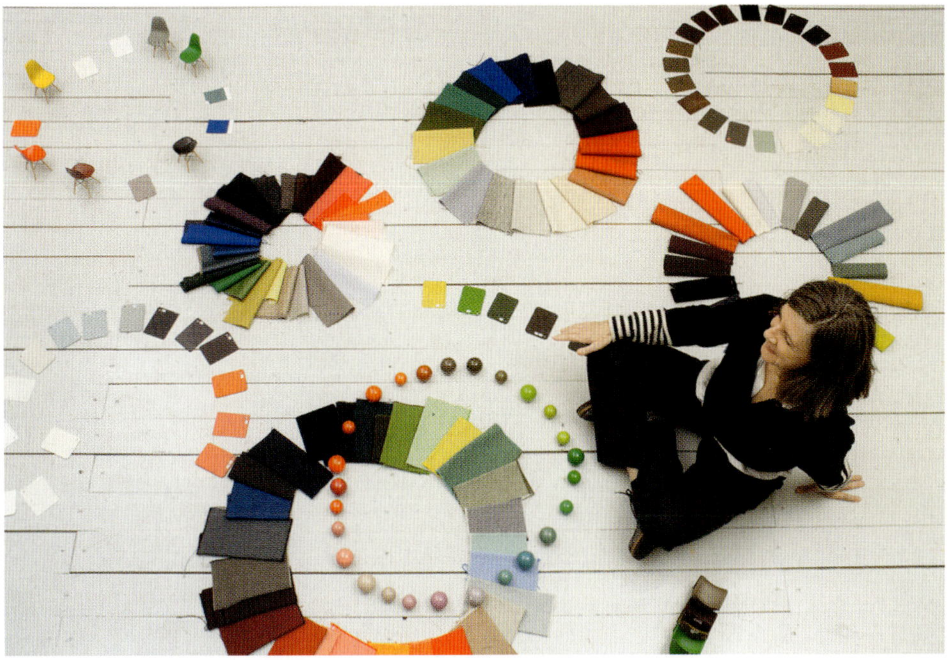

Industrial designer Hella Jongerius working on the color design for Vitra Colour.

42 FLAT COLOR

Color that is solid and completely uniform with no gradations or shading

Examples of flat color can be found throughout history in the decorative arts, illustration and graphic arts, animation and digital arts, as well as fine arts. The hallmark of mid-century graphic design, flat color is the main feature of the flat design trend.

Flat color was used to produce posters, cartoons, and comic strips as early as the mid-1800s. The style was firmly established by the late 1920s with the release of animated films that used flat art for the painted cels.

The earliest color comics were printed using screens cut for each color. The expense of manually cutting the screens resulted in a limited palette. Today, "flatting"—filling in areas of line art with flat color—is done digitally by a professional "flatter," and the color choices are infinite. Depending on the style of the creator, comics and graphic novels can be published as flat color or highly rendered by a colorist.

The use of flat color is a stylistic choice for artists and graphic designers.

SEE ALSO:
Gradients

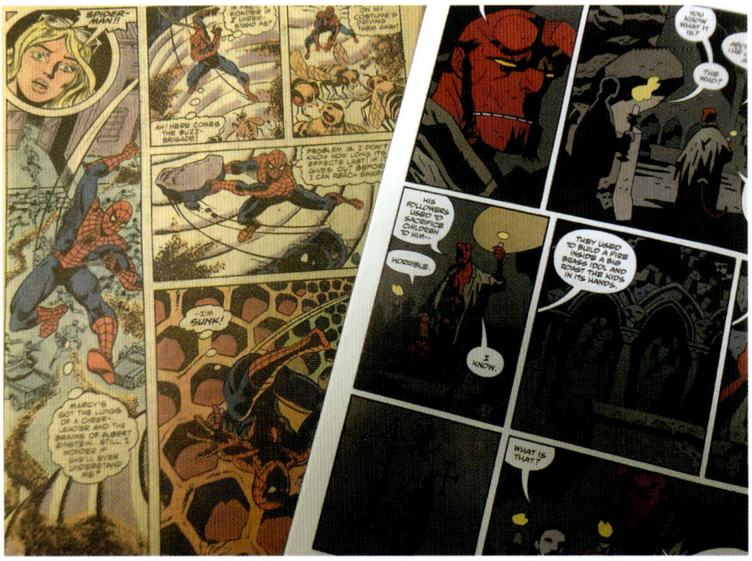

Art by Jim Mooney and inks by Pablo Marcos for an issue of *The Spectacular Spider-Man* from the 1970s. A 2008 *Hellboy* issue (story and art by Mike Mignola).

Woodblock print (c. 1830), by Utagawa Kuniyoshi. When Japan reopened trade with the West in 1854, the flat color of Japanese woodblock prints became a source of inspiration for artists of the late 1800s.

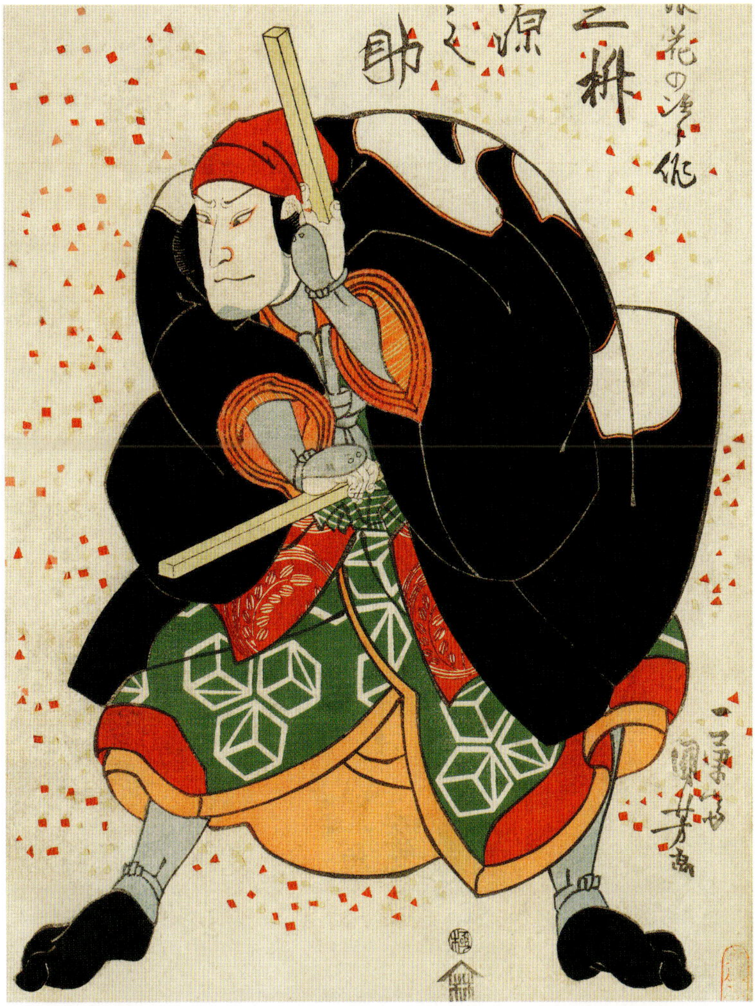

Little Big Painting (1965), by Roy Lichtenstein, a brushstroke rendered in flat color.

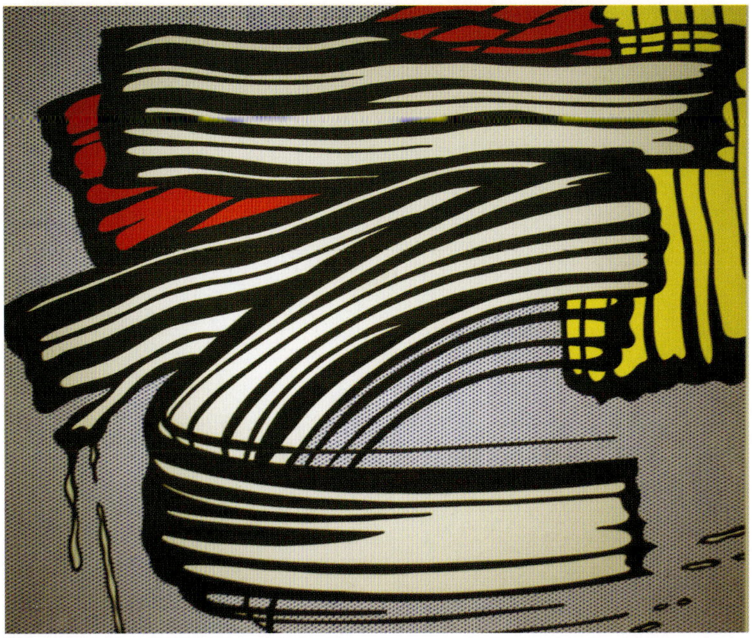

43 FLUORESCENCE

The property of absorbing light at one wavelength and emitting light at a longer wavelength

Fluorescence is a type of luminescence that is an important aspect of many lighting systems. Fluorescent tubes are now increasingly being replaced by LED lighting systems, but even some of these use fluorescence as a way to obtain a light source with better color-rendering properties.

Consumers are more familiar with fluorescence through its use with clothing and plastic materials to create very bright and vivid safety clothing and signs. Very often fluorescent materials absorb in the nonvisible region of the spectrum and emit light in the visible region. This can create colors that are very vivid and highly saturated. Although fluorescence is often considered to be an artificial phenomenon, some materials (even human teeth!) exhibit fluorescence naturally.

A related phenomenon was used to create the neon lights used to illuminate cities beginning in the 1930s. With neon lighting there is no actual fluorescence. Rather, the neon gas emits light when electricity is passed through the electrodes in the neon-filled glass tube.

SEE ALSO:
Human Visual System
Safety Colors

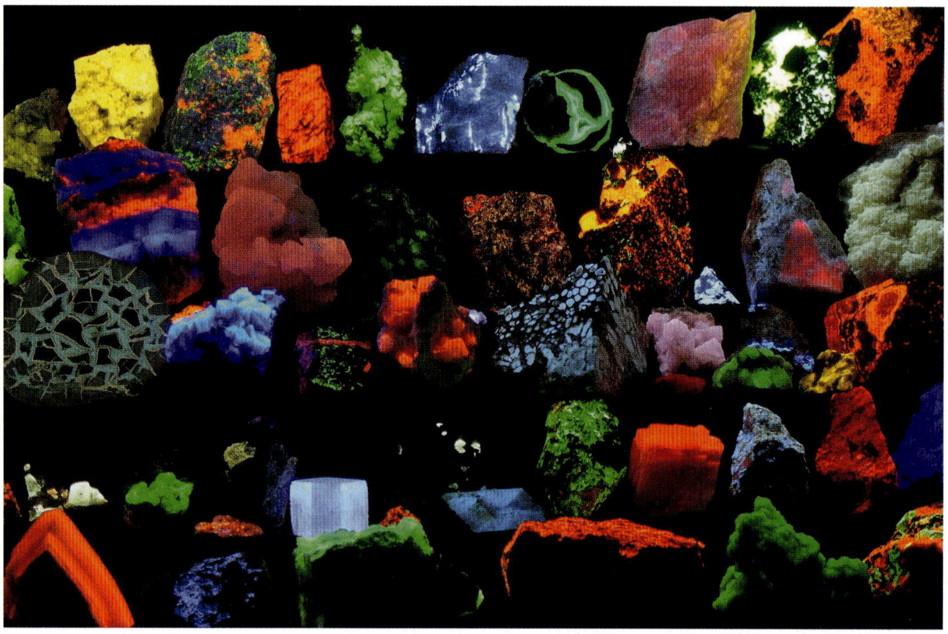

A collection of naturally fluorescent minerals.

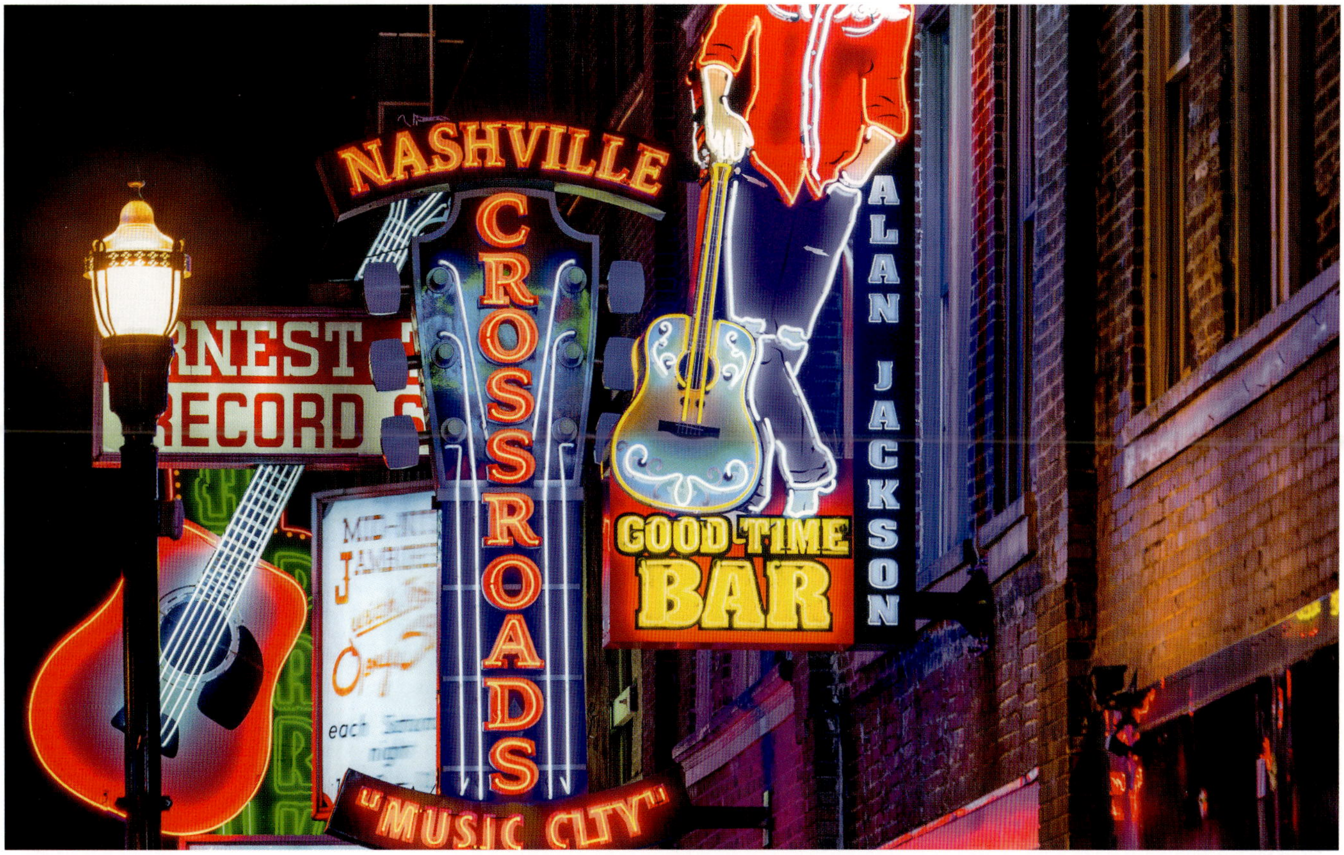

In a related phenomenon, neon lighting shines on lower Broadway in Nashville, Tennessee.

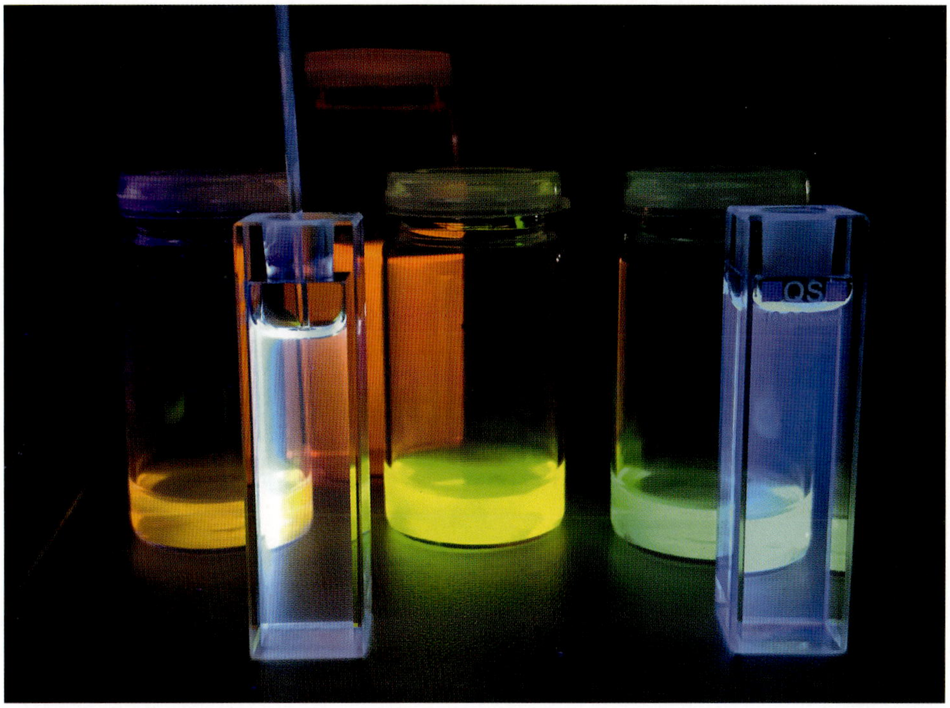

Many materials absorb ultraviolet light, which is invisible to humans but emits light in the visible region of the spectrum.

44 GAMUTS

The range of colors that can be created by a colorant or a color-forming system

Some say that we can generate all possible colors from three color primaries. Whether we use subtractive mixing or additive mixing, this is not, in fact, possible. However, it is possible to create all hues but not all at high chroma.

If the primaries are carefully selected, then it is possible to generate a wide range of colors. The range of colors that can be created by a set of colorants or a set of lights when mixed is called the color gamut.

The gamut of a typical RGB (red/green/blue) display is defined by a triangle in chromaticity space. It is impossible to generate colors outside of the RGB system's triangular gamut. Note, however, that even some of the chromaticities inside the triangle might not be achievable. This is because color gamuts are 3D and the chromaticities within the gamut cannot be shown at all lightness levels.

Different RGB systems have different gamuts. Most commercial display systems are based on the sRGB system; its gamut is less than half of all the possible chromaticities that can occur in the world. One of the reasons consumers don't notice this limitation is because materials (e.g., plastics, paints, prints, textiles) in the world with very high chromaticities are rare. In 1980 Michael Pointer measured the gamut of manufactured materials and showed that the so-called Pointer's gamut is not very much larger than the sRGB gamut. It is possible to generate chromaticities outside of the Pointer's gamut using special technology such as fluorescence or lasers.

If a small set of colors is carefully selected, it is possible to generate a wide range of colors, but not all high-chroma colors.

SEE ALSO:
CMYK
Palette
RGB

FURTHER READING
Color and Light (2010), by James Gurney

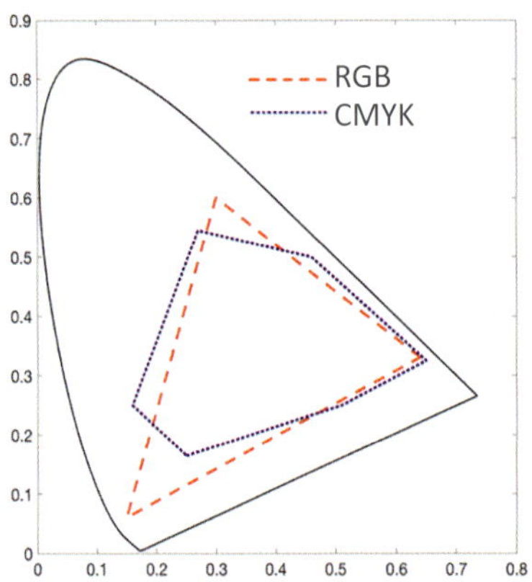

Comparison of the CMYK gamut (dotted line) with the sRGB gamut (solid line) in CIE chromaticity space.

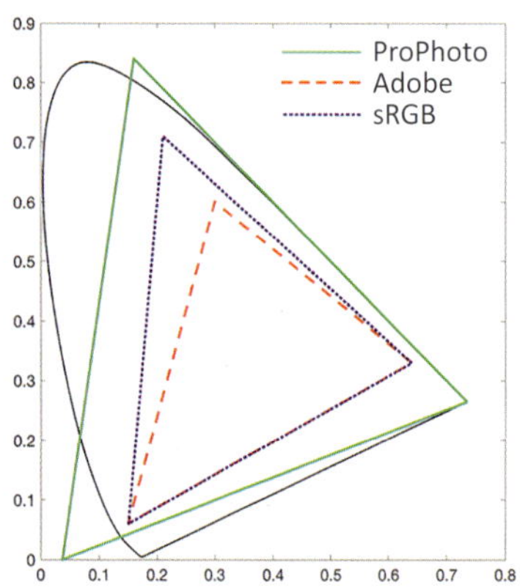

The CIE diagram showing the gamut of ProPhoto, Adobe RGB, and RGB.

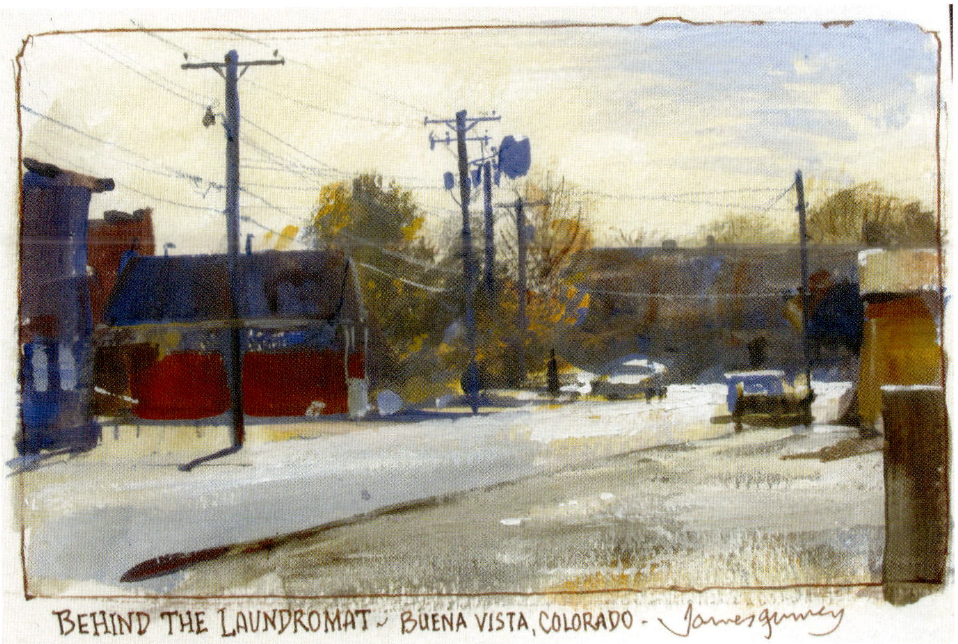

Behind the Laundromat, a painting by James Gurney illustrating the narrow gamut produced by using yellow ochre, Venetian Red and ultramarine blue.

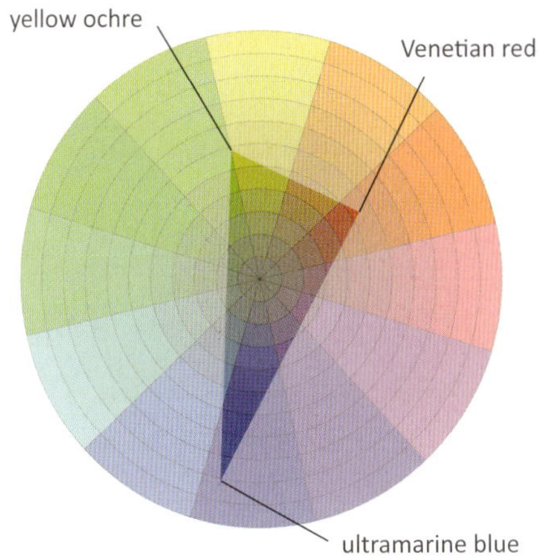

GAMUT MAPPING

This gamut map by James Gurney shows the area of the color wheel that is defined by boundary lines between the three paint primaries of yellow ochre, Venetian red and ultramarine blue used in his painting.

RED-YELLOW-BLUE GAMUT

Trying to mix a vivid purple from red and blue primaries in paint, inks, and dyes can be frustrating because the subtractive primaries of RYB traditionally taught starting in preschool result in a reduced gamut, especially between red and blue. The amount of chroma lost is dependent on the properties of the pigments and the quality of the primaries selected.

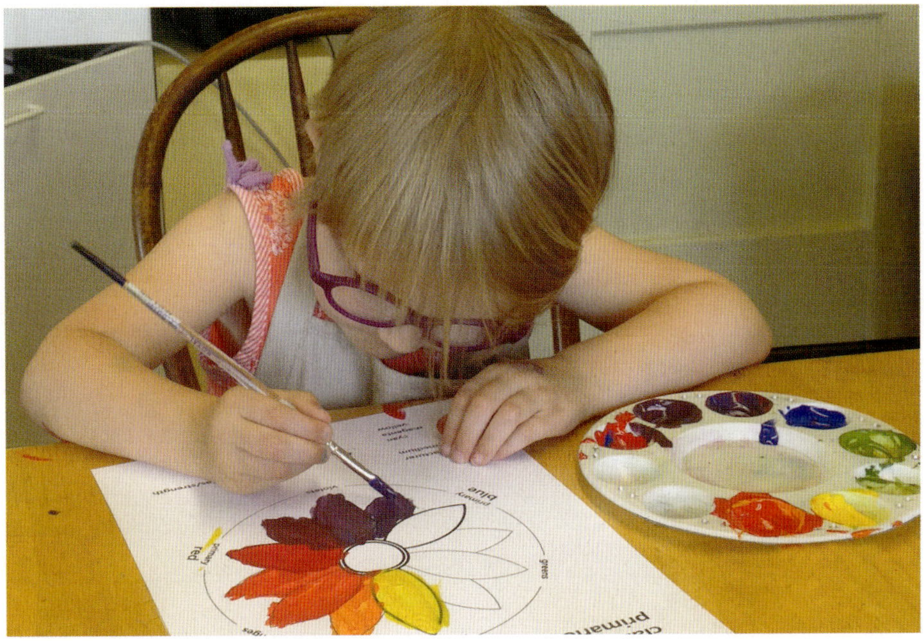

45 GEOGRAPHY OF COLOR

The influence of local materials, climate, and traditional construction techniques on the chromatic character of vernacular architecture around the world

Based on the color analysis method developed by Jean-Philippe and Dominique Lenclos, the geography of color refers to the variations found in specific parts of the world where the use of color in the built environment depends on the local climate and availability of building materials, as well as the cultural traditions and belief systems of the area.

SENSE OF PLACE

People develop deep connections to places based on the characteristics of the natural and built environment, how they interact with them, and how their surroundings make them feel. In areas with a strong chromatic sense of place, the use of color can either enhance or diminish the sense of place.

Awareness of the site-specific geography of color can both inspire and inform design decisions.

SEE ALSO:
Environmental Color Design
Sustainability

FURTHER READING
Colors of the World (2005), by Jean-Philippe and Dominique Lenclos

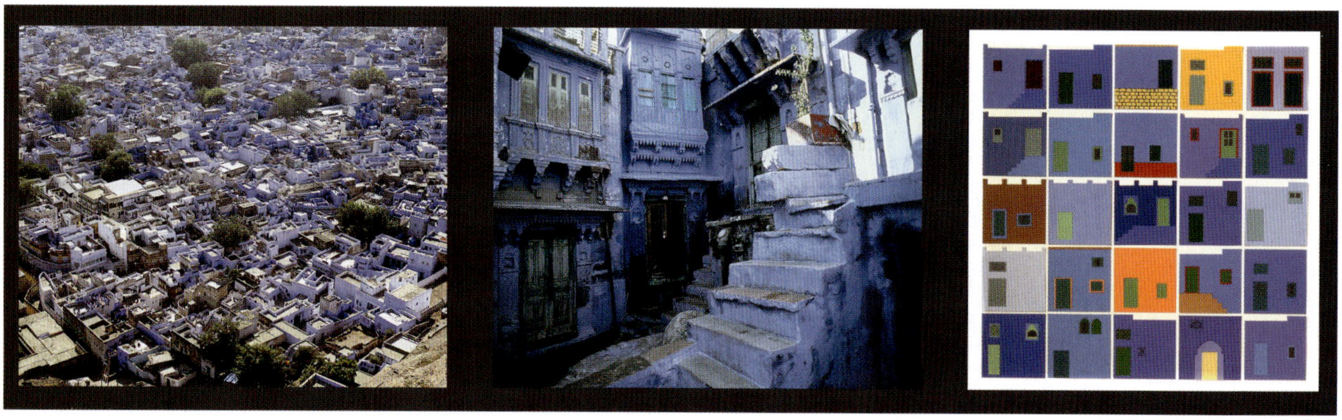

"Blue City" of Jodhpur, India. Three examples of the research documentation by Jean-Phillipe and Dominique Lenclos.

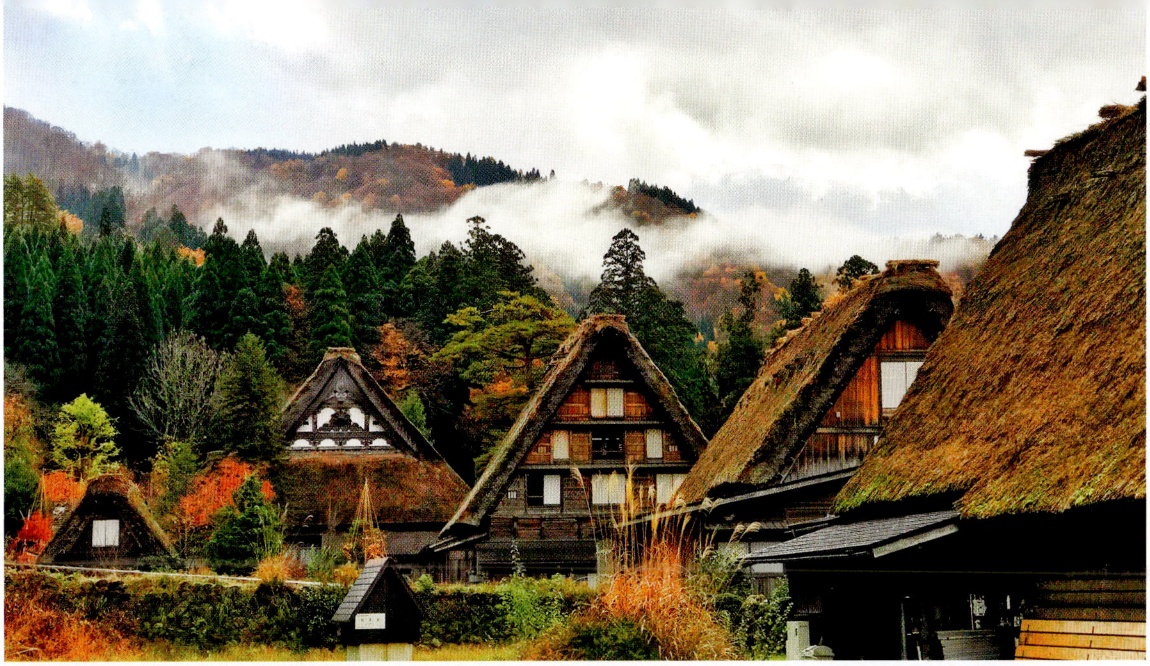

Traditional Japanese architecture: wood and clay tiles.

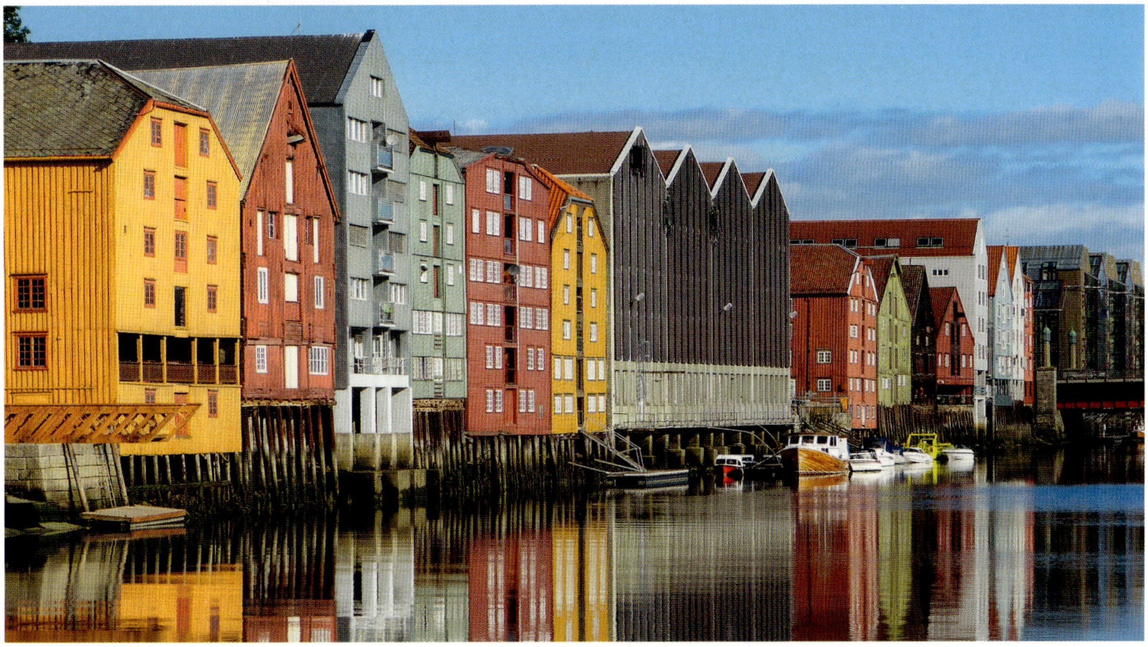

Trondheim, Norway: painted wood.

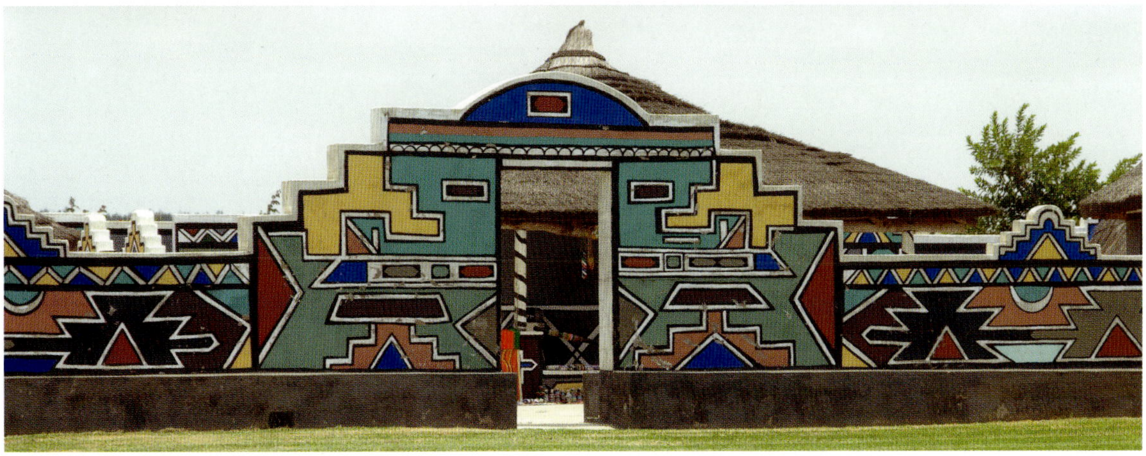

Traditional Ndebele architecture in South Africa: soil and cow dung.

46 GOETHE'S *THEORY OF COLOURS*

An influential book on color by Goethe published in German in 1810 and translated into English by Charles Eastlake in 1840

In 1810 renowned poet, playwright, novelist, and statesman Johann Wolfgang von Goethe (1749–1832) published his seminal work on color, *Zur Farbenlehre (Theory of Colours)*. Although the book was somewhat controversial in his times, it has been highly esteemed by many, including J.M.W. Turner, Wassily Kandinsky, Novalis, Werner Heisenberg, Kurt Gödel, Ludwig Wittgenstein, and Hermann von Helmholtz.

Goethe's treatise is a step-by-step exploration of color phenomena through an extensive sequence of detailed observations and experiments. He wasn't seeking to measure, categorize, model, or explain color, but, as he writes, "The blue of the sky shows us the basic law of chromatics. Let us not seek for something behind the phenomena—they themselves are the theory."

Furthermore, Goethe challenges the reader to engage. We must do these experiments, he urges—just like color itself, they cannot be grasped by reading about them. Goethe begins with the elusive colors that we experience physiologically, such as afterimages. He continues with the ephemeral colors that arise out of colorless conditions, like sunsets and prismatic colors. Then he investigates the permanent colors found in material substances, both inorganic and organic.

Goethe argued that colors are not "contained" in white light any more than they could be contained in darkness. He showed this most convincingly in his prism experiments. For example, by swapping the positions of brightness and darkness in traditional prism experiments, he produced the "inverse spectrum"—a perfect complementarity to Newton's well-known spectrum, with magenta in the center instead of green. Goethe didn't dismiss Newton's discovery but contended that it was only one aspect of color. It upset him that the entire realm of color had been reduced to this one perspective.

Goethe brought a contextual wholeness to the field of color study.

SEE ALSO:
Newton's *Opticks*

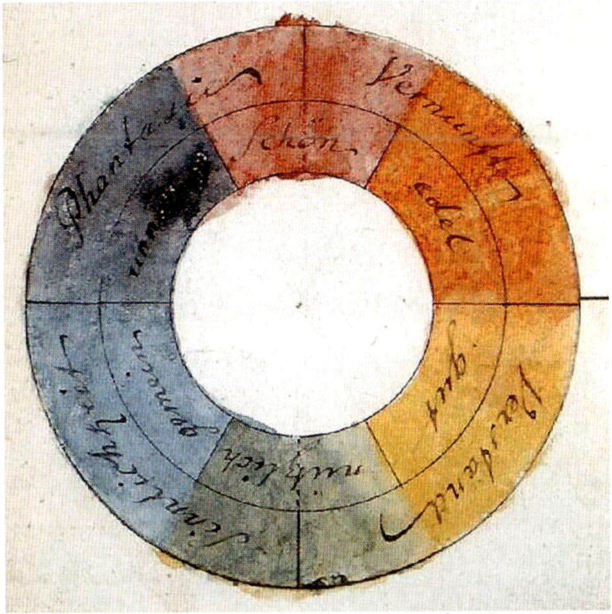

Goethe's color wheel.

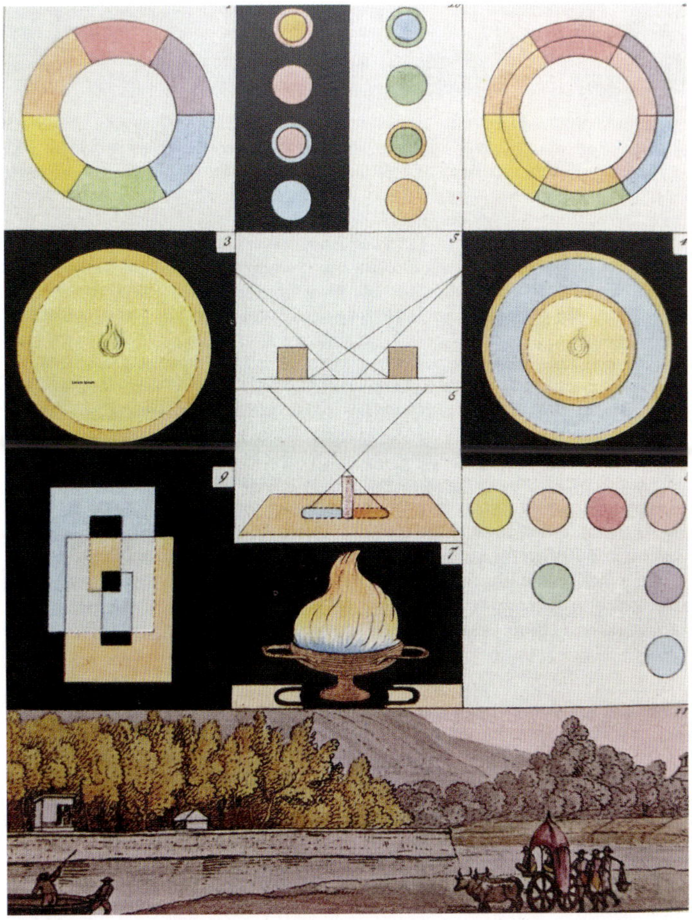

Illustrations of color phenomena from *Theory of Colours*.

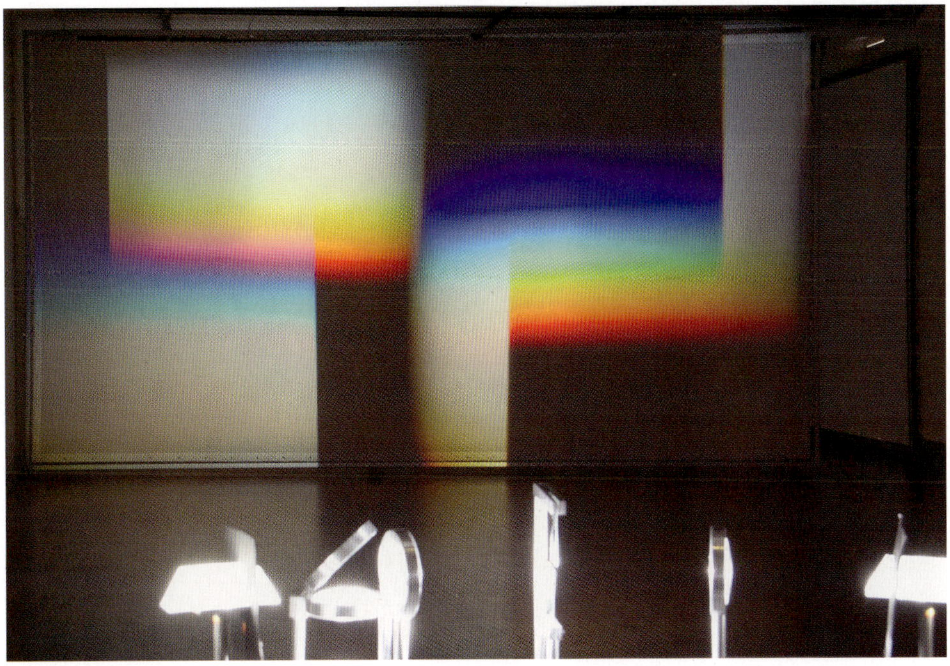

Demonstration of Goethe's inverse spectrum using prisms, lights and mirrors. Designed by the Science Section at the Goetheanum in Dornach, Switzerland. Photo by Mattias Rang.

47 GRADIENTS

The smooth blending of one color into another

Natural gradients are all around us. Found in plants, animals, flowers, and the sky, natural gradients can inspire artists and designers to integrate smooth blends of colors in their work.

In fabric dyeing, and more recently in hair dyeing, the gradient effect is called *ombre* from the French word for "shaded." The popularity of the ombre effect comes and goes, but the process stays the same: dip dyeing for different lengths of time.

In painting there are many ways to mimic the effect. Wet-on-wet blending, dry brushing between two colors, and scumbling are just a few of the techniques used to smoothly blend colors from one to the other in paint.

In computer graphics, the traditional gradient tools include linear and radial gradient options. These basic options are available in most design, drafting, and drawing programs and can be easily used to quickly create backgrounds with a gradient.

More complex gradients can be constructed using software options such as the free-form gradient tool and the gradient mesh tool in Adobe Illustrator.

SEE ALSO:
Color Scales
Color Schemes
Flat Color

Linear gradient and polar gradient.

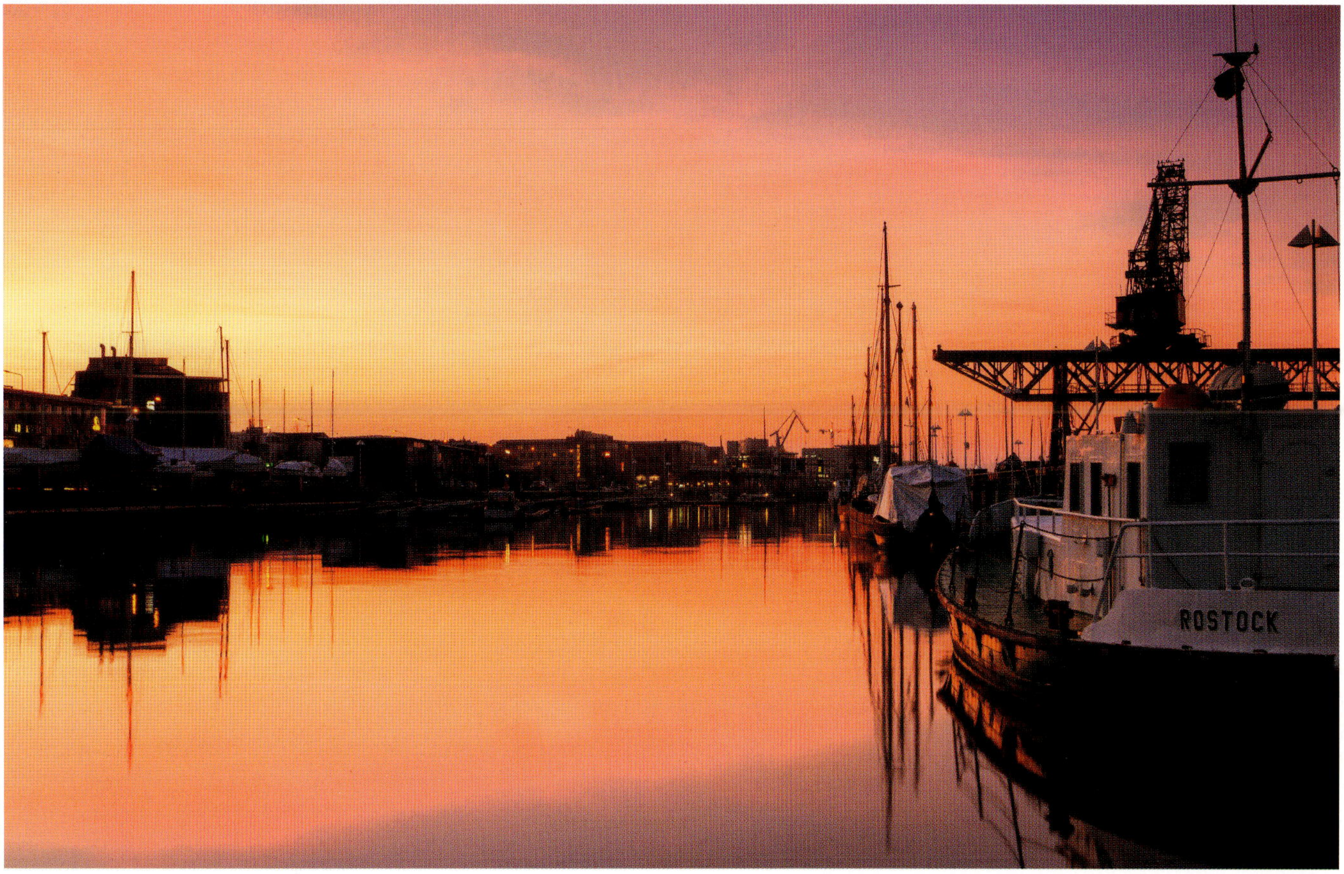

Sunset gradient

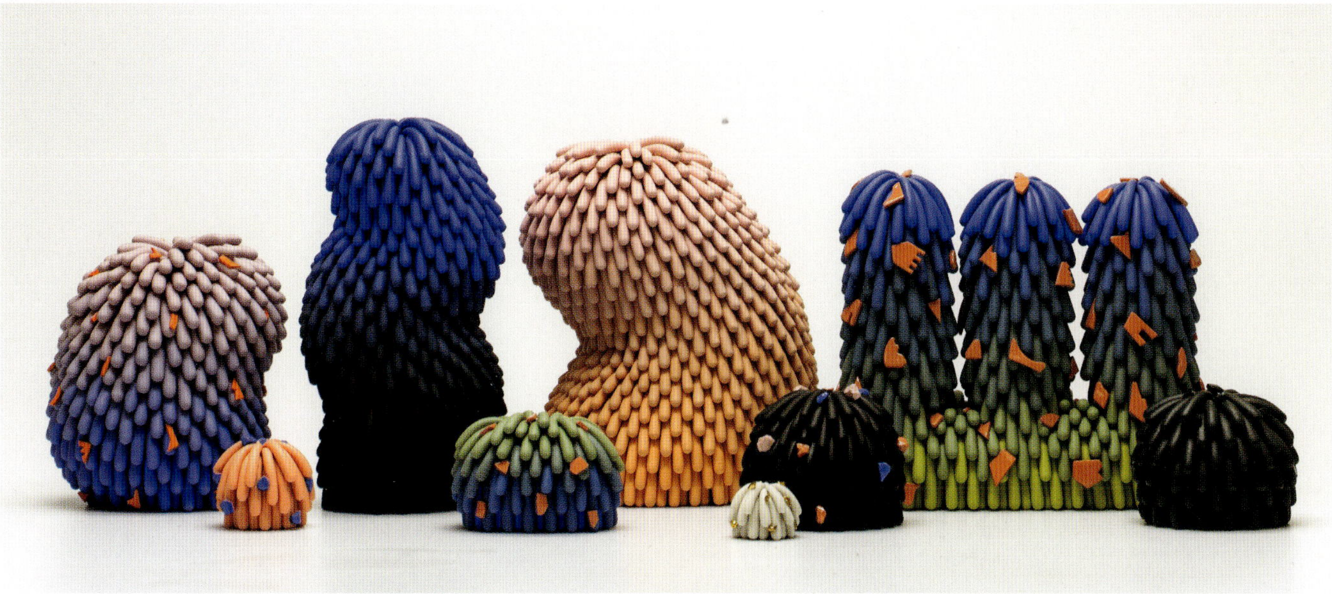

Stranger (2019), use of gradients in ceramic sculptures by Linda Lopez.

48 GRISAILLE

A painting technique executed in shades of gray or other neutral color

Grisaille is a term that derives from the French word *gris*, which translates as gray. This technique, as used particularly by Flemish artists in the fifteenth century, is an oil painting technique where a composition is painted entirely in gray tones before successive layers of transparent glazes are painted on top. The purpose of the underpainting is to structure a light and dark gradient to identify the relationship between forms.

The technique has decreased in popularity in the modern era as new materials and techniques have been introduced, but the concept of identifying a gradient of light to dark relationship continues to be a foundational tool for artists and designers.

SEE ALSO:
Black and White

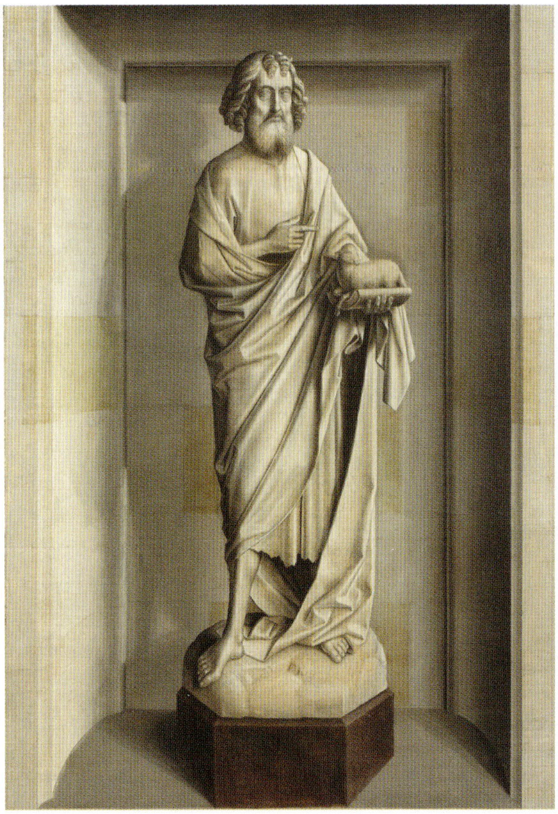

Saint John the Baptist (1475), Dieric Bouts.
Because sculpture was more expensive than painting, the grisaille technique was often used to mimic sculptures.

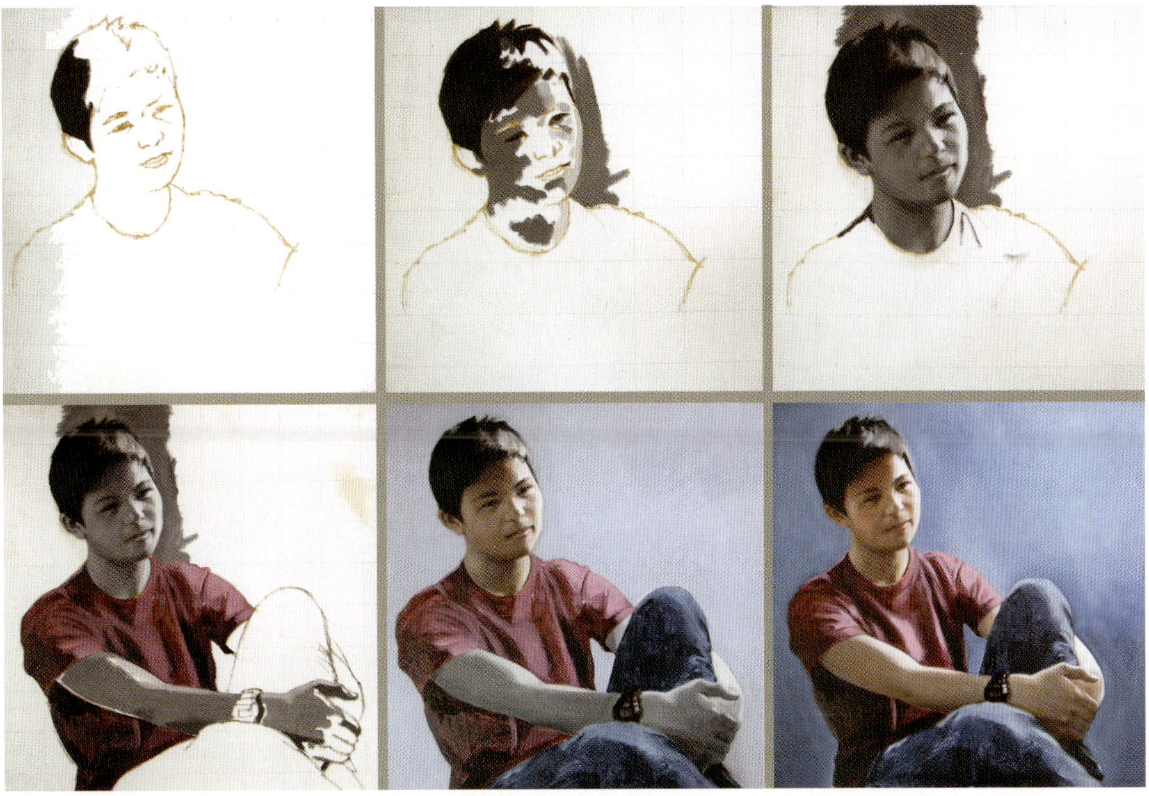

Portrait of Dai (2017), oil painting by Matt Harvey showing the process of grisaille underpainting.

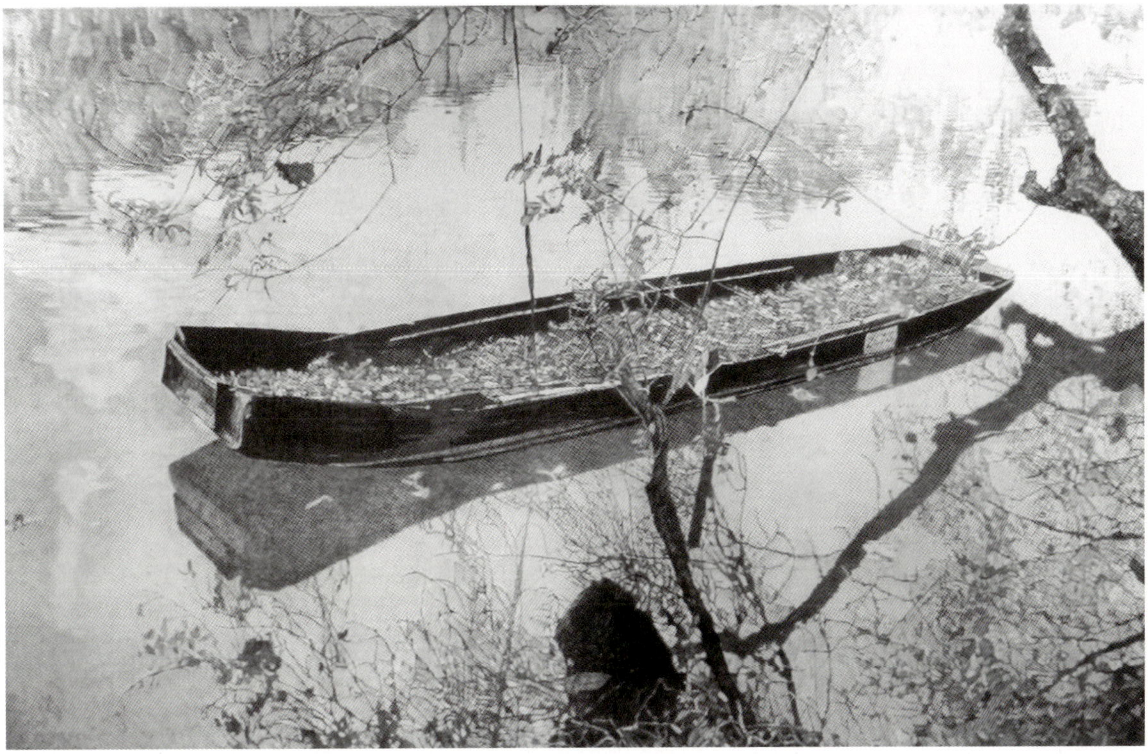

November on the Seine (2015), oil painting by Hugo Bastidas.

49 HARMONY

The aesthetics of color relationships

The aesthetics of color is a topic that has been studied for centuries with many attempts to define rules to ensure harmony. Though often described as a balance of separate but related parts, creating harmony is ultimately dependent on the personal decisions of the artist or designer.

Traditionally, most teaching about color harmony was focused on hue relationships, illustrated by simple geometric shapes such as triangles, squares, and rectangles positioned in a hue circle. Identifying hue relationships—such as monochromatic, analogous, complementary, split-complementary, triad, tetrad, and so on—has been defined as color harmonies and positioned as a foundational concept of traditional color theory. But how do these relationships really work?

Although various hue combinations can be used to produce strong aesthetic responses, there are several issues with the traditional teachings. First, hue is only one of the color attributes. To achieve a harmonic combination of colors, lightness and chroma also need to be carefully considered. Second, an aesthetic response to color combinations depends on several factors, including individual preferences, cultural preferences, and the context in which the design or work of art is positioned.

If related elements in art are considered harmonic, unrelated elements can be discordant. Discord can be used to provoke a deliberate challenge to the harmonic order.

From antiquity to the present day, attempts to quantify our cultural and personal response to color have fallen short. What is harmonic for one person may be discordant for another. Perhaps the complexity of color relationships is best left as a mystery?

SEE ALSO:
Balance
Color Schemes
Context
Hue Circle
Palette

"What dreams and great works of art had in common: mystery."
—*Hermann Hesse*

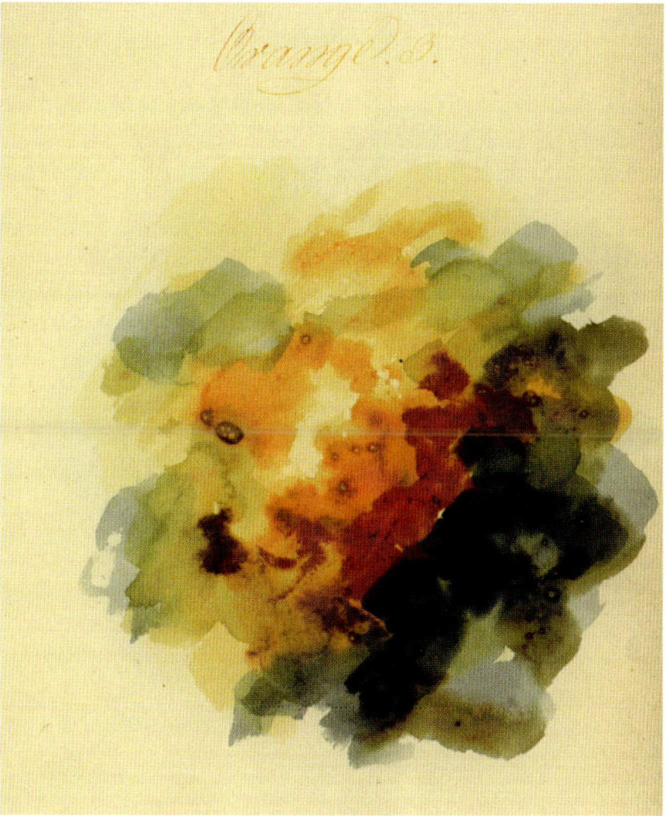

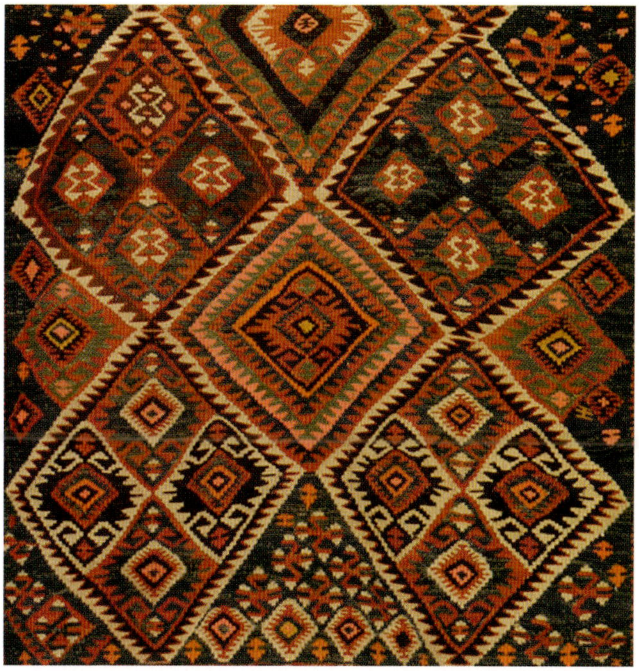

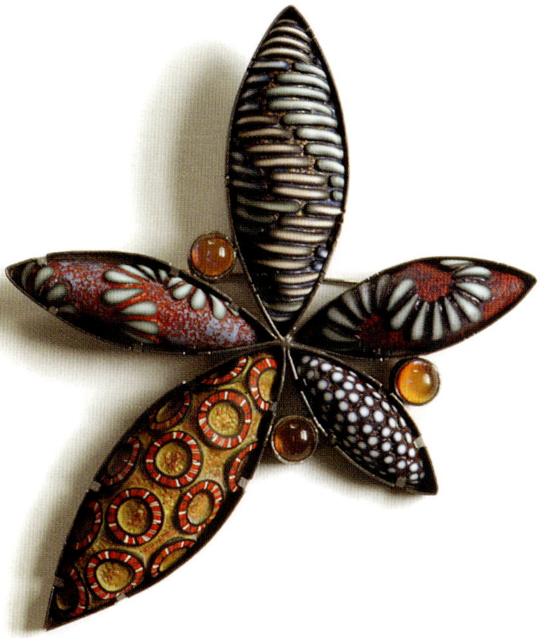

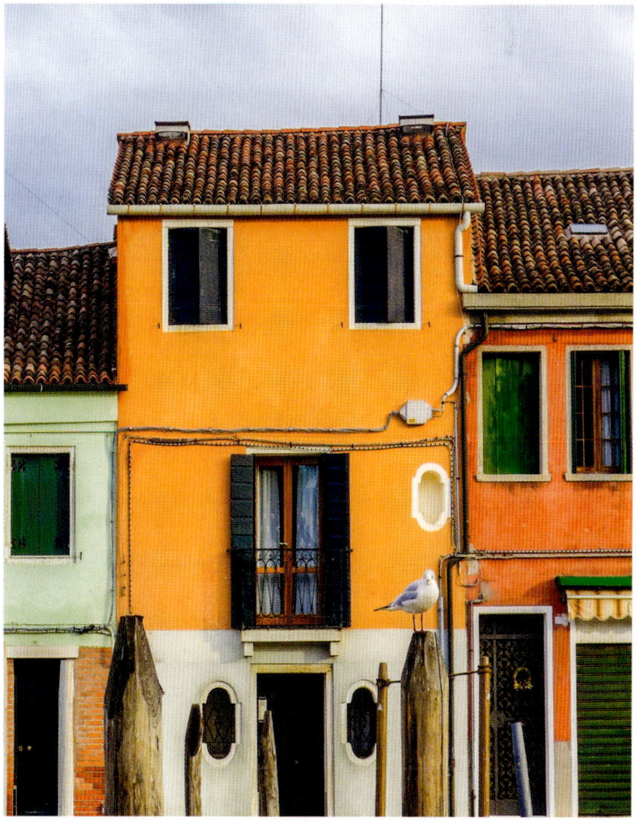

Top Left: Illustration from An Essay on Light and Shade, on Colours, and on Composition in General (1805). Watercolor painting by Mary Gartside. Top Right: Detail of vintage Turkish Kilim rug. Bottom Right: Canal facades. Venice, Italy. Bottom Left: Flower Pin #84 (2019). Polymer, silver, antique glass beads, stainless steel brooch by Steve Ford and David Forlano.

50 HUE ANGLE

The position of specific hues in polar relationship to a 360-degree hue circle

There are two major types of hue-angle identifiers: those based on CIELAB, such as LCh, and those based on the RGB system for monitors, such as HSV and HSB. The hue angle represents all the colors on the hue plane at that position in color space.

LCh = Lightness, Chroma, Hue
HSV = Hue, Saturation, Value
HSB = Hue, Saturation, Brightness

	HSB/HSV	LCh
Monitor Red	0°	35°
Monitor Yellow	60°	90°
Monitor Green	120°	130°
Monitor Cyan	180°	195°
Monitor Blue	240°	300°
Monitor Magenta	300°	0°

Although it is often necessary to use cartesian coordinates in specifying color, the advantage in becoming familiar with the polar coordinate system is that the attributes map onto our color vision experience much more closely than cartesian coordinates such as L*, a*, and b*.

SEE ALSO:
CIE System
Hue Circle
RGB

WEBSITES
Color of Art Pigment Database
Handprint

CONSTANT HUE PLANE

Hue angles define vertical slices, known as constant hue planes, that are cut through a 3D color space. The example, at right, shows the circle of hue angles and red hue plane of the RAL system. In the red hue plane shown, the lightness increases from bottom to top and the chroma increases from left to right.

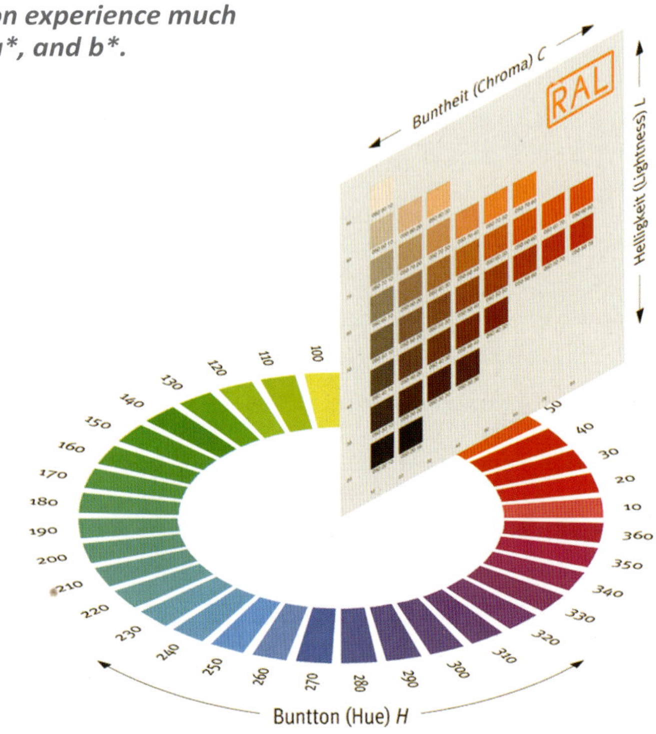

HSB/HSV hue angles of a monitor based on RGB Yellow at 60°.

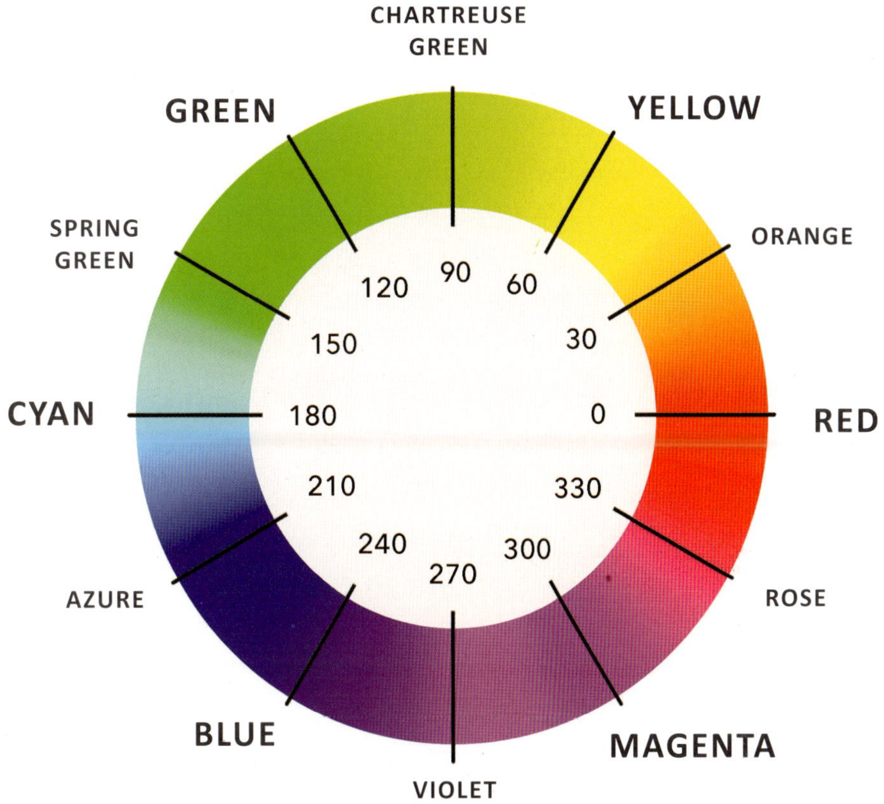

A painter's version of an LCh hue circle designed by Peter Donahue, aka color.nerd, based on a color wheel by Bruce MacAvoy on the Handprint website.

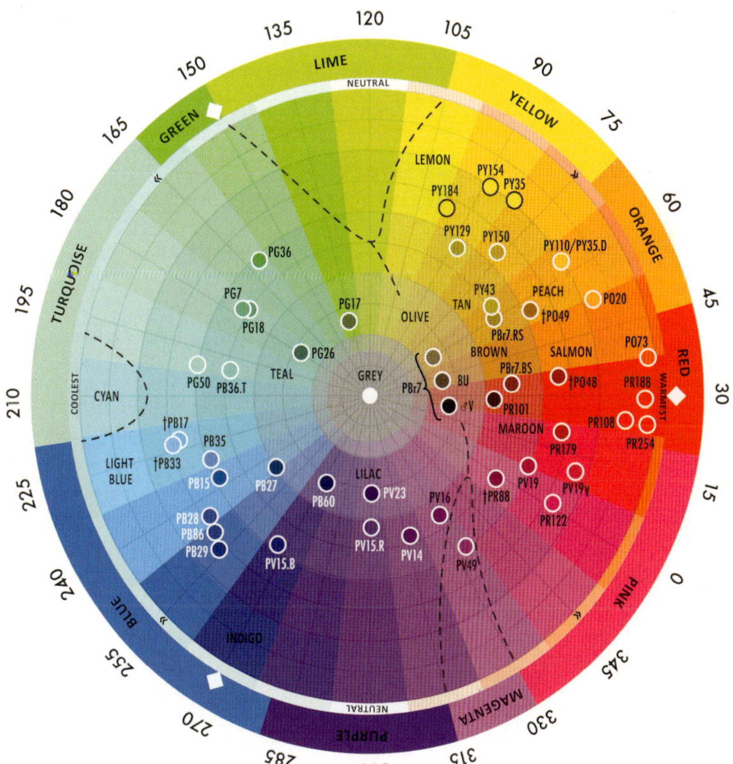

51 HUE CIRCLE

A circular arrangement that divides the spectrum into segments and illustrates the natural order of the spectral and nonspectral hues

Our perception of hue has a circular nature. This was first noticed by Newton, who observed that the short- and long-wavelength regions of the spectrum are somewhat similar visually. Newton is credited with introducing the hue circle, or hue wheel, though circular arrangements of color were introduced earlier by, for example, Aron Sigfrid Forsius and Robert Fludd. Newton arranged seven hues—red, orange, yellow, green, blue, indigo, and violet—around the circle.

Over the centuries since Newton's work, many different hue circles have been produced. Some of these purport to work as color mixing aids and begin with three so-called primary colors being equally spaced around the circle. Simple six-hue wheels have a secondary color interspaced between each pair of primary colors. Such wheels can be constructed starting with red, yellow, and blue (traditional artists' primaries); cyan, magenta, and yellow (optimal subtractive primaries); or red, green, and blue (additive primaries).

There are other hue circles that don't begin with three primaries, such as the hue circle in the HSB (hue-saturation-brightness) color space or the hue dimension of the CIELAB color space. Hue circles can also represent contrast in that colors that are further away from each other on the circle will have greater hue contrast if seen together. Hue angles are often used to define the location of hues in the 360-degree circle.

Hue circles are commonly referred to today as color wheels, which unfortunately does nothing to combat the sometimes-held misconception that hue and color are synonyms.

Despite the many misconceptions, hue circles are useful for teaching students about the relationships between different hues.

SEE ALSO:
Hue Angles
Three Dimensions of Color

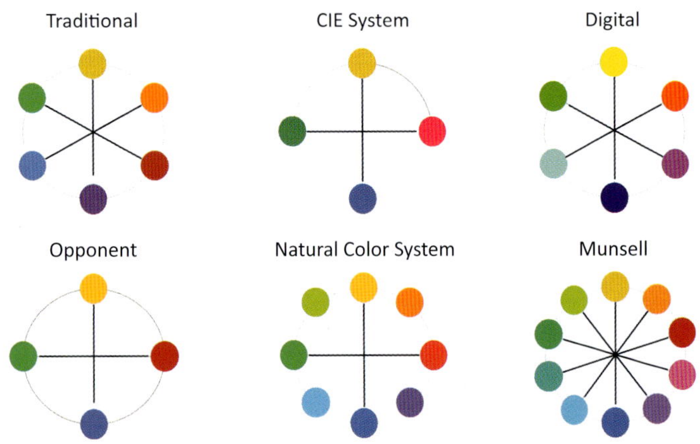

A comparison of hue circles shows the variations of hue placement in different color systems.

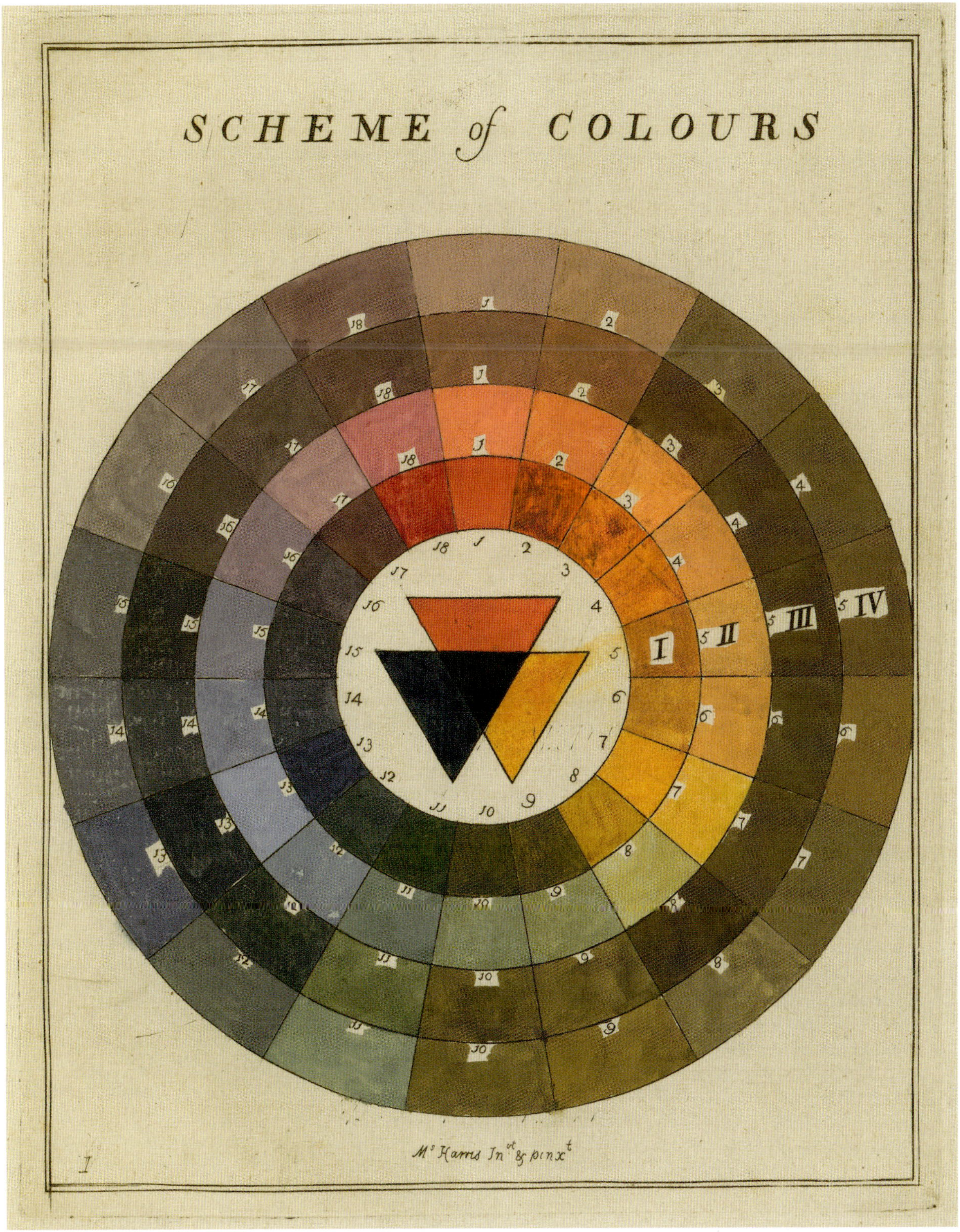

Hand painted hue circle in Exposition of English Insects by Moses Harris (1776), Smithsonian Collection. The use of a "spot" color in the section marked as 18 suggests that Harris was aware that the paint mixing system of red, yellow, blue primary colors produced dull purples.

52 HUMAN VISUAL SYSTEM

The eye and the brain are responsible for our perception of color

The eye is an approximately spherical structure whose primary function is to focus light on the back of the eye, known as the retina, where light-sensitive cells known as rods and cones are located. At the front of the eye, the cornea and the lens both act to provide focus. During normal levels of illumination (which we refer to as *photopic vision*), our color vision is mediated by three types of cone cells. These cells do not respond to single wavelengths, but the three types have maximal sensitivity at the short-, medium-, and long-wavelength parts of the spectrum, respectively.

At very low levels of illumination (*scotopic vision*), there is insufficient light to activate the cones; low-light vision is mediated by the rods. During scotopic, or rod, vision we can see only in shades of gray. Our brightness sensitivity shifts to shorter wavelengths so that objects that would normally appear red appear darker and objects that would normally appear blue appear lighter compared with photopic conditions. This is the Purkinjě shift.

The way that cone signals activate retinal ganglion cells means that the signals are combined and compared in the retina. This provides a physiological basis for visual phenomena such as contrast and opponency. The retinal ganglion cells send signals to the visual cortex, an area of the brain located at the back of the head. The visual cortex contains brain cells that respond strongly in response to visual stimuli.

The functional organization of the brain has been firmly established through many brain imaging studies, using techniques such as functional magnetic resonance imaging. Some visual effects (such as contrast) can be explained by our understanding of retinal processing, but other effects require us to delve deeper into how the brain processes the signals that it receives.

Although the primary function of the eye is vision, it was established at the beginning of the twenty-first century that a secondary function is to entrain our circadian system. Some retinal ganglion cells contain photoreceptors that send signals to the center of the brain, affecting the release of hormones such as cortisol and melatonin.

There is a growing interest in the effect of color and light on health and well-being.

SEE ALSO:
Limited Color Vision
Perception Triangle
Trichromacy

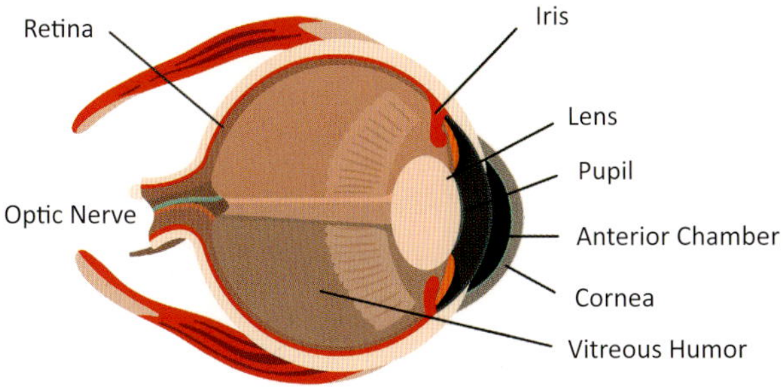

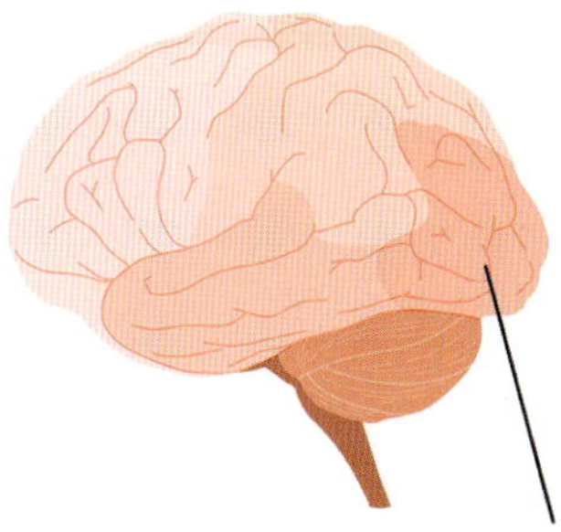

Top: The retina of the eye contains light-sensitive cells that respond to light and send electrochemical signals to the brain.
Left: An important fact about the brain is that different areas are responsible for different functions. The visual cortex—which color and vision are associated with—is located in the occipital lobe.

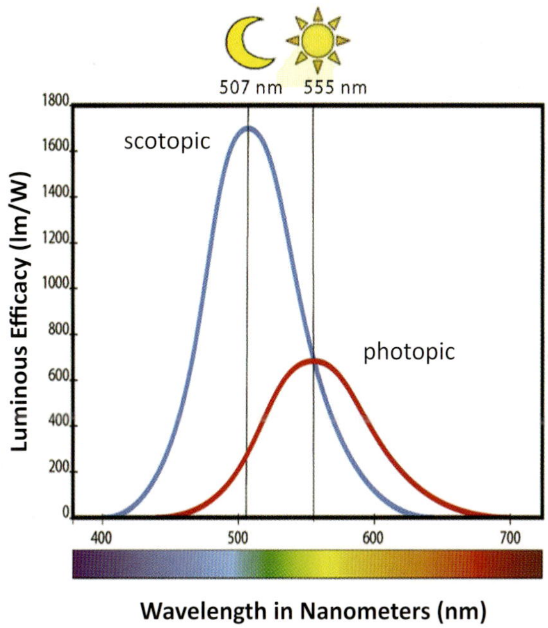

NIGHT VISION

The peak luminance sensitivity of the human eye tends to shift toward the blue end of the spectrum at low illumination levels.

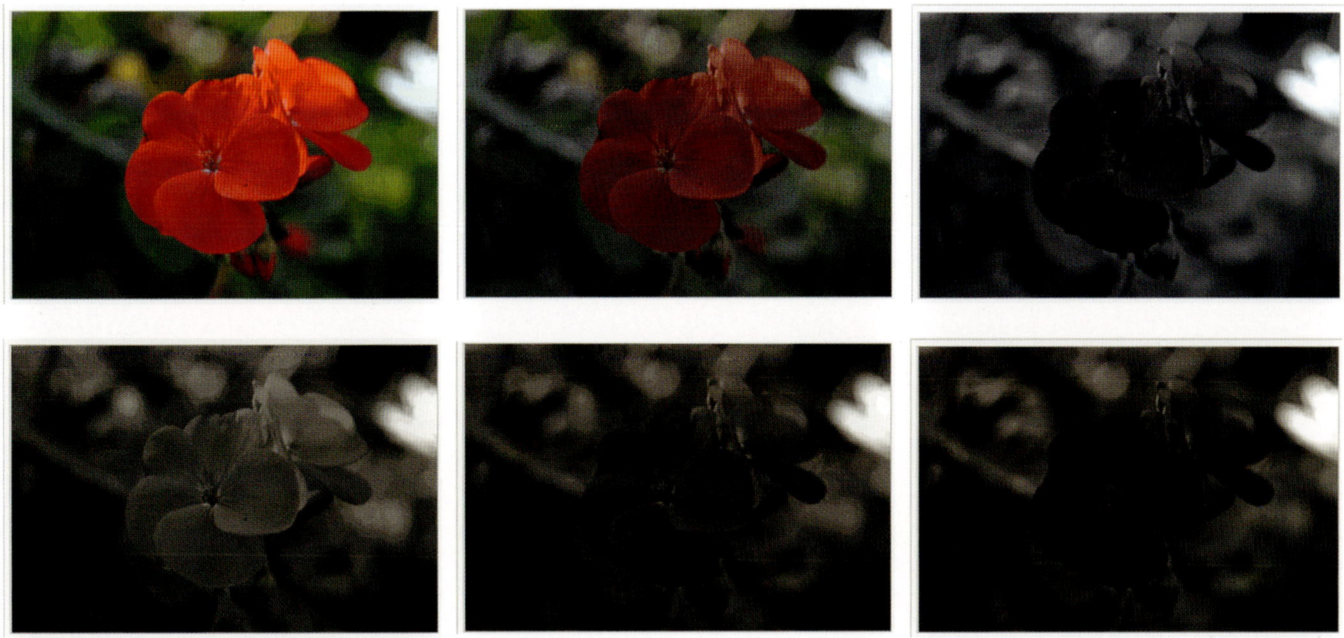

The Purkinjě shift was discovered by Jan Evangelista Purkinjě in 1819 when he noticed that his geraniums appeared red on a sunny afternoon, while at dawn they looked a darker bluish red. This observation led to the discovery that the eye has not one but two systems that determine how we see colors: one for overall bright light intensity (photopic), and one for dusk and dawn (scotopic).

53 IMPRESSIONISM

A nineteenth-century art movement that aimed to replicate visual sensations of light and shadow in paintings characterized by rapid brushstrokes of color

The term *impressionism* derives from a Claude Monet painting titled *Impression, Sunrise*. Along with Monet, notable impressionists include Georges Seurat, Paul Cézanne, Camille Pissarro, and Pierre-Auguste Renoir.

Based primarily in Paris, the impressionist painters are known for works they produced in the open air (*en plein air*) rather than in the studio, capitalizing on the recent invention of collapsible aluminum tubes. Renoir remarked that "without paint in tubes there would have been ... nothing of what the journalists were later to call Impressionists."

These innovative painters understood that one way to create the impression of a vivid chromatic hue was to juxtapose a hue next to its complementary hue. They rejected the method of mixing black or brown paint with a hue to create tonal variations and shadows. Instead, they employed small brushstrokes of complementary colors to construct chromatic shadows and establish a sense of depth in an image.

SEE ALSO:
Complementary Colors
Pointillism

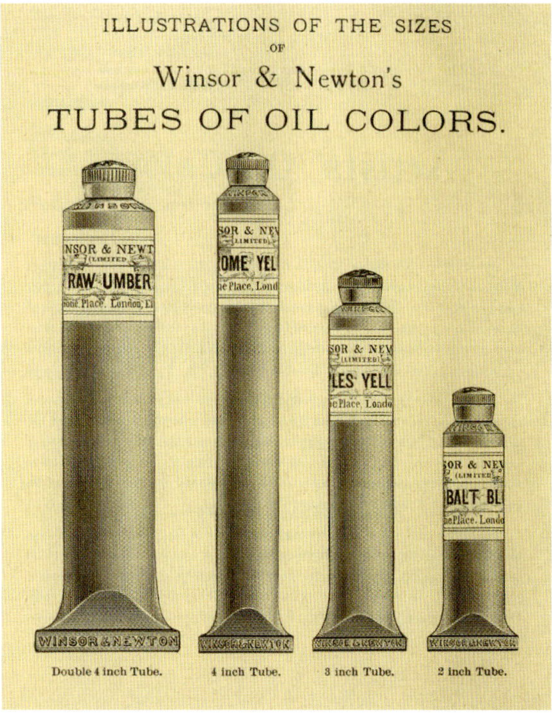

Advertisement from the late 1800s illustrating the early aluminum paint tubes which made it possible to paint "en plein air."

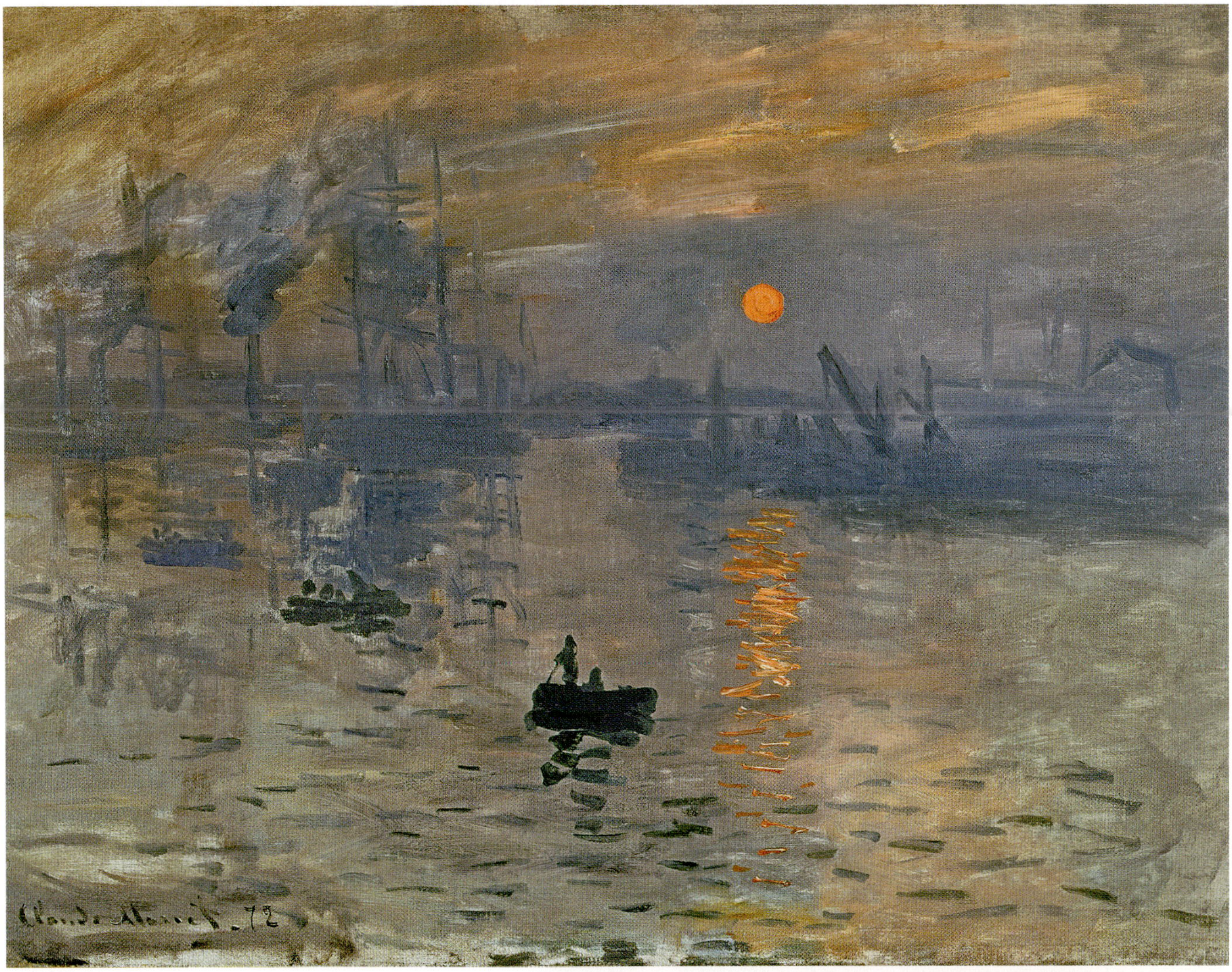

Impression: Sunrise (1872), by Claude Monet.

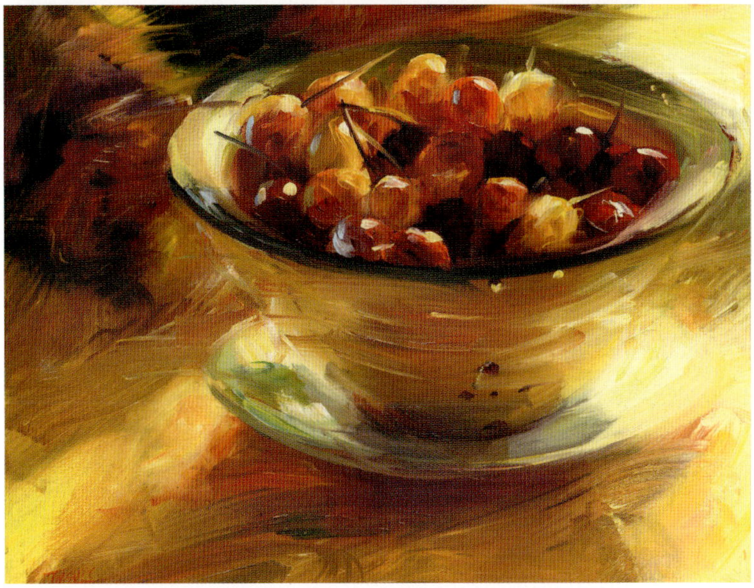

BROKEN COLOR

Just Picked, by Pam Ingalls. Contemporary painters use the painting technique of layering colors without physically blending them in order to create optical effects.

54 INFOGRAPHIC COLOR

The visual presentation of data in a pictorial or graphical format

Color can be used to enhance the legibility of information in graphs, charts, diagrams, maps, and graphic illustrations, but the use of color must complement—not detract from—the main purpose of the overall design. Clarity is the primary purpose of using color in data visualization (DataViz) and information visualization (InfoViz).

Accessibility of visual information and color meanings are key considerations in the design of infographics. For example, people with poor color discrimination or limited color vision due to age, injury, or ill health may struggle to decipher poorly designed color combinations, which could render the intended information illegible. On the other hand, insufficient consideration given to color associations (personal color preferences, cultural color biases and preferences) can make it more difficult for the viewer to assimilate the information embedded in the design.

When the design goal is to communicate clearly, use colors intentionally to strengthen the message.

SEE ALSO:
Accessibility
Color Scales
Flat Color
Gradients

The classic NYC subway map (1972) by Massimo Vignelli is an example of using color to convey information. But does it meet the current accessibility standards?

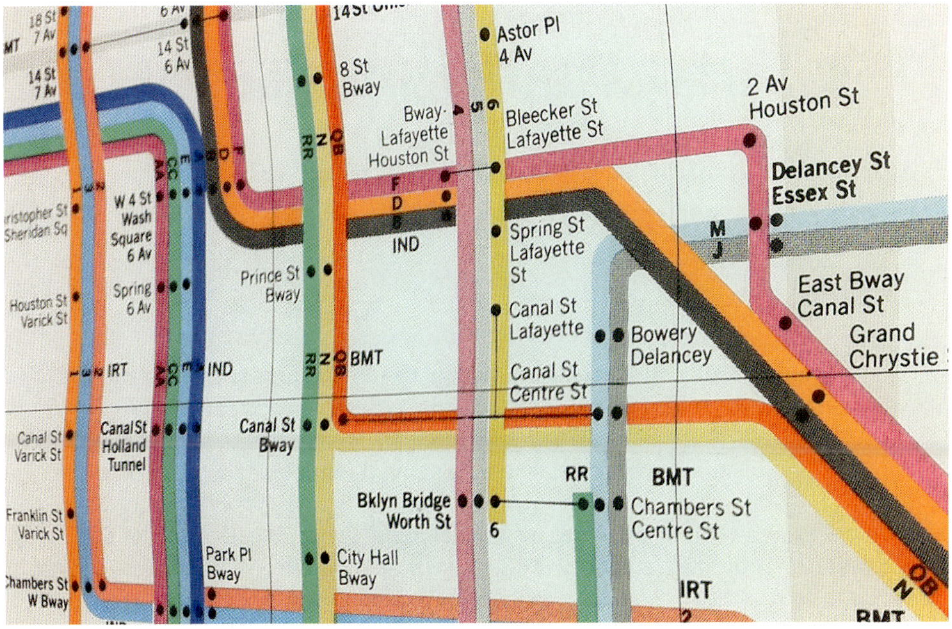

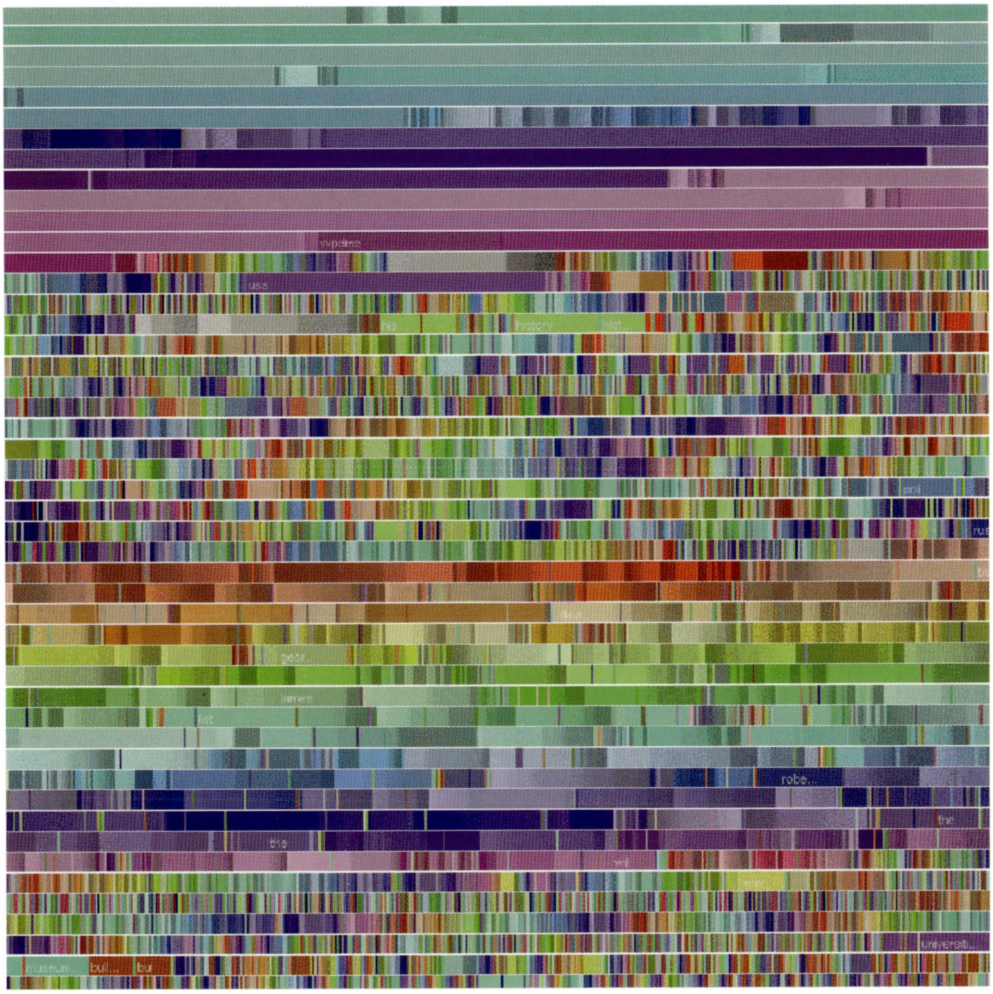

Data visualization using 'chromograms'. Editing activity over five months by user "Pearle" on Wikipedia. (Pearle is a robot). 2007. Fernanda B. Viégas

55 INTERNATIONAL KLEIN BLUE

A brilliant blue paint developed, and later patented, by the French artist Yves Klein

During the 1950s, Yves Klein, a leading member of the French artistic movement of *nouveau réalisme*, started to produce monochrome art where each painting consisted of a single color. Public reaction to these exhibitions was underwhelming, but Klein's response to this was to enter a period where he painted using a single color: blue.

Klein's 1957 exhibition in Milan, *Proposte Monochrome, Epoca Blue*, featured eleven blue canvases that used ultramarine blue pigment suspended in a synthetic resin. Klein worked closely with a Parisian paint specialist to develop this brilliant blue paint color. The new paint was a sensation and became known as International Klein Blue (IKB).

Later Klein blurred the boundaries between painting and sculpture by using naked female models smothered in his signature paint to impress their bodies on sheets of paper. In 1958 he exhibited absolutely nothing in an exhibition he titled *The Void*. However, he is perhaps most remembered for IKB.

Today Klein's art can be found in the Museum of Modern Art (New York) and the Tate Gallery (London), among other places.

SEE ALSO:
Brand Colors
Colorants
Emotion and Color
Symbolic Color

"Color is sensitivity in material form, substance in its purest form."
—*Yves Klein*

Klein developed his signature IKB paint, a previously unattainable brilliant blue color, from ultramarine pigment in the late 1950s.

In 1957 Klein exhibited several canvasses that were painted entirely using the new International Klein Blue (IKB) pigment.

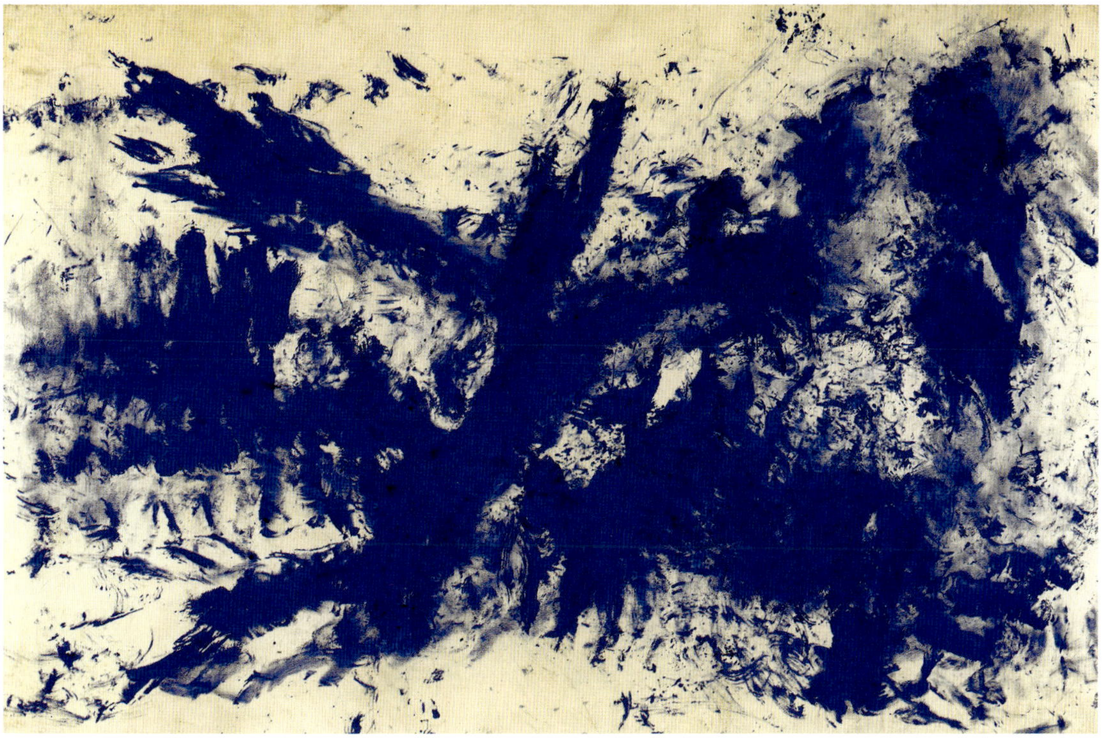

One of Klein's anthropometric art pieces (1960) where the paint was applied from people's bodies.

56 ITTEN'S *THE ART OF COLOR*

An influential book written by Johannes Itten, a Swiss artist, designer, educator, and color theorist

Johannes Itten (1888–1967) was appointed as one of the first teachers at the Bauhaus school in Germany, where he taught from 1919 to 1923. He played a key role in the development of the "preliminary course," which was designed to teach students the basic foundational concepts about composition, materials, and color.

In 1961 Itten published *The Art of Color*, a book on color theory that expanded on his earlier ideas. This influential book promoted a twelve-hue color wheel based on perceptually "pure" red, yellow, and blue color primaries that ignored many of the scientific developments of his contemporaries. Itten adhered to the view that all object colors were mixtures of red, yellow, and blue—a view held by most scientists until the mid-nineteenth century.

The Art of Color also promoted the idea of seven contrasts: hue, light and dark, cold and warm, complements, saturation, extension, and simultaneous contrast. His approach permeated much subsequent color education in the arts and the body of knowledge known as traditional color theory.

SEE ALSO:
Albers's *Interaction of Color*
Bauhaus
Contrast
Traditional Color Theory

"He who wishes to become a master of color must see, feel, and experience each individual color in its endless combinations with all other colors."

—*Johannes Itten*

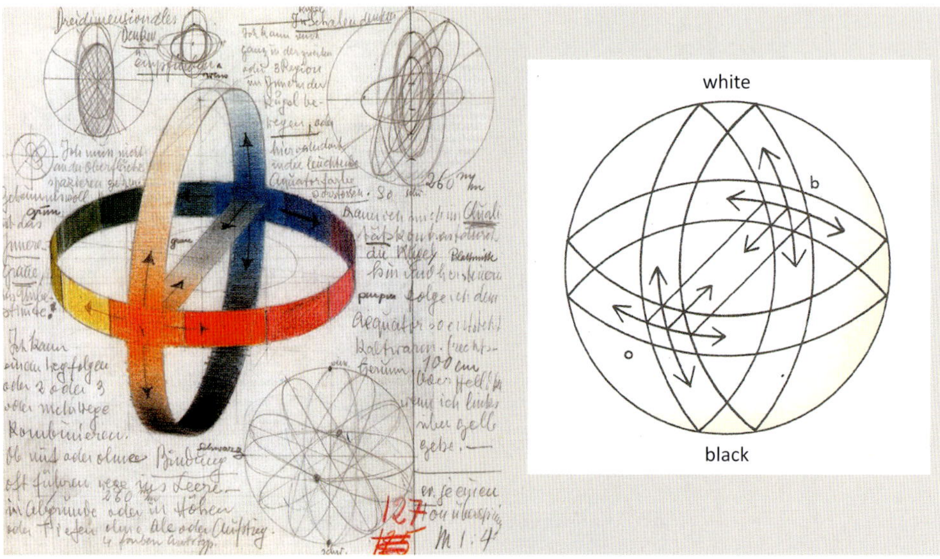

Itten's sketch of a color model from his diaries (left), and his drawing from *The Art of Color* (right), show the five principal paths of transition between two contrasting colors: two vertical paths, two horizontal paths and a diagonal path.

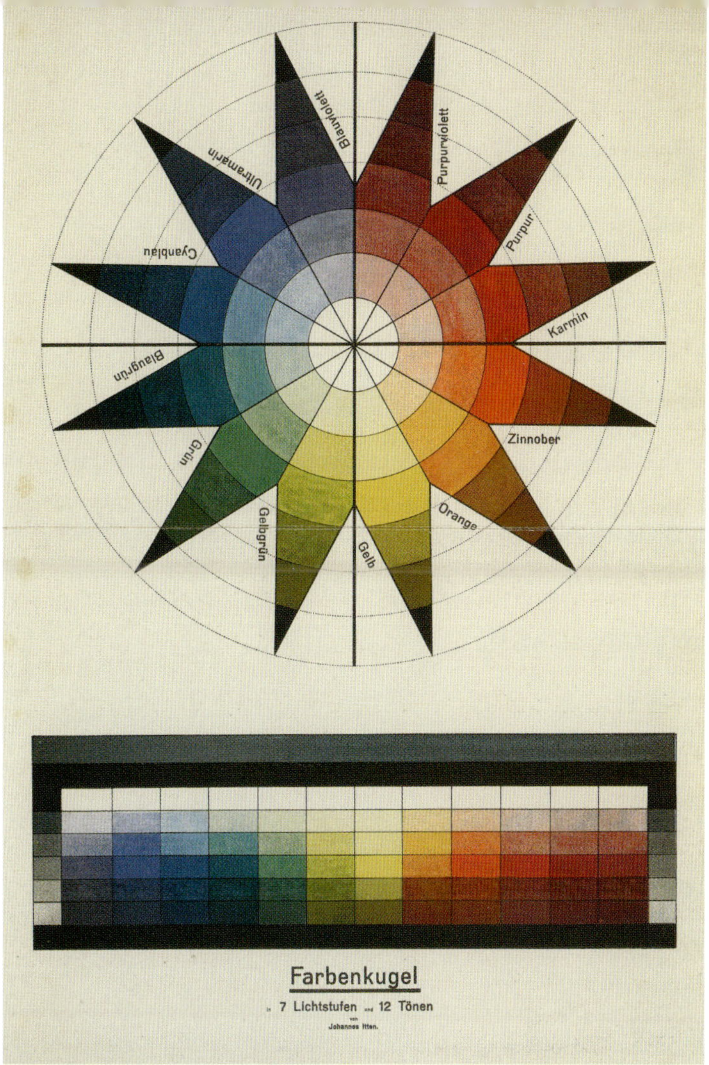

The Color Sphere (1921). This lithograph of Itten's Farbenkugel was published inside the cover of a book titled *Utopia* in 1921. In this version of his color star, Yellow is opposite Blue Violet.

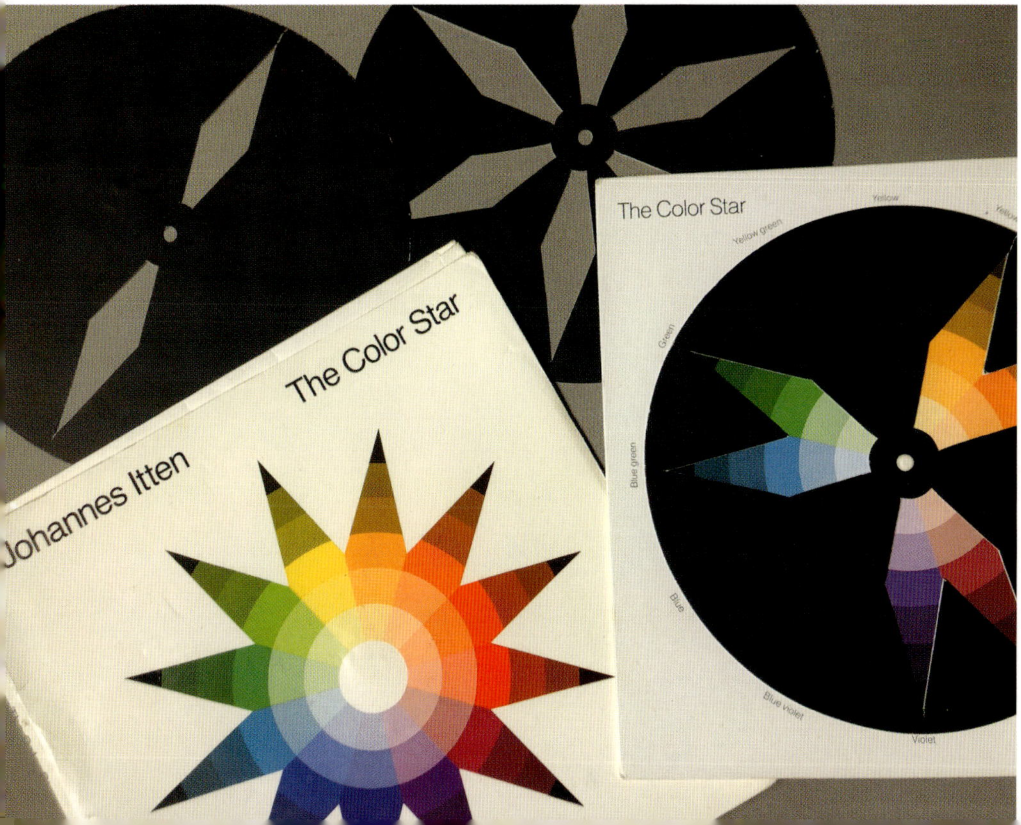

The Color Star (1986).
This color scheme tool has Yellow opposite Violet based on the color wheel from Itten's *The Art of Color*.

57 LED COLOR

A twentieth-century light source based on electricity passing through a semiconductor

Light-emitting diode, or LED, lights started to become practical in the 1960s, although initially they were not very bright and limited to a few colors (first red, then yellow and orange). They are based on a principle called electroluminescence, which was discovered in the early twentieth century. The red and yellow colors were originally produced by passing electricity through a substance called gallium arsenide phosphide. Early applications were indicator lights used in small electronic devices. The first commercially available blue-emitting LED was based on silicon carbide, but it was swiftly replaced by gallium nitride (c. 1990), for which Shuji Nakamura and colleagues received the Nobel Prize in Physics in 2014.

Early attempts to create white LEDs by mixing red, green, and blue light were only partially successful because the light produced had poor color rendering. A better spectral power distribution white was produced by including a phosphor as a coating. The idea was that the phosphor is activated by the LED light and produces light by fluorescence. This enabled very bright and efficient white LED lights with good color-rendering properties.

Modern LEDs are considered much more efficient and flexible than the older incandescent light sources that generated a lot of heat in addition to light. They have almost completely replaced incandescent lights and are replacing fluorescent tube lighting (which often contains the hazardous substance mercury). In addition to their efficiency and low running costs, LED lights can be easily switched to generate imaging displays for consumer devices, large screens, and applications in art.

Thoughtful use of the extensive color capabilities of LED technology is recommended. The luminosity of LED colors, coupled with the affordability and efficiency of the technology, has the potential to saturate the world in artificial color.

SEE ALSO:
Color Temperature
Lighting

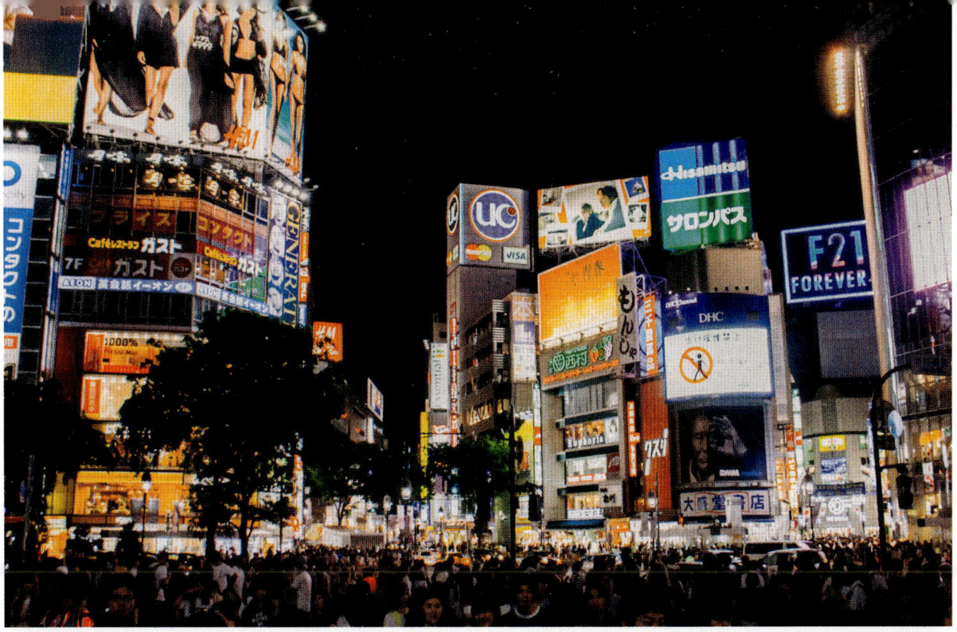

LEDs in the urban environment. Shibuya Crossing, Tokyo, Japan. LED screens are replacing billboards and signage all over the world.

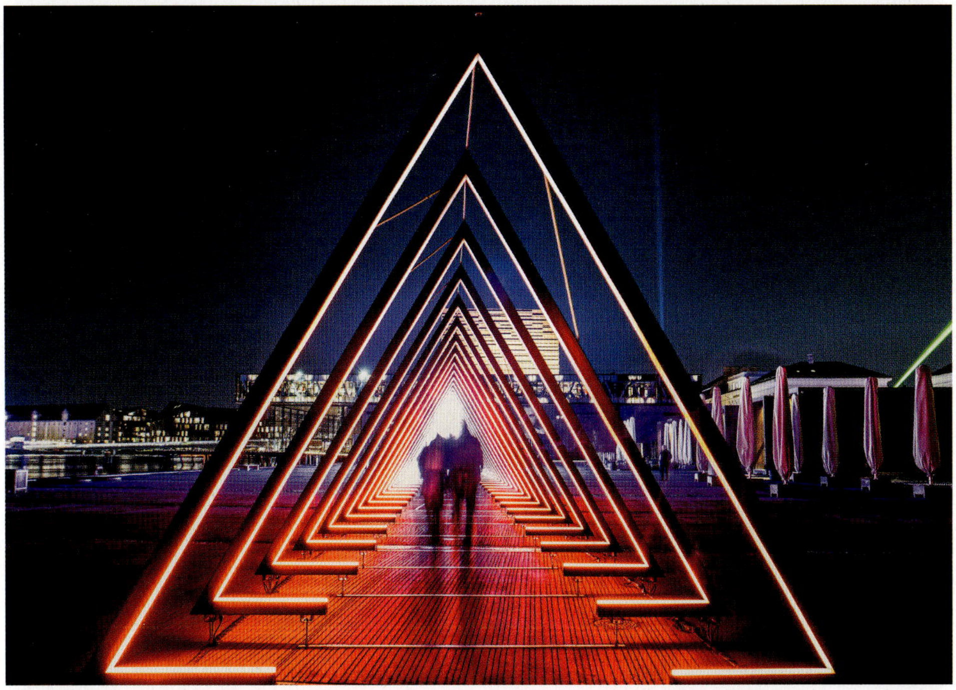

LEDs in public art. Copenhagen, Denmark – 2020. The light tunnel, or Gate of Light, installation consists of many triangular gates lit by LED bright lights.

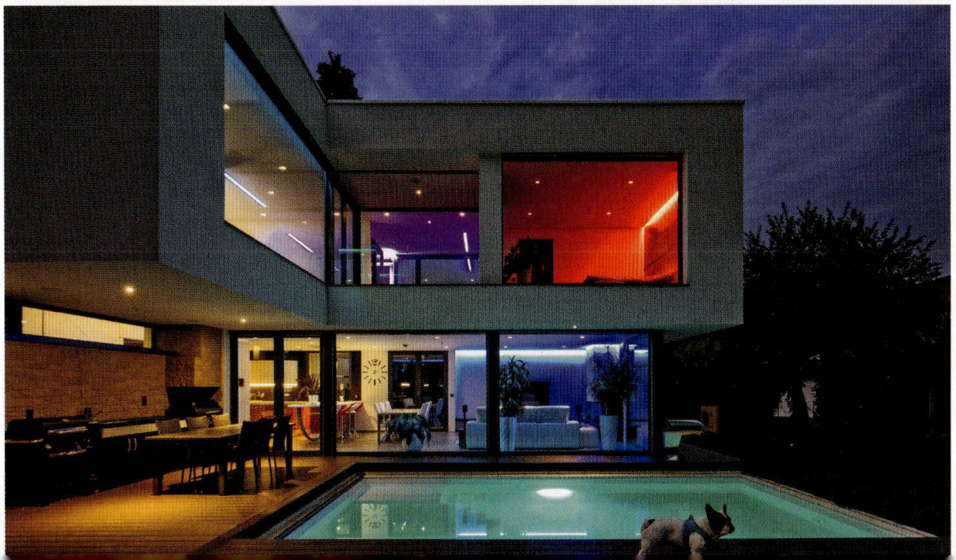

LEDs in private homes provide inexpensive and flexible lighting but more research is needed on the impact of LED lighting on health and well-being at home and in the workplace.

58 LIGHTING

The deliberate use of light to achieve practical or aesthetic effects

Humans have illuminated their environment for at least four hundred thousand years and possibly for one million years. For most of that time fire was used for both lighting and cooking. Candles have been used for a few thousand years, but it is only in the last few centuries that humans have developed efficient and effective manufactured lighting systems.

SEE ALSO:
Blue Light
Color Temperature
LED Color

The use of gas lighting and incandescent light sources transformed our cities and led to the idea that "the city never sleeps." However, the recent introduction of LED lighting has brought new efficiency and flexibility to our ability to illuminate our external and internal environments.

The color properties of light sources are determined by two different scales: correlated color temperature (CCT), which ranges from cool to warm, and color rendering index (CRI), which rates how close the light source is to natural daylight.

Light sources with energy distributions that vary smoothly with wavelength and are broadband tend to give better color rendering of objects than spikey or narrowband light sources. Methods exist to quantify the effect of a light source on the color constancy of objects. One such method is called the color rendering index (CRI), and this is often cited on commercial light sources. The proliferation of new LED sources, however, is bringing into question the suitability of such indices to correctly quantify the quality of modern commercial light sources.

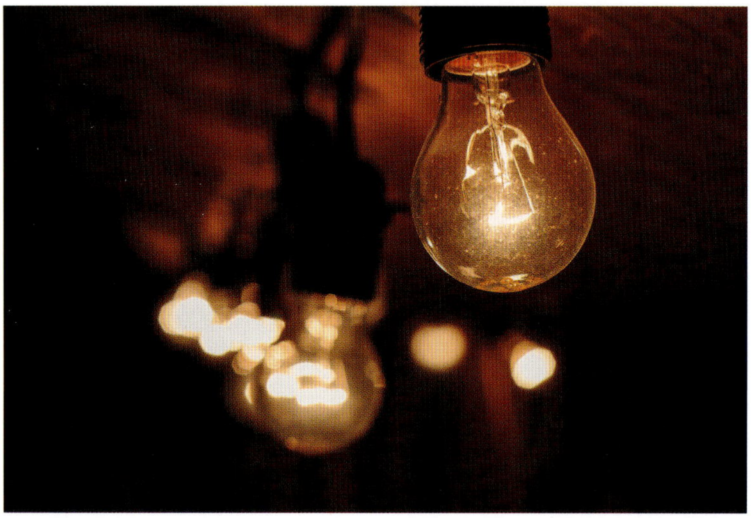

Commonly known as incandescent bulbs, tungsten light bulbs emit light when the tungsten filament is heated by electricity passing through it. The future of tungsten bulbs is in jeopardy due to the use of the more energy-efficient LEDs.

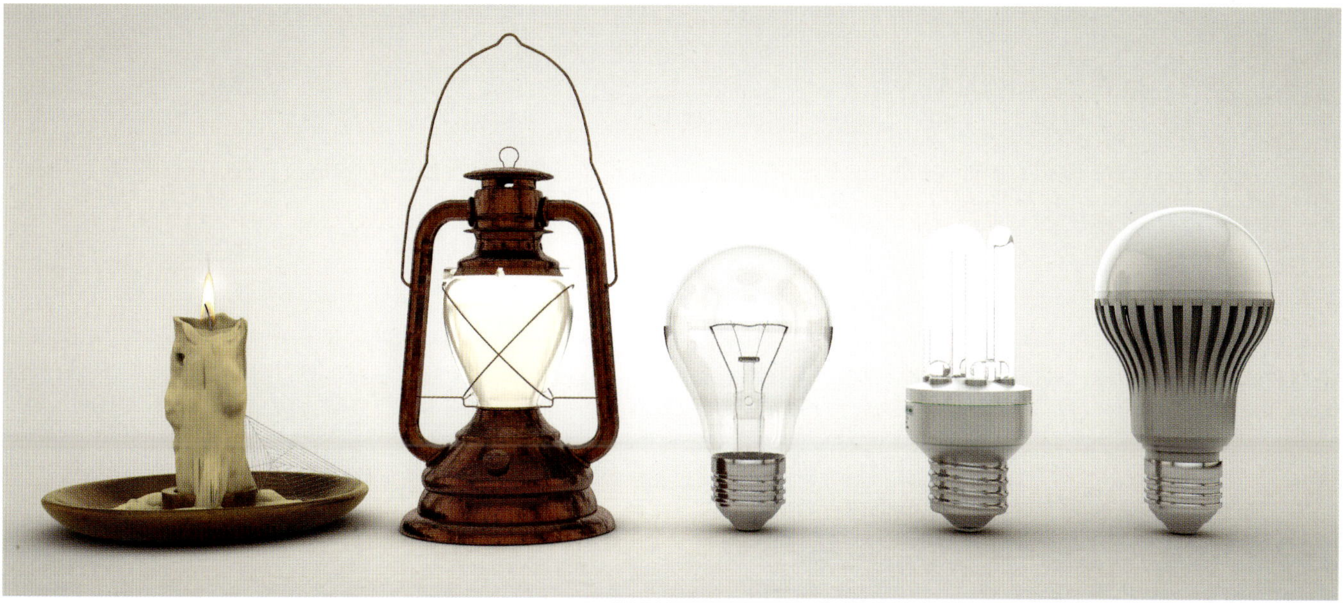

The technology of light sources has evolved from the simple candle (or firelight) through incandescent and fluorescent tubes to LED lights. LED is now becoming the dominant form of lighting in our built environment because it is energy efficient.

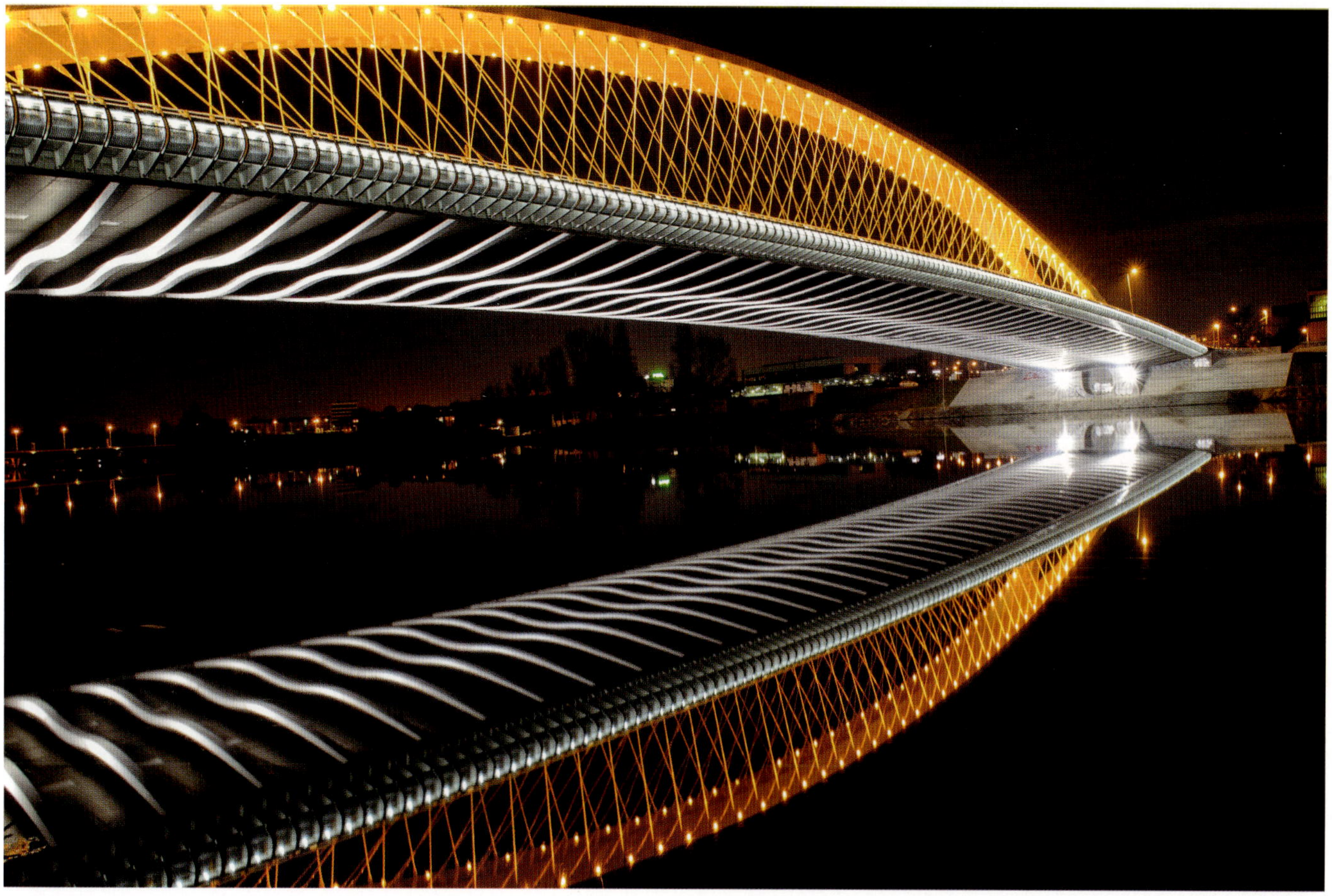

Dramatic use of light to generate an aesthetic effect.

59 LIGHTNESS

Lightness is one of the three main attributes of color and describes the extent to which an object or light source appears to reflect or emit more or less light

Lightness, also known as value, is a relative perception. Chromatically neutral objects that appear to emit a lot of light compared with other objects will likely appear white, and those that appear to emit little light compared with other objects will likely appear black.

The scale from black through gray to white is called an achromatic scale. Black is not strictly the absence of light, though objects that emit or reflect no light will almost certainly appear black. However, an object can reflect quite a large amount of light and still appear black if it reflects a lot less light than other objects in the scene. The terms *white*, *black*, and *lightness* are all relative, rather than absolute, terms.

All colors can be assessed in terms of their lightness, and awareness of this is often important for design. In terms of legibility, it is usually advisable, for example, that foreground (text) and background have a contrast in lightness because a contrast in hue alone can be very difficult to see or read.

The CIE defines lightness as "the brightness of an area judged relative to the brightness of an area that appears to be white or highly transmitting." Brightness is defined as "the amount of light perceived to be emitted or reflected by an area."

SEE ALSO:
Accessibility
Chroma
Three Dimensions of Color

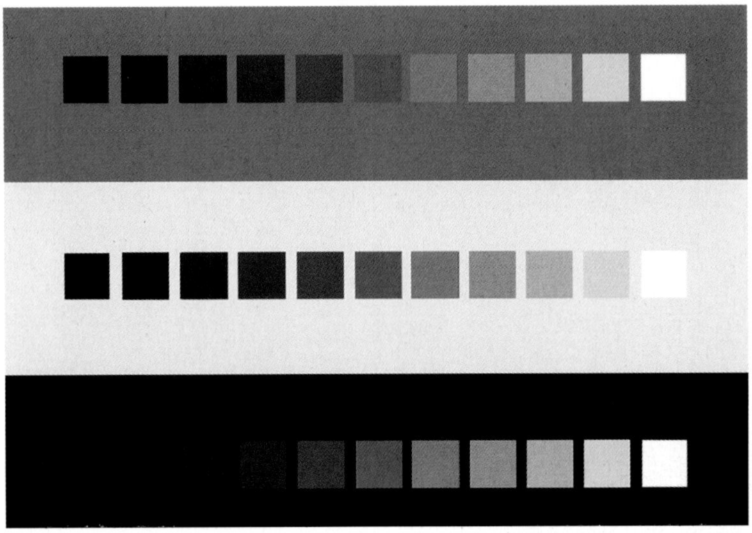

Effect of background on lightness perception and lightness scales.

The lightness scale in each case is identical and consists of an even scale of L= 0, 10, 20, 30, 40, 50, 60, 70, 80, 90, 100, but where is the biggest jump?

The phenomenon of "crispening" makes lightness intervals spanning the background lightness appear relatively large.

Comparison of lightness/value scales by David Briggs.

A. Munsell value scale designed to print accurate Munsell values on a specific printer.

B. Comparison of Munsell value with CIE lightness (L*) and Luminous reflectance percentages. Note that Munsell value 10 applies to a theoretical perfect diffuse reflector, while CIE lightness L* is based on luminance relative to an actual similarly illuminated standard white reflector. This almost, but not quite, perfect reflector is assigned a CIE lightness of 100, and consequently Munsell value 10 has a CIE lightness greater than 100 and a nominal Luminous reflectance greater than 100%.

C. Value scale of Denman Ross, as illustrated by Froelich and Snow (1905).

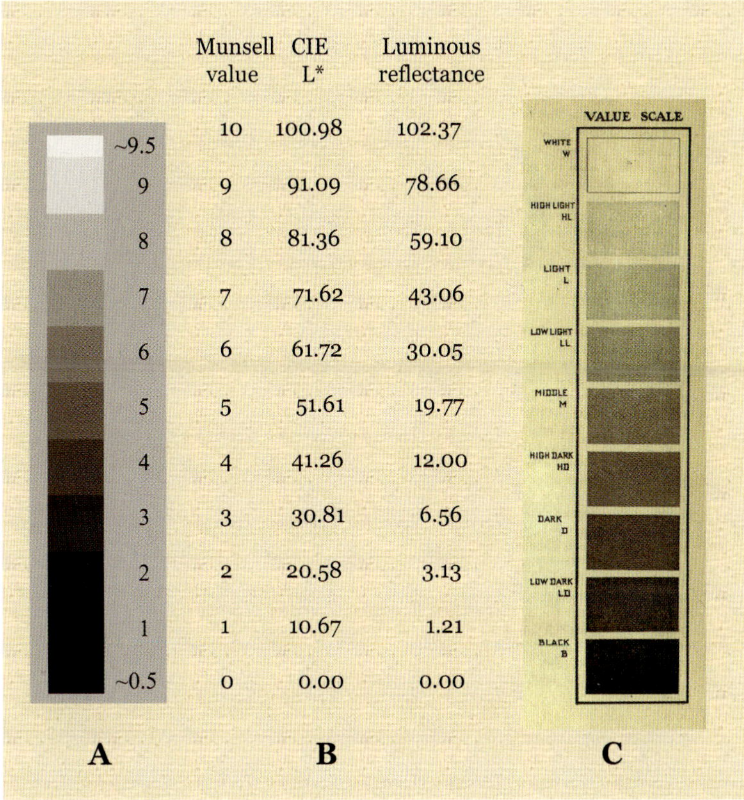

Munsell value	CIE L*	Luminous reflectance
10	100.98	102.37
9	91.09	78.66
8	81.36	59.10
7	71.62	43.06
6	61.72	30.05
5	51.61	19.77
4	41.26	12.00
3	30.81	6.56
2	20.58	3.13
1	10.67	1.21
0	0.00	0.00

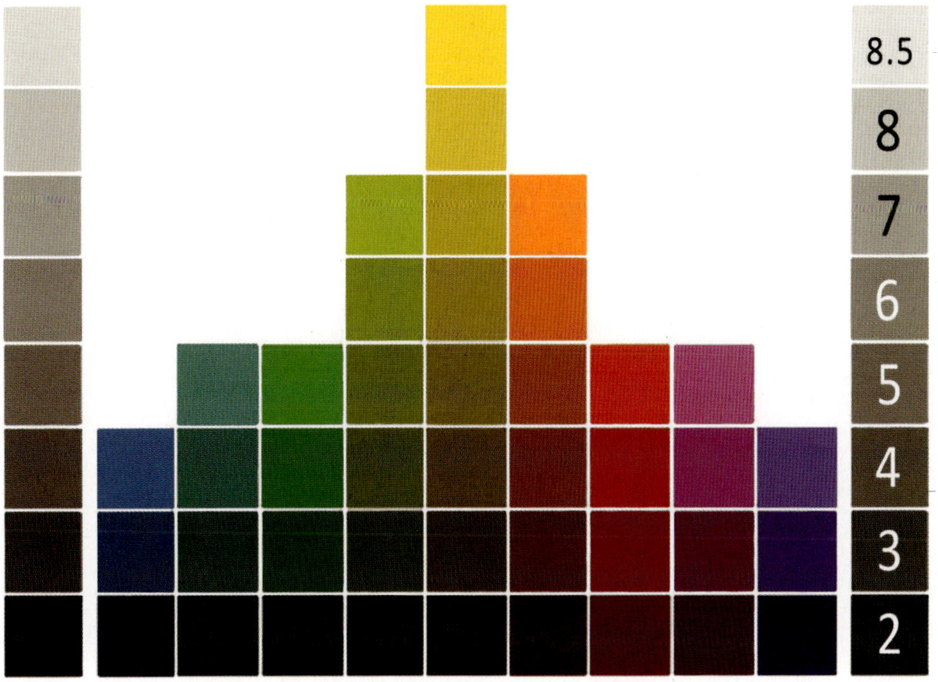

Comparison of the lightness/values of nine vivid hues at their highest chroma.

Note that the hues are not at the same lightness/value at their highest chroma. This chart shows nine high chroma hues at their respective lightness/value and the number of steps to reach lightness/value of 2.

60 LIMITED COLOR VISION

Physical condition of the retina of the eye leading to difficulty in discriminating between colors that other people can easily tell apart

The term *color blindness* is widely used. But it is a misnomer. Most people with this condition can see different colors; however, they have poorer color discrimination for certain parts of the color space. Because their color vision is limited, they are correctly called color-deficient observers.

Distinguishing between red and green is problematic for individuals with protanomaly (the milder form, or red weakness), protanopia (missing red cones, or red blindness), deuteranomaly (green weakness), or deuteranopia (green blindness). The difficulty distinguishing the amount of red or green in every color affects the perception of a whole range of colors.

In 1917 University of Tokyo professor Shinobu Ishihara published a set of printed colored images to be used as a diagnostic test for color vision deficiencies. During the test, a person is asked to read a number or trace a line in the image. In some cases, the number or line can be seen only by someone with normal color vision. In other cases, however, the number or line can be seen only by someone with protanopia or deuteranopia.

The Ishihara test is widely used in schools and other organizations because it is easy to administer and generally gives accurate results. However, care must be taken to ensure that a prescribed lighting environment is in place, because the wrong illumination conditions can lead to erroneous results.

For professions that require a high degree of accuracy in color discrimination, an additional test is used. The Farnsworth-Munsell 100-hue test is designed with intentionally small steps between colors to measure color acuity.

SEE ALSO:
Accessibility
Human Visual System
Trichromacy

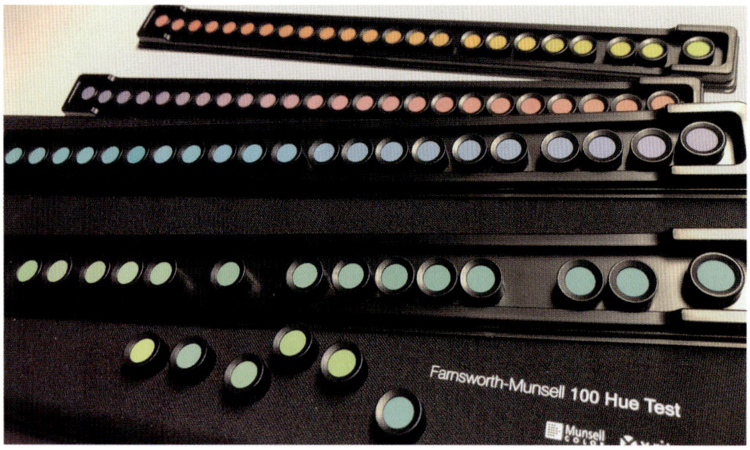

Individuals taking the Farnsworth-Munsell 100-hue test are asked to arrange a set of colored chips in order of hue.

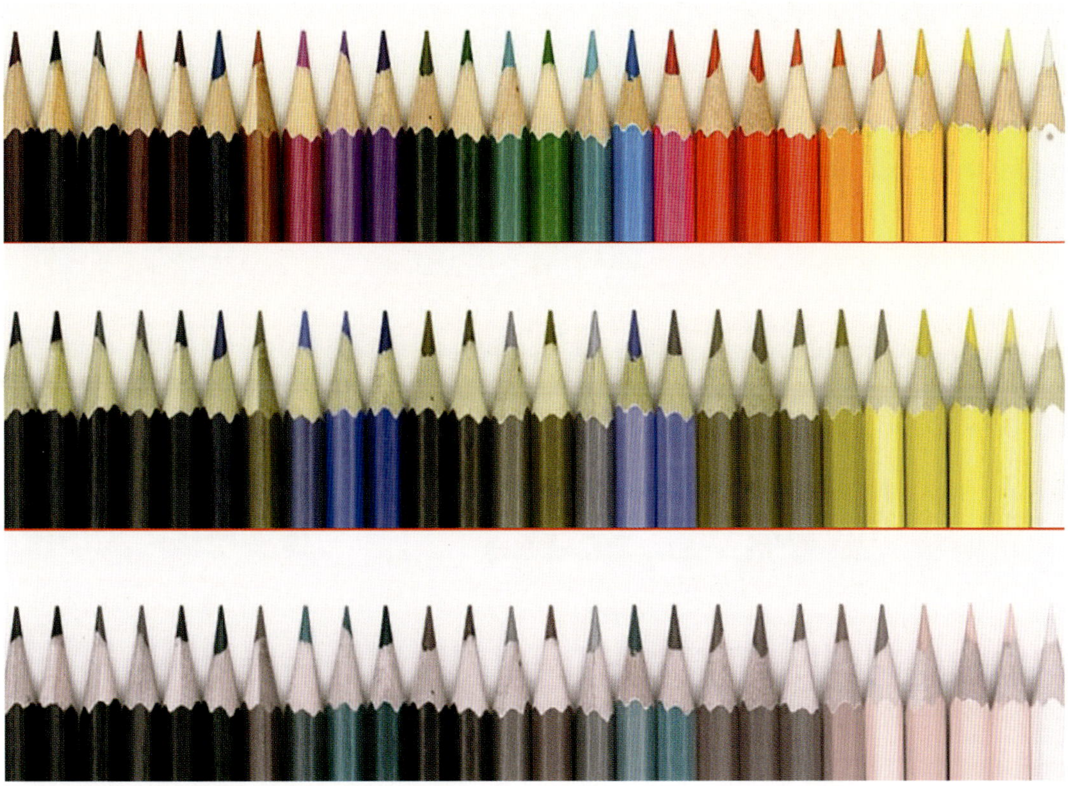

Simulations of how a set of colored pencils would look for someone with congenital color deficiency: normal vision (top), lack of long-wavelength cones (middle), and lack of short-wavelength cones (bottom).

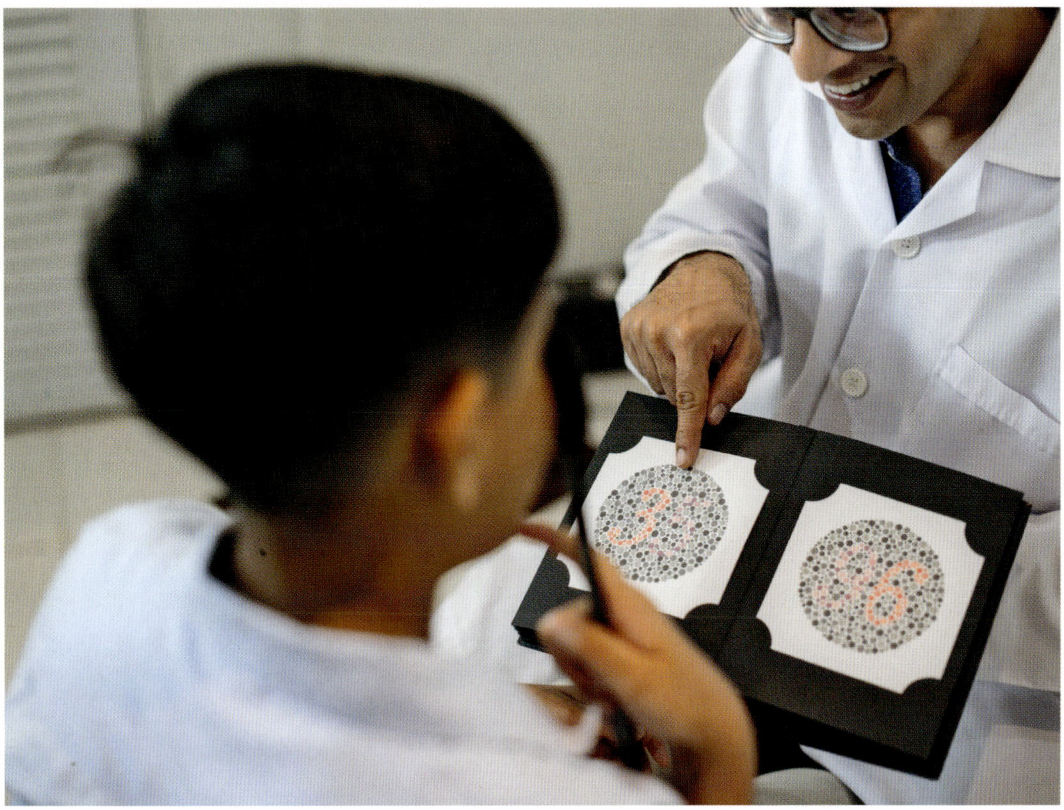

The Ishihara test is used as a screening test for color blindness. It is quick and inexpensive and can be used to identify the most common color vision deficiencies.

61 LOCAL COLOR

The perceived color of an object under noon sunlight without the influence of lighting, surrounding colors, or viewing conditions

Local color—also known as object color, inherent color, or nominal color—is one of the key factors that influences the perceived color of everything around us. Other factors that affect color include the lighting, viewing angle and distance, surrounding colors, surface texture, and shape of the objects.

One of the most enduring debates about color addresses the question: Is color a property of objects? The answer is complicated, but whether you believe that color is or is not a property of objects, all objects possess a "disposition" to absorb or reflect certain light waves, which are then channeled through our eyes and processed by our brains.

Colorimetry instruments are used to measure object color by recording the light reflected by an object or sample without the influence of outside factors.

SEE ALSO:
Color Measurement
Human Visual System
Shadows

"Colours in the Object are nothing but a Disposition to reflect this or that sort of Rays more copiously than the rest: in the Rays they are nothing but their Dispositions to propagate this or that motion into the Sensorium, and in the Sensorium they are Sensations of those Motions under the Forms of Colours."

—*Isaac Newton's* Opticks

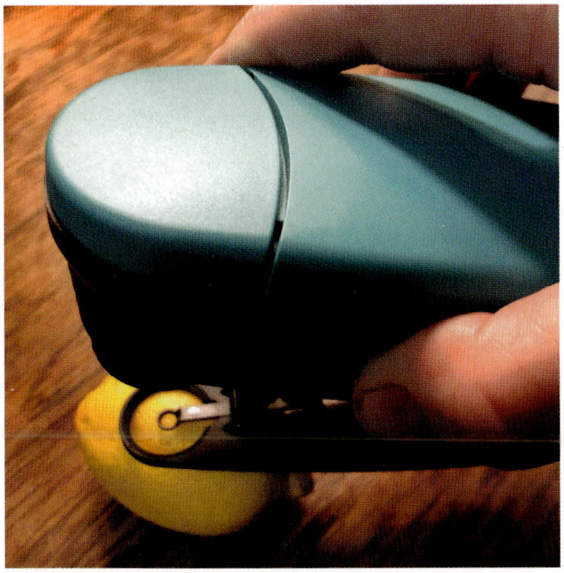

Measuring the local color of a lemon.

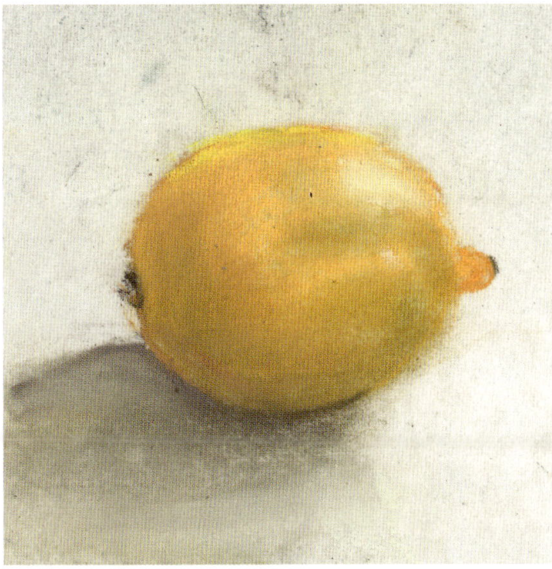

Noting the local color and shadows in a sketch of lemon by Greg Danielson.

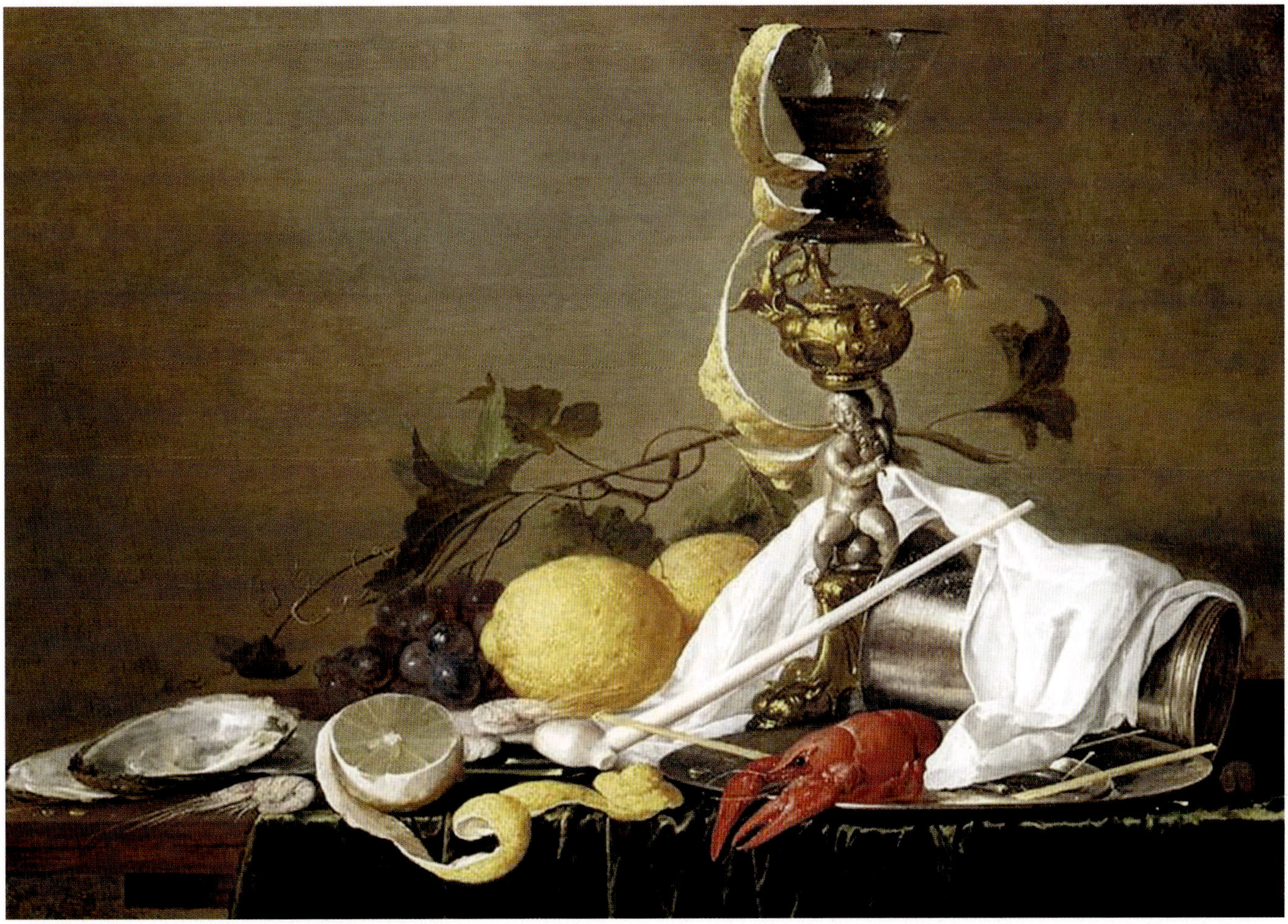

Still-Life (1642), oil painting by Jan Davidsz de Heem.

62 MAXWELL

Scottish scientist and mathematician who presented the first-ever color photograph

James Clerk Maxwell (1831–1879) was a renowned scientist who made notable contributions in the fields of electromagnetic radiation, magnetism, and statistical thermodynamics. He was also a leading figure in the nineteenth-century development of our understanding of how color vision works.

In the early nineteenth century, Thomas Young proposed that the human visual system operated using three channels. This became known as the trichromatic theory of color vision. We now know that the eye contains three classes of light-sensitive cells called cones. Maxwell developed mathematics and carried out experiments to provide evidence to support Young's proposal. Specifically, he showed that any stimulation of the cones could be achieved using an additive mixture of three monochromatic lights, thus inventing the field of colorimetry upon which the current CIE system is based.

The gamut of colors that can be achieved by additively mixing three primaries is a triangle. Maxwell was the first to show this triangular arrangement, and these triangular gamuts are known as Maxwell triangles.

To aid his research, Maxwell created a tool that became known as a spinning top or disk. Two or more colored disks are slotted together so that a percentage of each is visible. The inner circle disks are black and white. The outer circle disks are vivid hues. When the top is spun rapidly, the colors appear to blur together. He carefully recorded the different colors and proportions necessary to get the inner and outer colors to match. He found that the proportions that were seen as the best match depended on the observer. A few people with limited color vision gave very different answers.

SEE ALSO:
CIE System
Partitive Mixture
RGB

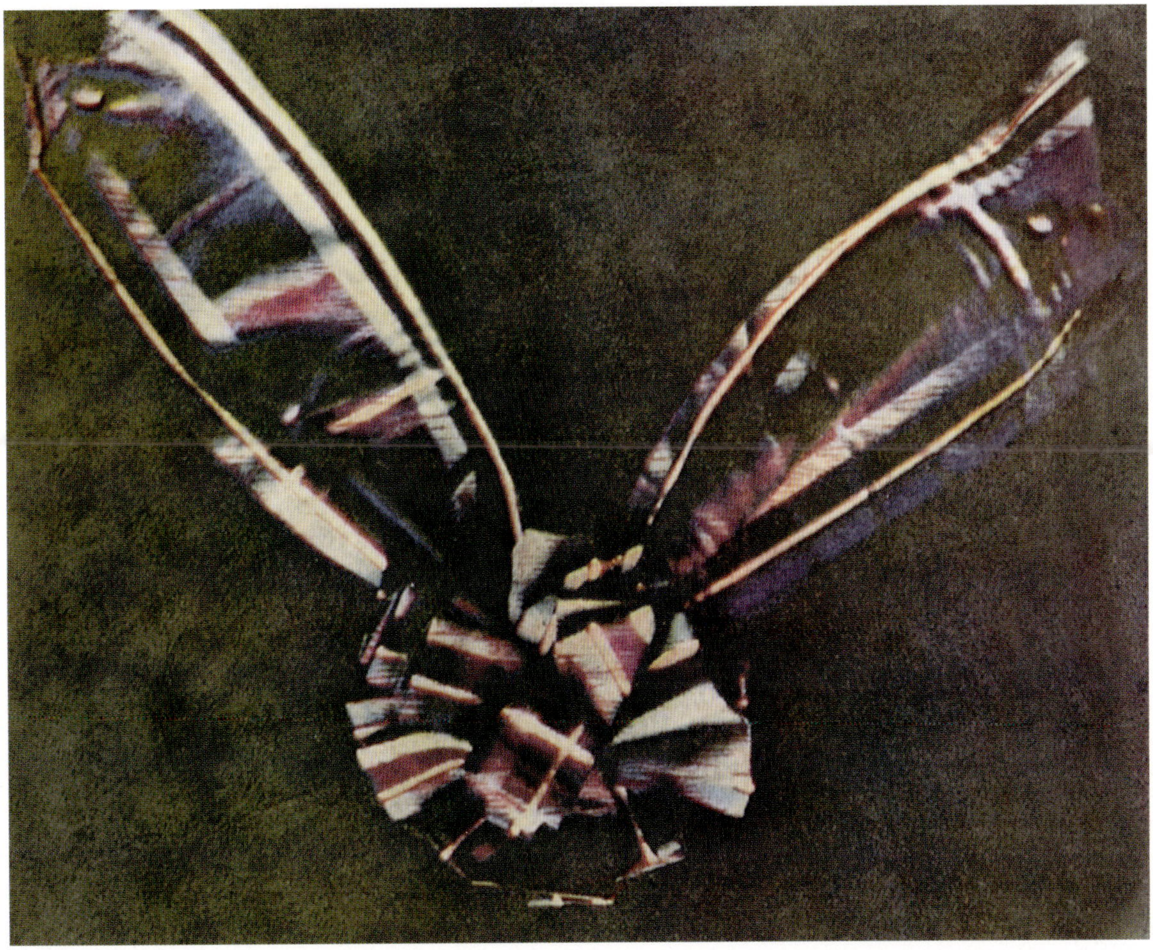

In 1861 Maxwell presented the world's first color photograph at the Royal Institution. The photograph was captured by Thomas Sutton, who took three images of a Scottish tartan through red, green, and blue filters. He then superimposed these three images using a projection system to create a color image, establishing the principles through which color imaging would later develop.

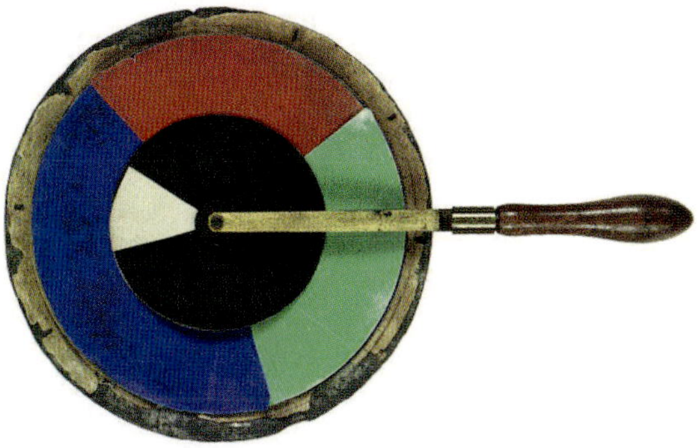

Maxwell pioneered the use of a spinner in experiments on optical, or partitive, mixing.

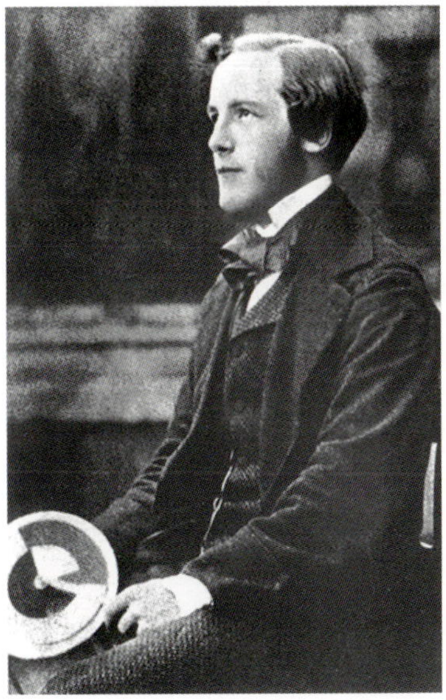

63 METAMERISM

Colors that match under one lighting condition can appear to not match under a different lighting condition

Two spectrally different stimuli can appear identical in color to an observer. For example, two cyan objects, one reflecting wavelengths in the cyan range and the other reflecting a combination of blue and green wavelengths, will match in one lighting condition but mismatch in another. This occurs because the human visual system is trichromatic; its response to a color stimulus is limited to the response of three classes of light-sensitive receptors in the eye called cones. If two spectrally different stimuli produce the same cone responses, they will appear to be identical in color if viewed in the same conditions.

The light that reaches the eye when we look at objects in our environment is a property of both the spectral distribution of the illumination and the spectral reflectance properties of the object. It is possible that the light reflected from two spectrally dissimilar objects when viewed in one light source generates identical cone responses in the viewer but that the light reflected from these objects when viewed in a second light source will generate different cone responses. In this situation the objects may match (appear to be the same color) when viewed under the first light source but then fail to match when viewed under the second light source. This is referred to as metamerism, and in this case can be described as illuminant metamerism.

Other types of metamerism exist including geometric metamerism (two objects match when viewed from one angle but fail to match when viewed from a second angle), size metamerism (two objects match when viewed from one distance but fail to match when viewed from a different distance), and observer metamerism (two objects match when viewed by one observer but not when viewed by a second observer). Note that metamerism requires the objects to be spectrally dissimilar. If two objects have identical reflectance spectra, they will likely be a match to an observer under all conditions if, for example, they are viewed in the same way (e.g., against the same background).

SEE ALSO:
Color Temperature
Human Visual System
Lighting

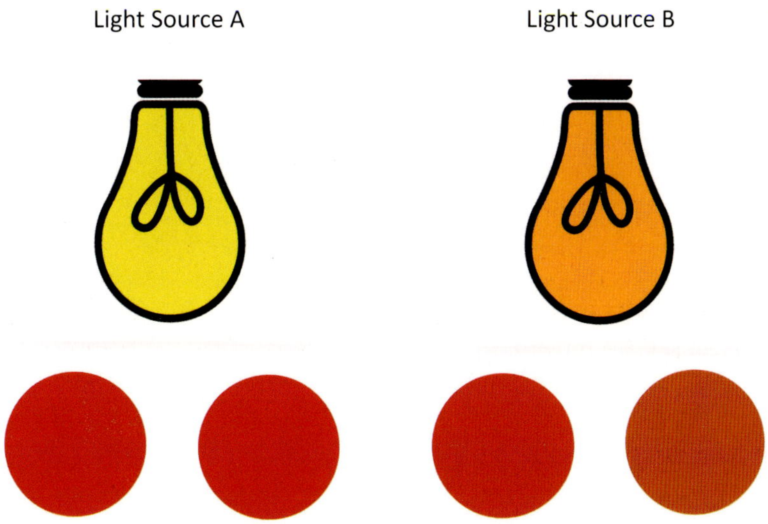

Objects match under one light source but look different under another light source if they have different spectral properties.

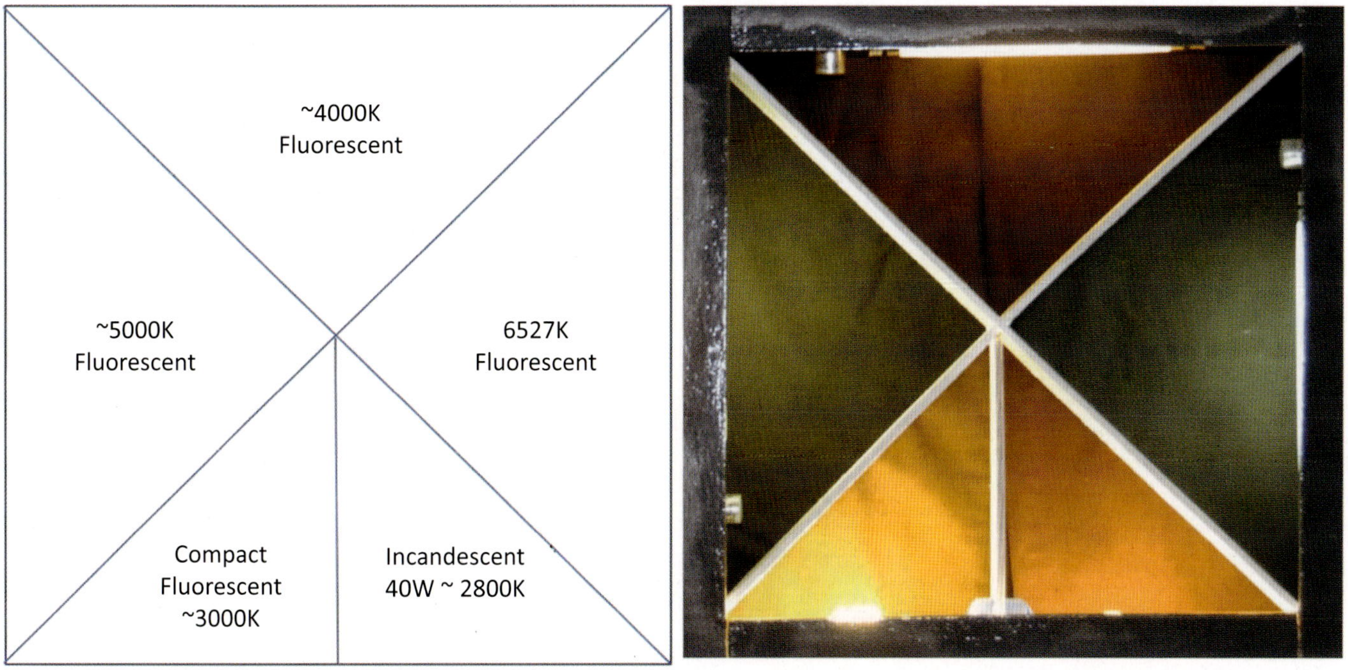

A booth used at the Color Science and Imaging laboratory, North Carolina State University, for testing the appearance of the same fabric under different lighting conditions can predict the effects of metamerism.

64 MONOCHROMATIC

A color scheme that features a single hue

A monochromatic color scheme, also known as harmony of dominant hue, is one where the component colors have the same hue but vary in lightness and chroma.

Art that contains a single hue was sometimes produced by expressionist artists; for example, in Picasso's blue period he produced paintings that only contained blue or blue-green. Note that sometimes it is a fine distinction between a strictly monochromatic color scheme and one that is analogous where the colors are similar, but not identical, in hue.

A monochromatic wash is also sometimes used in movies (or in advertisements for movies) to communicate a particular emotion or feel for a scene. In graphic design, a monochromatic color scheme can be both visually and cost effective. In science, the term *monochromatic* sometimes has a slightly different meaning; it refers to a single-wavelength light source.

SEE ALSO:
International Klein Blue
Color Schemes

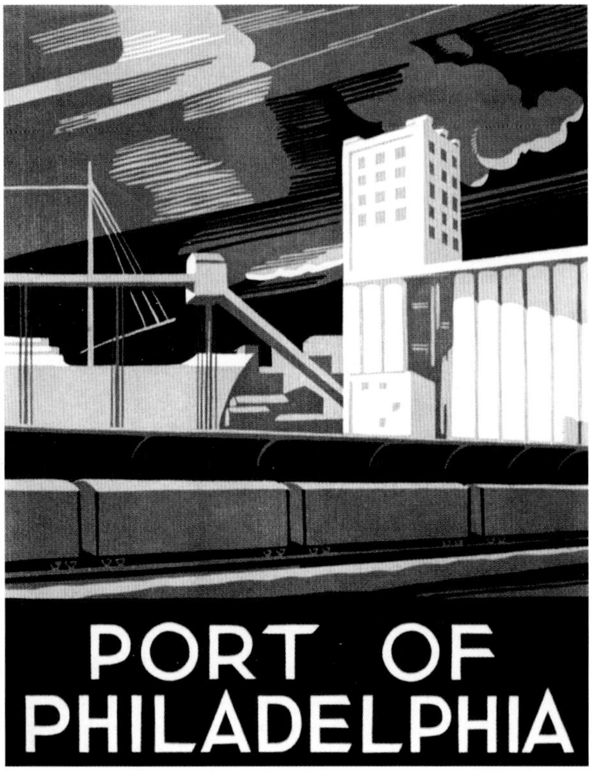

This WPA Poster uses a simple monochromatic scheme with a single blue hue shifting to black and to white.

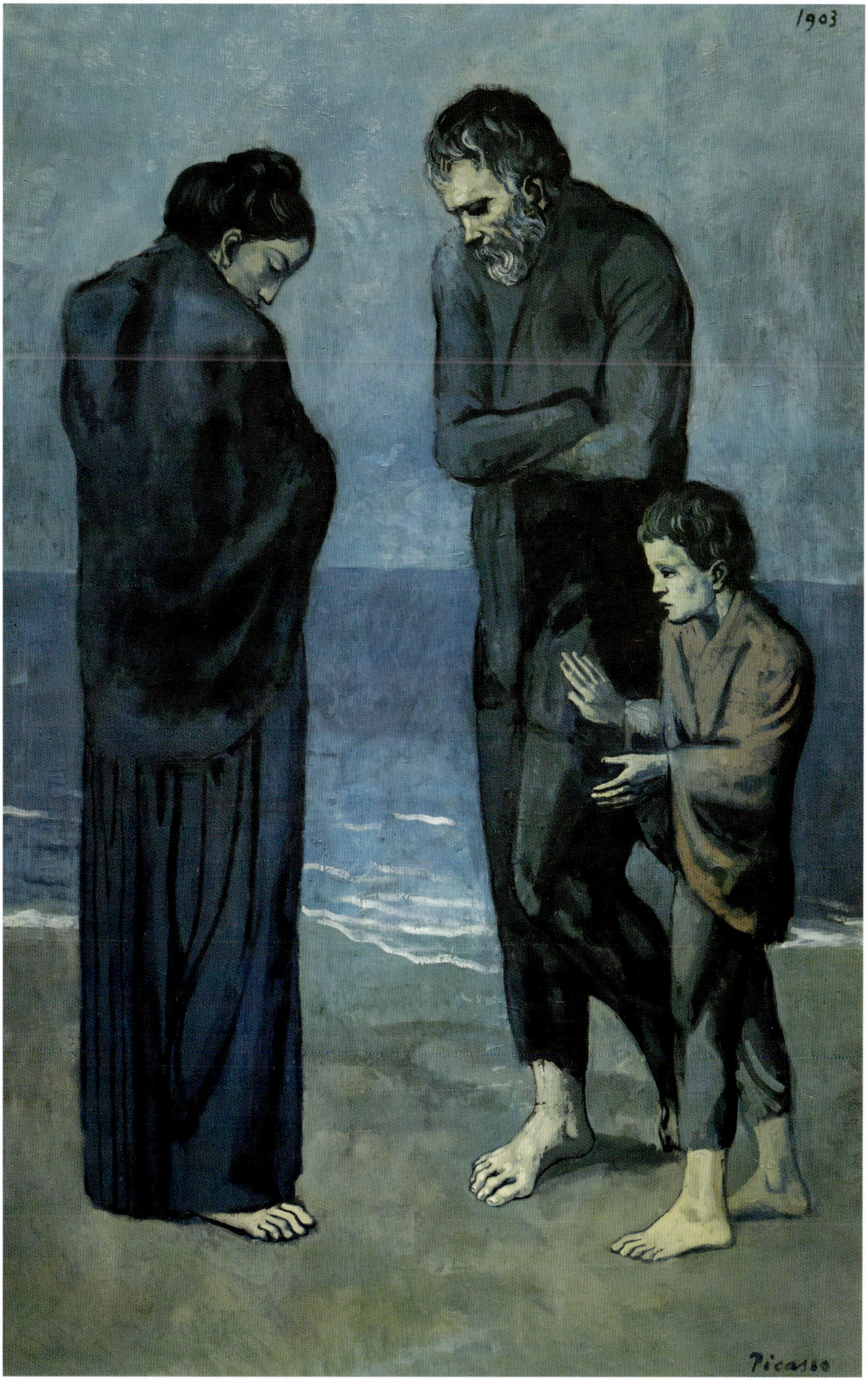

Tragedy (1903), oil painting by Pablo Picasso. A complex monochromatic scheme with many variations of blue.

65 MUNSELL SYSTEM

A color model and specification system created by the artist and art educator Albert Munsell in the early 1900s

Influenced by the science of color, Munsell based his color notation system on color perception rather than paint mixing. The Munsell system has five principal hues (red, yellow, green, blue, and purple) and three attributes, which he called dimensions (hue, value, and chroma).

Noting the need for accurate measurements to describe color variations, Munsell invented a photometer for determining value, equivalent in contemporary terms to lightness. To determine chroma, he used Maxwell disks to compare the visual color strength of colored papers. These measurements resulted in the system's distinctive asymmetrical arrangement of swatches around the central neutral axis.

The Munsell system is an example of a physical color-order system. The main purpose of such a system is numerical color communication. For example, the Munsell notation 5R 5/12 is a sample with Munsell hue of middle red, a middle value of 5, and a moderately strong chroma of 12.

Imagine that two people living in different countries have the same edition of the *Munsell Book of Color*. The first person can use the book to match a color with the closest sample and send the Munsell notation to the other person to locate in their version of the book. In this way, color has been communicated numerically. The fidelity of the communication is limited by several factors, including variations between editions and the limited number of samples in the system. Note that the number of colors that we can discriminate between far exceeds the number of samples in any such physical color communication system and therefore approximation errors may occur.

The Munsell system is the basis for the modern CIELAB system and remains of great historical and academic interest today. However, it has largely been superseded as a physical tool for color communication by more recent systems such as Pantone and the Natural Color System (NCS). Although its use as an industry standard is fading, the Munsell system continues to be useful for educating students about the perceptual attributes of color.

SEE ALSO:
Color Order Systems
Natural Color System
RAL System
Three Dimensions of Color

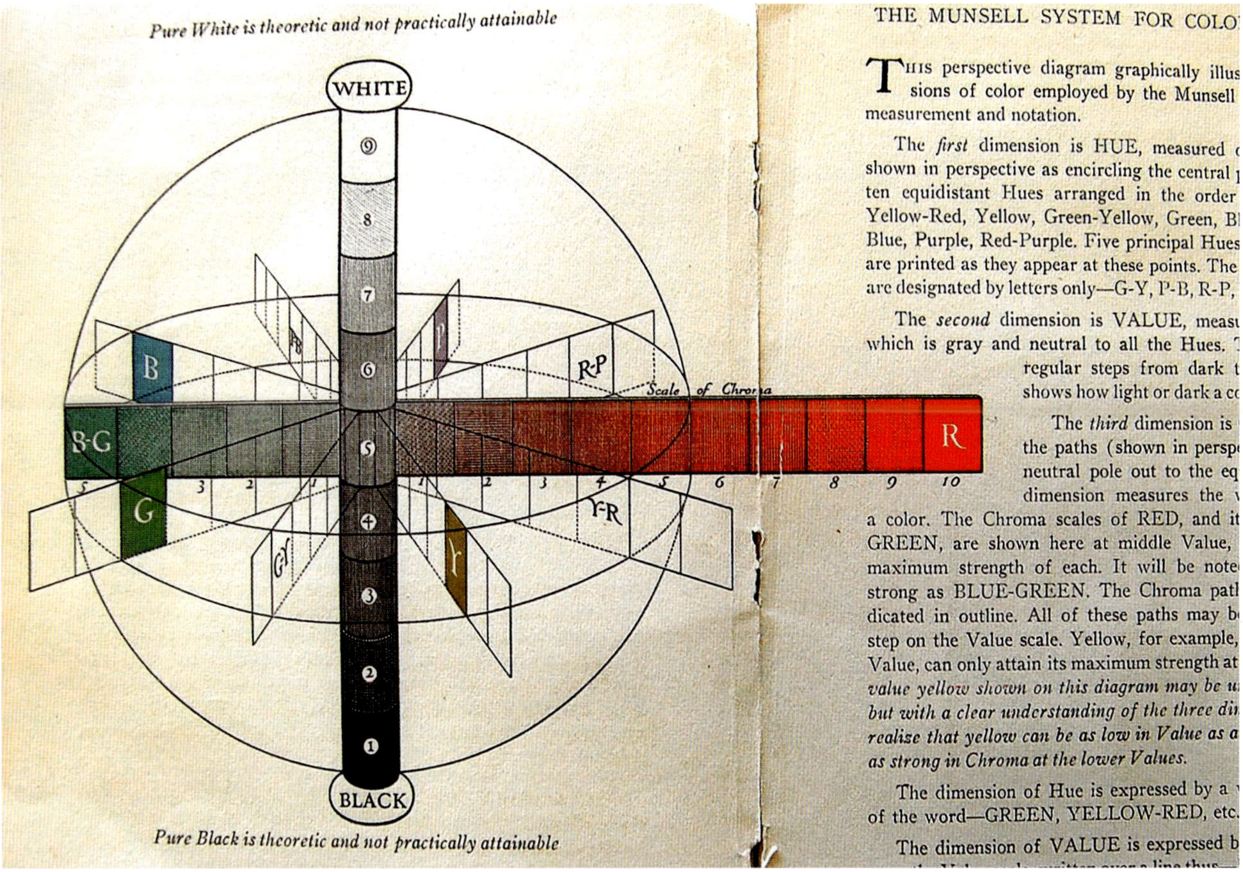

The Munsell system extends colors beyond a symmetrical spherical model (illustration in *A Practical Description of the Munsell Color System: With Suggestions for Its Use (1937)*, by Thomas M. Cleland).

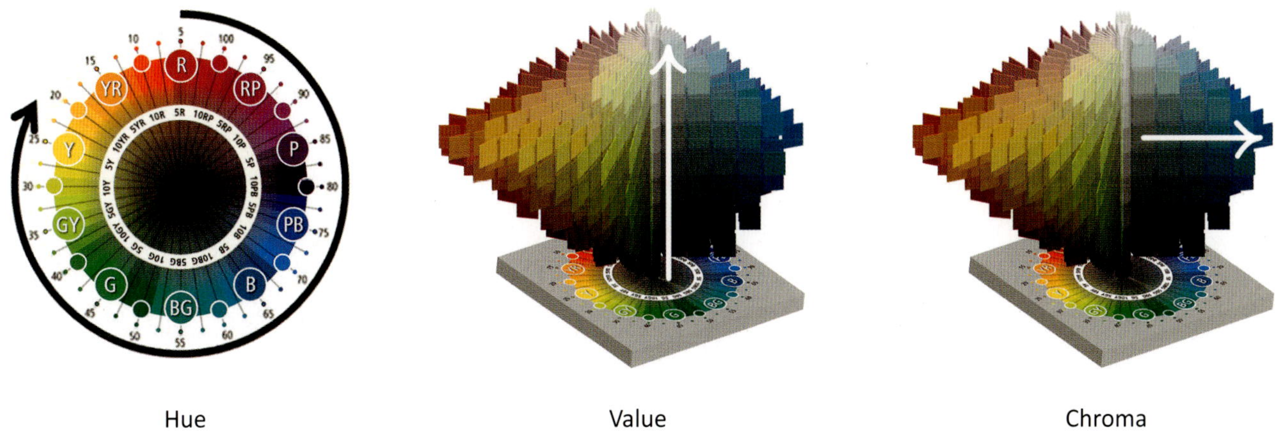

The system is based on perceptually even spacing in three dimensions that Munsell called hue, value (lightness), and chroma. Colors can shift in three directions: around the hue circle, up and down in lightness/value, and in and out from the central gray axis.

66 NATURAL COLOR SYSTEM

A proprietary tool for color communication and color description developed in Sweden in the 1960s

The Natural Color System's (NCS) perceptual color model is based on the color opponency hypothesis of color vision that was first postulated by Ewald Hering in 1892. It was developed by Anders Hård, Lars Sivik, and Gunnar Tonnquist in the Swedish Colour Centre Foundation in the 1960s and is based on the idea of six elementary color percepts. These six elementary percepts form three pairs of colors: white/black, green/red, and yellow/blue; the last four of these are also known as the unique hues. According to the NCS system, all color perceptions can be defined in terms of their similarity to these six elementary colors; a shocking pink color, for example, would be defined by its visual similarity to red, blue, black, and white.

NCS notation uses three values to define every color perception: degree of blackness (S), degree of chromaticness (C), and hue. In terms of hue, every color can be described by its similarity to two hue terms; for example, a color can be red or blue or red-blue, but it cannot be red-green because red and green are opponent colors in the system.

Unlike some other color models that are based on color mixing or other physical processes, the NCS system is based on color appearance, and any possible color appearance can be defined within the system. It is used in the industry as a tool for specifying and communicating color, and a physical system comprising 1,950 selected colors is available for standardization purposes. In the NCS notation the use of an S indicates that the color concerned is one of these 1,950 physical samples, for example, NCS S 1070-Y10R. The system added 100 samples in 2022 for a total of 2,050. It is widely used in Europe and is particularly popular in architecture and interior design applications.

SEE ALSO:
Character Zones
Munsell System
RAL System
Unique Hues

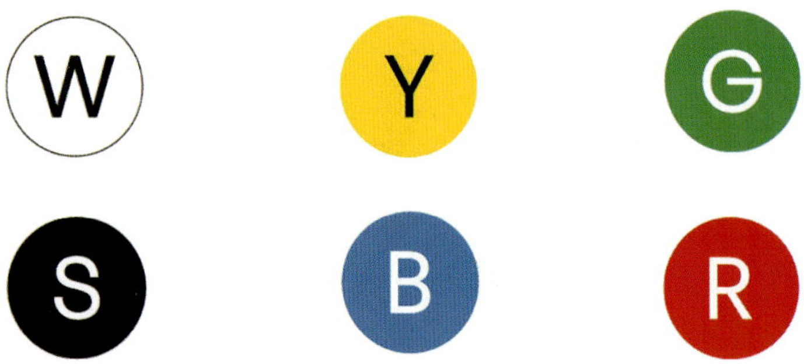

The NCS is based on Hering's three pairs of opponent colors: White/Black, Yellow/Blue, and Green/Red.

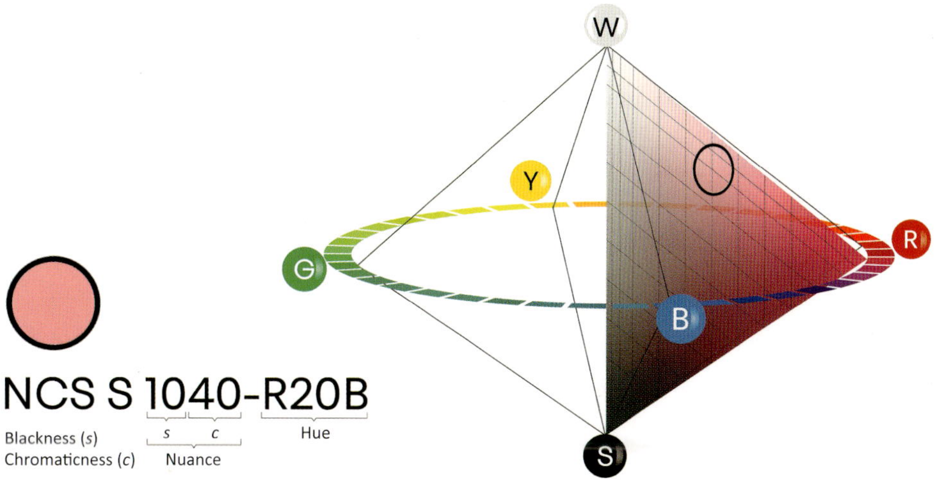

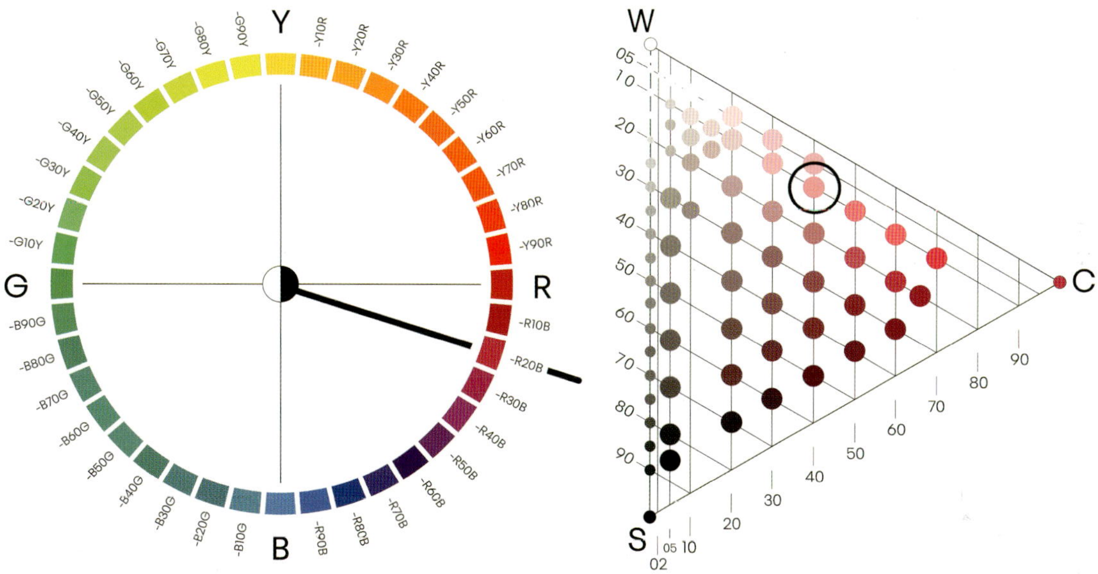

NCS notation: The standard colors of the Swedish national flag are specified using the NCS system.

The yellow is NCS 0580-Y10R, where Y10R is the hue, and the blackness and chromaticness are 5 percent and 80 percent, respectively.

The blue is NCS S-4095-R95B.

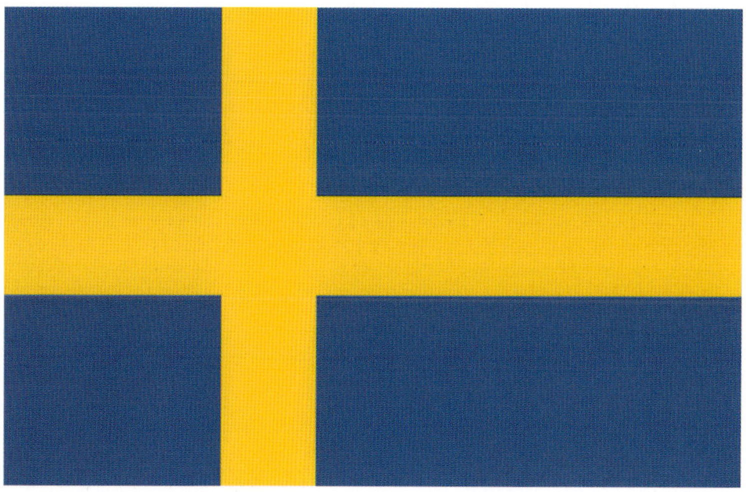

67 NATURE'S LIGHT

Sunlight and moonlight illuminating the natural world

The world around us is illuminated by the sun and the moon. Nature's light shifts in color over the course of the day, in different weather conditions, and from season to season due to the angle of the wavelengths and atmospheric conditions.

The CIE defines light as electromagnetic radiation that is visible, and this is generally taken to be the wavelength range of 360 nm to 780 nm. Note, however, that the precise limits of visibility depend on the viewing conditions, the intensity of the radiation, and the individual.

Light sources can be defined by their spectral power distribution. Natural daylight has a broad, even power distribution, whereas an incandescent light bulb has a distribution that increases markedly toward the longer (redder) wavelengths.

The color temperature of natural daylight can range from the warm light of 1900 Kelvin at sunrise and sunset to a cool 6000 Kelvin at noon.

SEE ALSO:
CIE System
Color Temperature
Electromagnetic Spectrum
Newton's *Opticks*
Rayleigh Scattering

"In nature, light creates the color. In the picture, color creates the light."

—Hans Hofmann

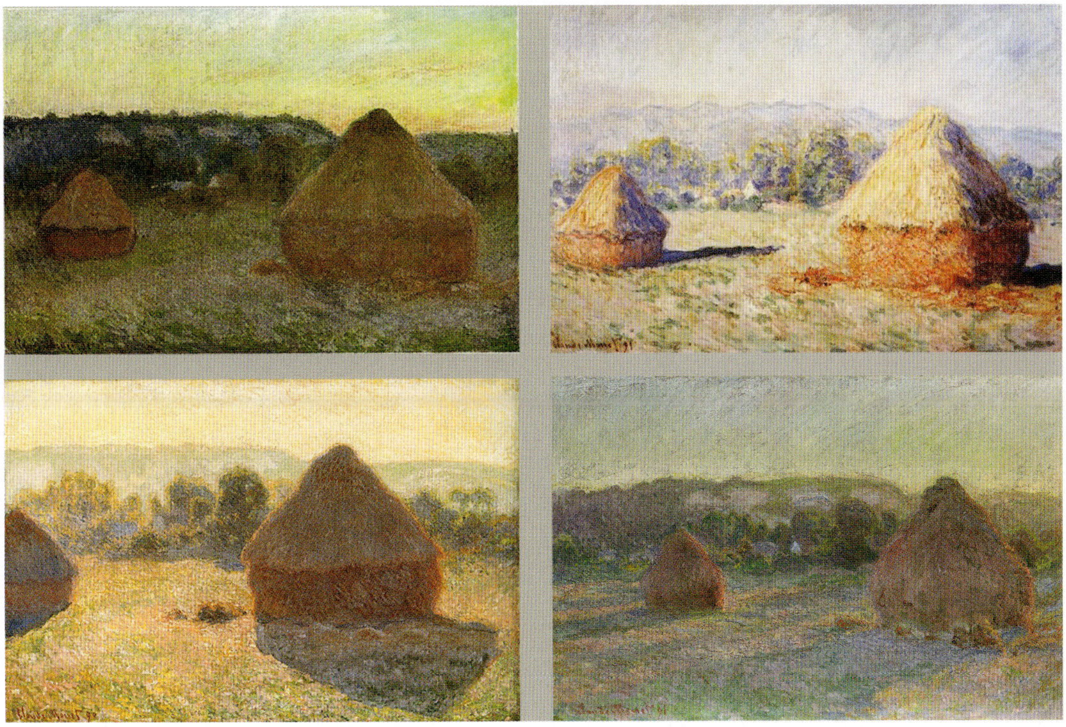

Haystack paintings at different times of the day by Monet.

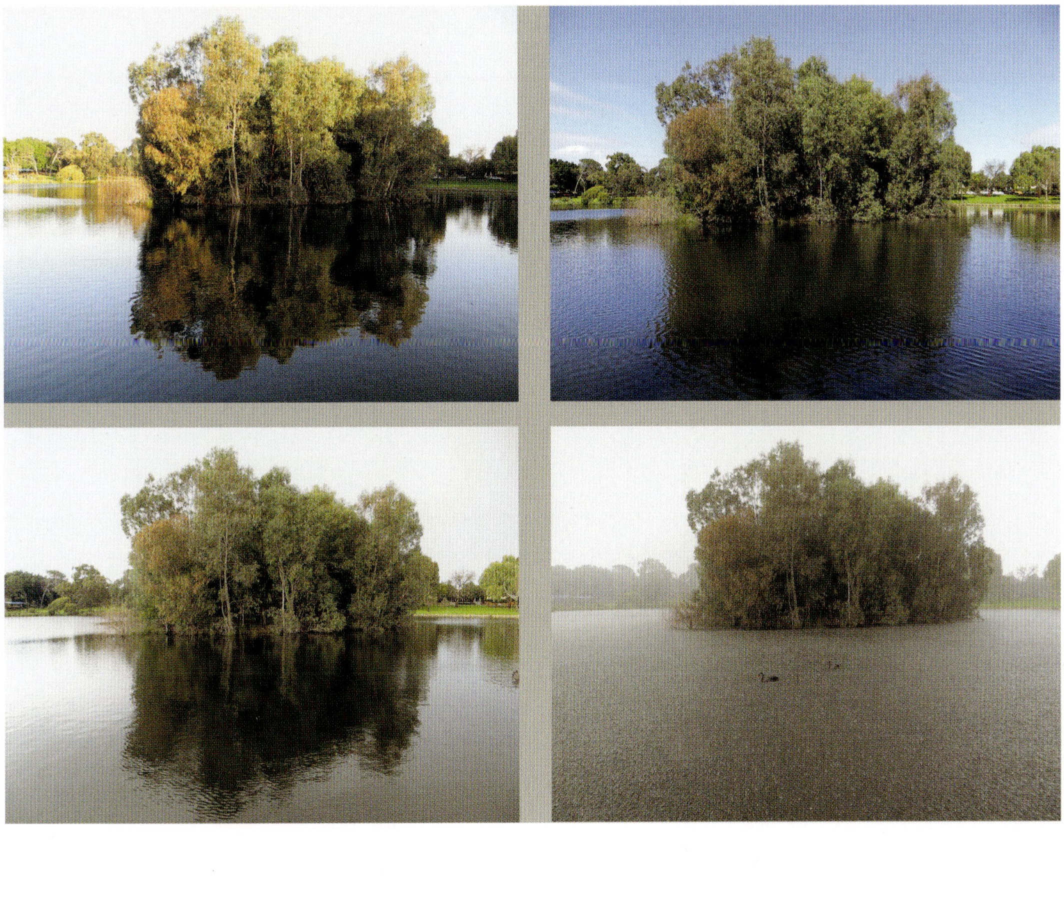

Lake photos at different times of the day and in different weather by Paul Green-Armytage.

68 NEAR NEUTRALS

Low-chroma colors that appear almost gray but have underlying hues

Sometimes called chromatic grays or chromatic neutrals, near-neutral colors are muted colors located close to the neutral axis in 3D color space. The underlying hue, or undertone, determines their position on the hue circle.

Due to their low chroma, the appearance of near neutrals can be strongly affected by lighting and surrounding colors. Side-by-side comparison under the same lighting conditions is necessary to establish the underlying hue.

SEE ALSO:
Lightness
Three Dimensions of Color
Undertone

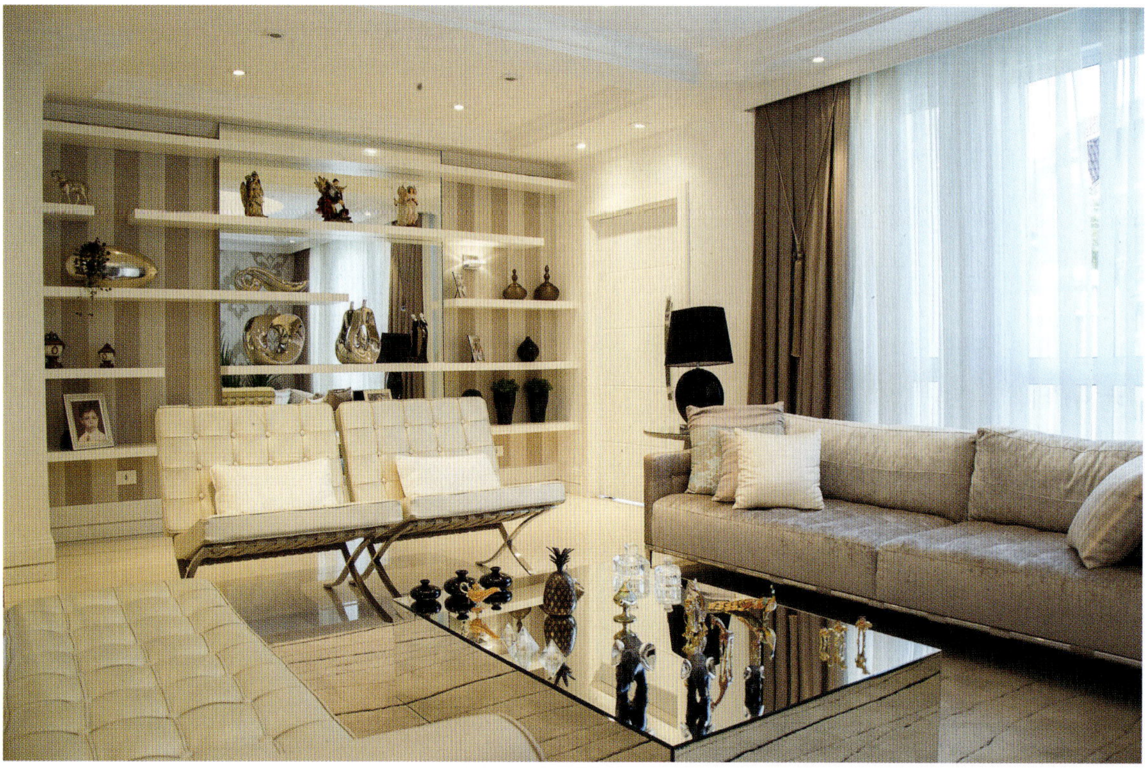

Near neutrals featured in the interior design of a living room.

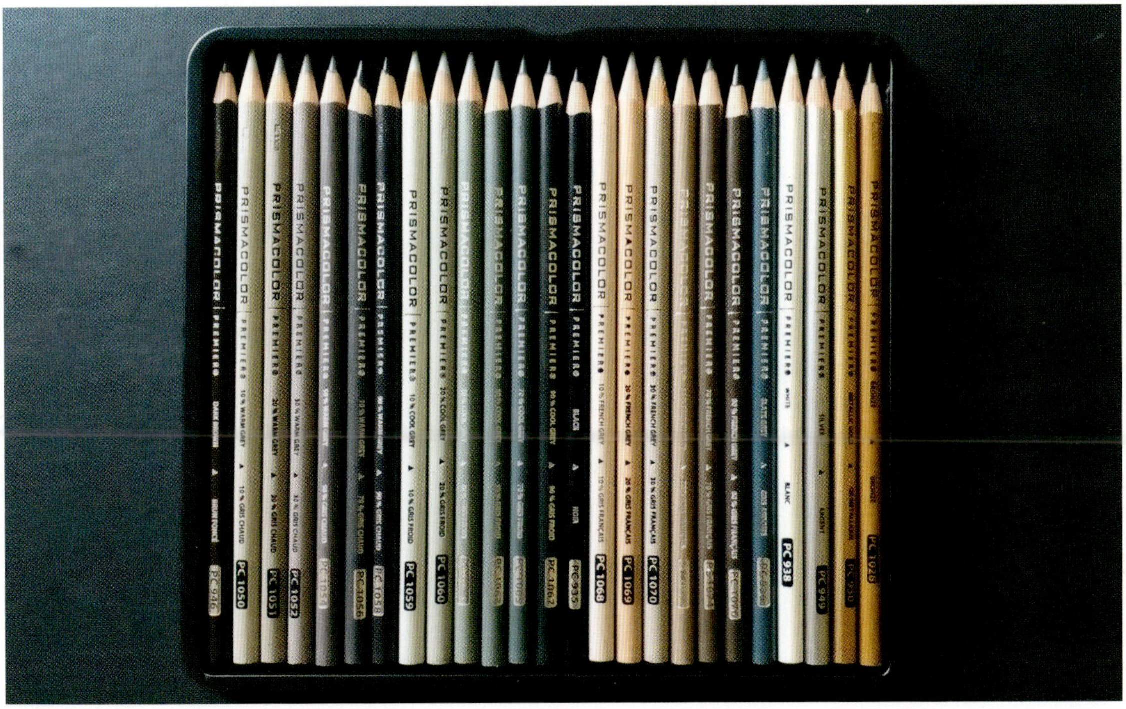

Prismacolor pencils in a set of near-neutrals.

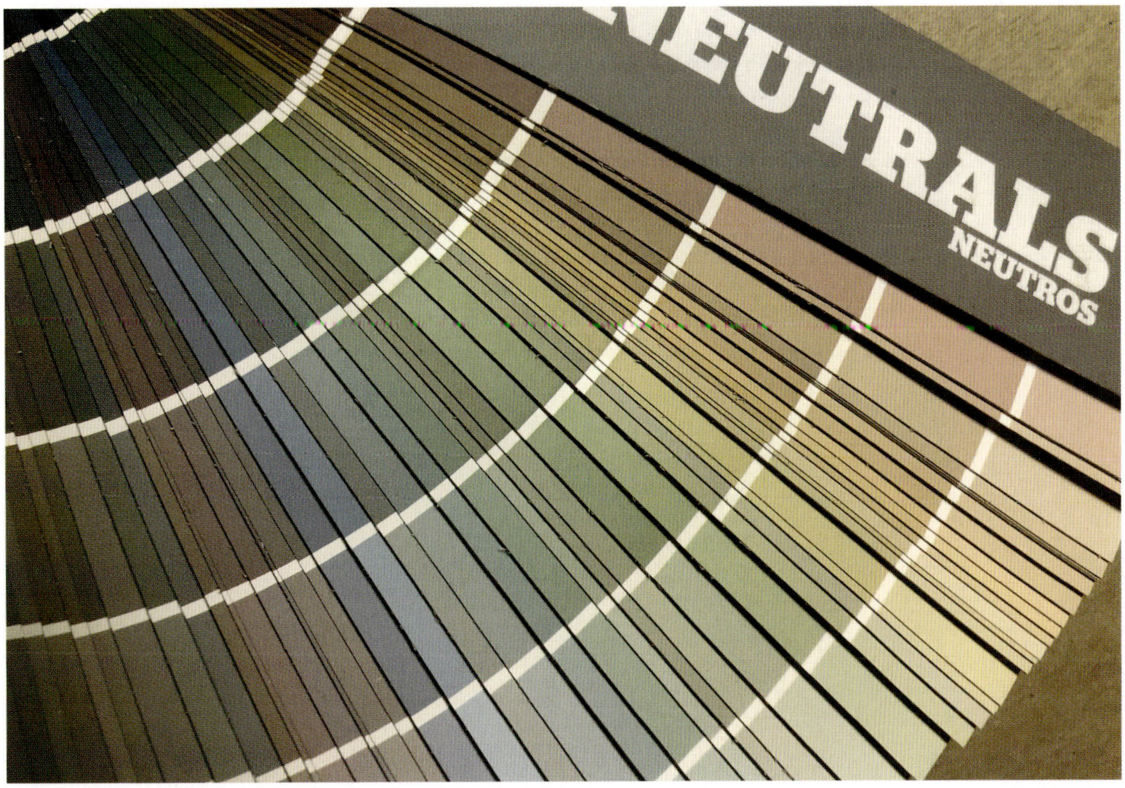

Neutrals paint fan deck from Sherwin-Williams.

69 NEWTON'S *OPTICKS*

Isaac Newton published *Opticks* in 1704 and profoundly changed the way we think about color

SEE ALSO:
Additive Mixture
Electromagnetic Spectrum
Spectral Hues

Isaac Newton (1643–1747) is famous for passing white light through a glass prism and noting that the white light separated into a band of different colors. However, he was not the first to perform this experiment. Prior to Newton it was widely believed that the reason that white light became colored as it traveled through the prism was because it picked up impurities from the glass itself.

Newton carried out two experiments to show that this was not the case. First, he passed white light through a prism and isolated some of the light that emerged (e.g., red light). Then he passed this red light through a second prism and demonstrated that its color was unchanged. In the second experiment, he repeated the procedure to generate a band of colored lights and passed these lights through a second (inverted) prism to reconstitute white light. The realization that when different-colored lights overlapped, they would generate light of a different color—which we now know as additive mixing—transformed how Newton's contemporaries thought about color.

Newton used the term *refrangibility* to describe how some colored light changed direction more than other colors when it entered the prism. We now know that it is the wavelength of light that causes this effect.

Newton also understood that hue perception is circular. He observed that some hues, such as purple and magenta, cannot be observed as single wavelengths.

Newton named the seven colors that can be observed in the visible spectrum: red, orange, yellow, green, blue, indigo, and violet. These are taught using the mnemonic ROYGBIV or, for the British, "Richard of York Gave Battle in Vain." The colors that Newton referred to as blue and indigo would be called cyan and blue, respectively, using contemporary language.

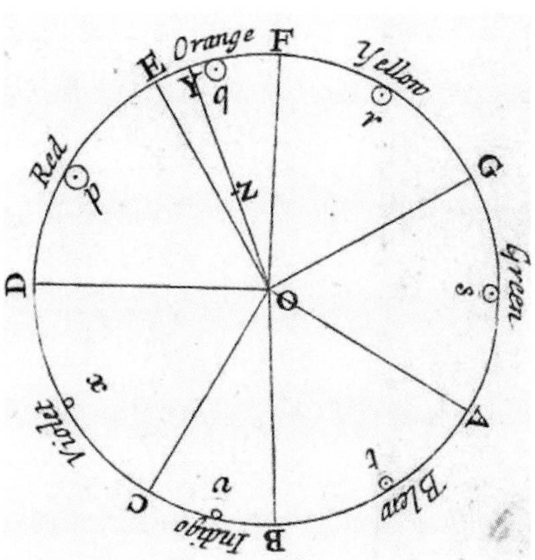

Newton's Color Wheel.

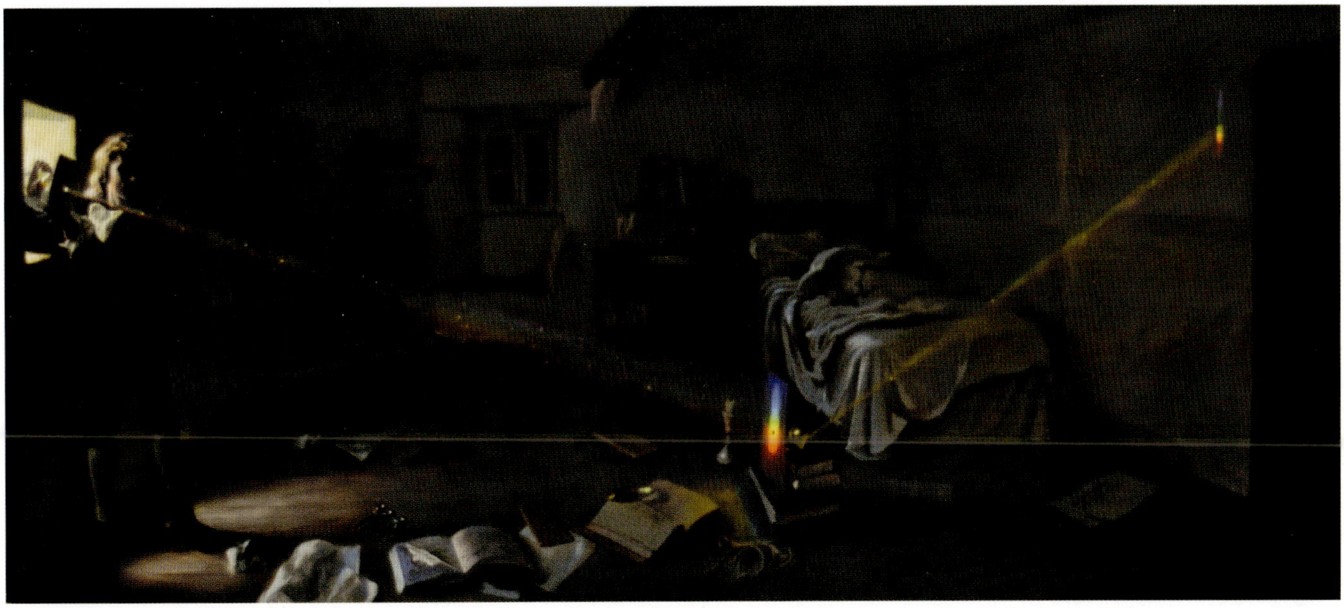

Newton disperses sunlight through a prism (painting by Sascha Grusche).

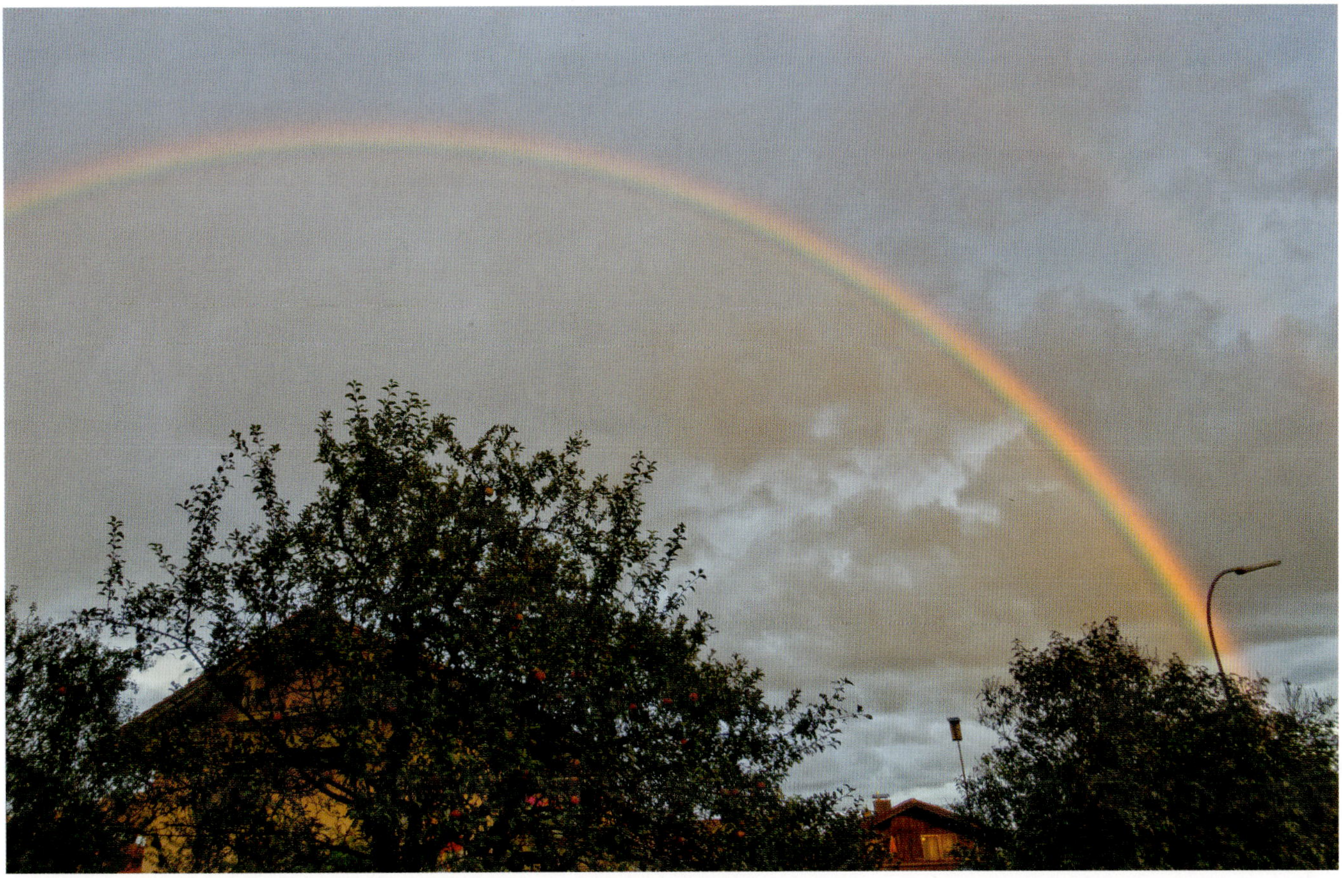

The same effect that Newton observed with a glass prism can also be seen in the rainbow. A rainbow forms because of diffraction of light by water droplets in the atmosphere. The order of the rainbow colors is often taught using the seven colors of Newton's color wheel.

70 OP ART

Abstract art characterized by geometric patterns creating optical illusions

Op ("optical") art artists of the 1950s and 1960s explored the phenomena of visual perception in abstract paintings that intentionally trick the eye by creating the illusion of motion and 3D space using only line and color.

Op art was the focus of *The Responsive Eye* exhibit at Museum of Modern Art in 1965, which included paintings and sculptures by artists such as Victor Vasarely, Richard Anuszkiewicz, Bridget Riley, Frank Stella, Ellsworth Kelly, Kenneth Noland, and Josef Albers.

In the exhibition catalog, curator William C. Seitz wrote, "The eye responds most directly when nonessentials such as freely modulated shape and tone, brush gestures and impasto are absent. These means muffle and distort the purely perceptual effect of lines, areas, and colors. ... Every work chosen for this exhibition, therefore, is entirely abstract."

Although the pinnacle of the movement was in the 1960s, the abstraction and optical effects of op art continue to influence artists and designers to this day.

SEE ALSO:
Advancing and Receding
Albers's *Interaction of Color*
Bauhaus
Flat Color

"The actual basis of color is instability."

—Bridget Riley

"Every form is a base for colour, everycolour is the attribute of a form."

—Victor Vasarely

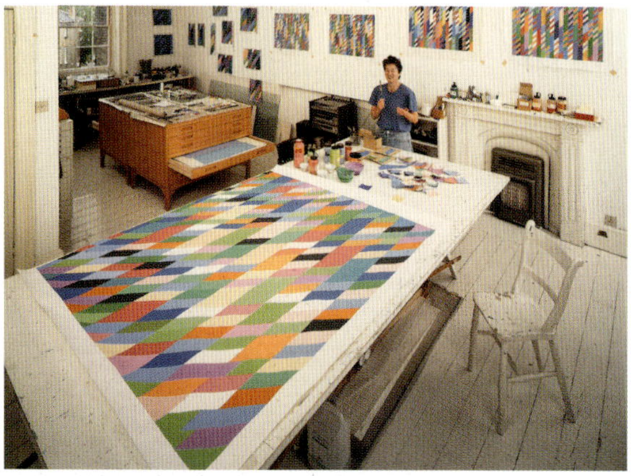

Bridget Riley in her London studio, 1992.

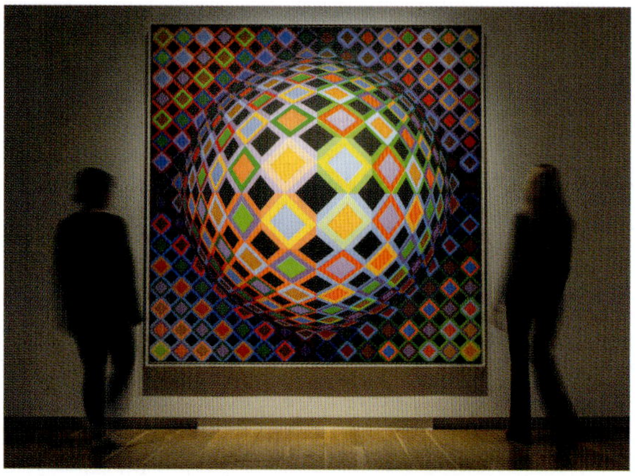

Vega-Multi (1976), painting by Victor Vasarely at the preview of the Mazzoleni gallery exhibit "Einstein in the Sky with Diamonds" in London in 2022.

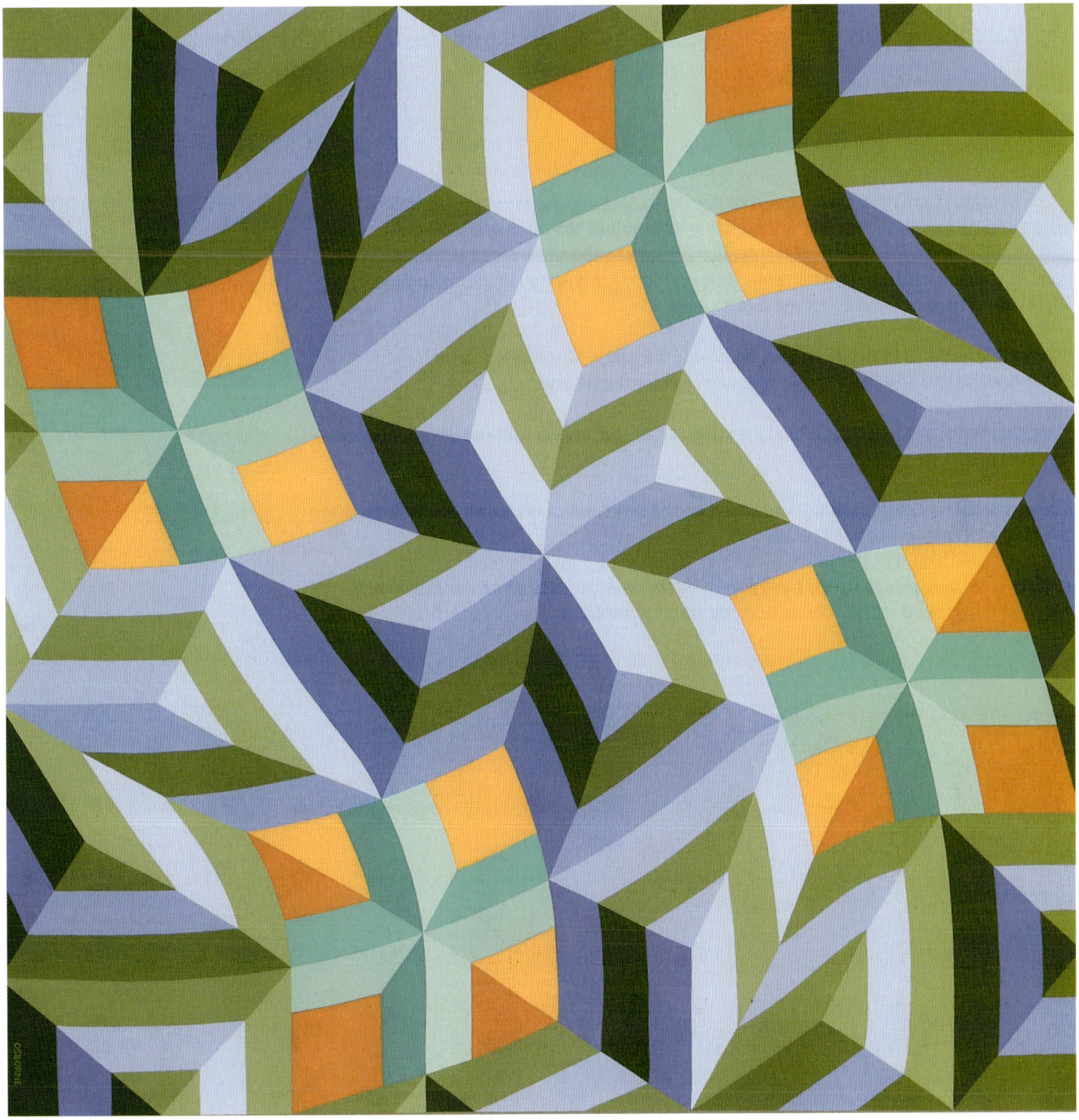

Crossways IX (2015–2020), by Roy Osborne.

71 PALETTES

The particular range of colors used by an artist or designer for a project

In the process of creating a work of art or design—using any medium or materials—artists and designers select a set of colors that determines the appearance and overall gestalt of the work. The palette refers to all the colors in the set, which can include vivid hues, chromatic neutrals, and achromatic colors. Some colors may be more dominant, while others may be used as accent colors.

In physical media such as paints, inks, and dyes, the range of colors available is dependent on the selection of colorants selected for the palette.

In digital media, the palette is more extensive due to the large gamut possible in display technologies.

In environmental design, palettes are based on the selection of materials and include the colors of natural and applied finishes.

Artists and designers often develop a signature palette that makes their work distinct and easily recognizable in any medium.

SEE ALSO:
Color Scheme
Colorants
Colorways
Gamut

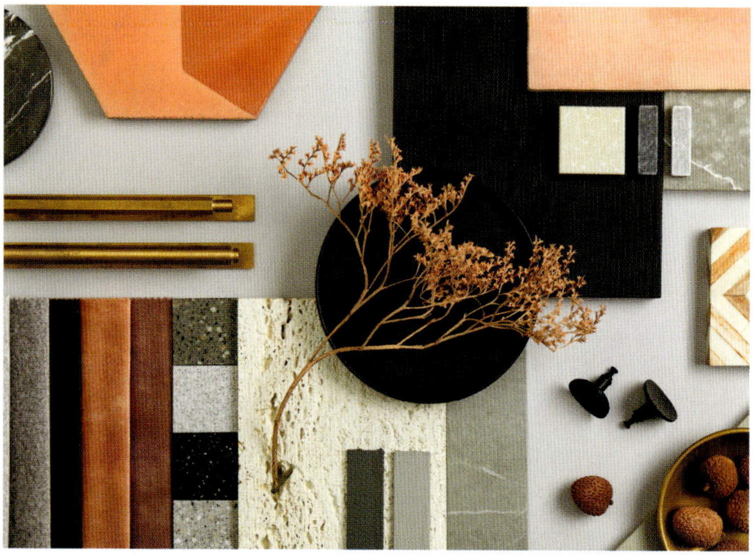

Interiors palette.
A limited palette for interiors that combines materials in natural and applied colors.

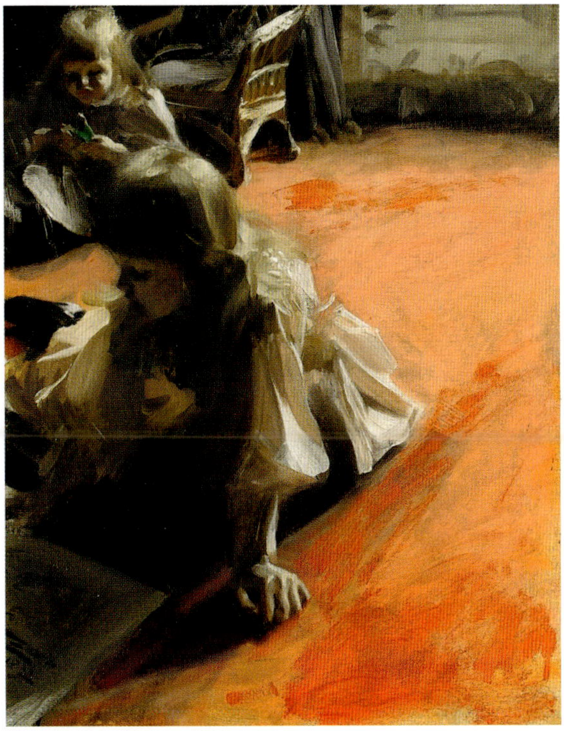

Limited palette.
A Portrait of the Daughters of Ramón Subercaseaux is an 1892 oil painting by Swedish artist Anders Zorn (1860–1920). Zorn restricted himself to a small number of pigments: Vermilion, Ivory Black, Flake White, and Yellow Ochre.

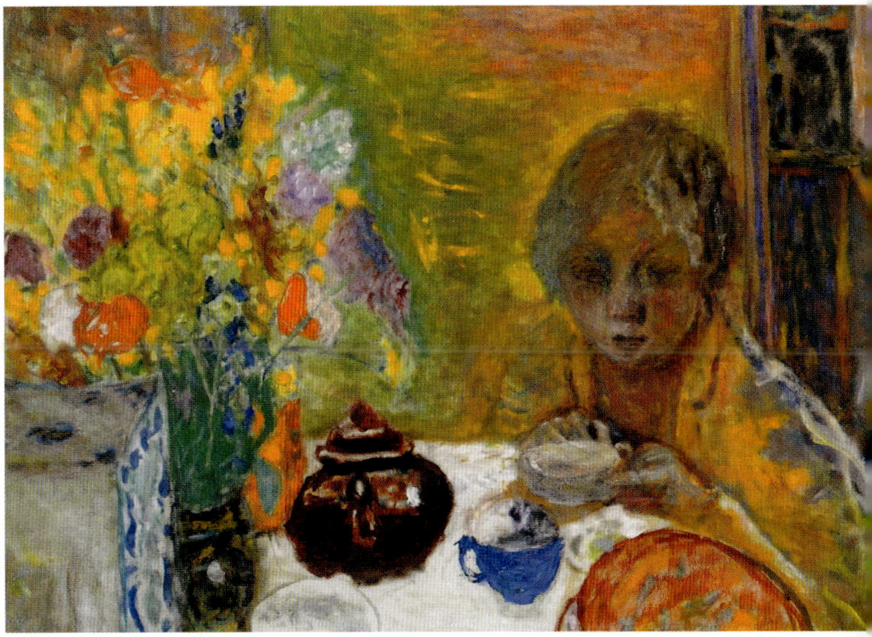

Full palette.
Le Dejeuner (1932), by Pierre Bonnard.

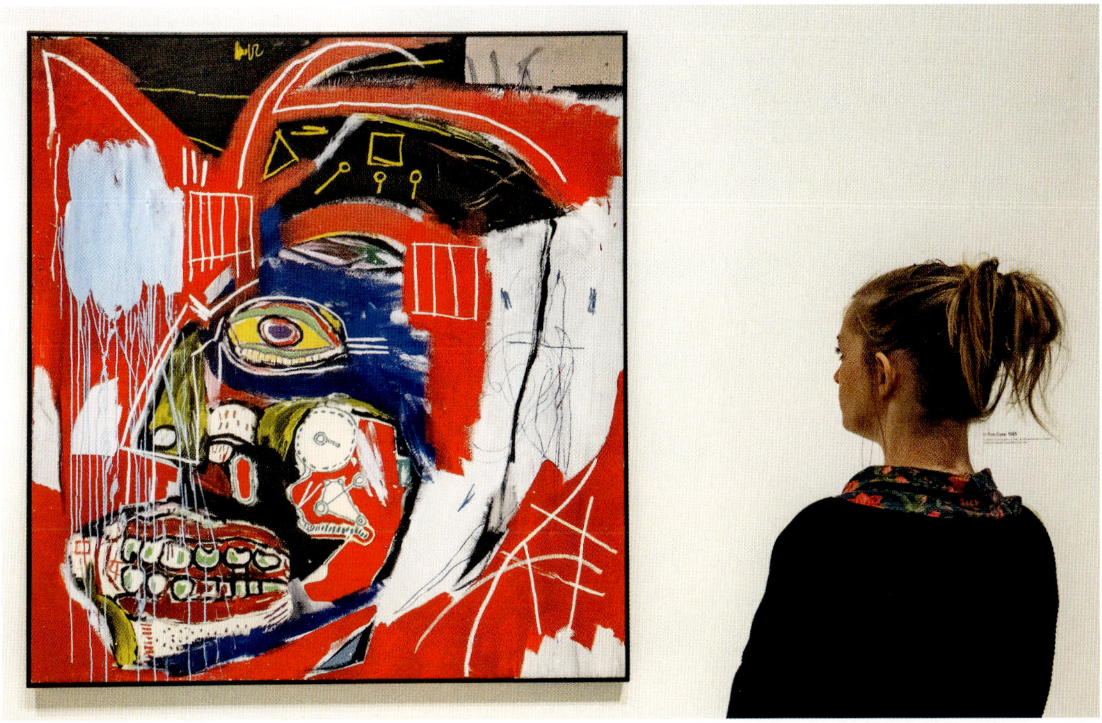

Narrative palette.
In This Case (1983), by Jean-Michel Basquiat.

72 PANTONE

Proprietary color communication tools designed for the accurate specification and communication of color

The Pantone company was formed in 1962 by Lawrence Herbert and is primarily known for its Pantone color communication tools. These tools are available in various forms including books and individual swatches but typically consist of a fan deck where each page contains colored samples that are similar in hue. These books or fan decks are produced to a high degree of reproducibility so that designers can identify a color in their deck and communicate the specific Pantone ID to a client with an identical fan deck.

Originally started as a printer ink company, the Pantone company now intentionally markets to designers. The Pantone Color of the Year announcements started in 2000 and lead the way in trendsetting colors for branding, marketing, and creative industries around the world. The Pantone Color System extends the idea to including a nominal recipe for making the color. For example, there is a Pantone process system where each color in the system has a CMYK recipe that indicates how much of the cyan, magenta, yellow, and black inks should be used to generate that color.

Other similar color communication tools exist, but Pantone is arguably the most widely known. It is used extensively in the graphic arts industries and to a lesser extent in the textile industry.

All physical communication tools suffer from having a limited number of samples. Some systems—such as the Natural Color System and Munsell—have an associated color space and specify colors using a nomenclature that relates to that space. However, the Pantone nomenclature is arbitrary with no way to determine how different colors compare with one another in a 3D color space.

The provision of a printing ink recipe in the original Pantone system has contributed to the widespread use of Pantone as a color communication and specification systems in the printing and graphic arts industries.

SEE ALSO:
CMYK
Color Management

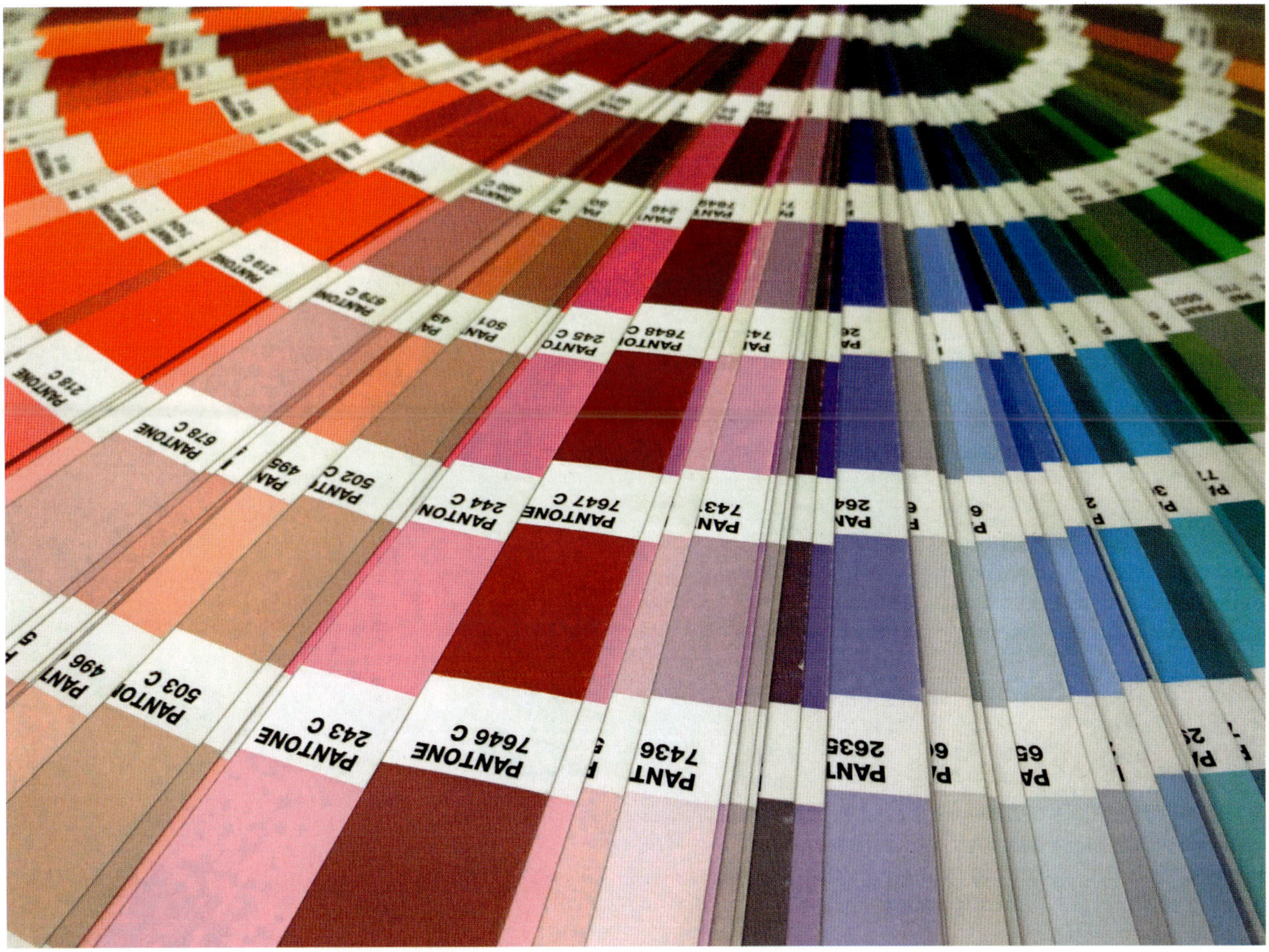

An example of a Pantone fan deck showing a range of different colors.

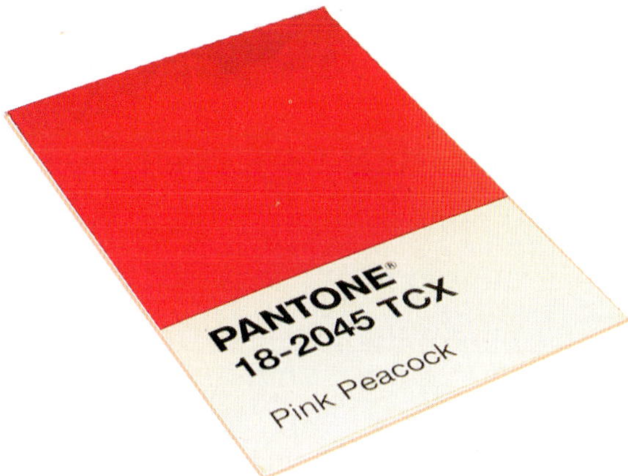

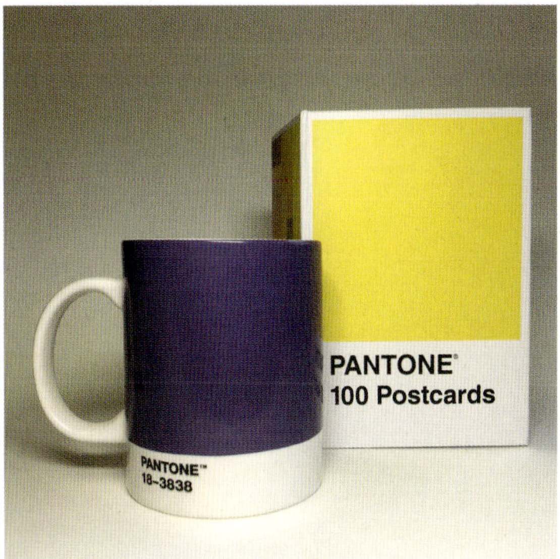

Pantone swatches are a recognizable brand used for color specification as well as product marketing.

73 PARTITIVE MIXTURE

The perception of color mixture that occurs due to spatial or temporal averaging of colors

In addition to the additive mixture of light and the subtractive mixture of paints, inks, and dyes, there is a third type of color mixture known as partitive, optical, or additive averaging.

The pointillist painters explored the effects of partitive mixture using small strokes of paint. The further away you stand, the more the distinct colors of the paint blend together. This technique is an example of spatial averaging.

Weaving is another example of spatial averaging. The distance required for the averaging of the colors is determined by the fineness of the threads. The thinner the threads, the quicker the colors optically mix.

Other examples of spatial averaging are the CMYK (cyan/magenta/yellow/black) printing process, which combines partitive and subtractive mixture, and digital displays that use partitive mixture of RGB (red/green/blue) pixels.

Temporal averaging is best demonstrated by the optical mixtures created by spinning disks. There are many disk designs, the most famous of which were those used by Maxwell in his explorations of color, where the slit in the circle of colored paper allowed for easy adjustment of the proportions.

In additive mixture of light, the result of a color mixture is lighter than the average lightness of the parts. In subtractive mixture, the result is darker than the averaging. In partitive mixture, the lightness of the mixture is closer to the average of the hue, lightness, and chroma.

Partitive mixture results in averaging the attributes of color.

SEE ALSO:
CMYK
Color Management
Maxwell
Pointillism
RGB

A Sunday on La Grande Jatte (1884), by Georges Seurat. Detail of a section in the upper left of the painting with an even finer detail showing the paint strokes.

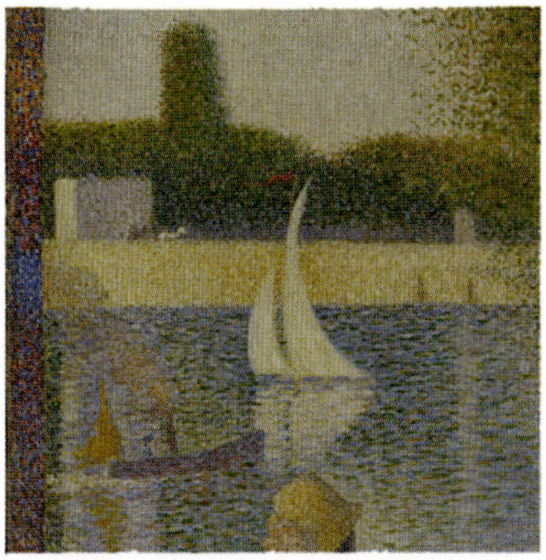

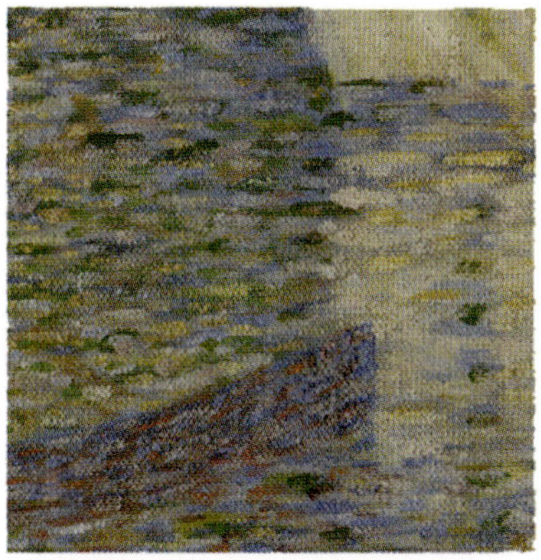

In plain weave, the even distribution of the two colors of the warp and weft optically blend together and appear to be a single solid color with only a small amount of variation.

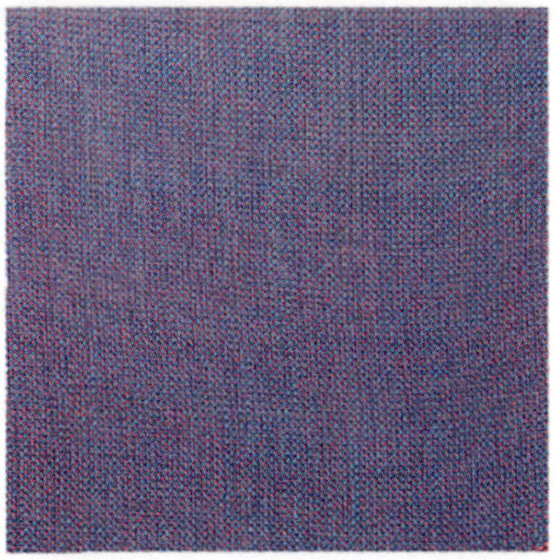

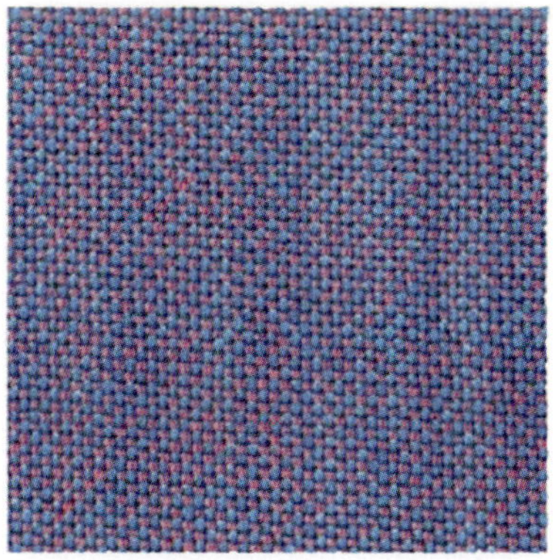

Brand color printed on metallic foil.

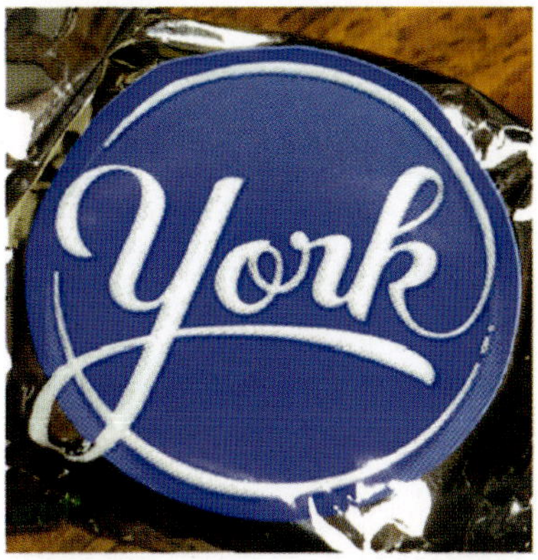

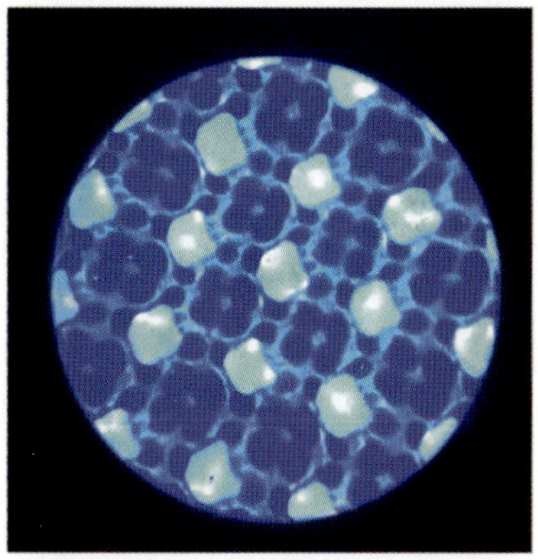

A dark blue color on an LED screen is another example of partitive mixture.

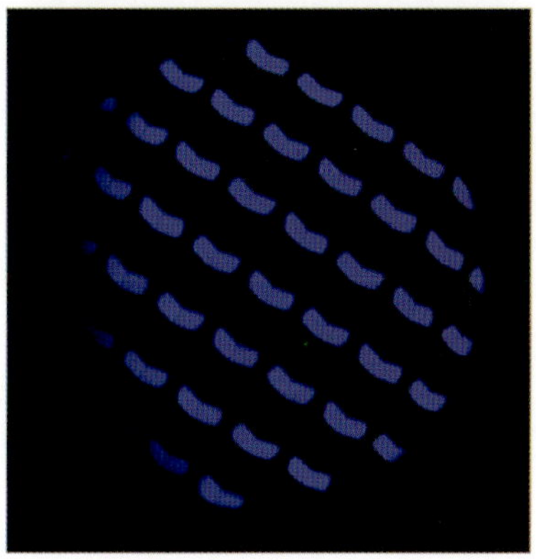

74 PERCEPTION TRIANGLE

The relationship between the light source, the object, and the observer in the perception of color

Generally, we see objects as being colored because of the brain's response to light that is reflected (or transmitted) by these objects. For this reason, the perception triangle—which indicates that light, object, and observer are all important—is traditionally taught. This is important because it reveals the insight that color is not simply a property of an object, although we often speak as if it is (for example, we might say that the bird is red whereas it would be more accurate to say that it looks red).

It is firmly established that the color appearance of an object often changes depending on the quality and quantity of a light source. An object's apparent color may also depend on the properties of the observer (e.g., when someone has limited color vision).

However, the perception triangle somewhat oversimplifies the complexity of color perception because we know that many other factors also contribute to color perception. For example, the color of an object may depend on the colors of surrounding objects (see, for example, Simultaneous Contrast and Bezold Effect) and on the colors that a person was previously looking at (e.g., afterimage colors). It is also possible, of course, to see color by looking at a light source directly.

The perception triangle is a good starting point when teaching about color. Whereas our everyday experience of color would often suggest that color is simply the property of an object, in fact we know that it depends on the lighting and the observer, in addition to many other factors including the context effects such as the surround.

SEE ALSO:
Bezold Effects
Context
Electromagnetic Spectrum
Human Visual System
Nature's Light
Simultaneous Contrast

FURTHER READING

Vision and Art: The Biology of Seeing (2014), by Margaret Livingstone

Color, Light, Sight, Sense (1985), by Moritz Zwimpfer

"When we see colors, processes are involved in this sensory experience which take place in three different areas, one after the other:

1-Physical events outside the human body (light)
2-Reaction of the visual organs to light stimulus
3-Occurrence of the visual experience in the brain."

Text and graphic by Moritz Zwimpfer.

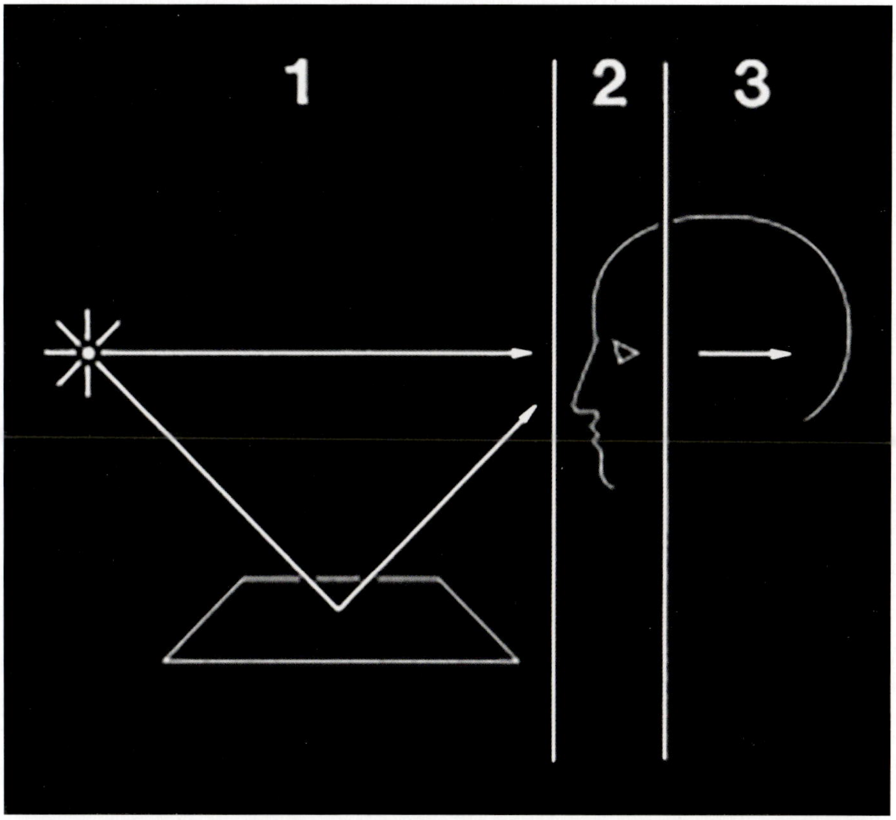

This illusion by the psychologist Akiyoshi Kitaoka plays tricks with our perceptual system. The strawberries appear to be reddish even though the pixels are gray.

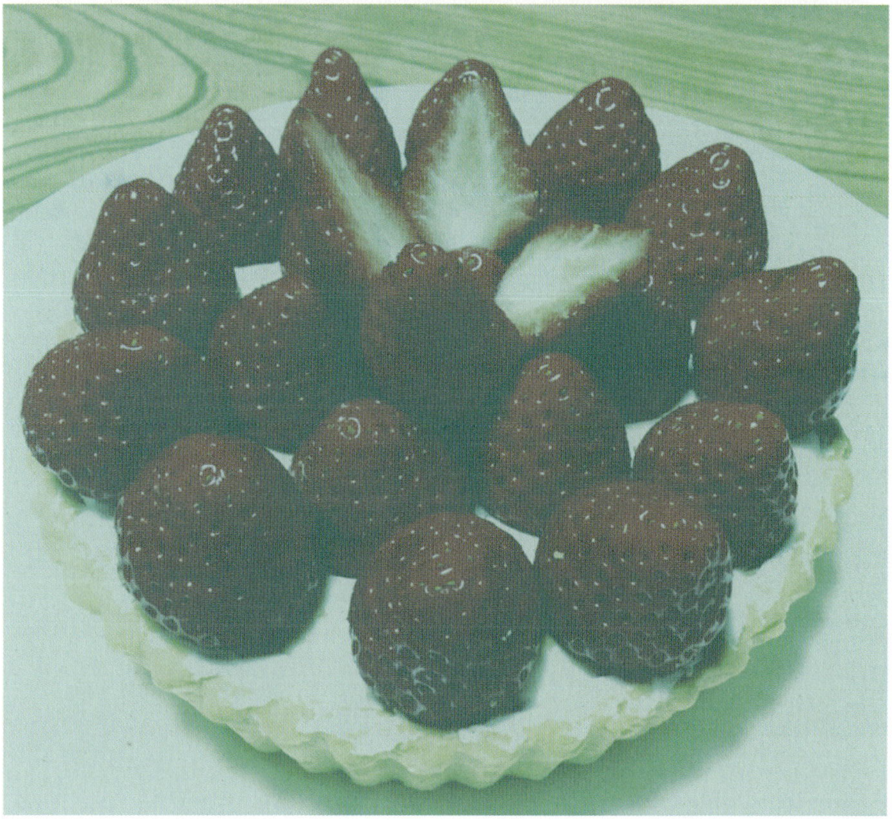

75 PERMANENCE

The ability of colorants to stay colorfast when exposed to light and heat

Most manufactured materials are colored because of the application of colorants that selectively absorb light. Over time, exposure to heat or light can cause the colorant molecules to break down, and this destroys the chromophore—that part of the molecule that absorbs light. This can lead to pigments or dyes that are said to be "fugitive." They will fade over time.

The selection of colorants that give permanence is often an important consideration when choosing colorants for a particular application. Colorants that are applied to clothing, for example, need to be washfast, meaning that they remain permanent under the hot and wet conditions under which clothes are washed. Colorants for products that are used outside, or for outside artwork, need to be chosen so that they have high lightfastness.

Many famous pieces of art were made using fugitive dyes and pigments, and the original colors have faded. Manufacturers now label the pigments with a lightfastness rating. The two main scales to measure lightfastness are the Blue Wool Scale and the ASTM scale. The Blue Wool Scale operates from one to eight, one being extremely poor lightfastness and eight being the absolute maximum lightfastness possible.

SEE ALSO:
Chemistry of Chromophores
Chromophobia
Colorants

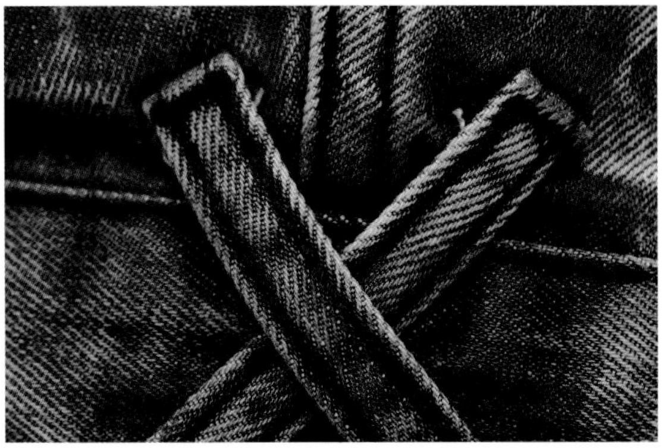

In addition to light and wash fastness, rub fastness is also a concern for certain products. However, poor rub fastness can sometimes produce favorable aesthetic effects.

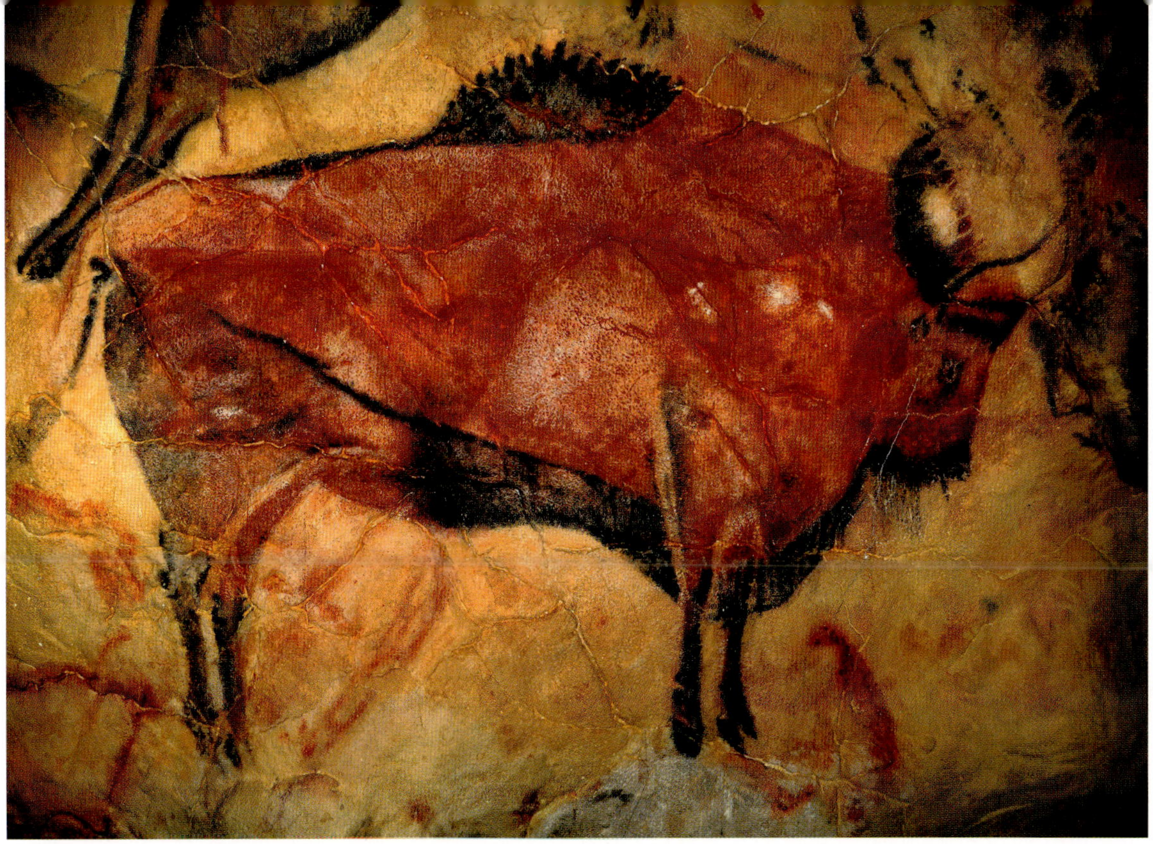

Although the colorants used were probably quite fugitive, the lack of exposure to light or heat in these cave paintings from Altamira in Spain have lasted for more than thirty thousand years.

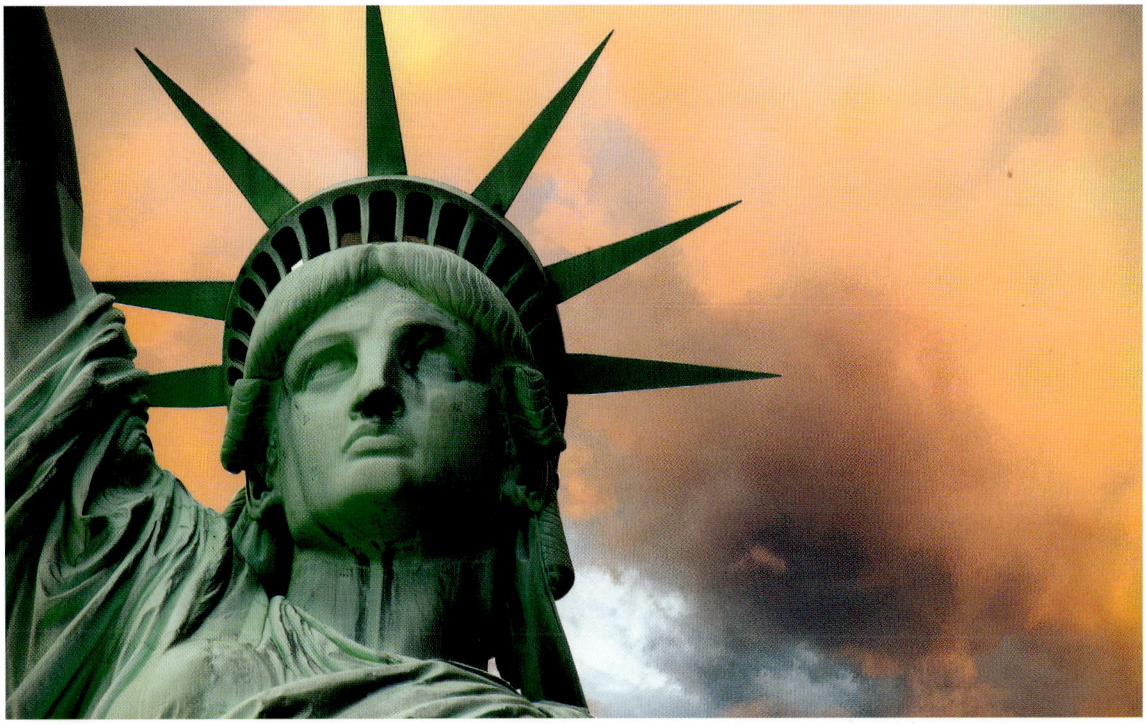

Weathering can sometimes create permanence in color. The Statue of Liberty (1886) is made of copper and was originally brown. However, exposure of the copper to the elements and the polluted air resulted in a reaction that oxidized the copper and produced the iconic green color by the early twentieth century.

76 POINTILLISM

A technique in painting whereby small, distinct dots of color are applied to form an image

Pointillism was a new method of painting that emerged toward the end of the nineteenth century and is primarily associated with the artists Georges Seurat and Paul Signac. Whereas impressionism was an attempt by artists to represent their subjective responses, pointillism was a post-impressionist movement that involved a much more technical approach.

The artists Van Gogh, Pissarro, and Kandinsky also experimented with this technique. When different colors of paint are mixed, there is an inherent loss in chroma that results in some dullness in the mixed colors. Pointillists avoided this dulling of the mixtures by placing dots of unmixed paint on the canvas close to one another. The idea was that these separate dots of color would then be blended by the eye to create more striking colors. For these reasons pointillist paintings often appear brighter than traditional paintings using paints that have been blended.

Pointillism is also referred to as divisionism by some, though there is a distinction. Whereas pointillist paintings are primarily dots of paint, divisionist paintings are short strokes of paint.

The method by which modern devices mix red, green, and blue light to create colored emissive displays is based on a similar principle albeit on a smaller scale so that the individual dots cannot be seen by the naked eye.

SEE ALSO:
Impressionism
Partitive Mixture

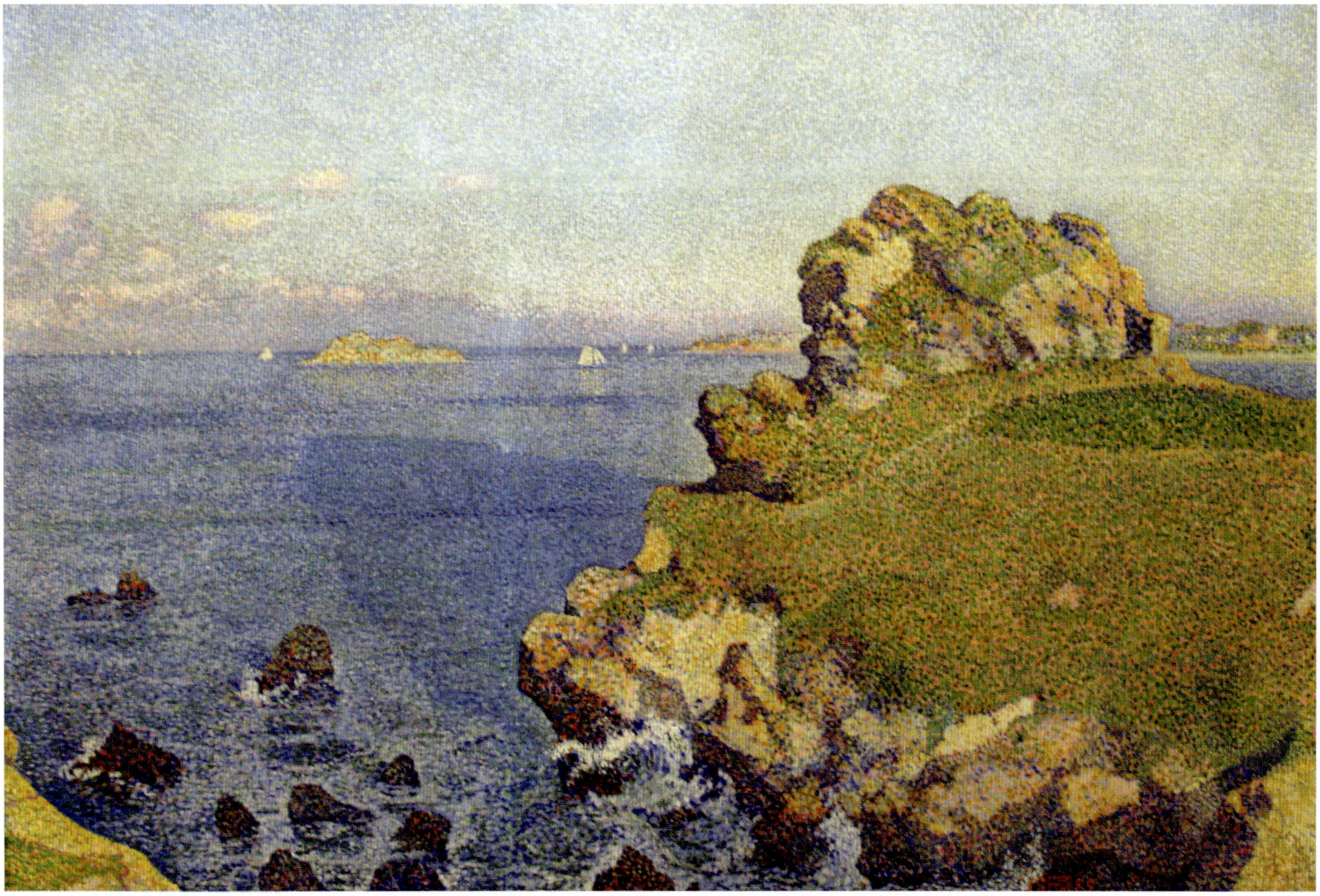

The 'Per-Kiridy' at High Tide (1889), by Théo van Rysselberghe.

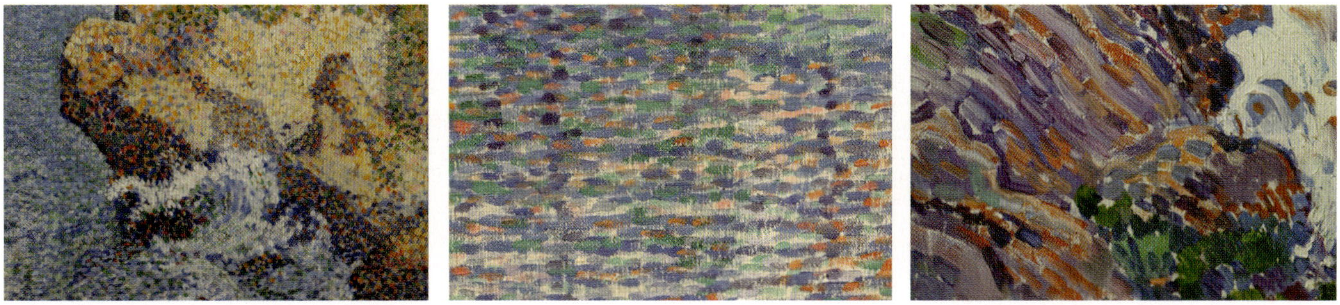

Details from three Théo van Rysselberghe paintings illustrating three different periods of his work: pointillism (1889), divisionism (1899), and fauvist (1905).

77 PRIMARY COLORS

A set of colored lights or colorants that can be combined to generate a range of different colors

Although it is sometimes stated that a set of three color primaries can be mixed together to create any color, it is a fact that this is not possible. It is possible to create any hue, but there is inevitable loss of chroma or saturation when mixing colorants or colored lights, respectively.

The largest range (or gamut) of colors that can be created with three light primaries occurs with red, green, and blue lights. Consequently, most emissive devices (computer displays, phone displays, etc.) use red, green, and blue primaries. However, there is some variability in the actual choice of red, green, and blue between different devices and manufacturers, and this is one of the reasons for lack of color fidelity in imaging systems.

Although red, yellow, and blue are still sometimes taught as the optimal subtractive primaries, this is an outdated concept and should no longer be taught. Optimal subtractive primaries should be red-absorbing (cyan), green-absorbing (magenta), and blue-absorbing (yellow). Red and blue pigments or dyes are poor choices as primaries because their absorption spectra are too broad. There is no reason why exactly three primaries should be used although at least three primaries are required in order to generate all hues. In printing, for example, a four-primary system consisting of cyan, magenta, yellow, and black is ubiquitous.

SEE ALSO:
Additive Mixture
CMYK
Gamuts
Munsell System
RGB
Subtractive Mixture

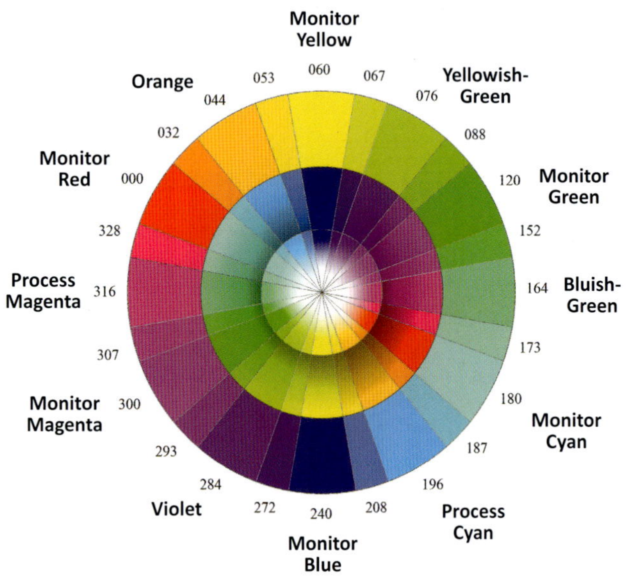

DEVICE DEPENDENT PRIMARY COLORS

It is often claimed that the digital primaries of the monitor (RGB) are the complements of the process primaries of the printer (CMY) and vice versa. Although this is a popular concept it is not accurate. broadly representative of the physical colorants employed for printing, as distinct from the secondary colors of the RGB monitor colors, often called cyan and magenta, which are distinctly greener and more purple, respectively.

Note that because hue angle (H) is defined using nonlinear RGB, opposite hue angles are not exact additive complementaries except on the R-Cyan, G-Magenta, and B-Yellow axes.

Composition C (No. III) with Red, Yellow and Blue, 1935.
Piet Mondrian

The traditional paint primaries of Red, Yellow and Blue were a signature of the painter Mondrian.

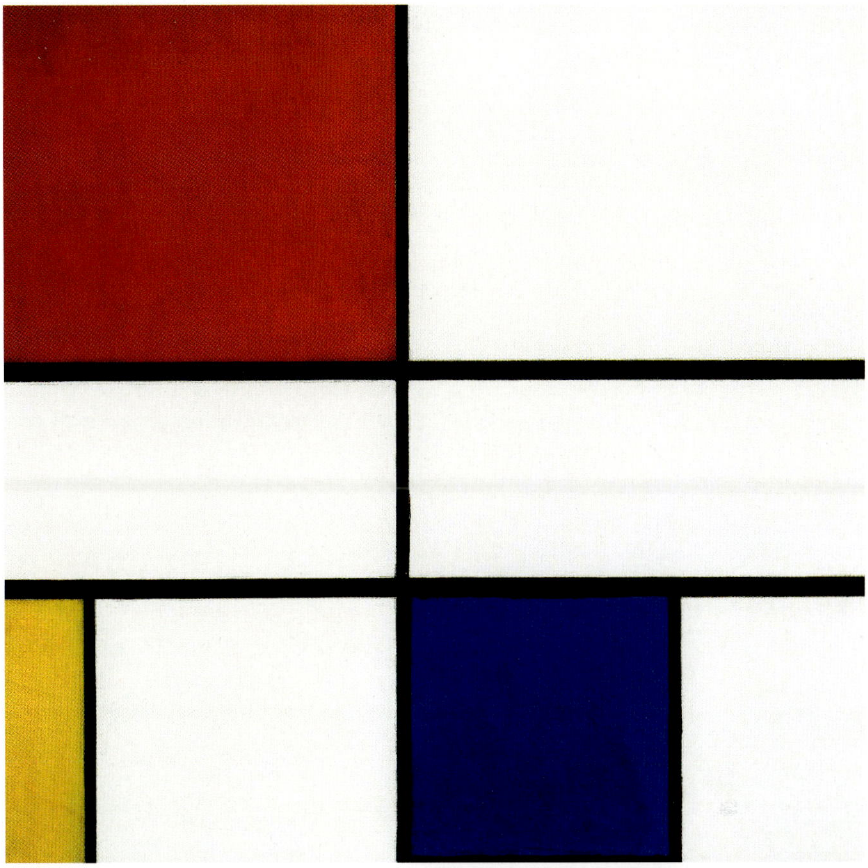

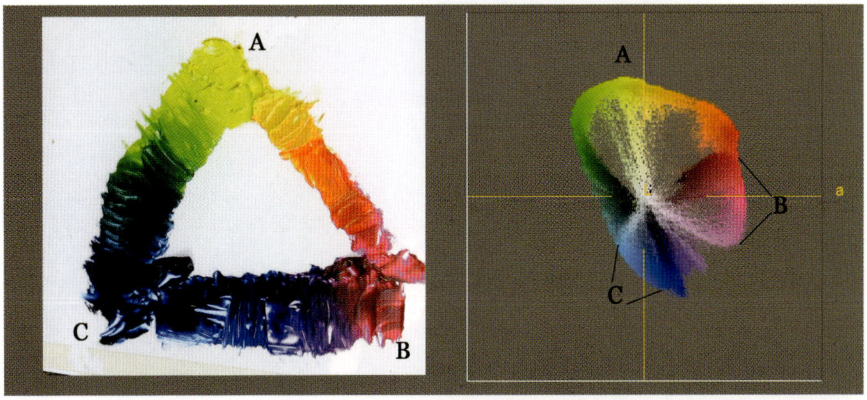

Mixtures of (A) Lemon Yellow, (B) Quinacridone Magenta, and (C) Phthalocyanine Blue (Green Shade) oil paints.

Photographed colors in a*b* plane of L*a*b*space. Each pair of paints mixes along a line that is convex outwards, keeping relatively high in chroma.

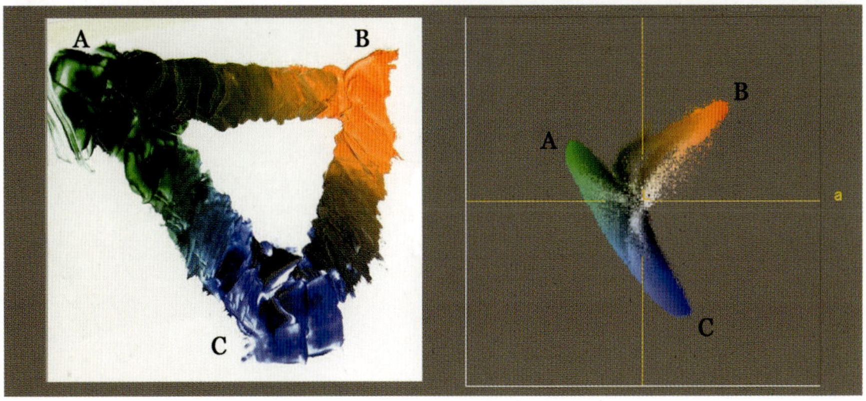

Mixtures of (A) Phthalocyanine Green (Yellow Shade), (B) Cadmium Orange, and (C) Ultramarine Blue oil paints.

Photographed colors in a*b* plane of L*a*b*space. Colors on each mixture line move away from high chroma.

78 RAYLEIGH SCATTERING

The scattering of light by the molecules and particles in air

Matter interacts with light in several fundamental ways. Light may be absorbed, transmitted, or scattered. When light is scattered due to the interaction with material, the light changes direction. When light interacts with particles that are small (up to about a tenth of the wavelength of light), the scattering that occurs is referred to as Rayleigh scattering. This is distinct from scattering (known as Mie scattering) that occurs with larger particles, such as pigment particles in a paint.

Rayleigh scattering was named after the nineteenth-century physicist Lord Rayleigh (1842–1919) and most commonly occurs in gases where the particles or molecules are sufficiently small. The reason that the sky is blue is because of Rayleigh scattering of light by the atmosphere. Rayleigh scattering affects short-wavelength light much more than long-wavelength light, and therefore it is blue light from the sun that is scattered by the atmosphere and travels toward our eyes.

Rayleigh scattering also explains red and yellow appearances of the sky as we look toward a sunrise or sunset. In this case, the light from the sun is traveling toward our eyes, but it is the short-wavelength light that is removed from the light that reaches us because of scattering.

SEE ALSO:
Atmospheric Perspective
Electromagnetic Spectrum
Nature's Light

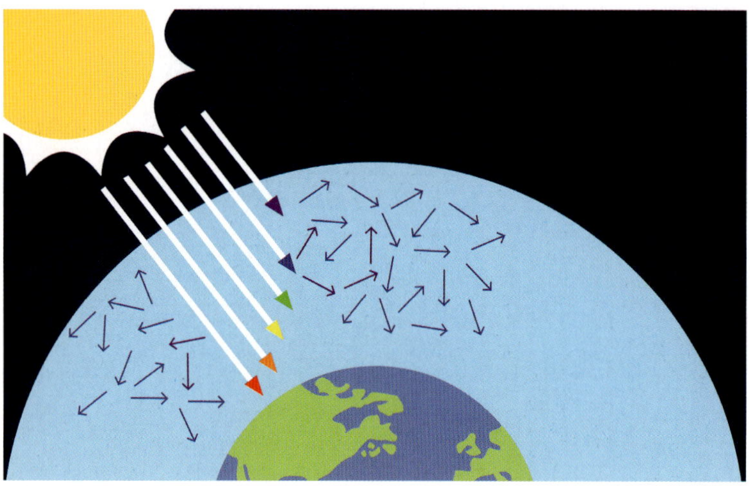

The short wavelengths of light are scattered by the atmosphere, which results in blue skies.

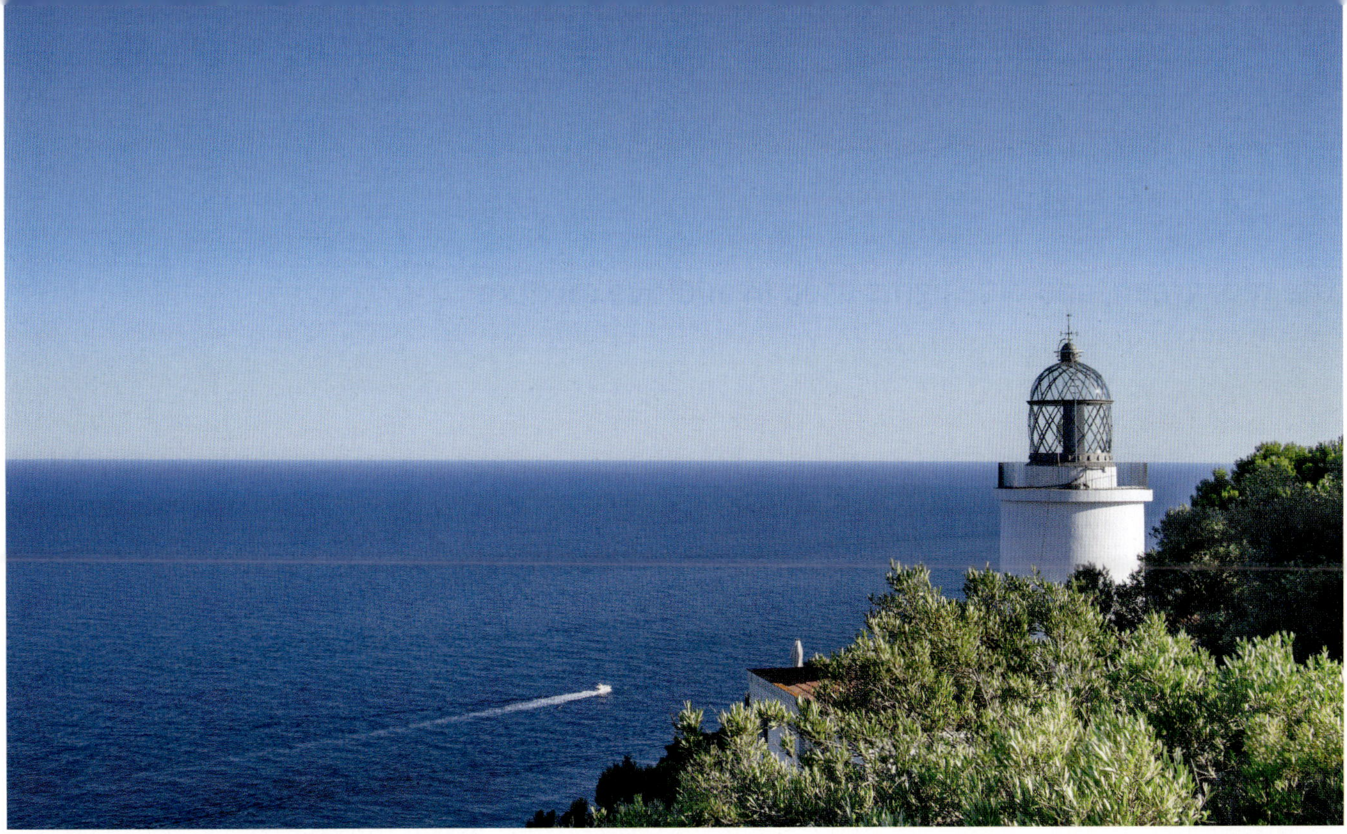

Rayleigh scattering is responsible for the blue color of the sky. The shorter wavelengths of light from the sun are deflected by particles in the atmosphere and reach our eyes. The color of the ocean is blue because it reflects the color of the sky and because longer wavelengths of light are absorbed more strongly than shorter wavelengths by water.

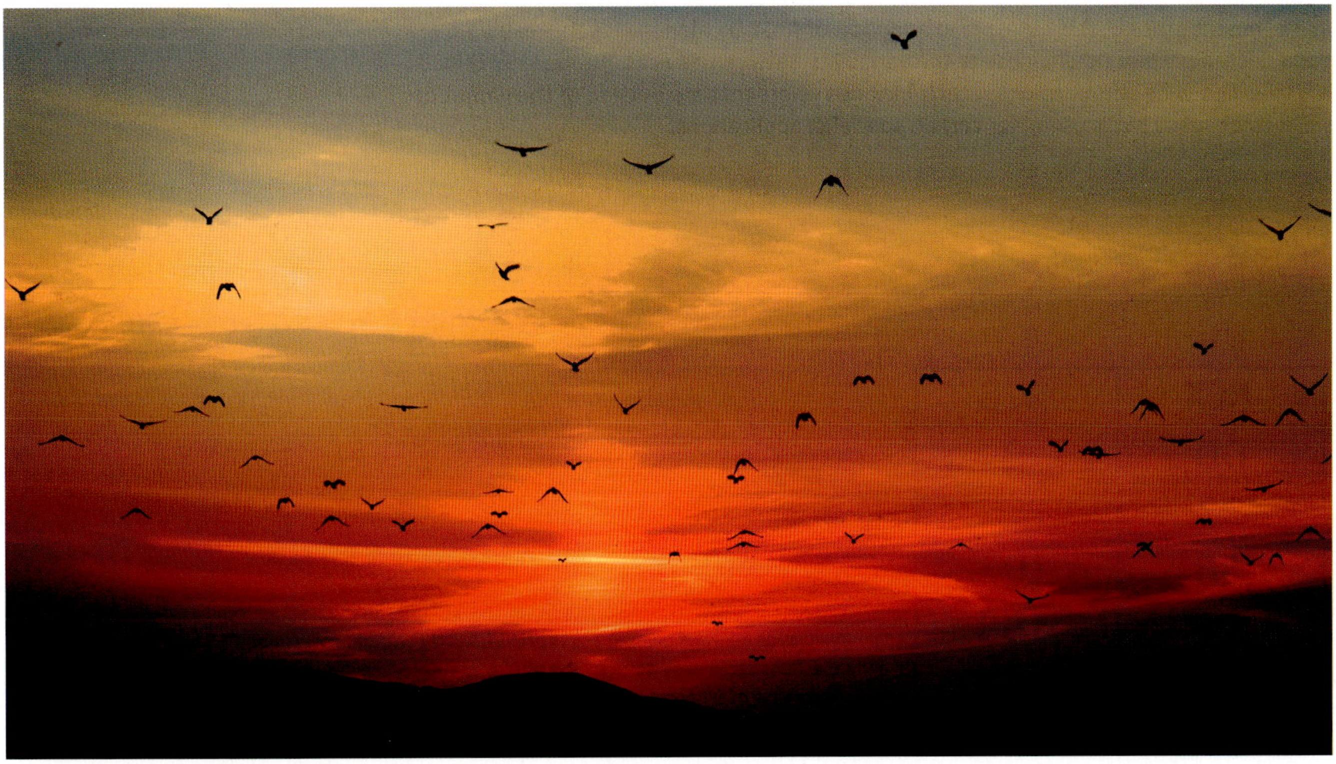

The same process of Rayleigh scattering that causes the sky to be blue can produce red and yellow colors at sunrise and sunset.

79 RGB

The red, green, and blue lights used in additive mixture

In the modern digital world RGB (red/green/blue) specification of color is ubiquitous. However, there is no single universal RGB standard. In most digital systems, a color is represented by 256 levels of each RGB, which leads to about sixteen million RGB combinations. Each RGB value is an integer in the range 0–255. This level of precision is more than sufficient for most consumer applications, although some specialist displays and cameras allow a greater bit of depth.

There is wide variability in the color primaries used by different devices; this means that RGB is usually device dependent. If we display the same RGB values on two different displays, we will probably display two different colors. Color management is the process of working to compensate for this device dependency to achieve color fidelity.

Various standard RGB color spaces exist including Adobe (1998) RGB and sRGB. The sRGB space is particularly important in modern digital imaging systems. Many emissive displays have primaries that are close to the sRGB standard, and many cameras produce RGB values that are similarly close to sRGB. In the absence of a more sophisticated color management process, the widespread adoption of sRGB by manufacturers enables a good degree of color fidelity despite the variability between devices. Adobe (1998) RGB is a so-called wide-gamut color space. It includes colors that are outside of the gamut of sRGB color space but is useful for certain specialist applications.

SEE ALSO:
Additive Mixture
Color Management

HEX	RGB
00	0
33	51
66	102
99	153
CC	204
FF	255

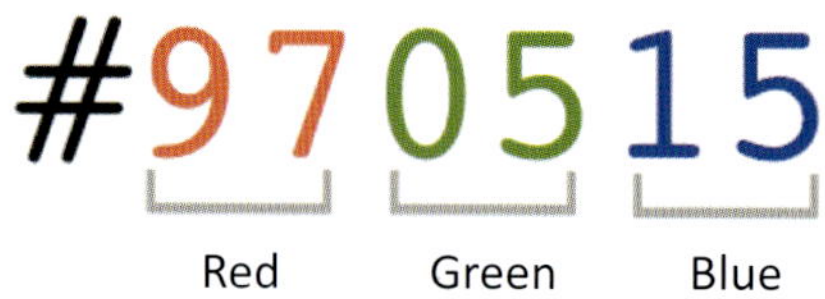

Hex color is code for RGB. In this system the 0–255 decimal values of each RGB value are represented by two characters in the hexadecimal system. In the above example, the hexadecimal red value of 97 corresponds to 151 in decimal (9*16 + 7). The advantage of this system is that every color is represented by only six characters.

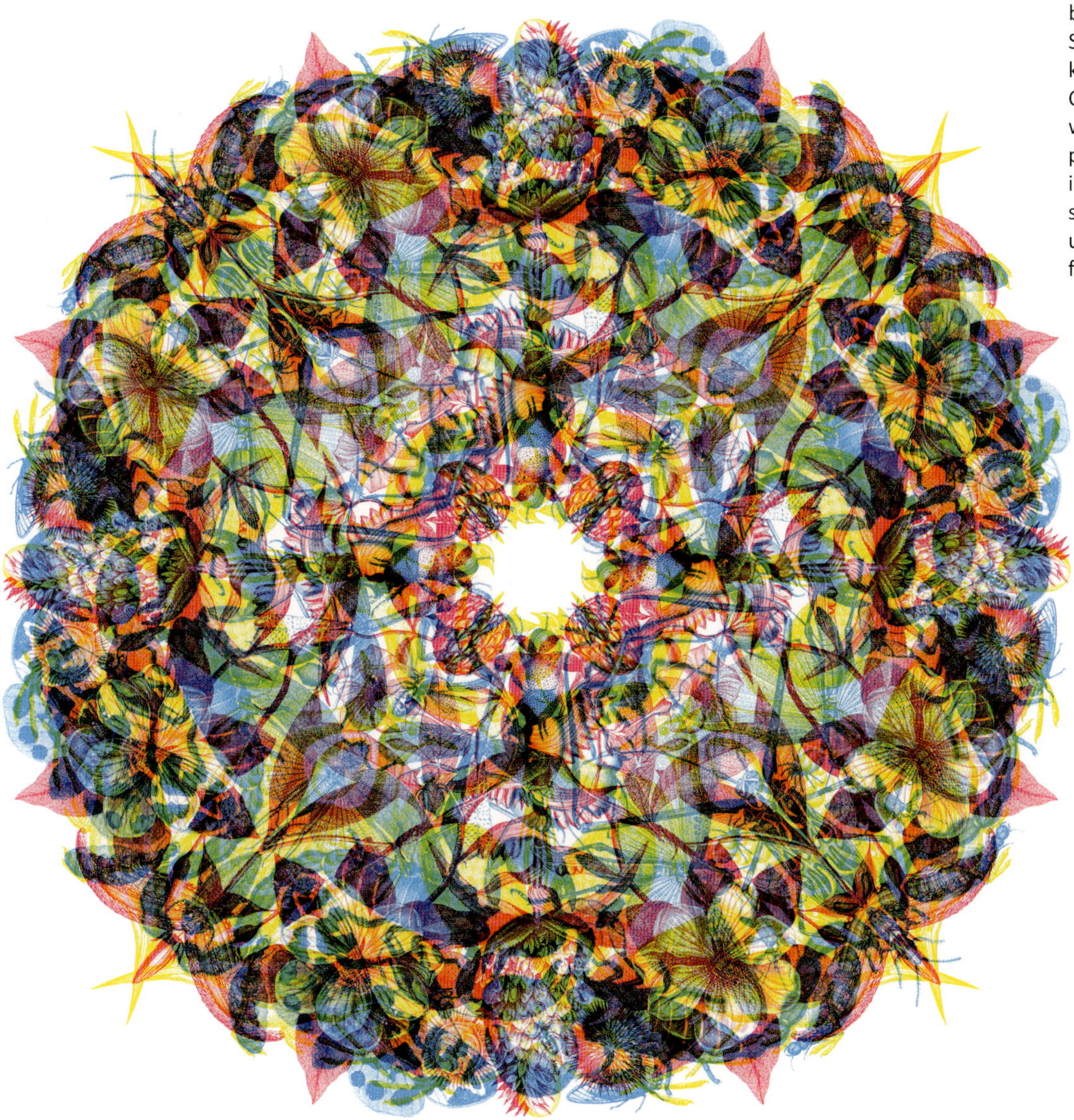

Rosone N.3 (2010), by Francesco Rugi and Silvia Quintanilla known collectively as Carnovsky. Designs for wallpaper and other products are printed in layers of CMY which separate when viewed under RGB lights or filters.

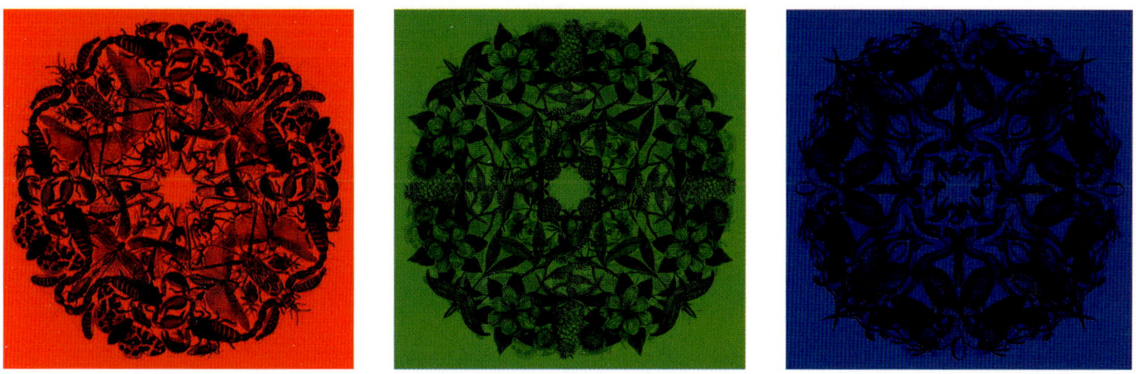

80 SAFETY COLORS

Standardized colors used to communicate levels of safety

The consistent use of color can enable us to identify hazards quickly and reliably. The American National Standards Institute (ANSI) 2535 has established rules for what different colors mean:

- Red = fire protection, danger of injury or death, and emergency stop
- Orange = moderate risk of injury
- Yellow = minor risk of injury and caution statements
- Green = safety equipment and first-aid equipment

Fluorescent yellow and orange colors are also used extensively for clothing in a safety context because of their high visibility. Extremely bright orange and yellow colors can be generated by using fluorescent dyestuffs. Fluorescence is where a material absorbs light at certain wavelengths and then re-emits the light at a longer wavelength, and this can increase the intensity of the light emitted in the orange or yellow region of the spectrum. Although fluorescence can also occur for other colors, fluorescent orange and yellow are used in a safety context because of their naturally high lightness values, which increases their visibility.

An important use of colors in safety is the use of red for stop and green for go in traffic lights. These colors are also used in similar ways with railway signals, shipping, and aeronautics. These safety associations are ubiquitous across the globe.

SEE ALSO:
Color Meaning
Fluorescence

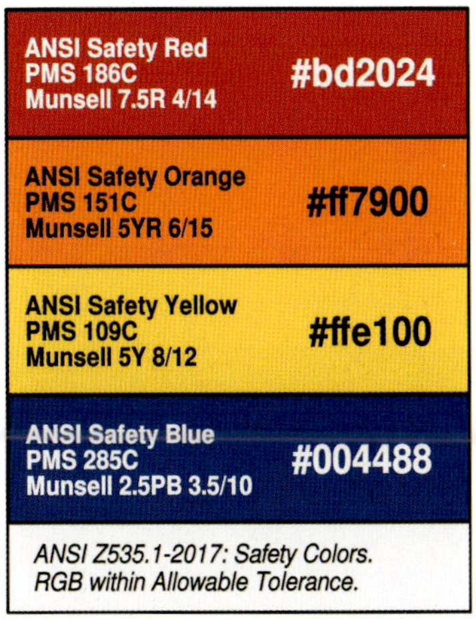

Examples of safety colors as defined by the American National Standards Institute (ANSI).

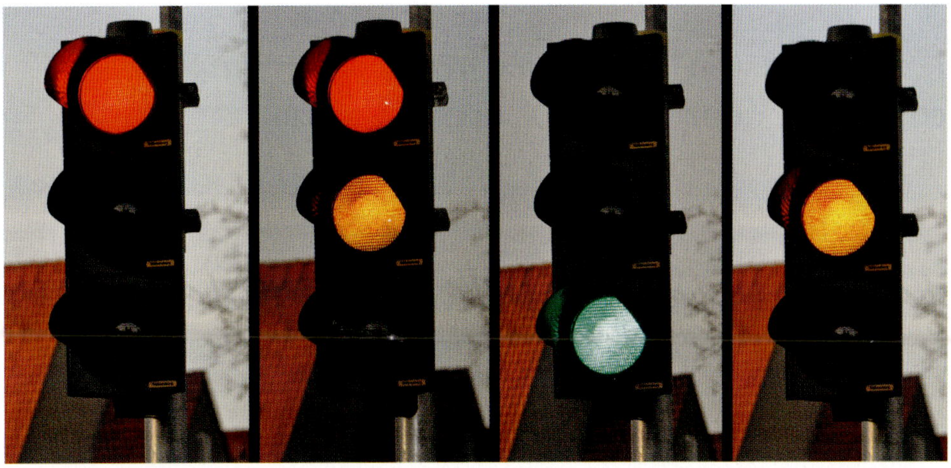

Red, amber, and green are the international standard colors of traffic light signals.

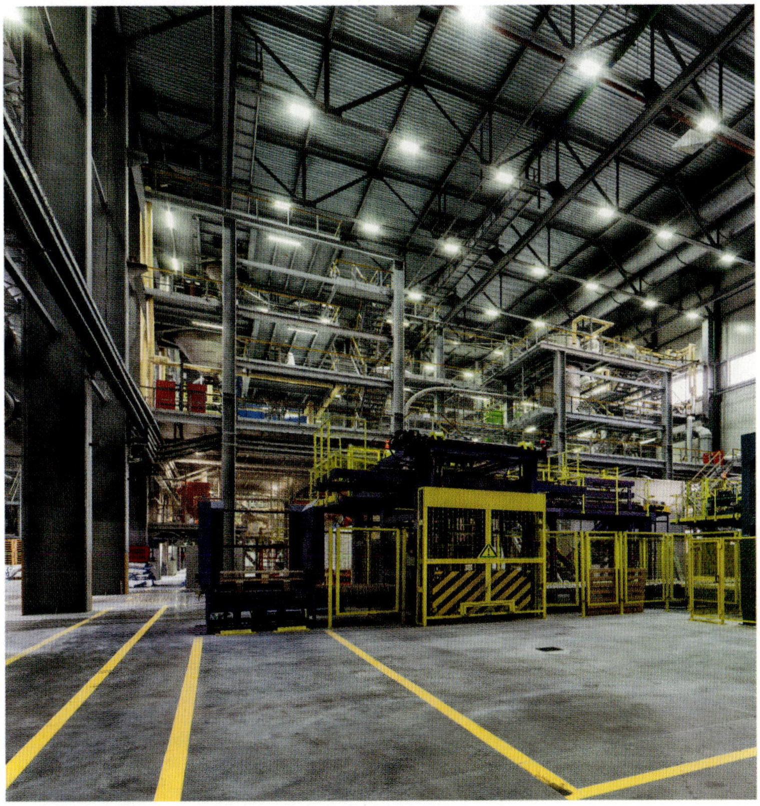

Bright yellow lines are used in this factory setting because they are highly visible and the color yellow denotes a hazard in this context.

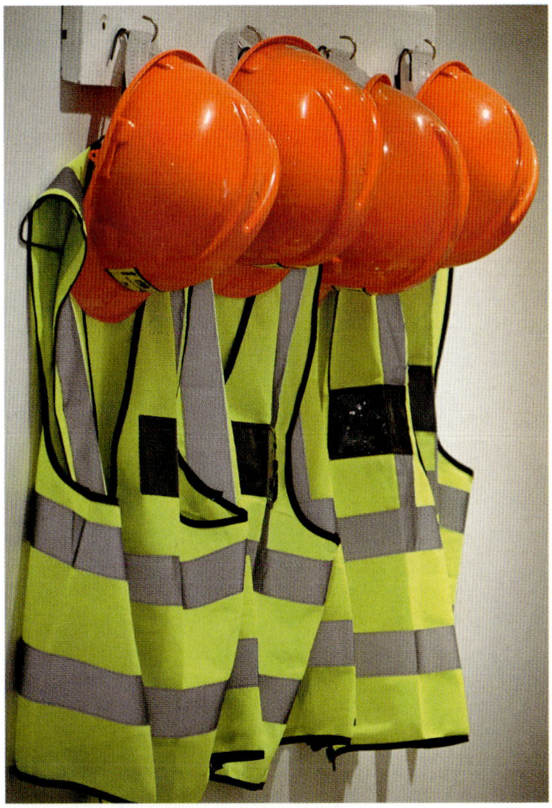

Fluorescent yellow is one of the ANSI/ISEA colors approved for safety vests.

81 SHADOWS

Areas where the light coming from a light source is completely or partially obstructed by an object

Realistic rendering of shadows requires understanding the various effects of lighting on the scene. In addition to light and shadow giving objects their form, the type of lighting and shape of the object are factors in the perception of color. The range between the darkest and lightest areas affects the overall effect of an image.

Cast shadow: shadow created by an object blocking the light source. A cast shadow has a hard edge close to the object that becomes softer the further it is from the object.

Core or form shadow: shadow on the surface of an object opposite the light source. A core shadow is lighter than a cast shadow, with a softer edge. Depending on the shape of the surface, a core shadow can be a gradient.

Crevice shadow: the darkest shadow in the space opposite the light source, between the object and the surface.

Highlight: lightest spot on the surface where the light is focused.

Penumbra: area of partial shadow between the cast shadow and full illumination.

In computer graphics the process of adding shadows by rendering an image using the light's point of view is called shadow rendering or mapping.

SEE ALSO:
Chiaroscuro
Gradients

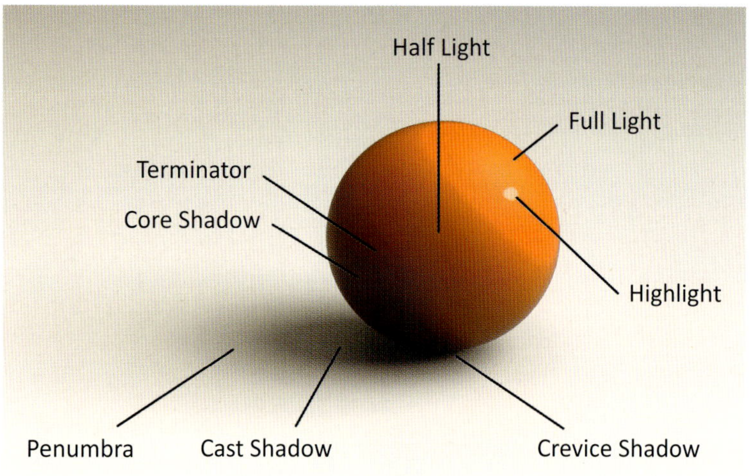

Shadow terms

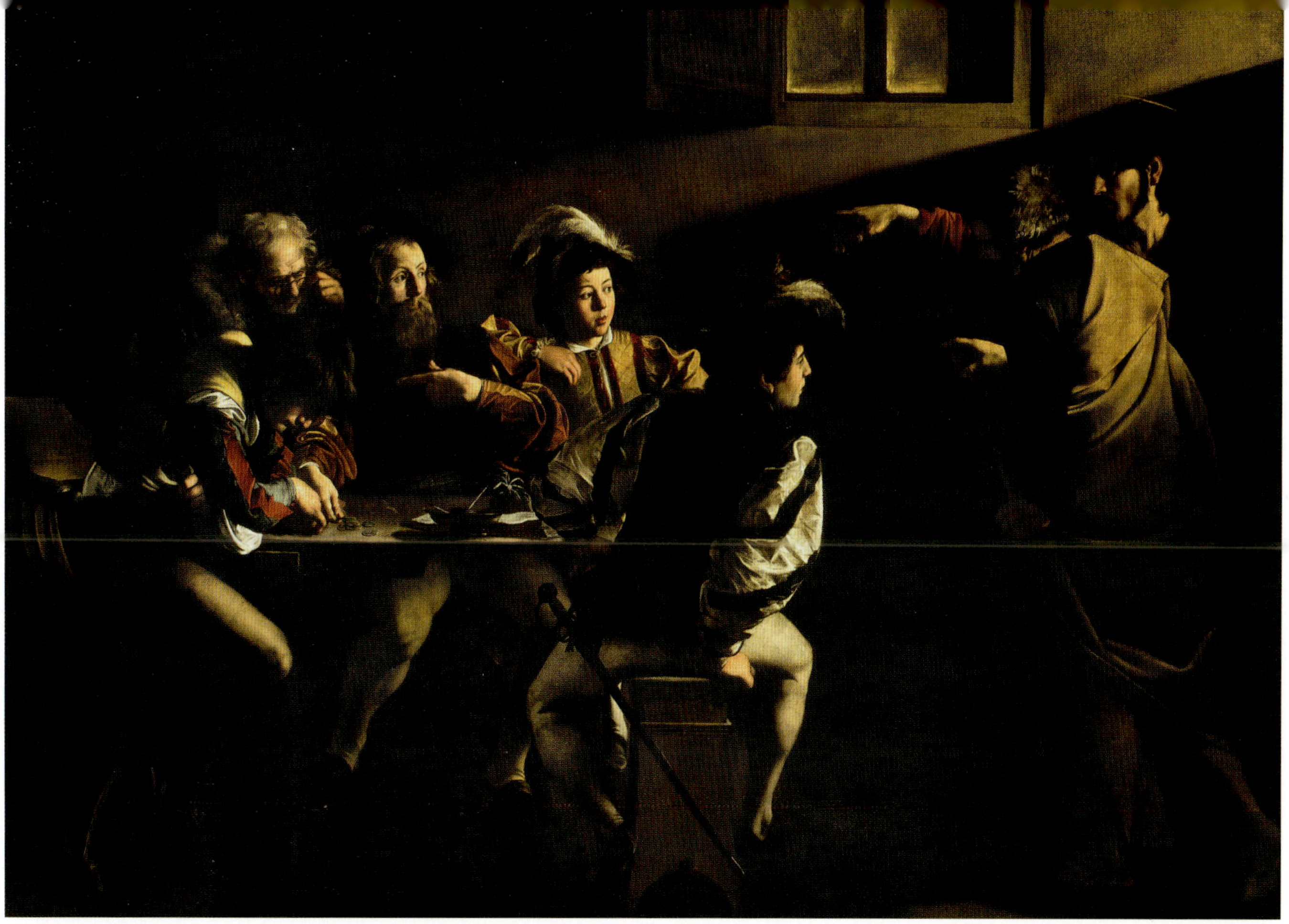

The Calling of Saint Matthew (1600), by Caravaggio.

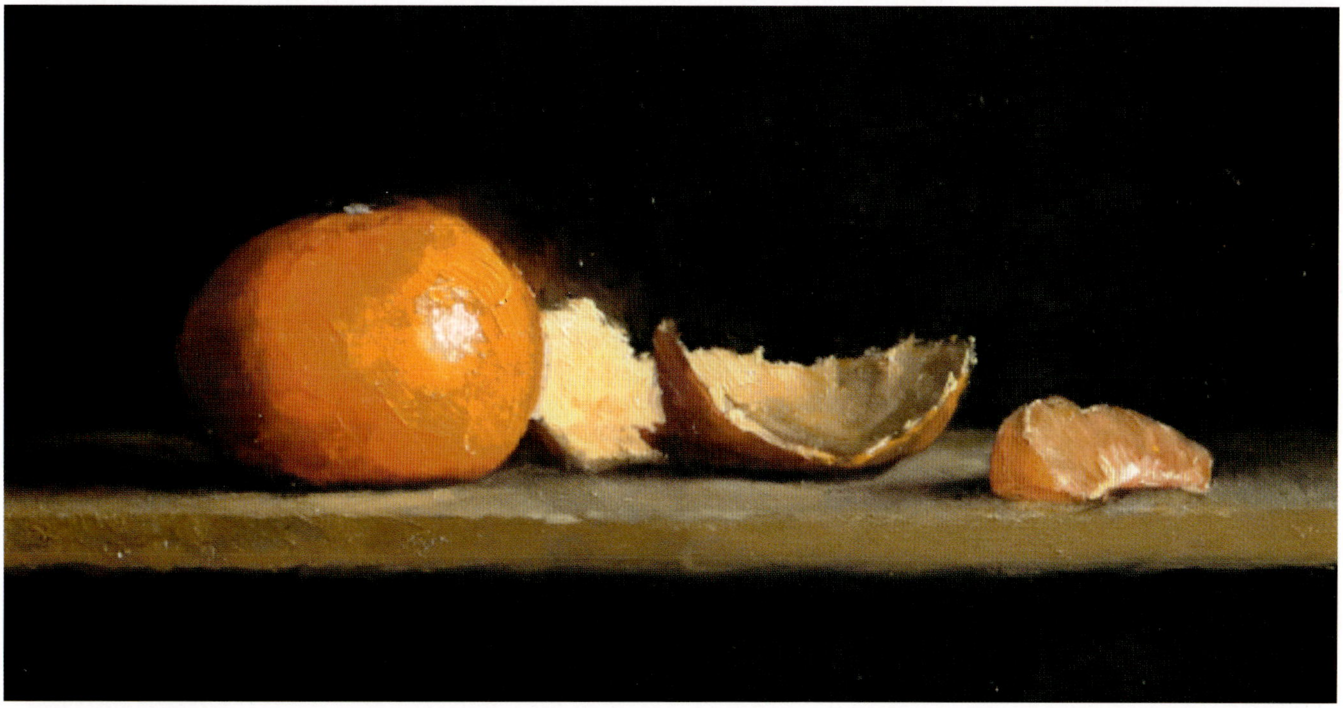

Painting by Paul Foxton.

82 SIMULTANEOUS CONTRAST

A perceptual shift in color that occurs when the color appears to move toward the opposite color of the surround against which it is seen

Color is a perception rather than a fixed property of an object or patch. As such, the color of an object or patch can change depending on the conditions in which it is viewed, leading to various color appearance phenomena. One of the most well-known color appearance effects is simultaneous contrast where two colors placed side by side will contrast with each other by appearing to take on the attributes of the opposing hue.

Imagine a nominally gray patch is placed on one of two backgrounds: One is red and one is blue. The gray patch on the red background will contrast with the red and appear greenish or cyanish. However, the gray patch on the blue background will appear yellowish. Note that although contrast is often expressed in terms of hue, there can also be contrast in lightness and/or chroma.

Simultaneous contrast is only one of many well-known color appearance phenomena. Mach bands, named after physicist Ernst Mach (1838–1916), exaggerate the lightness contrast at the borders of progressively lighter shades of gray. This is also known as the fluting effect due to its similarity to the shadowing on fluted columns.

Contrast occurs because of the way in which the human visual system processes light information. Cone responses from one part of a scene are effectively compared with cone responses from neighboring parts of the scene. This results in color perception being spatially relative.

Research is ongoing, and although many contrast effects can be explained by retinal processing, by such retinal processing, it is also suggested that higher-level cognitive processes could play a role.

SEE ALSO:
Albers's *Interaction of Color*
Bezold Effect
Human Visual System
Successive Contrast

"Why do two colors, put one next to the other, sing? Can one really explain this? No. Just as one can never learn how to paint."
—*Pablo Picasso*

Lightness contrast: The horizontal bar above looks lighter on the left and darker on the right because of the dark to light gradient of the background.

Mach bands: The image of Mach bands on the right illustrates the fluting effect.

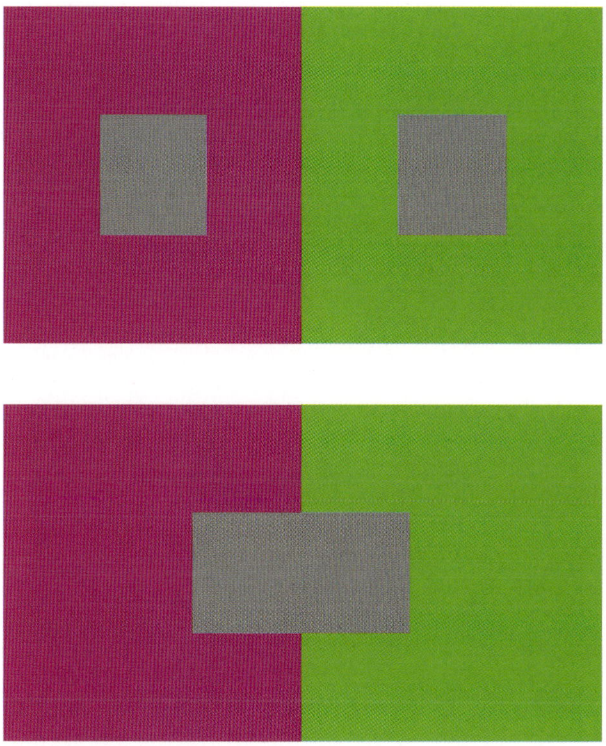

Hue contrast: In the Albers style image, the two small squares are physically the same but look different because of the different hue backgrounds.

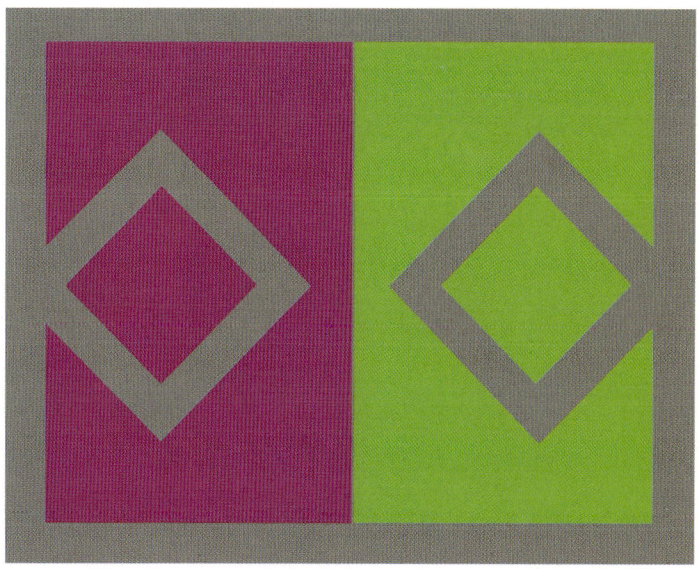

Hue contrast: The same colors are used in this image, designed by Paul Green-Armytage to heighten the contrast effect.

83 SPECTRAL HUES

Hues that are present in the spectrum of colors produced by splitting sunlight with a prism

The range of wavelengths that are visible to humans is approximately 360 nm to 780 nm. Seen together these wavelengths appear white. If we consider single wavelengths—or narrow bands of wavelengths—from this range, we typically perceive bands of color. These are known as the spectral hues and include reds, oranges, yellows, greens, cyans, blues, and violets. We experience this phenomenon whenever we see a rainbow in the sky or when light is passed through a glass prism.

The spectral hues such as yellow can be produced from single wavelengths, but it is also possible to produce a yellow from an additive mixture of other wavelengths. For example, a mixture of red and green lights can make yellow. The yellow produced by an additive mixture of red and yellow is no less real than the yellow that results from single-wavelength light.

Note that the wavelengths themselves are not colored. The spectrum in the image on the next page, top left, only appears on the surface of the counter, not in the air between the prism and the counter.

There are other hues we can experience that do not occur in the spectrum. These nonspectral hues include purples, magentas, and violet reds. The nonspectral hues occur only when we see several short and long wavelengths of light coincidently. For example, if we additively mix short (bluish) and long (reddish) light, we can see purples and magentas.

SEE ALSO:
Additive Mixture
Electromagnetic Spectrum
Newton's *Opticks*

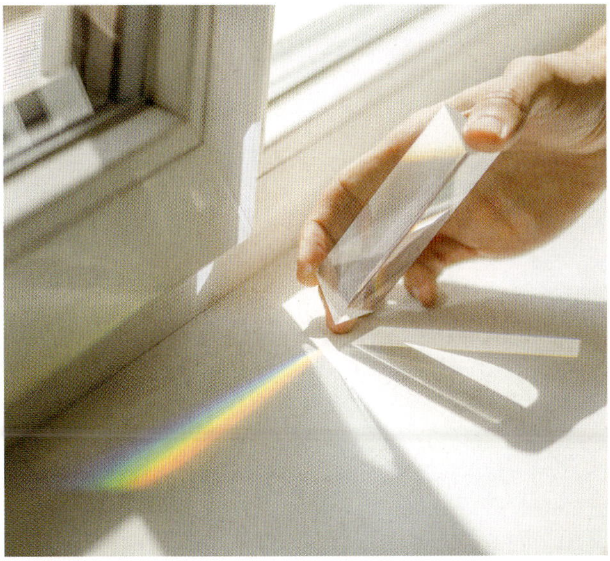

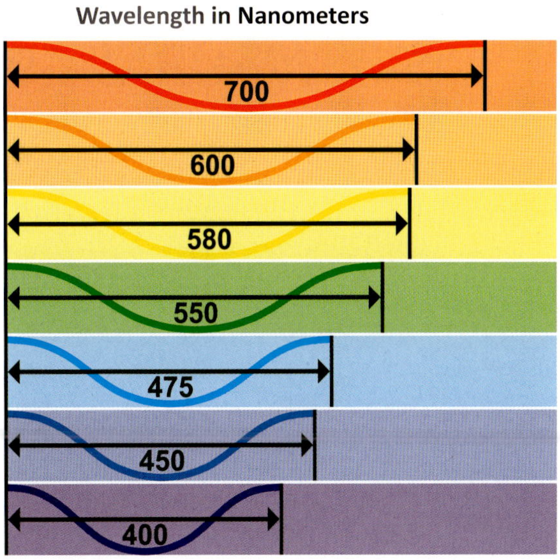

A prism splits sunlight into wavelengths measured in nanometers from 400 nm to 700 nm.

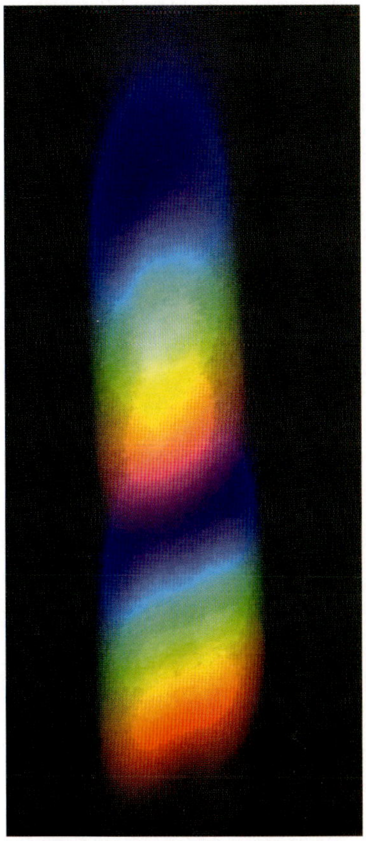

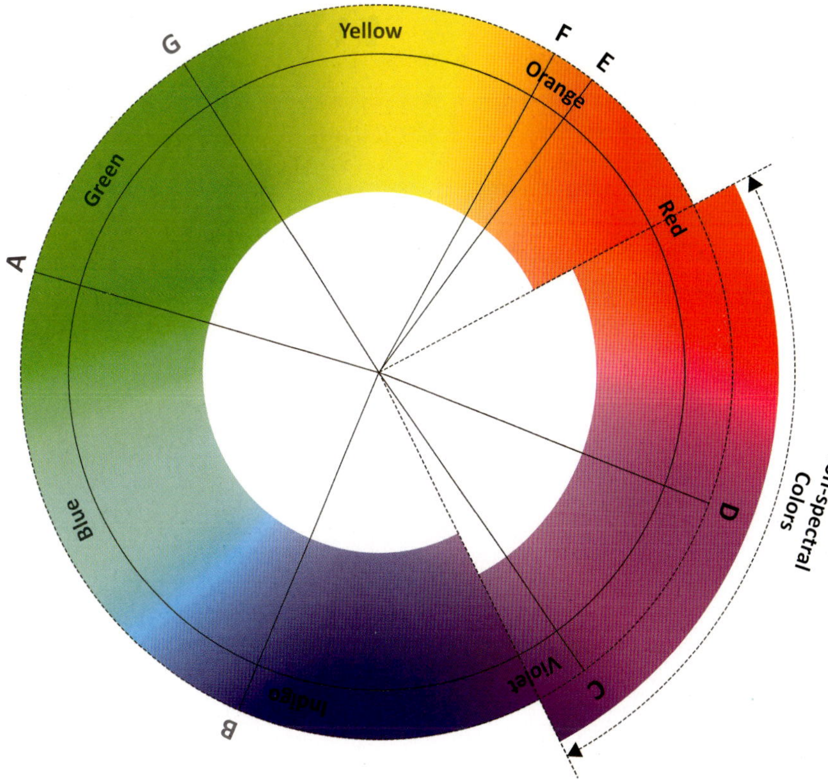

The overlap of the red end of the spectrum with the violet end of the spectrum produces colors that are not on the spectrum.

84 STRUCTURAL COLOR

Animals in nature produce color in three main ways: pigments, structural color, and bioluminescence

Structural characteristics in nature can lead to scattering of light. A good example is eye color in humans. Brown eyes occur in individuals who have high concentrations of the pigment melanin, which primarily absorbs the long visible wavelengths. Yet in the absence of melanin, the structural components of the eye scatter light and cause blue eye color. Butterfly wings and peacock feathers are some of the well-known examples of structural color in nature. Sometimes the structures result in light scattering, which typically can produce a blue color or, in conjunction with pigments, a wide range of colors.

SEE ALSO:
Electromagnetic Spectrum
Rayleigh Scattering

Structural color has been studied since the 1940s with the introduction of the electron microscope. In addition to scattering and diffraction, highly magnified images of natural structures led to an understanding of interference as a process for generating color.

In interference, multiple thin layers of a material where the distance between the layers is typically like the wavelength of light can produce unusual color effects. Interference between the light reflected by the different layers can result in specific wavelengths of light being preferentially reflected. The colors in soap bubbles and the colors that result from mixtures of oil and water are good examples of this effect.

Our understanding of structural color phenomena has led to commercial applications including antireflection coatings on lenses in eyeglasses, binoculars, and telescopes.

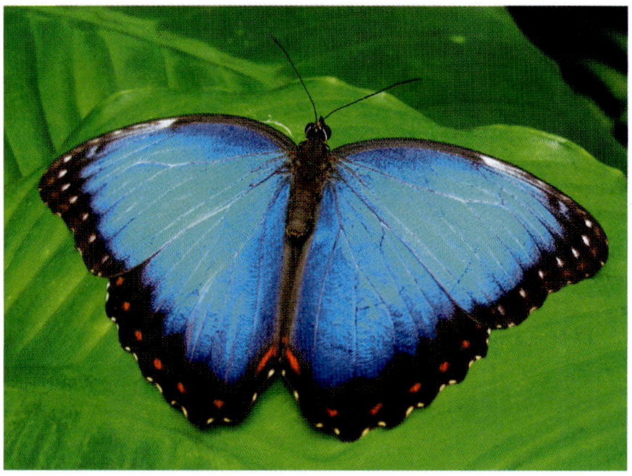

Structural characteristics are the primary source of the beautiful colors found in butterfly wings.

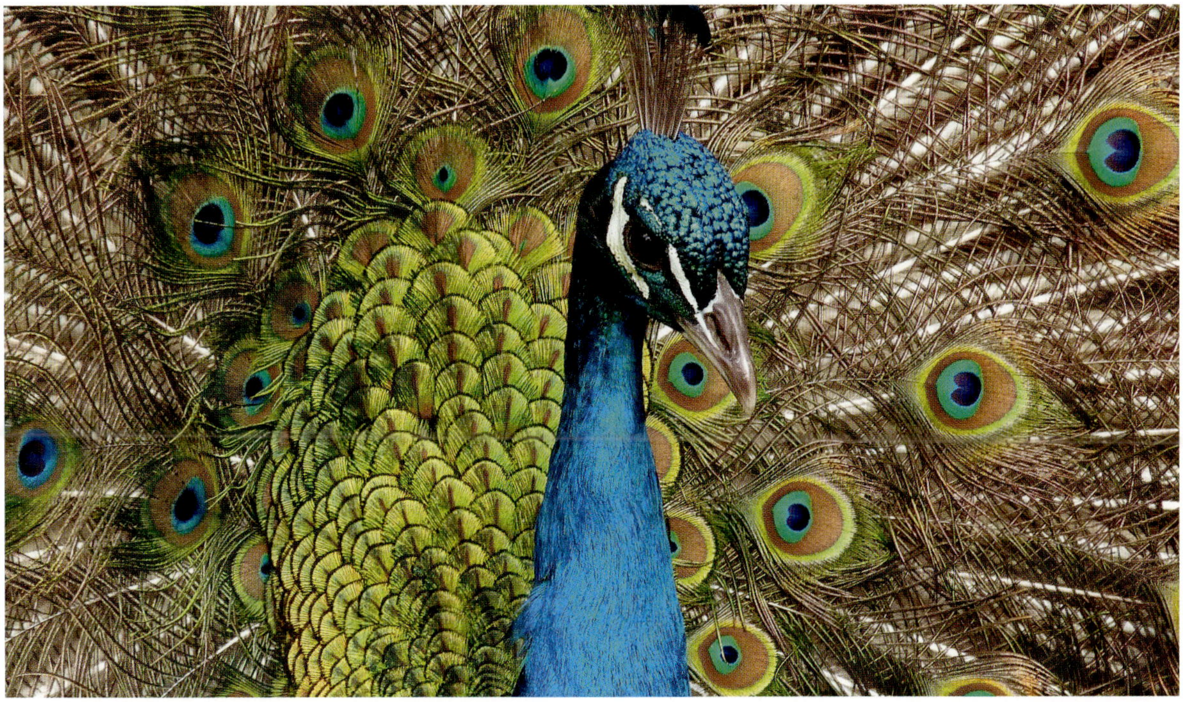

In peacock feathers the main colorant is a brown pigment. This is supplemented by structural aspects, which can result in a wide variety of vivid colors.

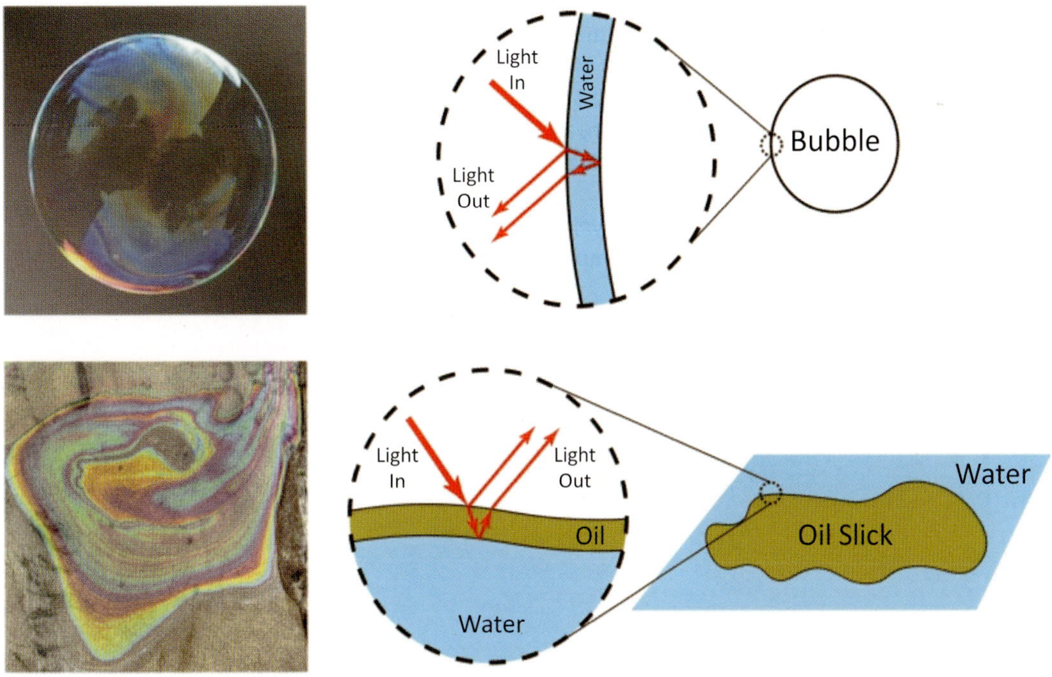

Diagram of structural color by George Degan for the Santa Barbara Museum of Natural History.

85 SUBTRACTIVE MIXTURE

The process and effect of combining colorants such as paints, inks, and dyes

The term *subtractive* arises because colorants absorb (subtract) light. The light that is not absorbed is the light that we see.

Traditional color theory teaches that the subtractive primaries are red, yellow, and blue and that paints or inks of these colors can be combined to create all other colors. However, it has been known for nearly one hundred years that it is not possible to make a full range of colors from three primaries.

The optimal subtractive primaries for minimizing saturation loss are cyan, magenta, and yellow, though unfortunately, the traditional red, yellow, and blue primaries of the subtractive system are still overwhelmingly taught in color education. The case for updating color education models to cyan, magenta, and yellow is important and timely, aligned with state-of-the-art tools and technologies.

A loss of chroma occurs when two colorants of different hues are mixed. The selection of primaries in any medium is based on minimizing the number of colorants used while also minimizing the loss of chroma.

Another way to offset the loss of chroma in a subtractive mixture is to start with six primaries rather than three. There are many variations of this concept; some recommend using two each of red, yellow, and blue. These are known as double or split primary systems. Others suggest adding orange, green, and violet (often called a secondary palette in paint) or an extended gamut (in printing).

The use of four-color printing (where cyan, magenta, and yellow inks are supplemented with black) is ubiquitous. Printing systems that use six or more inks are used for high-quality commercial printing.

Additive and subtractive color mixing are related. The optimal additive primaries are red, green, and blue, and the optimal subtractive primaries are red-absorbing (cyan), green-absorbing (magenta), and blue-absorbing (yellow) colorants.

SEE ALSO:
Additive Mixture
CMYK
Color Management
RGB

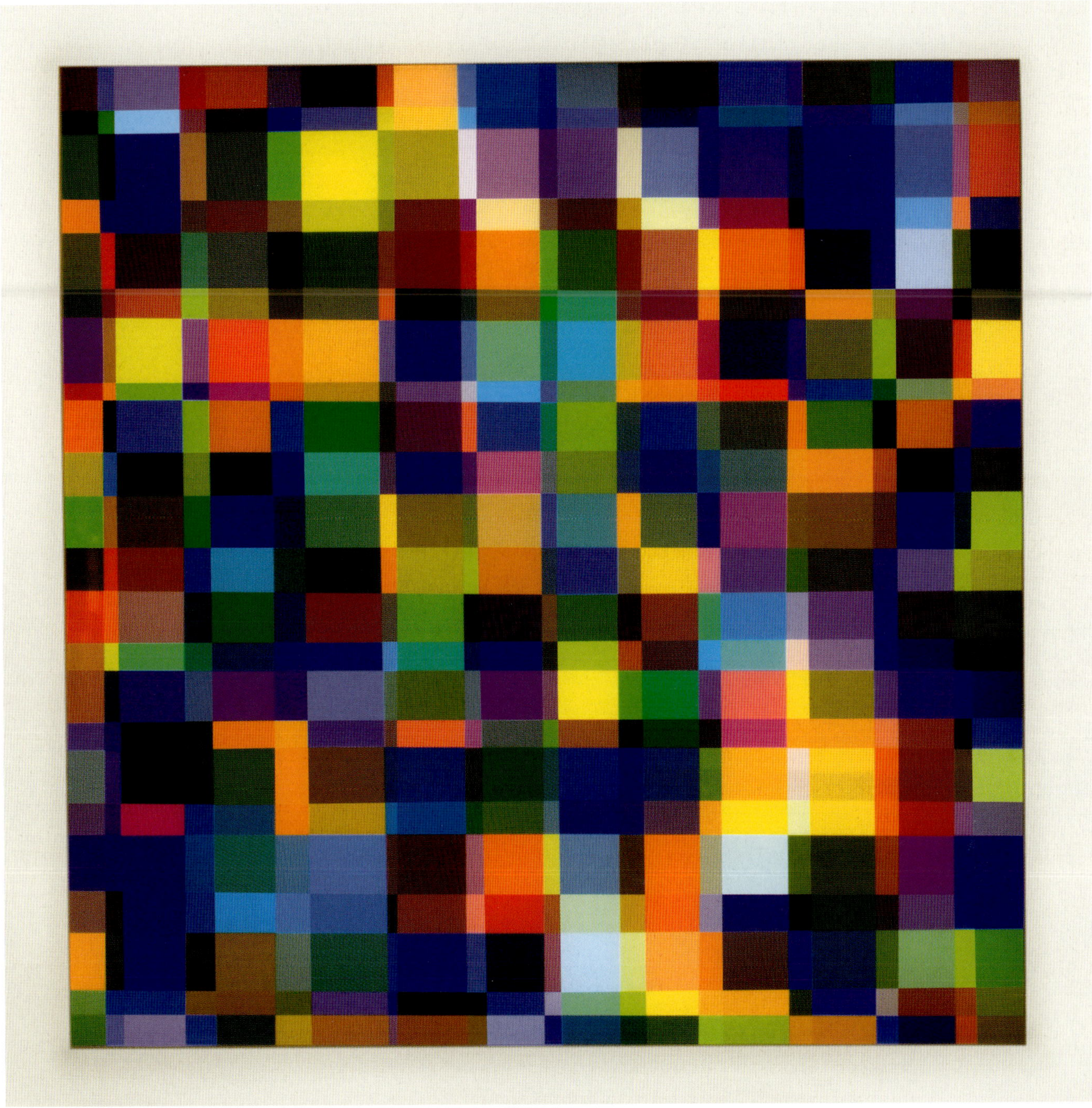

Color Test (576) (2017), by Spencer Finch.
LED lightbox, Fujitrans.

The Color Tests are made by layering and laminating two translucent grids of unique colors printed on Fujitrans to form a more complex grid with more complex colors. The overlapping gels result in subtractive mixtures.

86 SUCCESSIVE CONTRAST

A temporal effect in which retinal impressions persist following the removal of a stimulus, and color perception is influenced by the colors that were previously seen

If a red swatch is stared at for a short while and then removed to reveal a neutral or white background, a weak green or cyan color will be observed in its place. This successive effect, one perception of color followed by another, is commonly known as the afterimage.

Afterimage colors are the opposite of the colors that are originally viewed. Afterimages occur when the eye's photoreceptors (cones) adapt to overstimulation and lose sensitivity. For example, looking at a red swatch causes the long-wavelength sensitive cones to be stimulated; when the red swatch is removed, these long-wavelength cones will be less sensitive and a white background will appear to have a cyan or greenish swatch.

The existence of the afterimage effect was one of the phenomena that led to the opponent theory of color vision being considered alongside the trichromatic theory. The trichromatic theory is based on the existence of three photosensitive cones, but opponency—the idea that the cone signals are combined and subtracted from one another in the retina—is needed to explain certain visual phenomena such as afterimages.

It is important to consider your state of visual adaptation when making any critical visual color evaluations. Allow your eyes to rest for a few minutes following color observations.

SEE ALSO:
Human Visual System
Simultaneous Contrast

Stare at the X on the top for thirty to forty-five seconds. Try to relax and not move your eyes. Then look at the X in the white space below the image. It may take as long as ten seconds, and blinking may help. Try it again, but keep one eye covered or closed. When the afterimage colors appear, open your covered eye at the same time you cover your other eye. Go back and forth covering each eye. What happens to the afterimage?

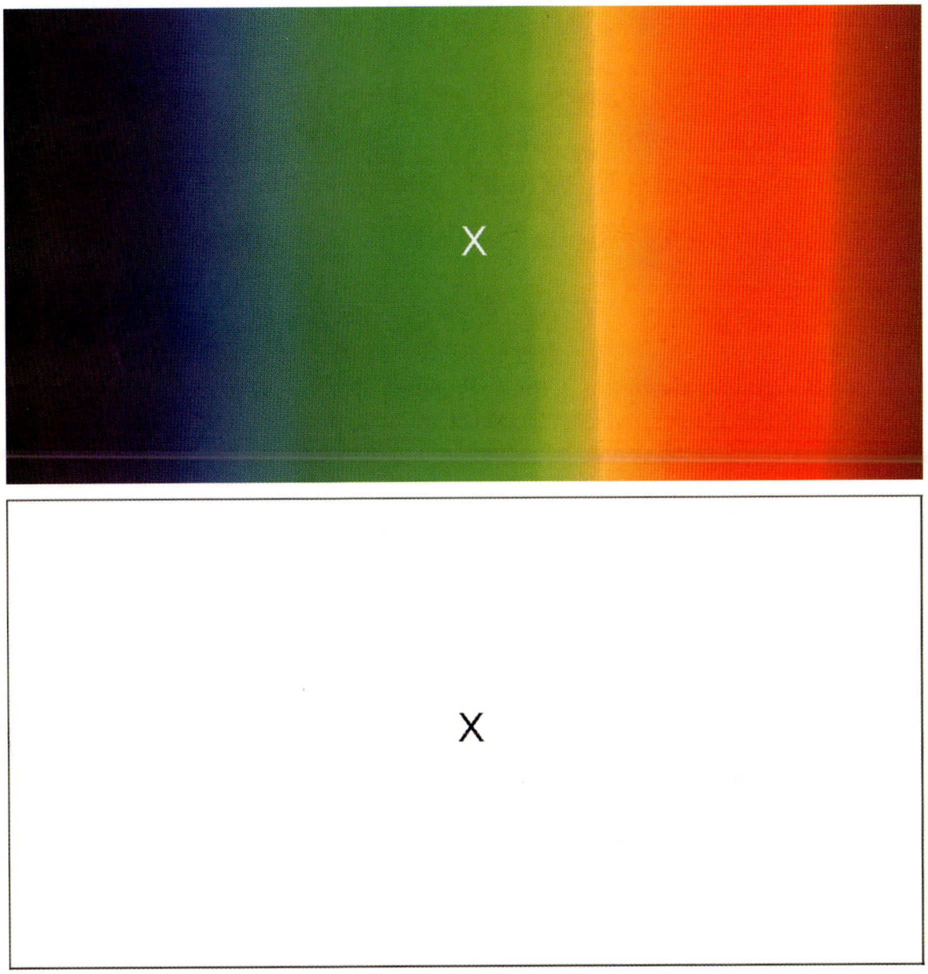

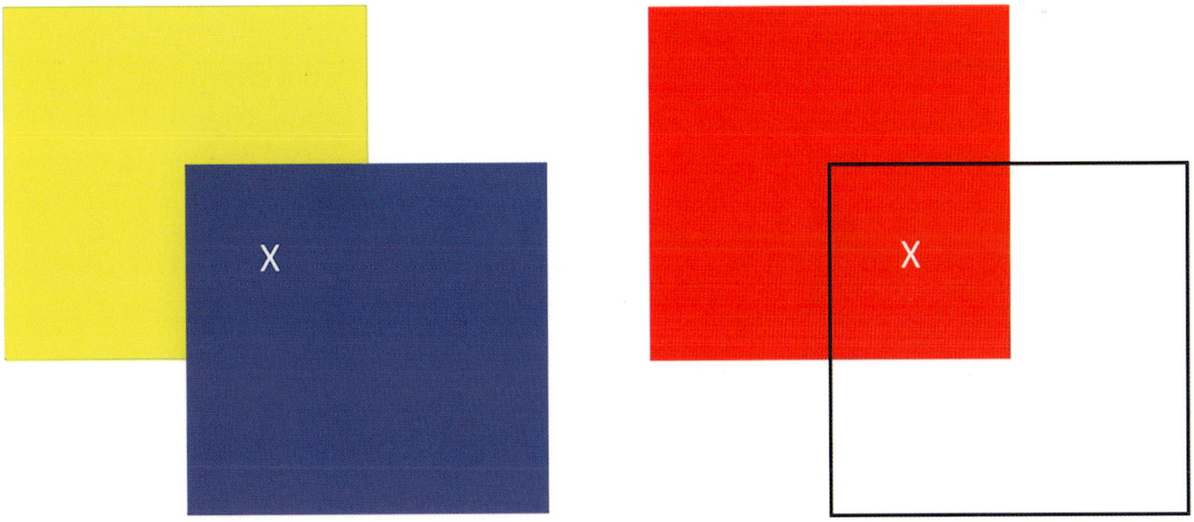

Stare at the X on the left for thirty to forty-five seconds. Try to relax and not move your eyes. Then look at the X on the right. Afterimage colors will appear if you continue to look at the X. It may take as long as ten seconds and blinking may help. Notice how the afterimage appears to float over the overlapping area. Afterimages are an example of film color.

87 SUSTAINABILITY

Efforts to reduce the environmental impact of the petroleum-based dye industry by developing economical natural colorants

There is a growing awareness of the environmental impact of manufacturing products using synthetic textiles, dyes, and food colorants. To provide an alternative to the use of synthetic colorants, several initiatives around the world are tackling the issue of producing affordable sustainable colorants from natural sources.

The first synthetic color was mauveine, a derivative of coal tar discovered by William Henry Perkin in 1856. Today 99 percent of the colorants used in industrial applications come from fossil fuels. Because synthetic dyes are cheaper to produce than natural dyes, the textile industry is responsible for 20 percent of global water pollution—due to the toxicity of synthetic dyes and their resistance to biodegradation.

There are three types of natural dyes: plant based (such as woad and indigo), animal based (such as cochineal and murex sea snails), and mineral based (such as ochre and lapis lazuli). Because plant-based dye production requires large areas of land, state-of-the-art biotech researchers are experimenting with manufacturing natural colorants from fungi, algae, and bacteria. This research is not only focused on textile dyes but expanding into the development of natural food, drug, and cosmetic colorants as well.

Another aspect of sustainable color is the shift away from plastics and paints in favor of natural materials such as wood, stone, clay, and undyed fibers, especially in the design of the built environment.

The aesthetic decision to use natural materials can be a sustainable choice as well.

SEE ALSO:
Color Literacy
Environmental Color Design
Geography of Color

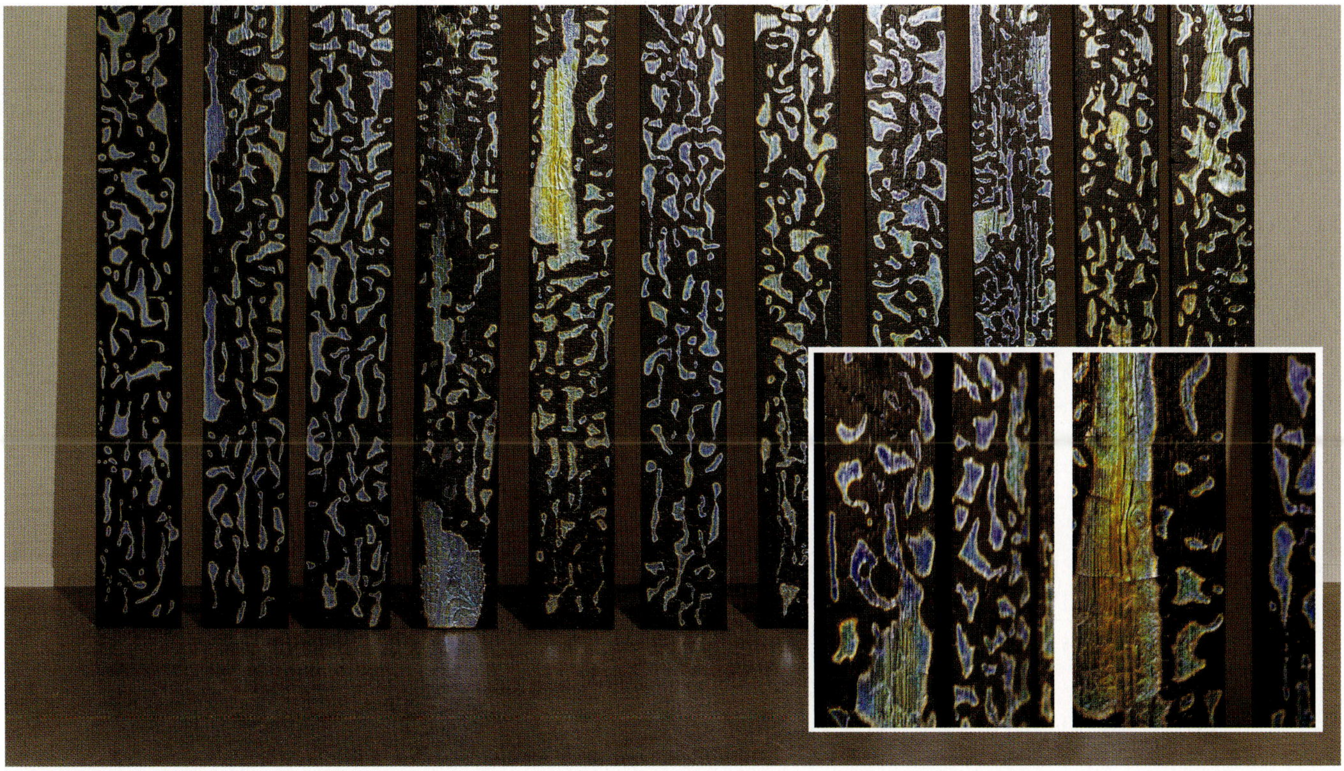

Shimmering Wood (2022). Konrad Klockars and Noora Yau. Sustainable structural color produced 100% from wood and applied on wood as a result of research at Aalto University's Structural Color Studio in Finland. (Photo by Esa Naukkarinen.)

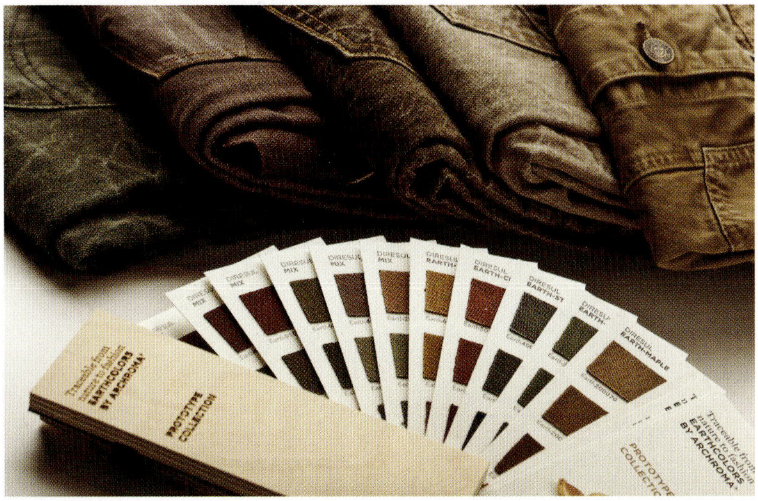

Earth Colors by Archroma. Research into sustainable dyes is ongoing in many companies in the textile industry.

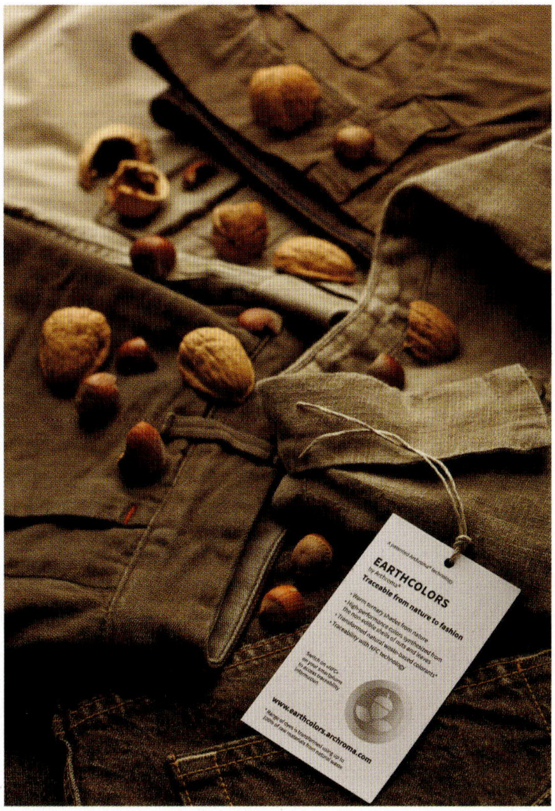

88 SYMBOLIC COLOR

Color that is intentionally used to communicate meaning based on individual, cultural, or universal associations

Color symbolism is context-dependent, influenced by changes over time across cultures around the world. Although there are few universal standards for colors as symbols with specific meanings—stop-sign red is an exception—there are common themes across many cultures.

Symbolic representations of religious concepts or articles may include a specific color with which the concept or object is associated. There is evidence to suggest that colors have been used for ceremonial purposes as early as 90,000 BC.

Diversity in color symbolism occurs because color meanings and symbolism evolve over time on an individual and cultural basis. Contemporary examples of evolving color symbolism include sports teams, organized movements, and social causes such as breast cancer that use color to unify groups.

SEE ALSO:
Brand Colors
Color Meaning
Emotion and Color

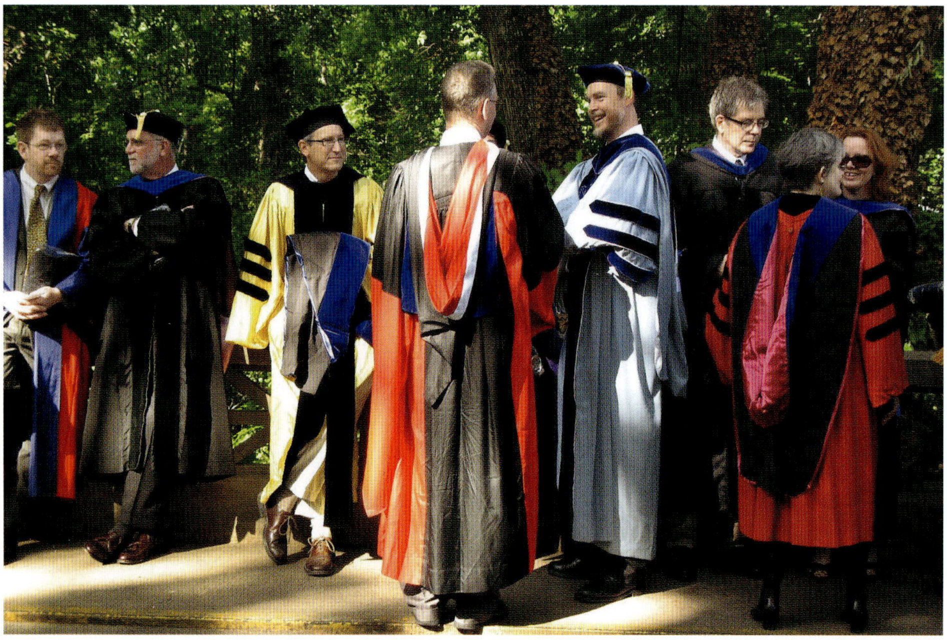

The colors of the regalia worn by faculty at college and university graduation ceremonies are an example of symbolic color.

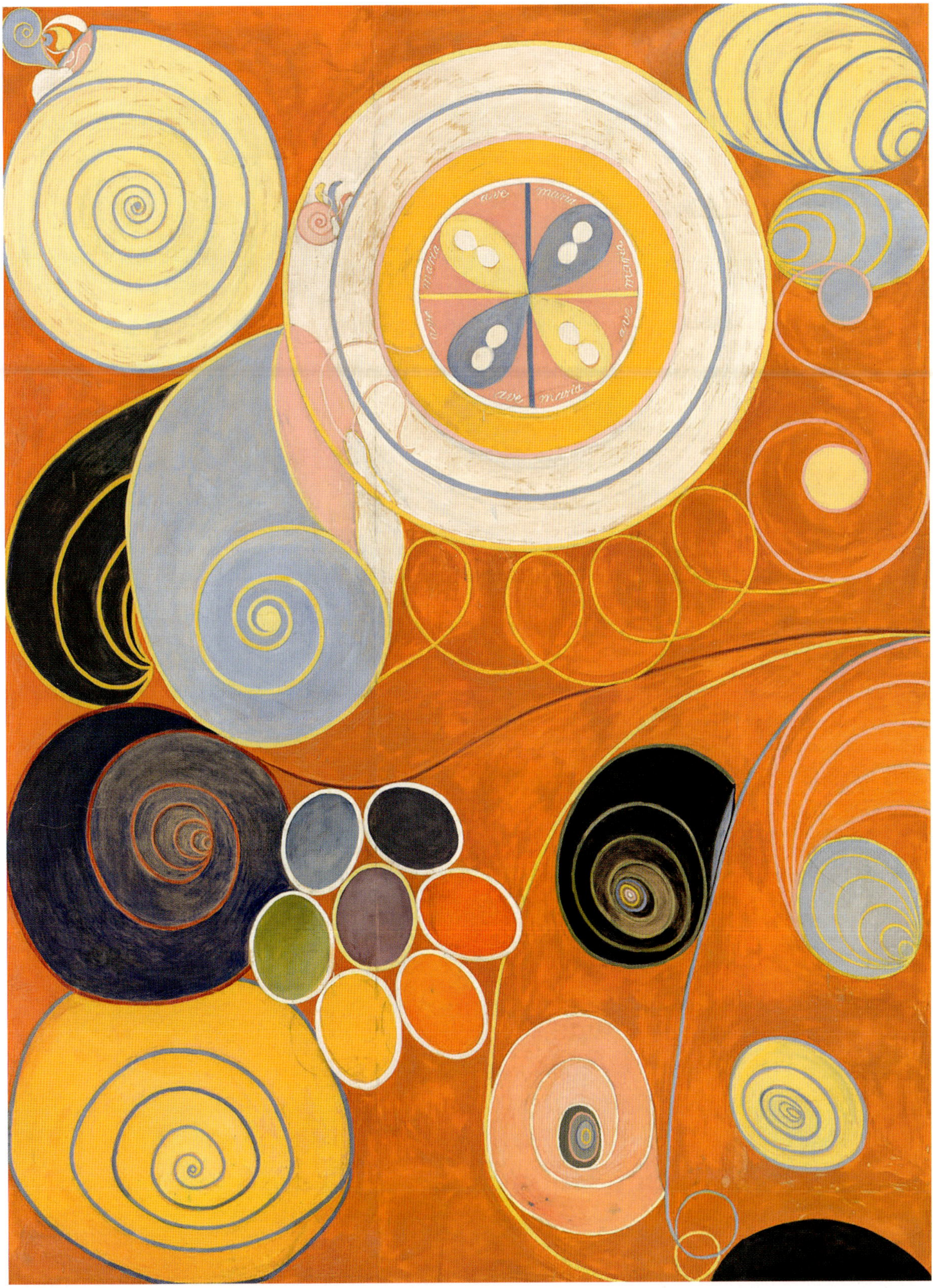

The Ten Largest, Youth (1907), by Hilma af Klint.
Klint developed a symbolic language of color at the turn of the last century for the Paintings for the Temple series.

89 SYNESTHESIA

The phenomenon whereby stimulation of one sensory pathway (such as hearing) leads to involuntary experiences in another sensory pathway (such as vision)

Interest in synesthesia goes back to Ancient Greece, and interest in the association between music and color remains to this day. Although research is expanding, the neurological cause of synesthesia is still not clear.

The most common type of synesthesia is grapheme-color synesthesia, where synesthetes perceive letters and/or numbers as being inherently colored. Chromesthesia is another color-related condition where everyday sounds or certain musical notes can trigger the perception of color.

It has been argued that synesthesia may be a source of creativity in artists. Wassily Kandinsky was a Bauhaus master artist who famously associated colors with shapes. It is now believed that Kandinsky was a synesthete. Composers Franz Liszt and Nikolai Rimsky-Korsakov disagreed on the colors of musical keys. While he was conducting, Liszt once told the orchestra that they should make the music bluer or a deep violet. Today, the musical artist Pharrell Williams is open about his synesthesia.

Note that a distinction is made between art created by synesthetes and art that is intended to evoke synesthetic associations in nonsynesthetic viewers. The most famous piece of work that is thought to evoke synesthetic associations is the 1940 Disney animation film *Fantasia*.

Although synesthetes tend to have different associations from one another, there are some general consistencies and participants are usually consistent with their own associations.

SEE ALSO:
Emotion and Color
Human Visual System

FURTHER READING

The Frog Who Croaked Blue: Synesthesia and the Mixing of the Senses (2009), by Jamie Ward

Synesthesia (2018), by Richard E. Cytowic

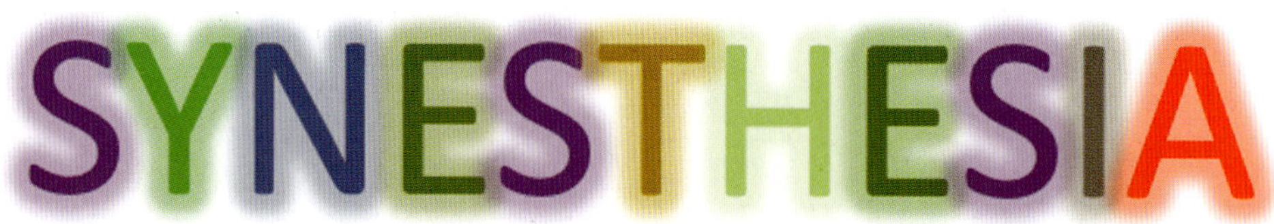

A representation of how a synesthetic person might see letters in color. It is also common to see numbers as colors. Although different people tend to have different associations, there are some typical consistencies and participants are usually consistent with themselves.

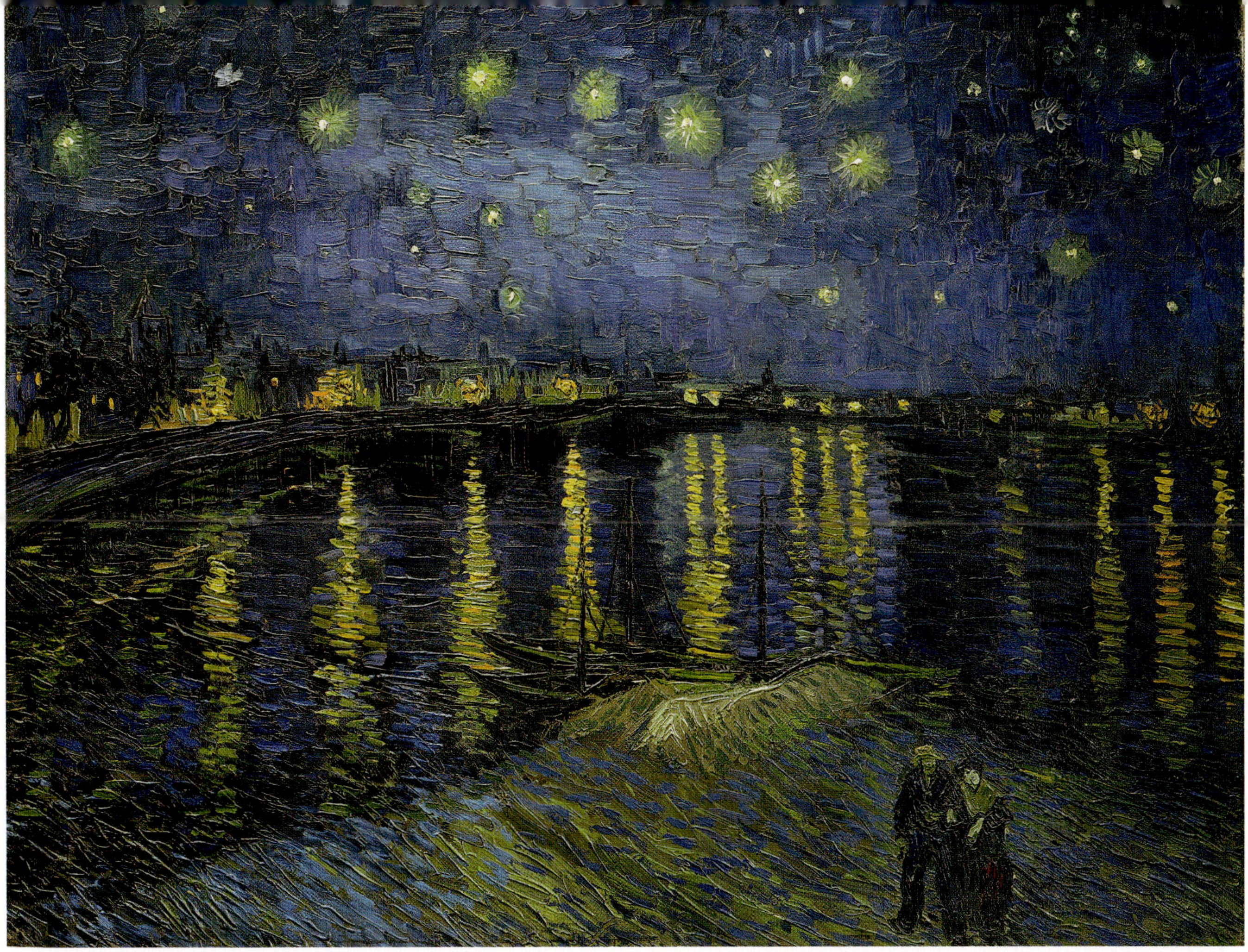

Starry Night Over the Rhone (1888), by Vincent Van Gogh.
Many art historians believe that Vincent van Gogh had a form of synesthesia called chromesthesia—an experience of the senses where the person associates sounds with colors.

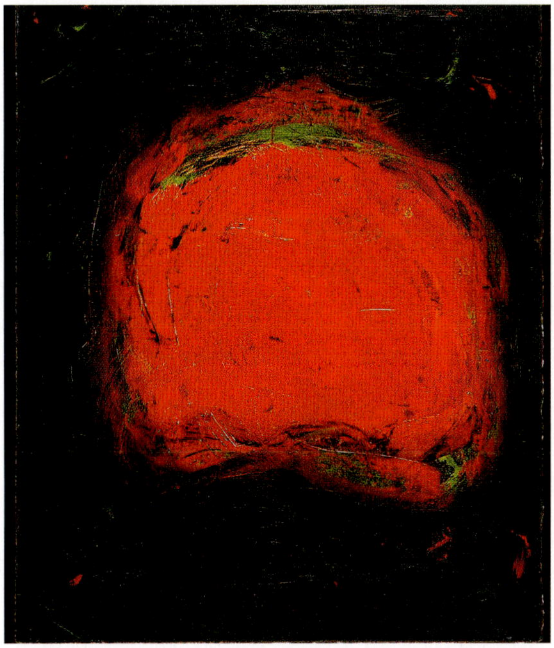

Vision (1996) is a painting by the synesthetic artist Carol Steen that was produced in response to her visual experiences during an acupuncture session.

90 TECHNICOLOR

An important development in the 1930s that led to a rapid increase in the use of color in the movie industry

Color movies began to be produced in the first quarter of the twentieth century with the Kinemacolor process, inspired by discoveries made by James Clerk Maxwell. The original Kinemacolor process was an additive system that used only two color primaries (red and green).

However, Technicolor dominated the industry between 1920 and 1930. There were several Technicolor systems. Technicolor I was similar to Kinemacolor and used a two-primary additive system. Technicolor II, III, and IV incorporated developments that would lead to a trichromatic subtractive system that could produce beautiful and vivid color images.

Many high-quality color movies were produced with Technicolor, but using the process was expensive due to the high cost of the cameras and the level of training required for the operators. Technicolor offered the equipment on favorable terms to a new animator named Walt Disney, and as a result movies such as *Flowers and Trees* and *Three Little Pigs* were truly groundbreaking. The full gamut of Technicolor was unleashed in *The Wizard of Oz*. Despite the technical superiority of Technicolor, it was eventually replaced by Eastman Color by the 1960s.

Today the use of color in the movie industry has shifted to digital technologies, though shooting on film is still preferred by some directors.

SEE ALSO:
Cinematic Color
Gamut
Palette

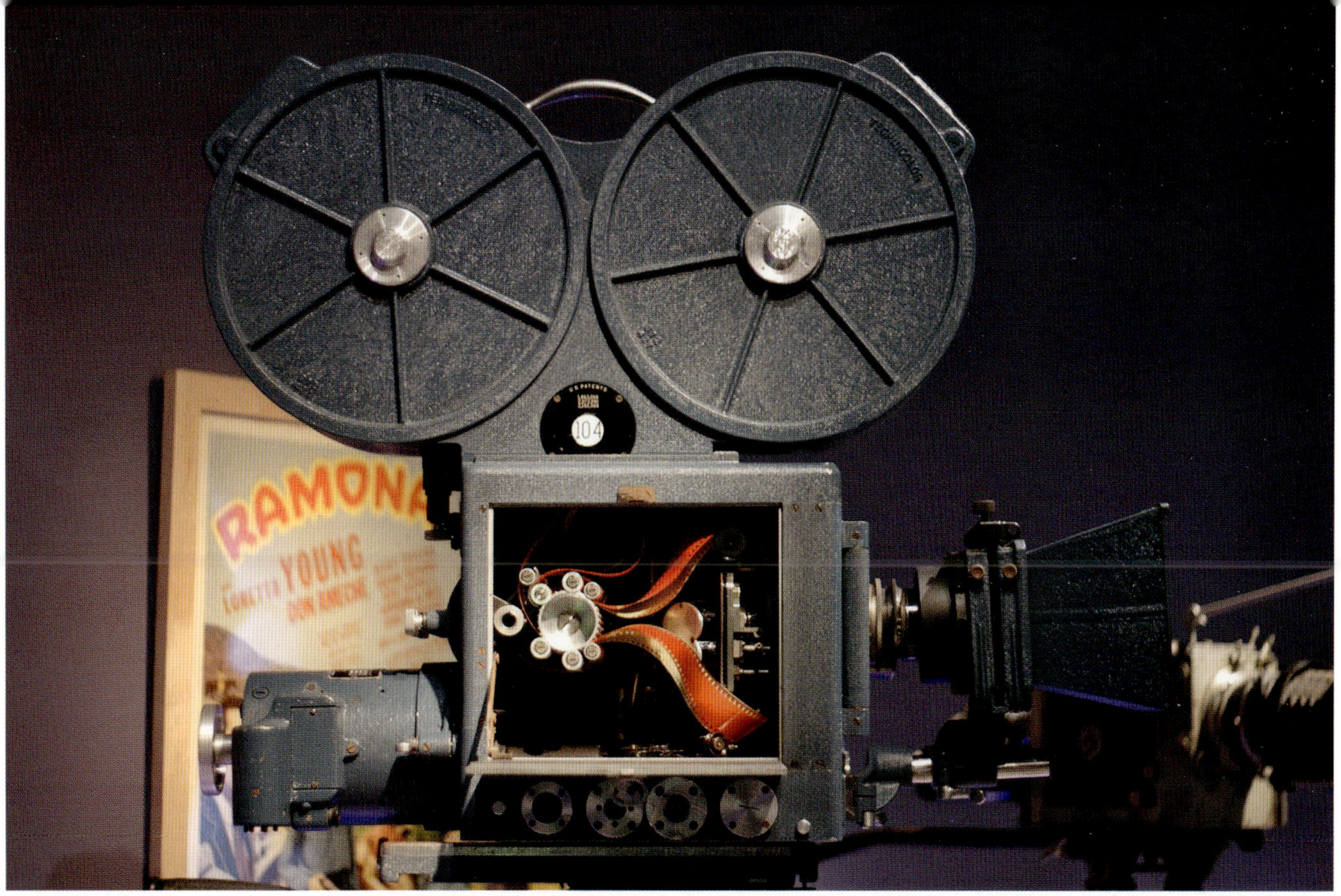

A 3-strip Technicolor camera from the 1930s. Two strips of 35 mm black and white film negative, one sensitive to blue light and the other to red light, ran together through an aperture behind a magenta filter, which allowed blue and red light to pass through. A third film strip of black and white film negative ran through a separate aperture, behind a green filter.

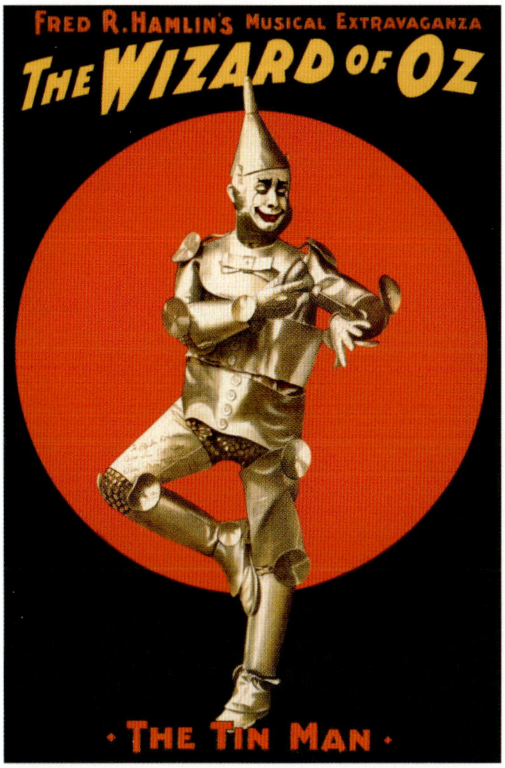

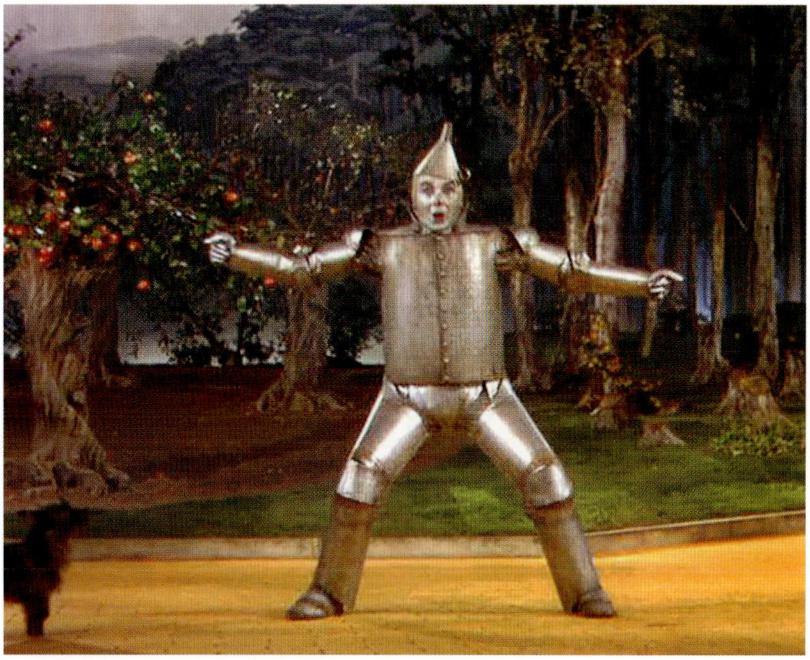

The Wizard of Oz showcased the capabilities of Technicolor. Produced by Metro-Goldwyn-Mayer in 1939, it greatly influenced popular culture and inspired many musicals and stage shows ever since.

91 TEXTURE

Surface characteristics of objects affect the perception of color

Texture is one of the key elements of art and design. The term texture is often described with terms such as rough or smooth, hard or soft, and matte or glossy. Everything around us has texture — both physical and visual.

Physical texture is the tactile quality of an object or artwork. It can be touched and felt. The physical texture of surfaces interacts with light and affect the perception of the color.

SEE ALSO:
Context
Local Color

ATTRIBUTES OF APPEARANCE

Cesia is a term for the aspect of visual appearance related to the perception of different spatial distributions of light. The word was proposed by Cesar Jannello in the 1980s. It is the same type of phenomena that Robert Hunt called geometric attributes of appearance. These surface attributes affect the perception of color.

Light that is not absorbed by an object may be reflected either sharply (mirrored) or diffusely (matte). Materials will also interact differently with light depending on whether they are more or less transparent, translucent, or opalescent, and, of course in different levels of darkness according to the light-dark axis.

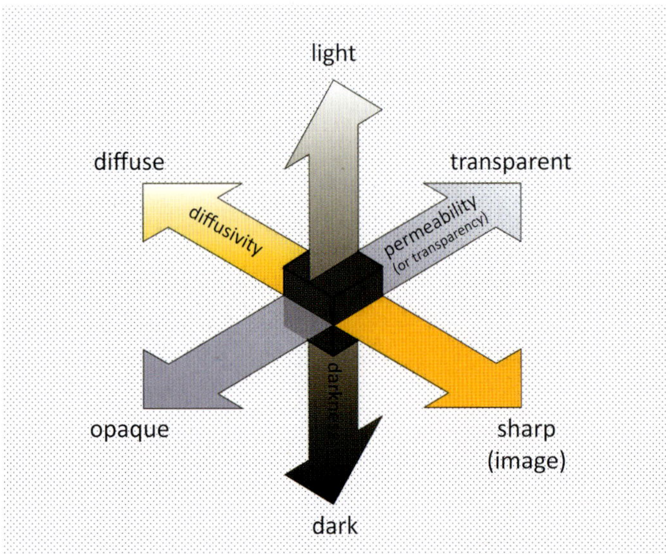

Systems of Cesia by Jose Caivano.

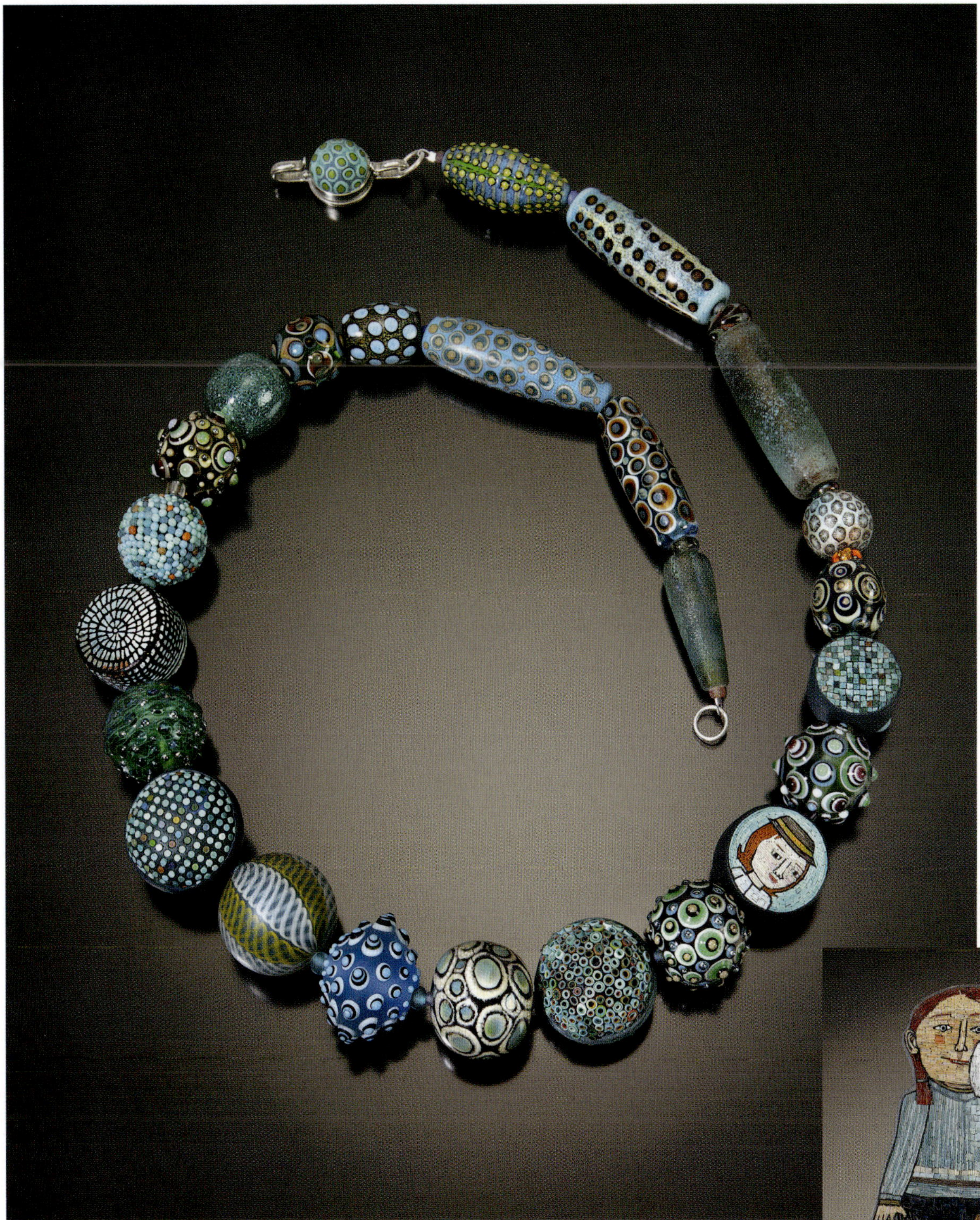

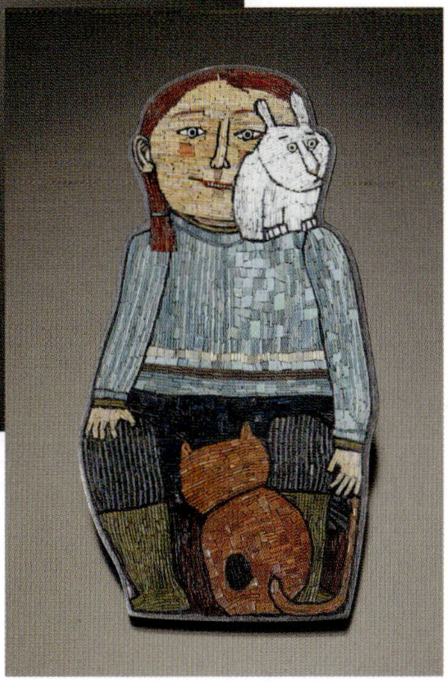

Texture is a key element in the work of contemporary art jewelers Cynthia Toops and Dan Adams.
(Above) Necklace (2020). Polymer, glass, by Cynthia Toops and Dan Adams.
(Right) Micromosaic Brooch (1.5" x 3.5" tall) Polymer, Silver, by Cynthia Toops.

92 THREE DIMENSIONS OF COLOR

Colors can be described according to attributes scaled in three dimensions—hue, lightness, and chroma—or three similar terms

The perception of color has three attributes. Although the terminology varies depending on the discipline, and the definitions are not the same, the three attributes of color can be described as:

1. Hue
2. Lightness (value, brightness)
3. Chroma (colorfulness, chromaticness, saturation, intensity)

Hue is the degree to which a color looks red, yellow, green, or blue. Lightness is the variation in the color from dark to light. Chroma is related to the visual power of a color from strong to weak.

According to this definition of color, white, black, and gray are colors, but they are colors that contain no chroma. The term *achromatic* is used to describe these colors. Black, white, and a full range of light to dark grays are achromatic colors.

It has been understood for centuries that any logical arrangement of colors according to these attributes will require at least three dimensions. The 3D nature of color is often represented as a color space. Several important color-communication tools (e.g., Munsell system, Natural Color System, RAL system) are based on this 3D arrangement.

This 3D concept can also be used to describe colors using natural language in a systematic and meaningful way; for example, we might describe a color as a light, strong red or as a light, weak blue. We can also describe the differences between colors in terms of these three attributes; thus, we might say that one color is darker, stronger, and bluer than another, for example.

Even though there are other appearance attributes that affect how we perceive the world—for example, objects can be opaque, translucent, or glossy—the topic of color in three dimensions is normally restricted to the attributes of hue, lightness, and chroma.

SEE ALSO:
Human Visual System
Munsell System
Natural Color System
RAL System

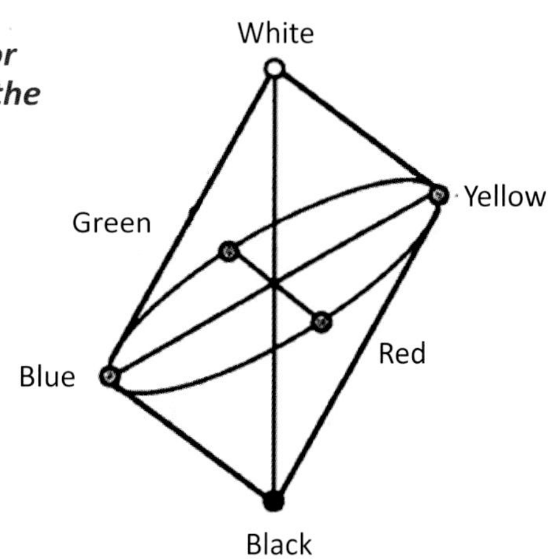

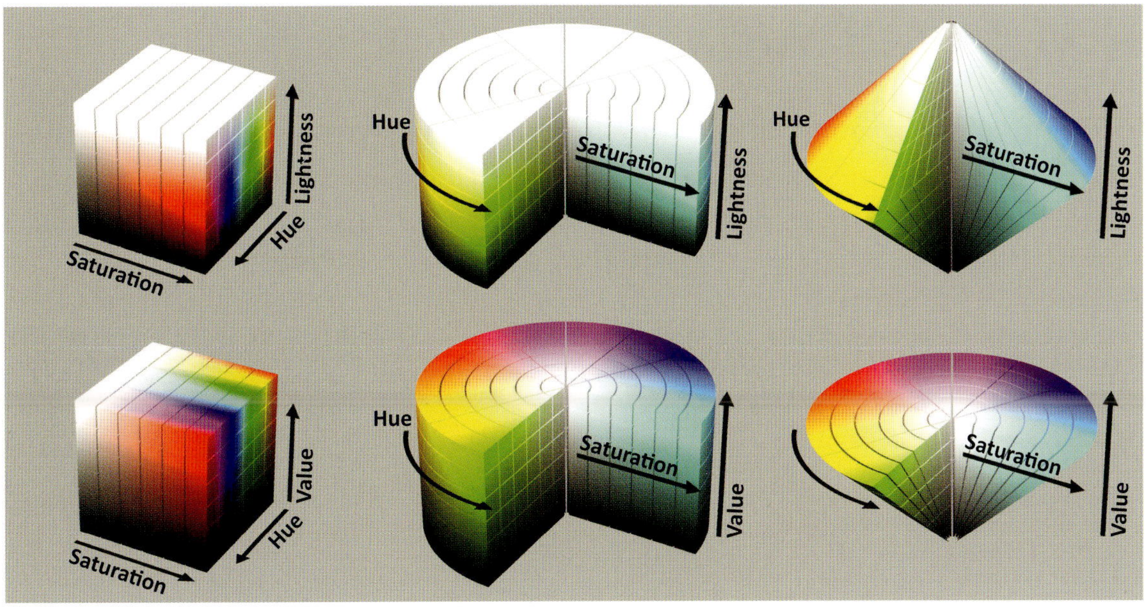

The attributes of color in a variety of 3D systems that use the term *saturation* instead of *chroma*.

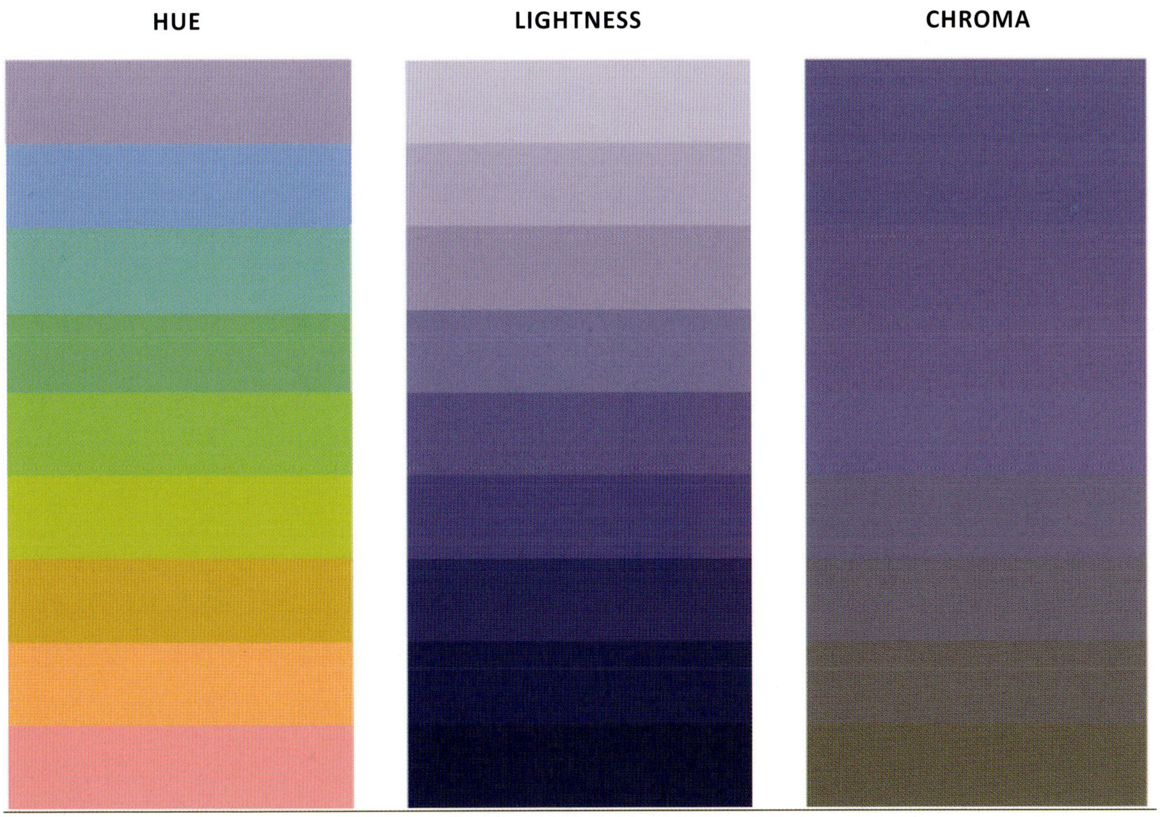

Examples of the range of each of the three attributes of color that are organized in three-dimensional models.

93 TINT, SHADE AND TONE

Variations of pure hues made by mixing with white, black, and gray

Traditionally, color theory has used the terms *tint*, *tone*, and *shade* to define a method of mixing hues with white, gray, or black pigments to create a larger gamut of monochromatic colors. Therefore, these terms have very specific meanings for artists.

In this methodology, tint refers to the colors that result from mixing a hue pigment with a white pigment; tone refers to the colors that result from mixing a hue pigment with a light, medium, or dark gray pigment; shade refers to the colors that result from mixing with a black pigment.

In more contemporary contexts, however, these terms are often used in different ways, and this can be a source of confusion. For example, the word *shade* is sometimes used as a synonym for color. In graphic design, the term *tone* can refer to variations in lightness. The technical term *tone mapping* is often used for the nonlinear relationship between the input to an emissive display and the light intensity that is output (also referred to as gamma).

- **Tinting** a vivid color results in colors that are described as pale.
- **Toning** a vivid color results in colors that are described as muted.
- **Shading** a vivid color results in colors that are described as dark.

Any color, not just vivid colors, can be tinted, toned, and shaded.

SEE ALSO:
Character Zones
Color Meaning
Subtractive Mixture
Three Dimensions of Color

Faber Birren's triangle shows the relationship between the pure hues and black, white, and gray, as well as three ways to mix a tone.
TINT = Color + Black
SHADE = Color + White
TONE = Color + Gray, Tint + Black, Shade + White

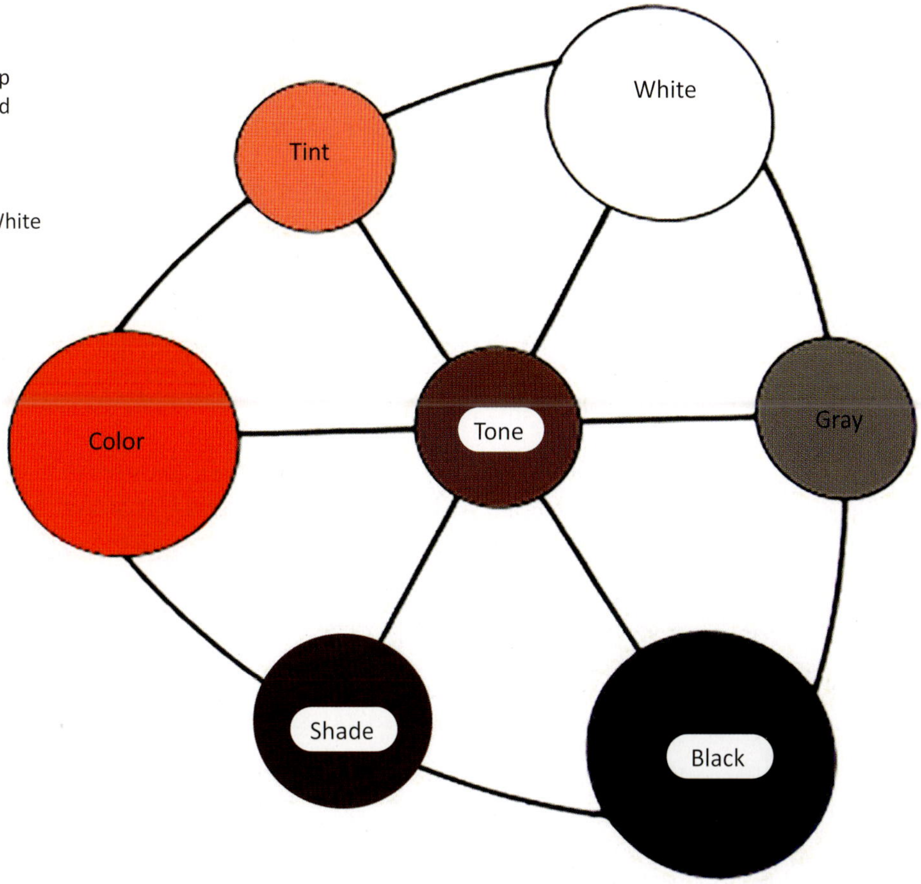

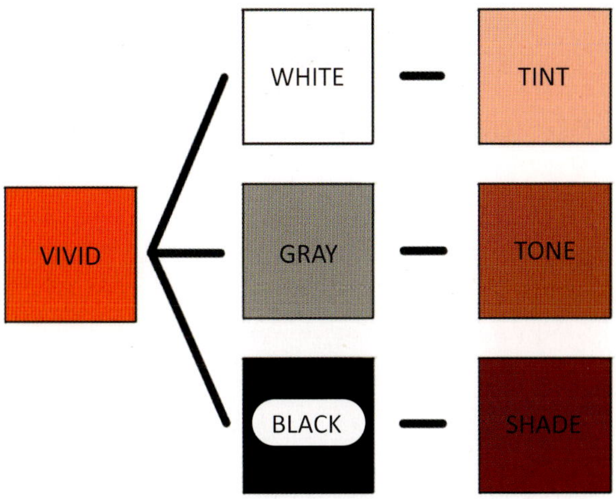

Left: A tint, tone, and shade of a Vivid Red. The tone of Vivid Red is a Muted Red.

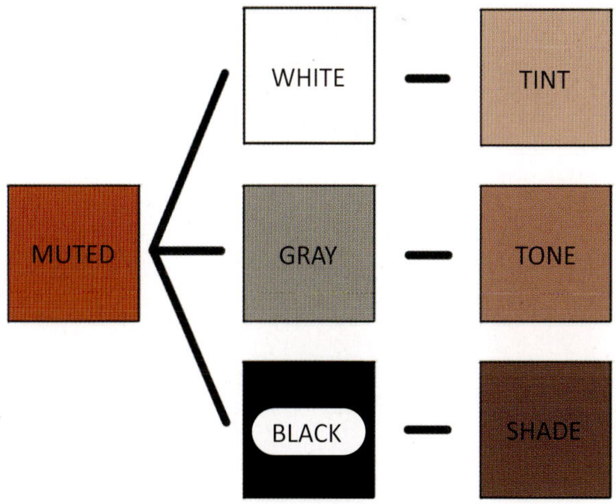

Right: A tint, tone, and shade of a Muted Red.

94 TRADITIONAL COLOR THEORY

An ambiguously defined body of knowledge that has been traditionally taught in art and design schools for many decades

Although the exact curriculum is not precisely defined, traditional color theory typically includes some or all the following topics: color naming, color mixing, color circles, color harmony, and color meaning.

A great many people contributed to the ideas that are traditionally taught as color theory. For example, Goethe, Michel Eugène Chevreul, Wilhelm Ostwald, Albert H. Munsell, and Johannes Itten all made important contributions to a topic referred to as color harmony, which concerns the aesthetic relationships between colors.

Itten was particularly influential on the concept of hue circle and the use of this tool to teach aspects of color harmony and color mixing.

When viewed through a contemporary lens, some of the concepts that have been taught—and, in fact, continue to be taught—are difficult to reconcile with practice. It is still sometimes taught that three color primaries can be mixed to generate all other colors, whereas in practice it is known that this is not possible.

The STEAM movement is an opportunity to align color teaching in the arts with state-of-the-art science and technologies.

There are many concepts in traditional color theory that can be expanded to reflect the topics and technologies relevant in the twenty-first century.

SEE ALSO:
Additive Mixture
Color Harmony
Subtractive Mixture

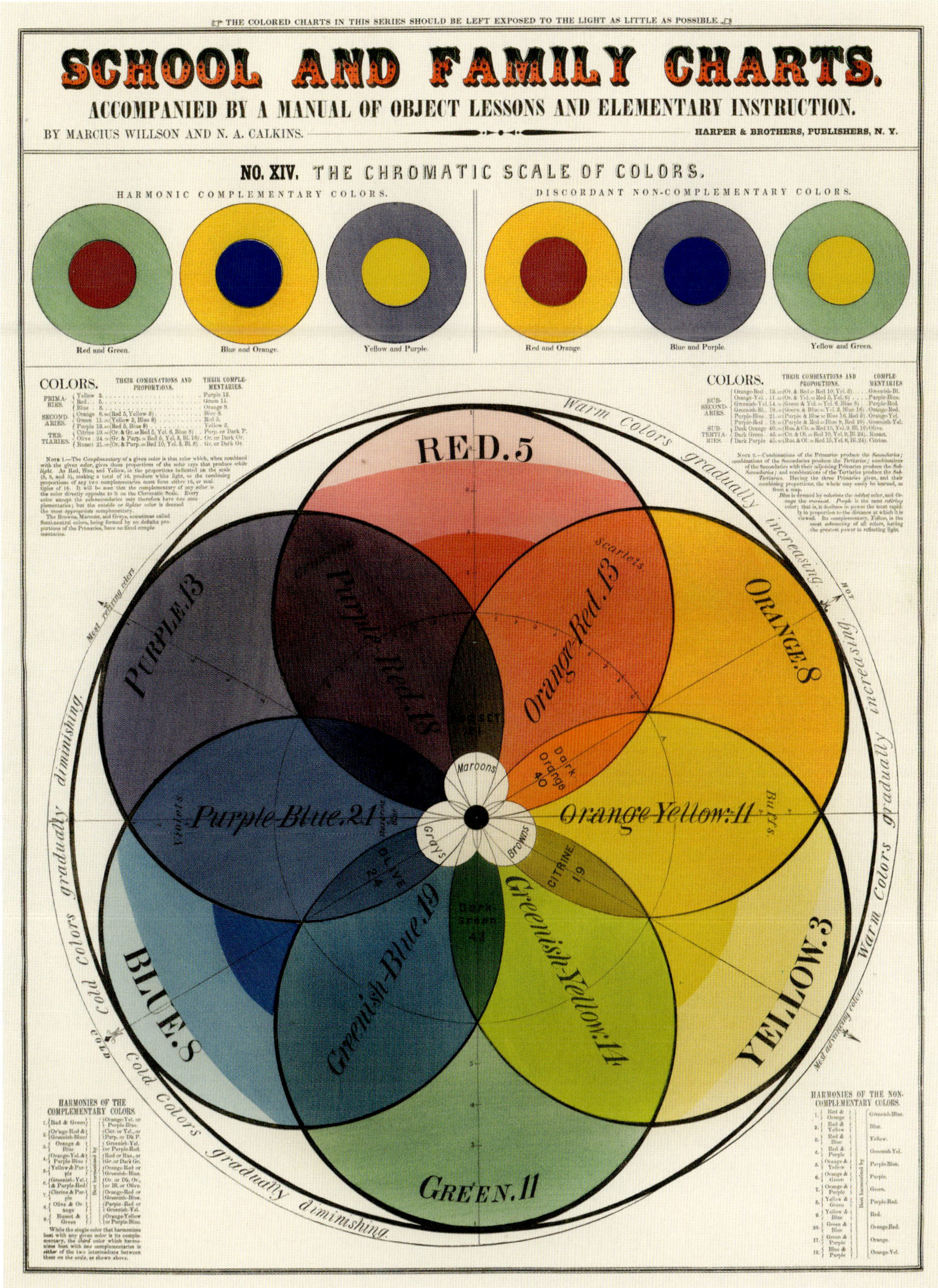

The elements of traditional color theory as shown on a classroom poster from 1890.

95 TRANSPARENCY EFFECT

The pictorial illusion of overlapping transparent layers to represent multiple perspectives

A transparent material allows light to pass through and provides the opportunity to see what is behind the material. This is literal transparency. The illusion of transparency is defined by the intentional use of colors and shapes to suggest overlapping planes and multiple viewpoints.

Renaissance and baroque painters used the transparent layers of paint to create nuanced surface effects for skin tones, atmospheric conditions, and fabrics such as silk. In the early twentieth century, cubist painters used the illusion of transparency to build up visual layers representing objects shifting in space and time. Modernist painters used transparency to add the illusion of depth to compositions made with flat planes of color.

There are three types of transparency effects:

- Two colors can both appear transparent with the illusion of material behind both colors.
- One color can appear to be transparent on top of the second color, which appears opaque.
- The relationship of colors can be ambiguous with no visual clue about which color, and shape, is on top of the other.

The element of ambiguity is critical to the success of transparency effects aiming to represent multiple perspectives.

SEE ALSO:
Advancing and Receding

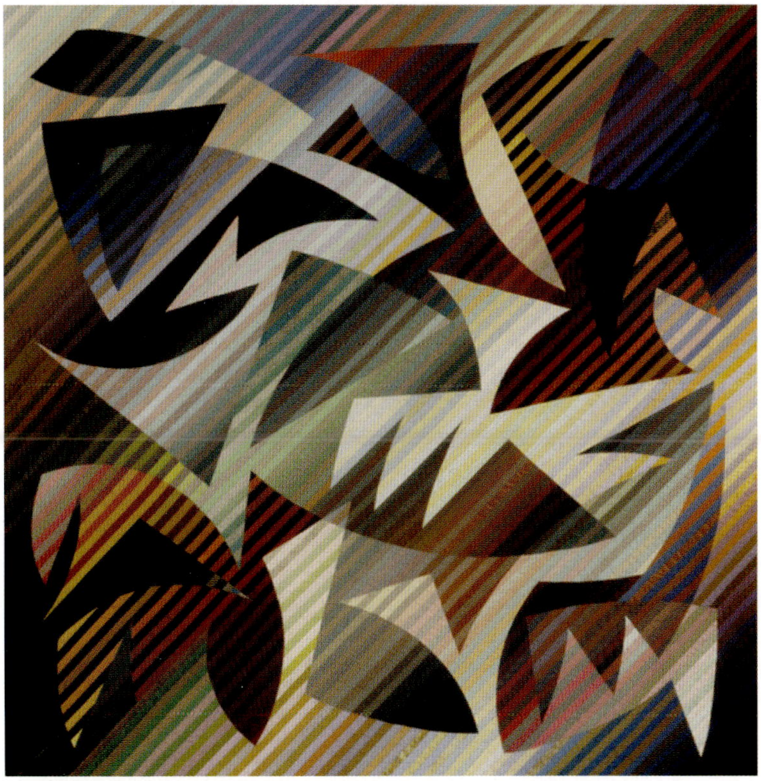

The Metaphysics of Action (Entropic Forms) (1994), a contemporary art quilt by Michael James.

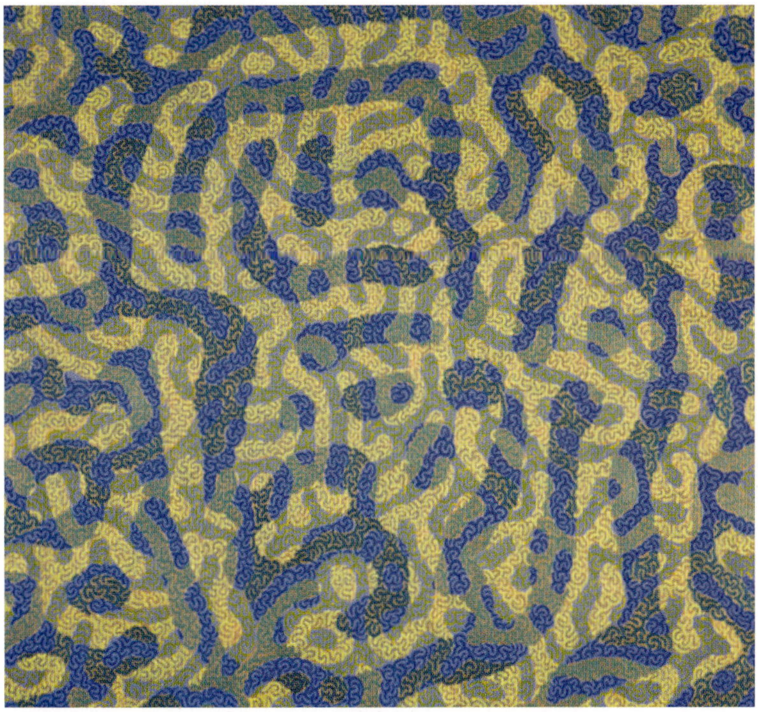

Explanatory Gap (2010), an acrylic painting by Andrew Werth.

96 TRICHROMACY

Human vision is mediated by three types of light-reception cells called cones in the retina of the eye

Most humans are trichromatic, which means that their vision is mediated by three types of light-reception cells called cones in the retina of the eye.

Trichromacy is the normal condition for most people. The fact that most of us have three types of cone cells in the eye is the reason that it is possible to generate a wide range of colors (and all hues) using three lights or three colorants in mixture. Some people have only two classes of cone, and this is one of the most frequent causes of so-called color blindness where people can see color but have limited color discrimination ability.

Toward the end of the twentieth century, it was discovered that some people—almost always female—have four types of cone class. There is some evidence that tetrachromats may have enhanced color discrimination. Note that tetrachromacy can also be commonly found in many species of fish and birds.

SEE ALSO:
Human Visual System
Limited Color Vision
Synesthesia

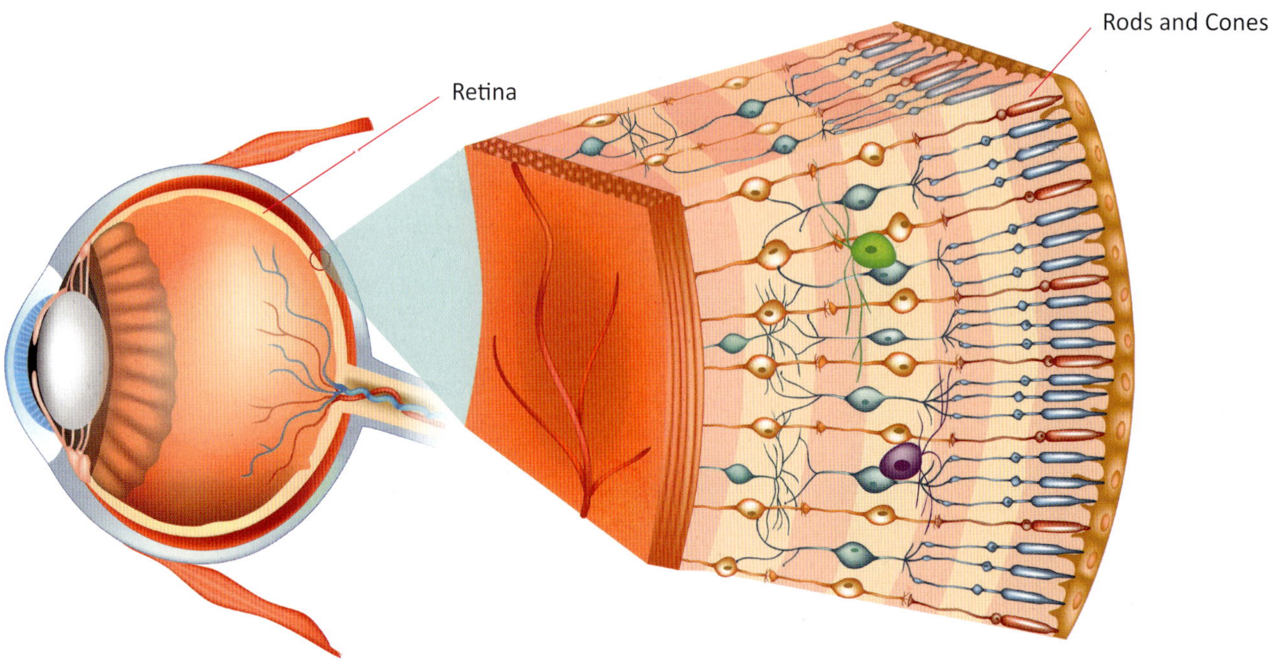

Diagram of the eye with rods and cones. The trichromatic nature of our vision stems from the fact that most of us have three types of cones in the retina.

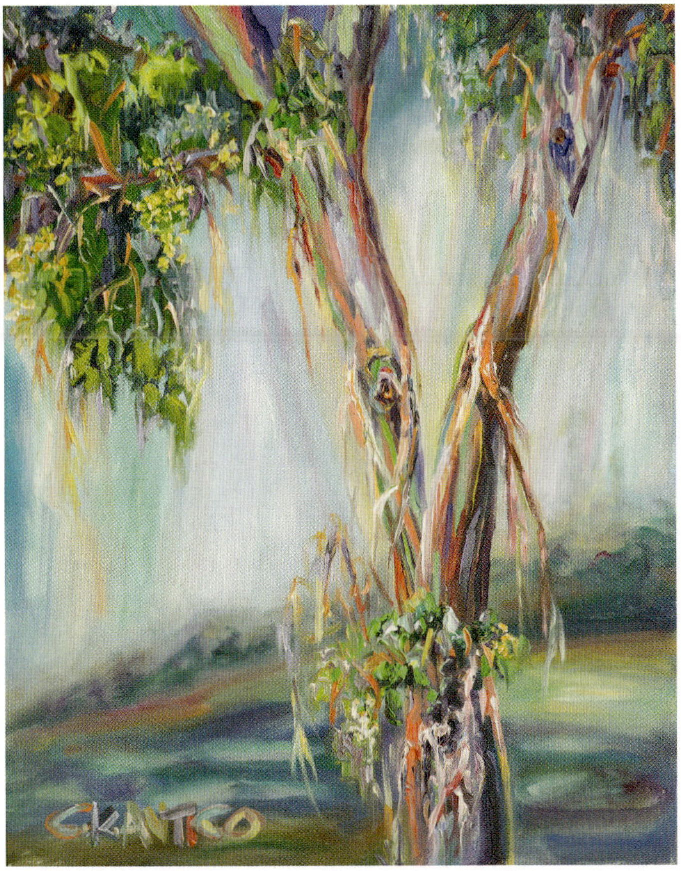
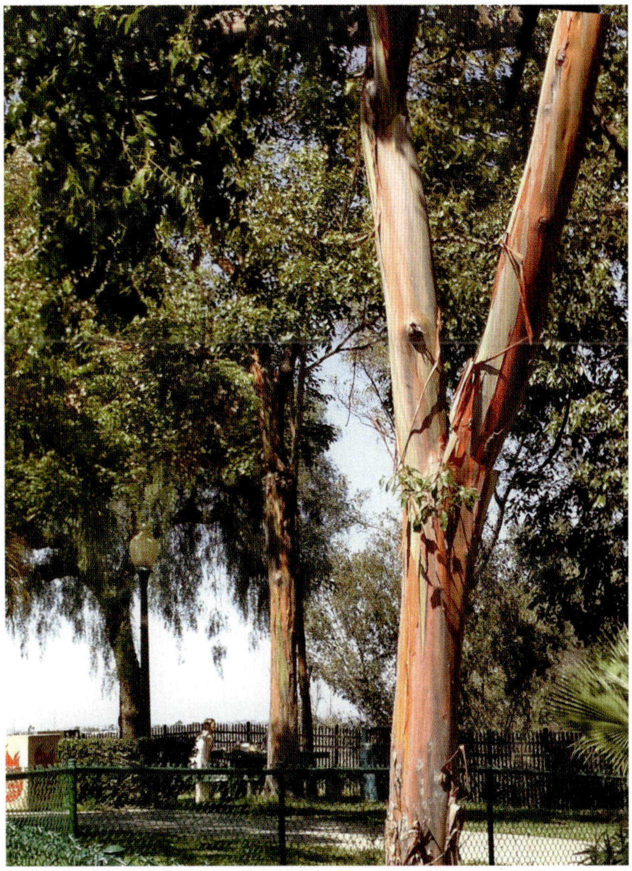

Rainbow Eucalyptus (2016).
Oil painting by the artist and tetrachromat Concetta Antico with a photo of the same species of tree by Robert Linsdell.

TETRACHROMACY

A very small percentage of people have a fourth cone. Tetrachromacy may give us a different way to perceive the world and may lead to interesting artistic outcomes in the same way that synesthesia has given some artists an enhanced view of the world. (For example, it is believed that the Bauhaus artist Kandinsky was synesthetic.) On the other hand, tetrachromacy may not always be an advantage. Color imaging technologies (such as cinematography and emissive displays) are predicated on the idea of trichromacy and may not work so well for tetrachromats.

97 UNDERTONE

The underlying hue of a low-chroma colored sample

Colors can be described by three attributes using terms such as lightness, chroma, and hue. The hue of most samples can be described by a hue name—for example, red, yellow, or green. However, for samples of low chroma it can be difficult to identify the underlying hue. It can also feel unnatural to describe a sample as "red" if the sample is close to gray.

In several industries—most notably the cosmetics industry and the interior design industry—the term undertone is often used to describe the hue of a sample. In cosmetics, many people have an undertone that is between red and yellow. People with a redder undertone have a hue angle less than about forty-five degrees, and those with a yellow-greener undertone have a hue angle greater than forty-five degrees.

In the paint industry, near-neutral paints are particularly popular for use in offices and in homes. The term *undertone* is often used to differentiate between different near-neutral paint samples.

The undertone is sometimes described as warm or cool, but this can be misleading because the appearance of color is relative to the context such as the lighting and surrounding colors.

SEE ALSO:
Hue Angle
Near Neutrals
Warm and Cool

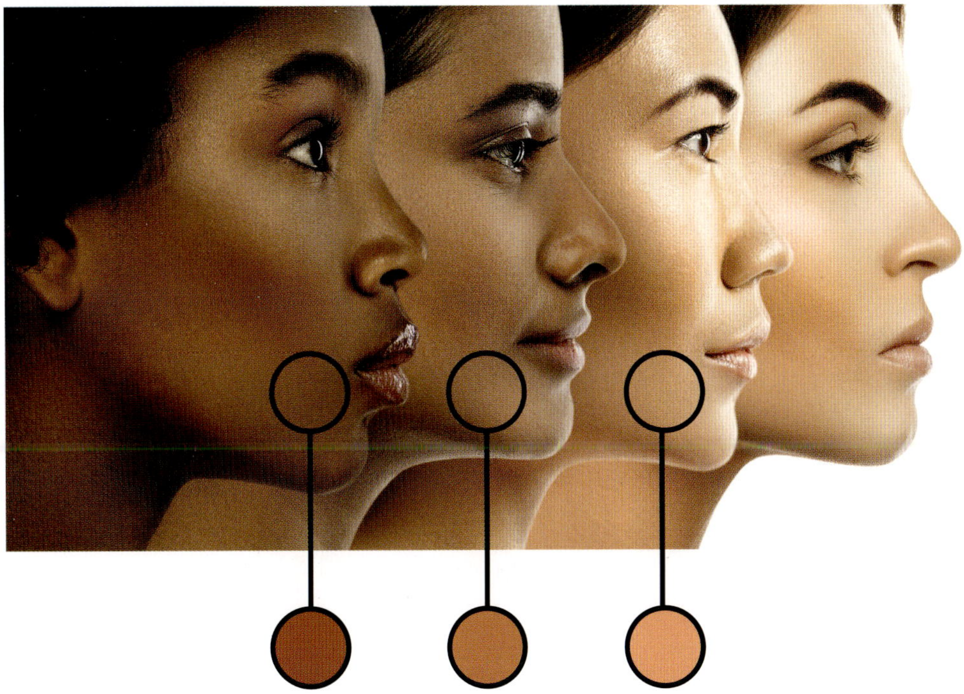

Undertone is a major element in the cosmetics industry. Skin ranges in undertone between a CIELAB hue angle of about twenty-two degrees to about sixty-eight degrees. The undertone is more apparent when shown against a white background.

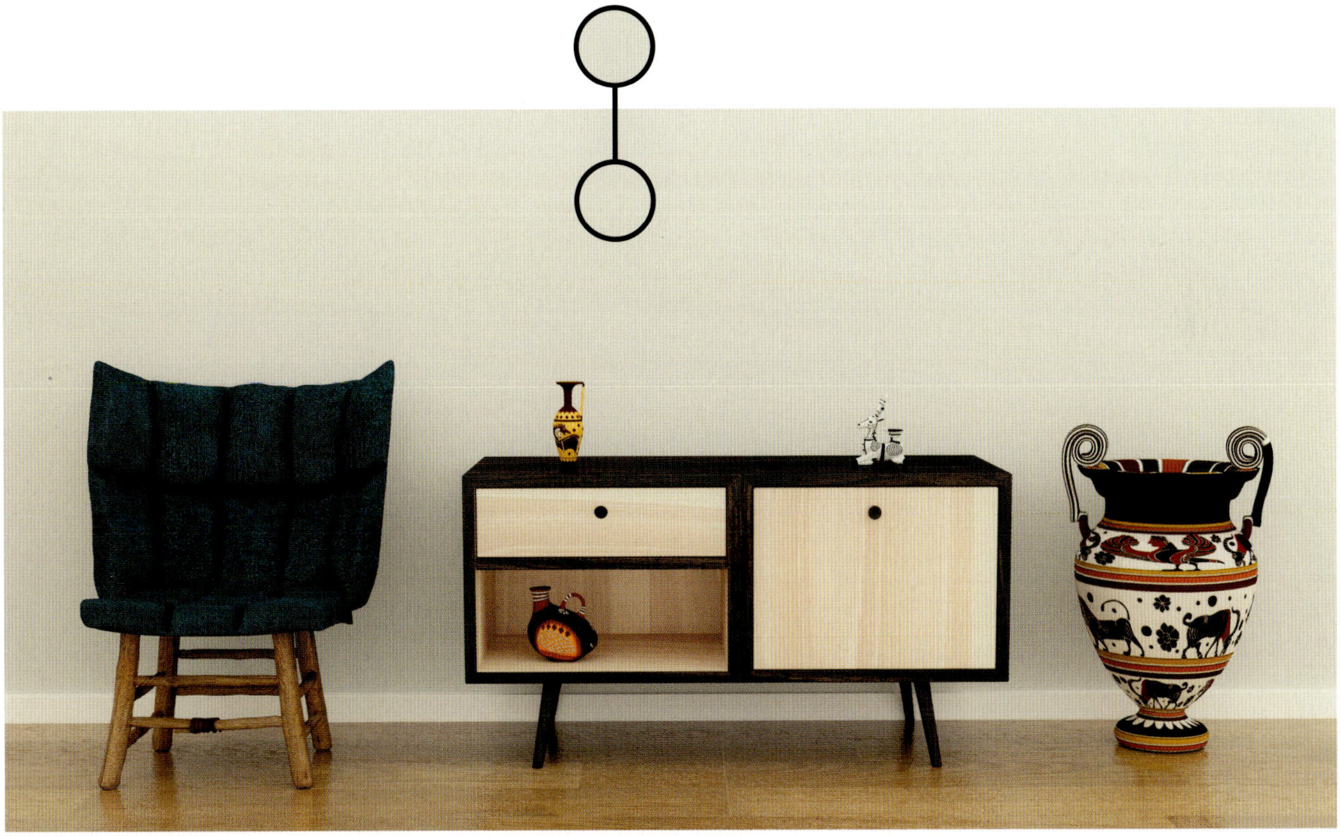

The wall paint in this image has a yellow-green undertone with a CIELAB hue angle of about 110 degrees.

98 UNIQUE HUES

Colors considered to be perceptually pure without any evidence of other hues

Ewald Hering first defined the unique hues, sometimes known as psychological color primaries, as red, green, yellow, and blue. Hering's observation was that these four colors cannot be simultaneously perceived. Unlike the unique hues that appear pure, other colors always appear as combinations of these unique hues. For example, orange can be perceived as a mixture of red and yellow.

Hering's system is based on two sets of opposite or opponent colors: red/green and yellow/blue. These two pairs of opponent colors, along with a white/black pair, form the basis of the Natural Color System.

Note, however, although physiological opponency is clearly a mechanism that contributes to the phenomenon of unique hues, the actual opponent colors in the visual system are not the same as the unique hues.

If an observer is asked to adjust the wavelength of light so that it appears to be a yellow that is neither reddish nor greenish, they will be able to do so repeatedly to within a few nanometers.

Although unique blue, yellow, and green exist in the spectrum, there is no unique red in the spectrum. All the reds in the spectrum are too yellowish to be considered a unique red. Unique red is a nonspectral color.

SEE ALSO:
Natural Color System
Three Dimensions of Color

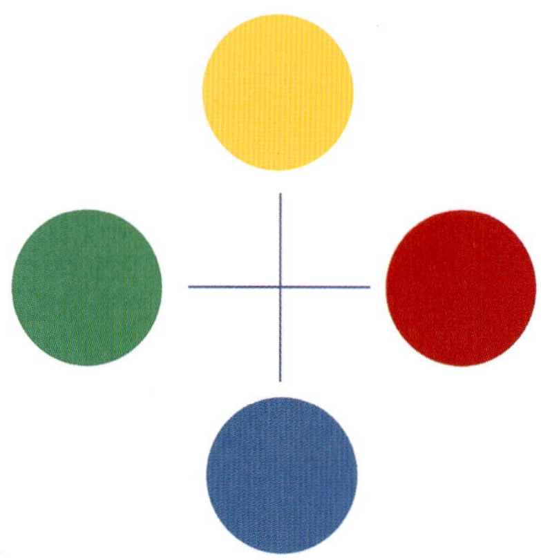

The basis of unique hues is physiological. It is known that channels that correspond closely to the opponent pairs red/green and yellow/blue are found in the human visual system neurophysiology.

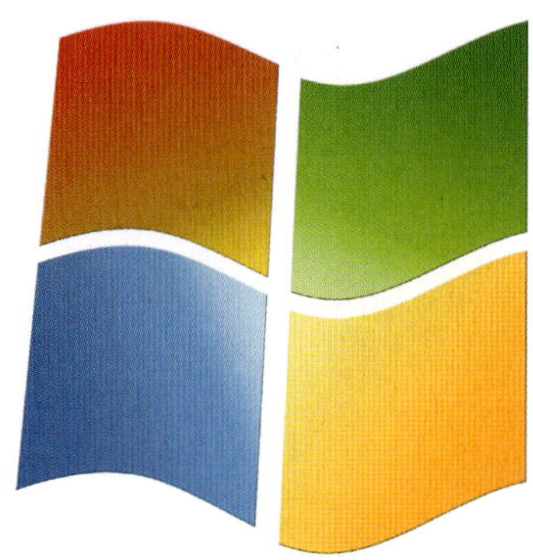

The four unique hues have particular visual saliency and can often be found in combination in logos (including those of Microsoft, eBay, and Google) and in tetradic color harmony schemes.

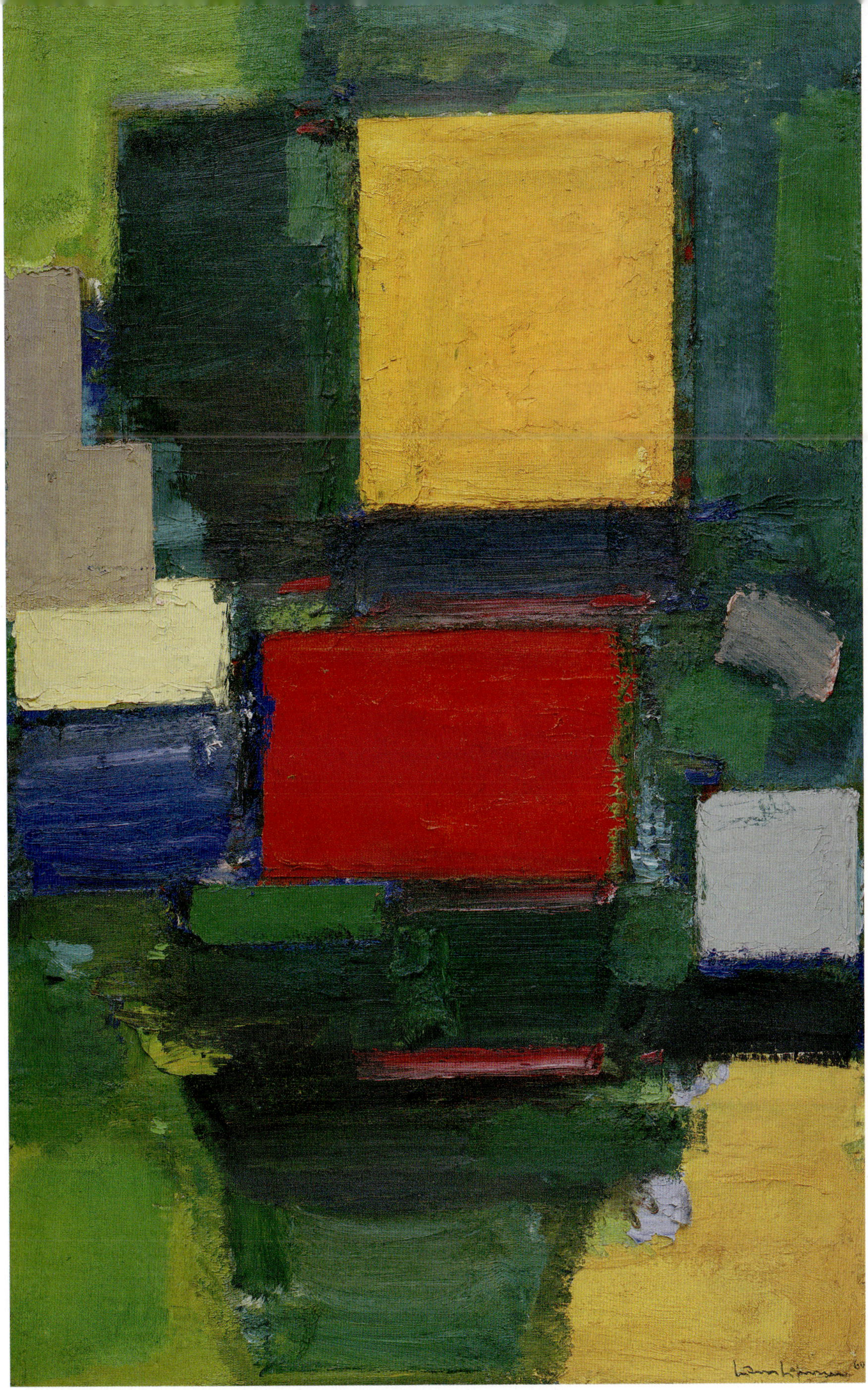

The Gate (1959-60), by Hans Hofmann.

99 WARM AND COOL

The colors of objects and lights can appear warm or cool mainly depending on their hue

The concept of warm and cool colors dates to the early eighteenth century. In 1813 Charles Hayter produced the first hue wheel that represented half of the hues as warm colors and the other half as cool colors. Reds, yellows, and oranges were considered warm, whereas blues and greens were considered cool. Although there is still some dispute over the warmest and coolest colors and whether all colors (apart from the achromatic scale) can be considered either warm or cool, it is often useful to describe colors as appearing warmer or cooler.

SEE ALSO:
Color Temperature

In some art and design fields, it is common to use the terms *warmer* and *cooler* to discuss the relationship between the color of objects. In interior design, the terminology can describe the psychological feeling of a space, especially with respect to the quality of the lighting. Light at a low color temperature, for example, is considered warmer than light at a higher color temperature.

One of the problems in describing colors as warm or cool comes into play when describing blues. There is no consensus for describing a blue leaning toward red as either warm or cool. The same is true of orange. A shift in which direction—toward red or yellow—would be a cooler orange?

***For clarity in communication, it is better to describe a shift in hue by naming the hue it moved toward, rather than using the terms* warm *or* cool.**

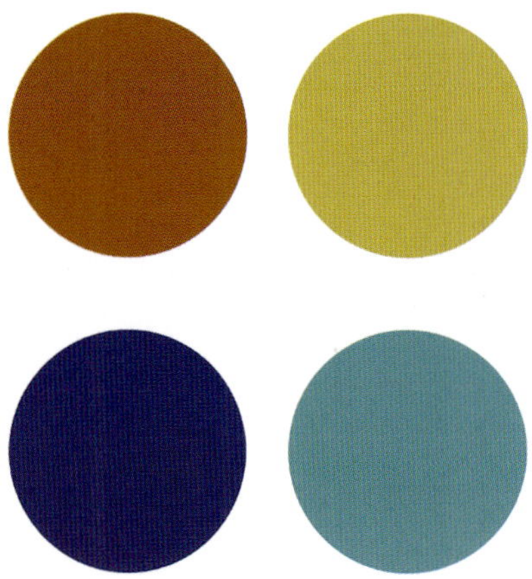

Many people might agree that the yellowish circle on the right is warmer than the one on the left. However, it is far less clear with the two blues. Which of the blues looks warmer to you? It is often better to say that the right-hand blue is redder and the left-hand blue is greener.

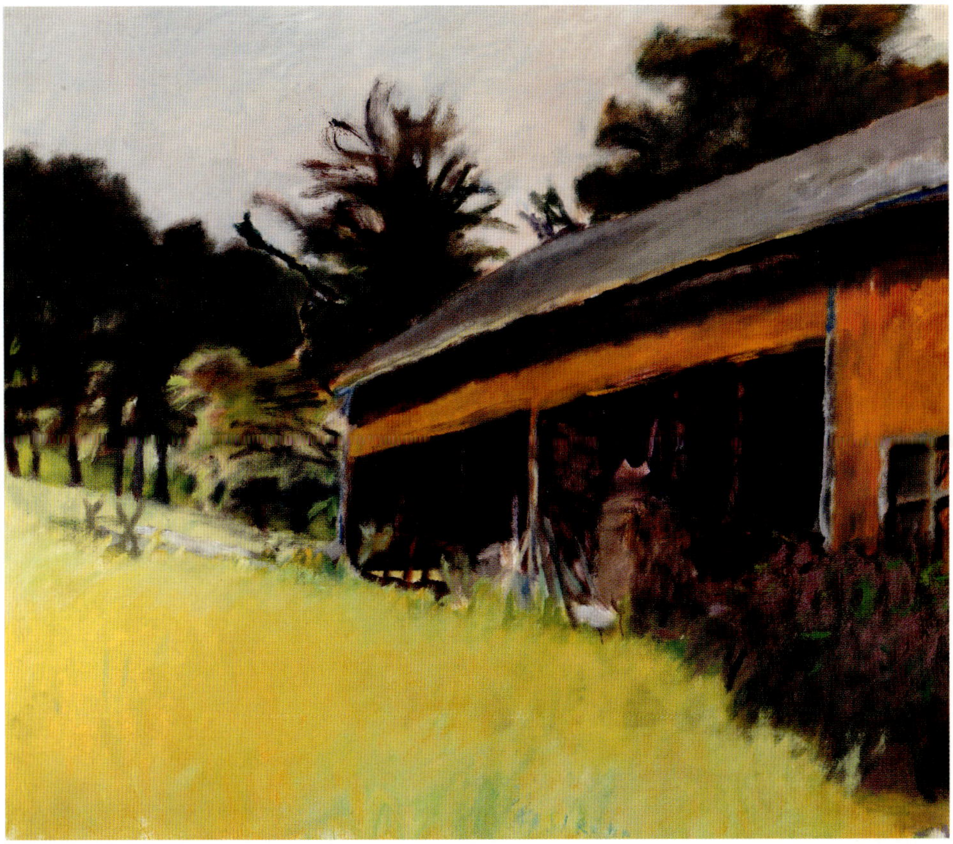

High Summer (1972), by Wolf Kahn.

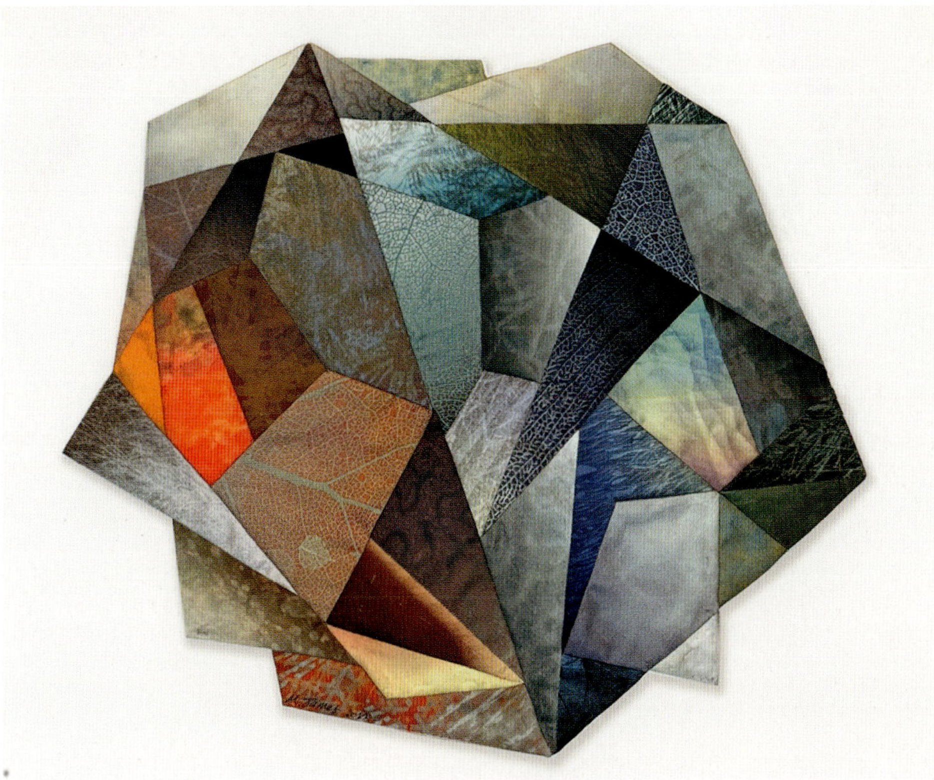

Coda (No.16). (2022) Hand-pieced quilt by Michael James.

100 WHITE BALANCE

The setting that ensures color fidelity in an image by establishing a baseline for the color of white in cameras and monitors

The goal of performing a white balance is to render neutral colors (such as white and gray) appropriately, usually according to a specified color temperature.

White balance is a feature of high-end digital camera systems and can typically be set manually or automated. In the case of automatic white balance, the camera software will use algorithms that are inspired by an understanding of the human process of color constancy. Often such automatic algorithms try to ascertain the color temperature of the ambient illumination.

For emissive displays, the white balance of the display can usually be adjusted using settings on the display. White balance is an important feature in most color management pipelines that ensure color fidelity when color images are transmitted between different imaging devices. The unknown state of the white balance of many consumer displays is a challenge for retailers who are concerned with color fidelity on the internet.

SEE ALSO:
Color Management

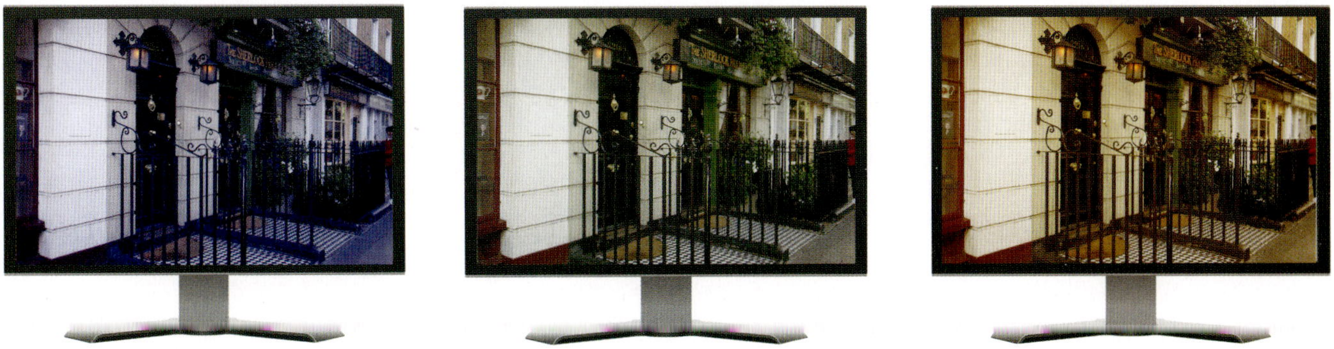

The same image is displayed on three emissive displays, which have different white points. The display on the left is set to a lower color temperature, and the display on the right is set to a higher color temperature, relative to the middle display.

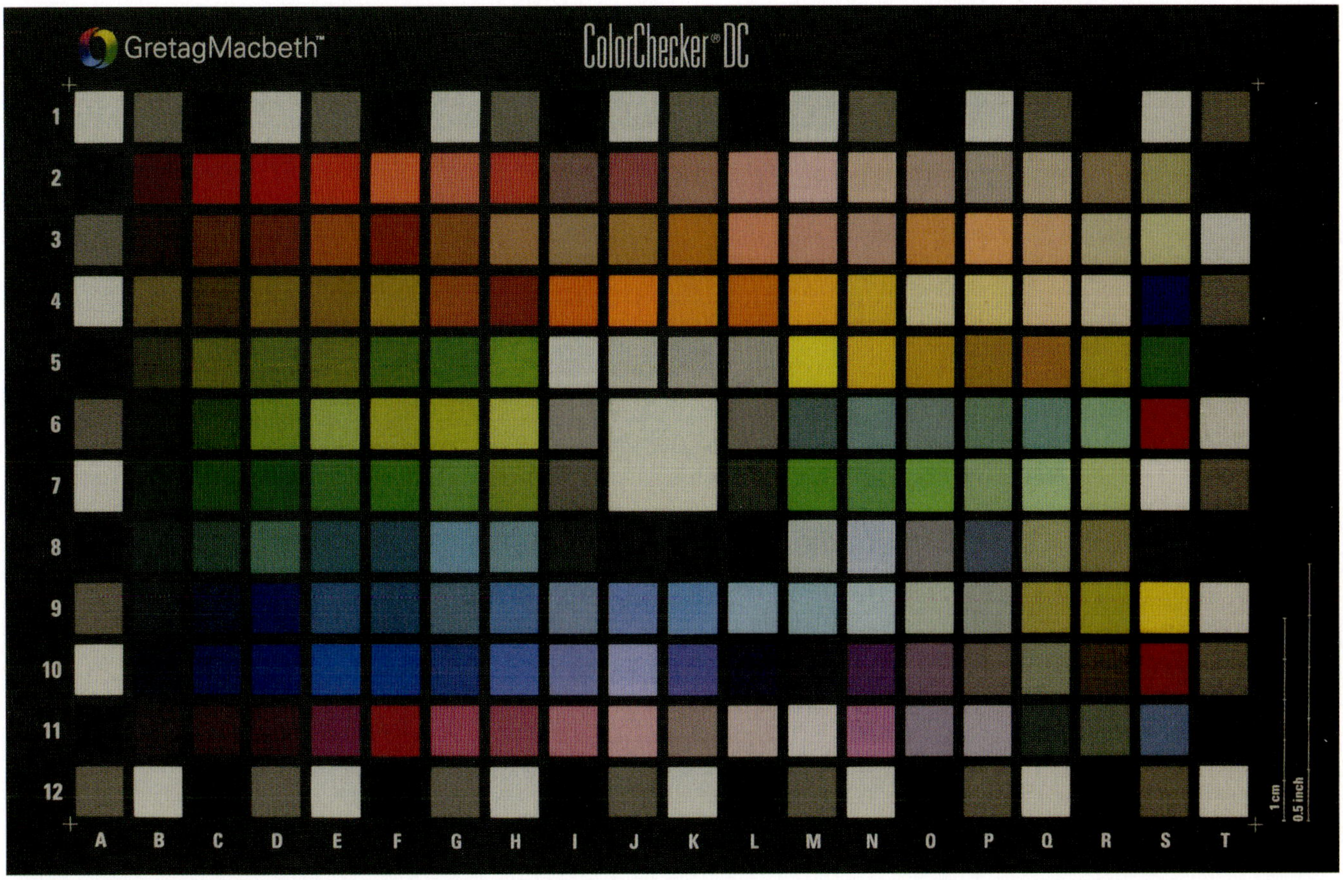

Special color-checker charts have been designed to enable a digital camera to be color calibrated. Part of the calibration of a camera involves setting an appropriate white point with respect to the illumination. Because the spectral reflectance factors of the patches on the color checker are known, both white balance and gamma correction can be achieved.

Acknowledgments

At Rockport Publishers, we must thank many people, especially Joy Aquilino for suggesting we coauthor this book, Jonathan Simcosky and John Gettings for keeping us on track, and David Martinell for his immense help during the layout process. A book on color would not be complete without images to accompany the text so we need to give a huge thank-you to the many designers, artists, architects, and photographers who gave us permission to include their work in the book. A special thank-you to the members of the Joint ISCC/AIC Colour Literacy Project team for their contributions to the book and to Robert Hirschler, Luanne Stovall, and Karen Triedman who reviewed drafts and provided critical feedback.

Maggie Maggio and Stephen Westland

I would like to thank all my students over the years who asked questions I could not answer. Their curiosity inspired my deep dive into the universe of color. I would like to thank Stephen Westland for inviting me to coauthor this book. I am grateful for his wide-ranging expertise on the complex subject of color, his dedication to dispelling misconceptions, and his commitment to expanding our understanding of color to meet the evolving needs of the twenty-first century. Working together over the past two years has been a pleasure. Finally, I must thank my husband, Chuck Maggio, for his support and patience during the times when the deadlines loomed large and all my attention was focused on this book. **—MM**

I would like to thank Maggie Maggio for making the hard work and long hours that went into putting this book together enjoyable and rewarding. Without Maggie I could never have written this book. I would also like to thank all of my students over the many years from whom I have learned so much; it is, with them in mind, that I have written this book. Finally, I must thank Jane and Tyler for their endless patience during the many evenings when I needed to engage with Zoom calls. **—SW**

About the Authors

Maggie Maggio is a designer, artist, and art educator who has studied, taught, and worked with color for over forty years. Her personal explorations into the science of light and pigments led to the creation of workshops for artists and designers who want to incorporate the latest research in color science into their creative practice. As a member of the board of directors of the US Inter-Society Color Council (ISCC) and co-chair of the International Color Association Study Group on Color Education, Maggie focuses on bridging between the art, science, and industry of color and advancing color literacy for the twenty-first century. She is the current chair of the Joint International Color Association/ISCC Color Literacy Project, advocating for the integration of art and science in color education programs worldwide.

Stephen Westland is Professor of Color Science and Technology in the School of Design at the University of Leeds (UK). He was previously head of the School of Design at Leeds (2006–2013). His research interests are color design, color vision, and color measurement, and he has published over 250 peer-reviewed papers, book chapters, and books about these topics. He is a Fellow of the Society of Dyers and Colourists and was President of the Society in 2019. In 2008 he was awarded the Davies Medal from the Royal Photographic Society (London) for his color research. He has won numerous research grants from both government and industry and has recently worked with AkzoNobel, Colgate, and Unilever on color-related projects. He holds several visiting professorships including at the University of Texas (US) and Huazhong University of Science and Technology in Wuhan (China).

Photo Credits

(t=top, b=bottom, l=left,r=right, m=middle, a=all)

11: (t) NASA, ESA, CSA, and STScI. Image processing: J. DePasquale, A. Pagan, and A. Koekemoer (STScI); (b) Westland/Maggio **13:** (t) Courtesy of Dr. Anya Hurlbert; (b) Westland/ Maggio **14:** Westland/Maggio **15:** (t) Agefis on Unsplash; (b) Westland/Maggio **17:** (t) Dave Meeker, (left) Zátonyi Sándor, (ifj.) Fizped/Wikimedia Commons (WC), (r) Nuria Estape **18:** Westland/Maggio **19:** Andrew Neuhart **20:** Westland/ Maggio **21:** (t) Album/Alamy Stock Photo; (b) Westland/Maggio **23:** Dennis Jarvis/ WC **24:** (r) Westland/Maggio; **25:** Jeffrey Lloyd Dever **27:** (b) Westland/Maggio **28:** Transferred from en.wikipedia/WC **29:** (t) Tegula/Pixabay **31:** (a) Westland/ Maggio **33:** (t) Bequest of King Ralph/ WC; (b) National Archives and Records Administration, Records of the National Park Service/WC **35:** (b) Gorodenkoff/ Shutterstock **37:** (t) Squirrel photos/ Pixabay; (b) AdrianaGórak/WC **38:** James Vaughn/Flickr **39:** (t) Nedd3_89/Pixabay; (b) Guy Bell/Alamy Stock Photo **41:** (a) Westland/Maggio **43:** (t) Maxx Studio/ Shutterstock; (l) Wikimediaimages/ WC; (bottom) Westland/Maggio **45:** (t) Galleria Nazionale d'Arte Antica/WC; (b) Emmanuel Douzery/WC **47:** (a) Westland/ Maggio **49:** (t) David Batchelor; (b) ger- alt/Pixabay **50:** (l) Westland/Maggio **51:** Holger Everding/WC **53:** (t) geralt/ Pixabay; (b) Compiled by Tommaso Buonocore **54:** (r) Nicoline Kinch **55:** Darri Lorenzen+ Elin Hansdottir **57:** Harald Arnkil **59:** (t) agefotostock/Alamy Stock Photo; (b) Rob Corder/Flickr **60:** Kira Yan/Shutterstock **61:** (t) Cars Down Under/Flickr; (b) catwalker/Shutterstock **62:** Westland/Maggio **63:** (t) Westland/ Maggio; (l) Westland/Maggio; (r) Amorn Suriyan/Shutterstock **65:** (t) Maxx Studio/ Shutterstock; (b) Ad Oculos/Shutterstock **67:** (t) Archivart/Alamy Stock Photo; (b) Ellen Divers **69:** (b) Westland/Maggio **72:** Westland/Maggio **73:** (b) Westland/ Maggio **74:** Westland/Maggio **75:** (b) Westland/Maggio **77:** (t) Rashchektayev/ Shutterstock; (b) Westland/Maggio **79:** (t) Andy Musa Chantu/Shuttertock; (b) Neale Cousland/Shutterstock **80:** Collage Kaffe **81:** (t) MBatty/Pixabay; (b) Fritzlorenz/ WC **82:** Westland/Maggio **83:** Paul-Green Armytage **84:** David Briggs **85:** (t) Silvestri Matteo; (b) Harald Arnkil **87:** (t) Ken Howard/Alamy Stock Photo; (b) Andreas Schwarz **89:** (a) Westland/Maggio **91:** (t) Eusebius/WC; (b) Orlagh O'Brien **92:** Juan Serra Lluch **93:** (t) Harkolufs/WC; (b) Hella Jongerius **94:** Purchase, Joseph Pulitzer Bequest, 1918/WC **95:** (t) Library of Congress original/WC; (b) Tim Evanson/ WC **96:** Hannes Grobe/AWI/WC **97:** (t) f11photo/Shutterstock; (b) Karolspacja/ WC **98:** Westland/Maggio **99:** (l, r) James Gurney; (b) Westland/Maggio **100:** Jean- Phillipe Lenclos and Dominique Lenclos **101:** (m) Bischoff49/Pixabay; (b) Dezalb/ Pixabay **103:** (l) Transferred from de.wiki- pedia by Andrei Stroe/WC; (r) Westland/ Maggio; (b) Mattias Rang **104:** Westland/ Maggio **105:** (t) JuliaBoldt/Pixabay; (b) Linda Lopez **106:** Dieric Bouts/WC **107:** (t) Matt Harvey; (b) Hugo Bastidas **109:** (t,r) Cllane4; (b,l) Linda Lopez; (b,r) Pfüderi/ Pixabay **111:** (t) Westland/Maggio; (b) Peter Donahue **112:** David Briggs **115:** (a) Westland/Maggio **117:** (t) Heritage Image Partnership Ltd/Alamy Stock Photo; (b) Pam Ingalls **119:** (t) Nick Sherman/Flickr; (b) Fernanda B. Viégas **120:** m-louis/WC **121:** (t) Lluís Ribes Mateu; (b) George Rex **122:** Westland/Maggio **123:** (b) Westland/Maggio **125:** (t) StockSnap/ Pixabay; (m) Roberto Rizzi; (b) alexandre zveiger/Shutterstock **126:** Pexels/Pixabay **127:** (t) haroldguevara/Shutterstock; (b) Stanislav Duben/Shutterstock **128:** David Briggs **129:** (t) David Briggs; (b) Jean-Phillipe Lenclos and Dominique Lenclos **130:** Westland/Maggio **131:** (t) Bru-nO/Pixabay; (b) chomplearn/ Shutterstock **133:** (l,r) Westland/Maggio; (b) Web Gallery of Art/WC **137:** (t) Westland/Maggio; (b) Renzo Shamey **139:** Peter Barritt/Alamy Stock Photo **142:** Westland/Maggio **143:** (t) NCS; (b) Westland/Maggio **145:** (b, 4 images) Paul Green-Armytage **146:** leemelina08/ Pixabay; **147:** (t) BlazingFirebug/Pixabay; (b) Westland/Maggio **149:** (t) Sascha Grusche/WC; (b) stux/Pixabay **150:** (l) Ian McKinnell/Alamy Stock Photo; (r) Stephen Chung/Alamy Stock Photo **151:** Roy Osborne **152:** Followtheflow/ Shutterstock **153:** (r) World History Archive/Alamy Stock Photo; (b) Hemis/ Alamy Stock Photo **155:** (a) Westland/ Maggio **157:** (a) Westland/Maggio **159:** (t) Moritz Zwimpfer (b) Akiyoshshi Kitaoka **160:** Pexels/Pixabay **161:** (t) Janeb13/Pixabay; (b) ParentRap/Pixabay **163:** (b) Robert Hirschler **164:** David Briggs **165:** (t) History & Art Collection/ Alamy Stock Photo; (c, b) David Briggs **166:** Westland/Maggio **167:** (t) EGL21/ Pixabay; (b) giani/Pixabay **168:** Westland/ Maggio **169:** (a) Francesco Rugi **171:** (t/r) Wikimediaimages/WC; (b/l) muph/ Shutterstock; (b/r) Tanya Paquet **172:** Westland/Maggio **173:** (b) Paul Foxton **175:** (t,c,l) Westland/Maggio; (r) Paul Green-Armytage **177:** (t/l) Mila Drumeva/ Shutterstock; (t/r) udaix/Shutterstock; (b) Westland/Maggio **178:** Garoch/ Pixabay **179:** (t) PeterKraayvanger/ Pixabay; (b) George Degan **181:** Spencer Finch **183:** (a) Westland/Maggio **185:** (t) Esa Naukkarinen; (b/l,b/r) Nuria Estape **186:** Uri Rosenheck/WC **188:** Westland/ Maggio **189:** (b) Carol Steen/WC **191:** (b/l) Prawny/Pixabay; (b/r) Tom McKinnon/ Flickr **192:** Jose Caivano **193:** (t) Dan Adams; (b) Cynthia Toops **194:** Westland/ Maggio **195:** (t) Dautmizer/WC; (b) Westland/Maggio **197:** (t) Jacobolus/ WC (b) Westland/Maggio **199:** rawpix- el 201: (t) Michael James; (b) Andrew Werth **202:** Westland/Maggio **203:** (a) Concetta Antico **205:** (t) BLACKDAY/ Shutterstock; Monoar CGI Artist/Pixabay **206:** (l) Westland/Maggio; (r) sipa/Pixabay **207:** Artepics/Alamy Stock Photo **208:** Westland/Maggio **209:** (t) Gift of the Sara Roby Foundation; (b) Michael James **211:** (a) Westland/Maggio

Index